THE LEGACY SITES

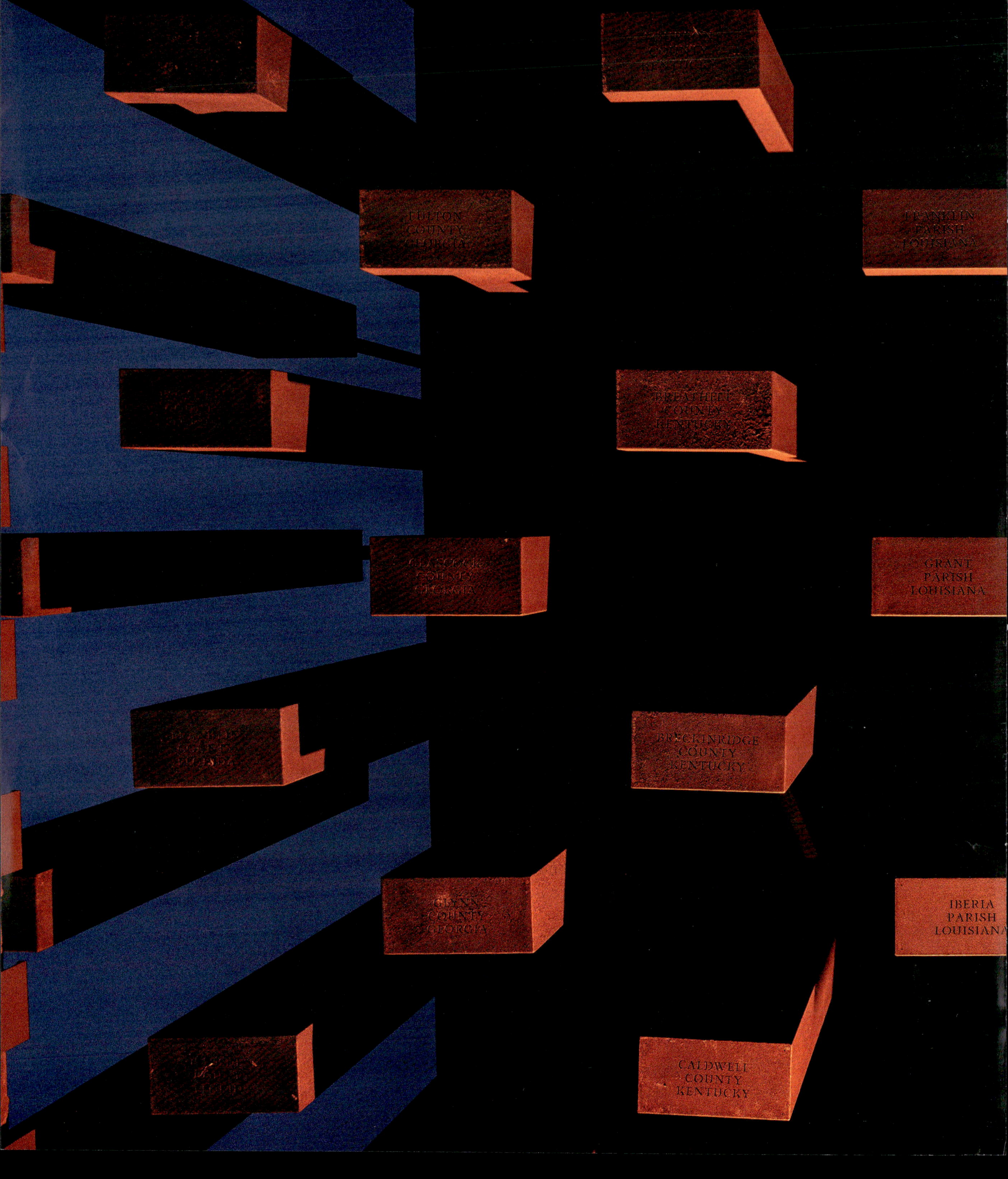
FULTON
COUNTY
GEORGIA
FRANKLIN
PARISH
LOUISIANA
BREATHITT
COUNTY
KENTUCKY
GLASCOCK
COUNTY
GEORGIA
GRANT
PARISH
LOUISIANA
BRECKINRIDGE
COUNTY
KENTUCKY
GLYNN
COUNTY
GEORGIA
IBERIA
PARISH
LOUISIANA
CALDWELL
COUNTY
KENTUCKY

THE LEGACY SITES

A HISTORY OF RACIAL INJUSTICE

Bryan Stevenson and the Equal Justice Initiative

Contents

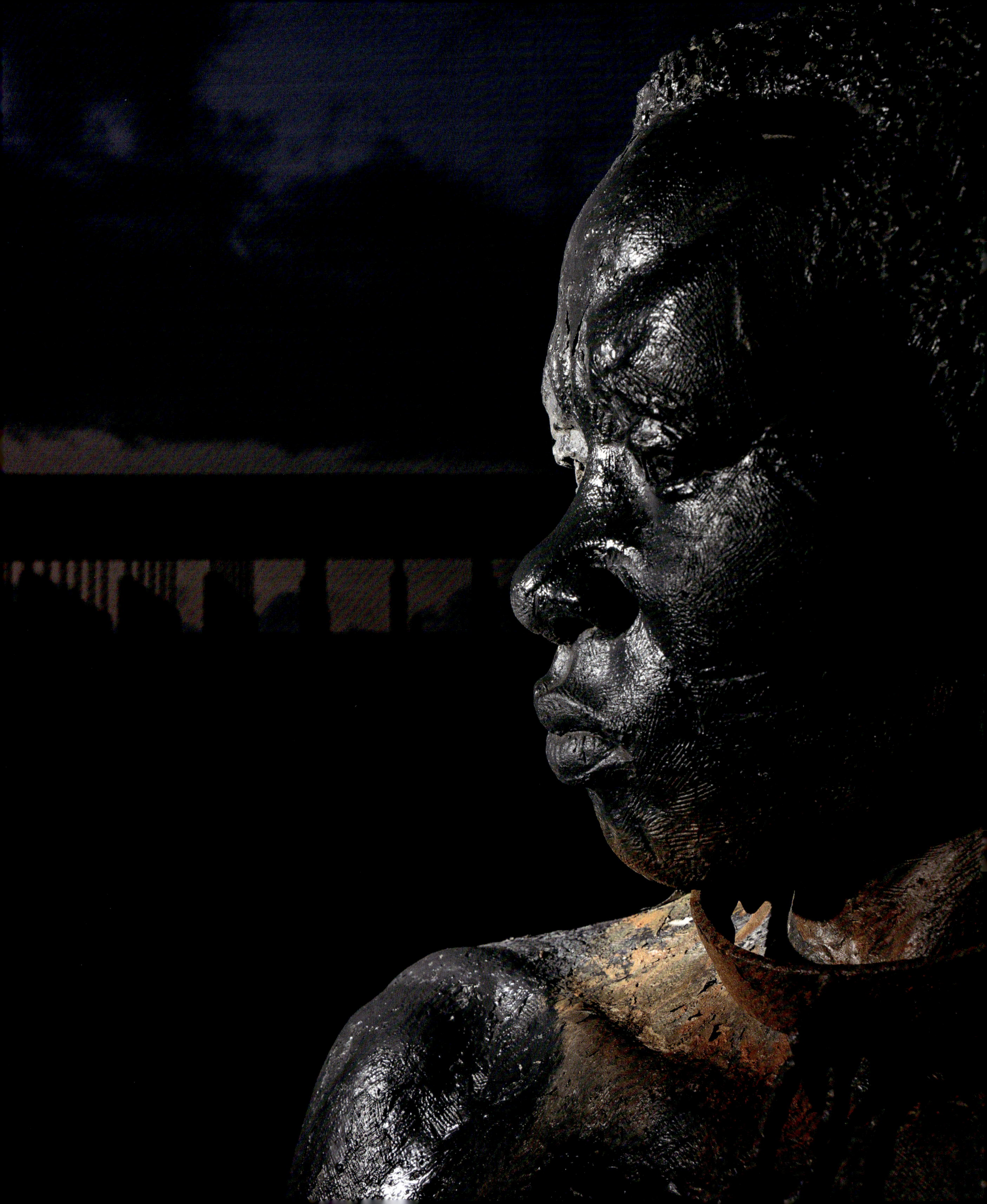

We will remember.
With hope, because hopelessness is the enemy of justice.
With courage, because peace requires bravery.
With persistence, because justice is a constant struggle.
With faith, because we shall overcome.

Foreword

In America, we have avoided honesty about the harsher parts of our history for centuries. The abuse of Indigenous Peoples who were here before Europeans, the enslavement of millions of Black people, a century of racial terrorism when thousands were lynched and millions threatened with lawless mob violence, and our not-so-distant history of codified racial hierarchy and segregation have all been topics many educators, historians, and elected officials sought to ignore. Too often we have looked away from essential parts of the American story and tried to minimize the harms of our history.

Our collective avoidance has allowed mistrust, misunderstanding, bias, and bigotry to fester and continue to undermine equality, freedom, and justice for all. Cultural institutions have frequently been complicit in this avoidance. Among the thousands of museums and historical sites in America, there is a startling absence of institutions that help us understand slavery and its legacy, the horrors of lynching and its implications for how we live today, and the degradation of Jim Crow and its lingering effects.

On a trip to Berlin, Germany, I was struck by the density of markers, monuments, and dedications to victims of the Holocaust. There are the Stolpersteine, "stumbling stones," bearing brass plates inscribed with the names of Jewish and Roma families who were forcibly taken to concentration camps, where millions were murdered. There is the extraordinary Memorial to the Murdered Jews of Europe near the Brandenburg Gate, a massive, compelling park sculpture that powerfully envelops visitors in the enormity of one of the worst tragedies of the twentieth century.

In Johannesburg, South Africa, I had a similar experience. The Apartheid Museum is an amazing cultural institution that forces visitors to confront the brutality of apartheid and the deadly system of racist rule that dominated South Africa for too long. There is a commitment to truth-telling that does not spare visitors from witnessing the violent oppression that Black Africans endured. Even before entering the museum, visitors are subjected to the humiliation of apartheid when they are issued an admission ticket that requires them to use the white or "colored" entrance. The magnificent Constitutional Court in Johannesburg, where Nelson Mandela ushered in a new era of racial equality in 1994, is surrounded by monuments and plaques recognizing those who suffered under apartheid rule.

In Kigali, Rwanda, there is a Genocide Memorial so determined to express the nation's grief that it holds human skulls. In other parts of the world, cultural institutions committed to reckoning with horrific histories of oppression, genocide, and human suffering provide critically important healing and transformation. There is a recognition that nations that have lived through inhumanity and cruelty on a massive scale cannot recover without a process of truth followed by repair, recovery, and reconciliation.

As someone who began his education in a racially segregated "colored school" before racial integration of public schools was finally achieved, I am disheartened that, despite important achievements and progress toward racial justice, we still contend with so much racial bias and bigotry in our nation. There is an assumption of incompetence or a presumption of dangerousness and guilt assigned to people of color who must navigate a multitude of challenges and obstacles because of our nation's history of racial inequality—a history we have failed to acknowledge or address adequately.

We are now confronting efforts by many to eliminate teaching, education, or even conversation about our history of slavery, lynching, and segregation. Some hope to ignore the past as if its tragedies and trauma can be eliminated by pretending it never happened. However, like with any illness, we will never become healthy by believing we are always well. We must confront the truth of our past for the sake of our future. Truth is the justice we owe to the ten million Black people who endured the immense suffering and constant sorrow of slavery in this country. Failure to fully acknowledge the 246 years enslaved people were brutalized and abused is not only dishonest, it is unjust.

Without memory, history's greatest crimes never happened. Avoidance of harsh history is convenient for those who want only pride and glory, but it is a perversion and distortion of true patriotism. To be great, a nation cannot root its character and strength in falsehoods and lies about our past. Without an accurate understanding of our collective failures, we can't even fully appreciate our achievements.

Some want to talk about the Tuskegee Airmen, Jackie Robinson, or the Navajo Code Talkers as symbols of American progress without detailing their abuse and mistreatment due to racial bigotry. Ignoring the racial injustice many people have had to overcome undermines their accomplishments and the heroic contributions they've made to the American story.

Memory is our only defense against repeating the misery of history.

We need cultural institutions uncensored by those who only want narratives of success and achievement. Millions of Black people in the twentieth century endured decades of pervasive humiliation and violent repression due to Jim Crow laws and racial bigotry. If we don't document this history fully, only those who lived it will remember the degradation and anguish of this era. Our silence becomes yet another insult and injury for them to bear.

The Legacy Sites were created to help advance an era of truth and justice in America. We believe we can free ourselves from the harms of history only by confronting our past with honesty and courage. There are so many things to learn about how our nation has sometimes failed that can strengthen our resolve to never fail again.

The Legacy Sites are about truth-telling. They are an invitation to everyone to learn our history, not to be condemned by it, but to be inspired to never repeat it. The National Memorial for Peace and Justice opened in 2018, the new Legacy Museum opened in 2021, Freedom Monument Sculpture Park opened in 2024, and Montgomery Square opened in 2026. These Legacy Sites will challenge us but also uplift and empower visitors to seek a better future free of the bigotry and bias that has so burdened us.

The Legacy Sites present a unique opportunity for visitors and every American to reckon with the painful components of our past. There is work that must be done. We must all acquire knowledge that is informed by an honest examination of our history. It is difficult but necessary to face the heartbreaking history of slavery, lynching, segregation, and racial injustice that has weighed on our nation for generations. It can be painful and uncomfortable to see the brutality and cruelty we have allowed in this country, but we ignore it at our peril.

The Legacy Sites don't just present the harm of history. A story of survival, determination, resiliency, and hope emerges from the difficulty of our past. This story of endurance and strength is important for us to understand if we are to eliminate racial bias in the twenty-first century.

If you want a future less burdened by bigotry and discrimination, more hopeful, and more determined to overcome racial inequality, I hope you will visit our sites again and again. Spend time with us, bring your friends and loved ones, join us in an important project that empowers us to overcome racial injustice in America.

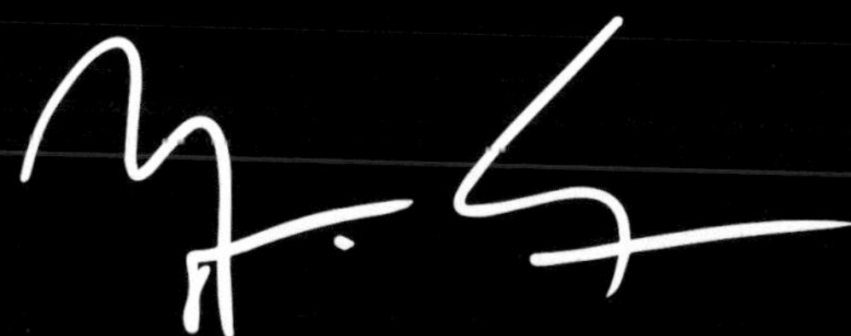

Bryan Stevenson, Executive Director, Equal Justice Initiative

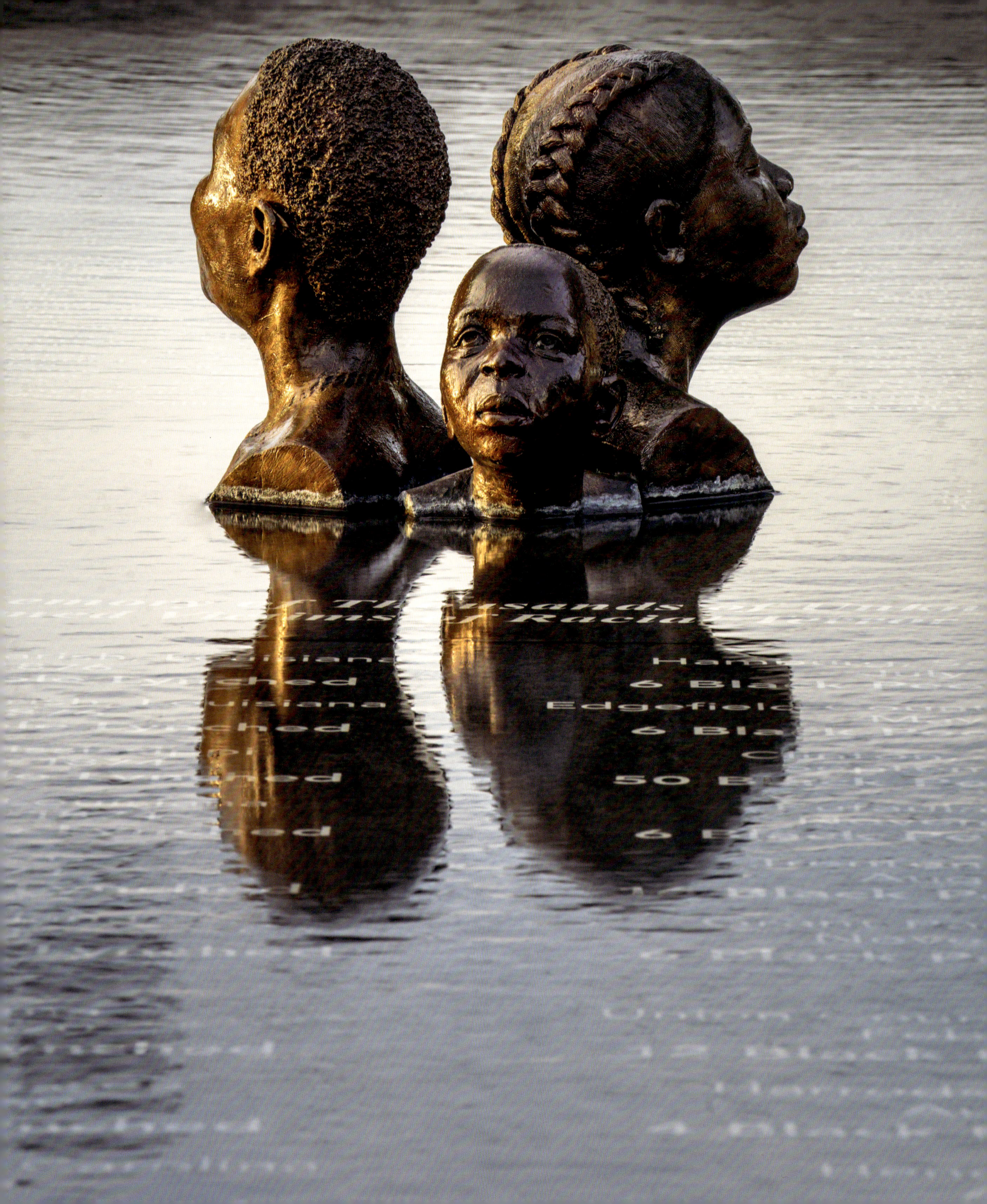

THE LEGACY MUSEUM

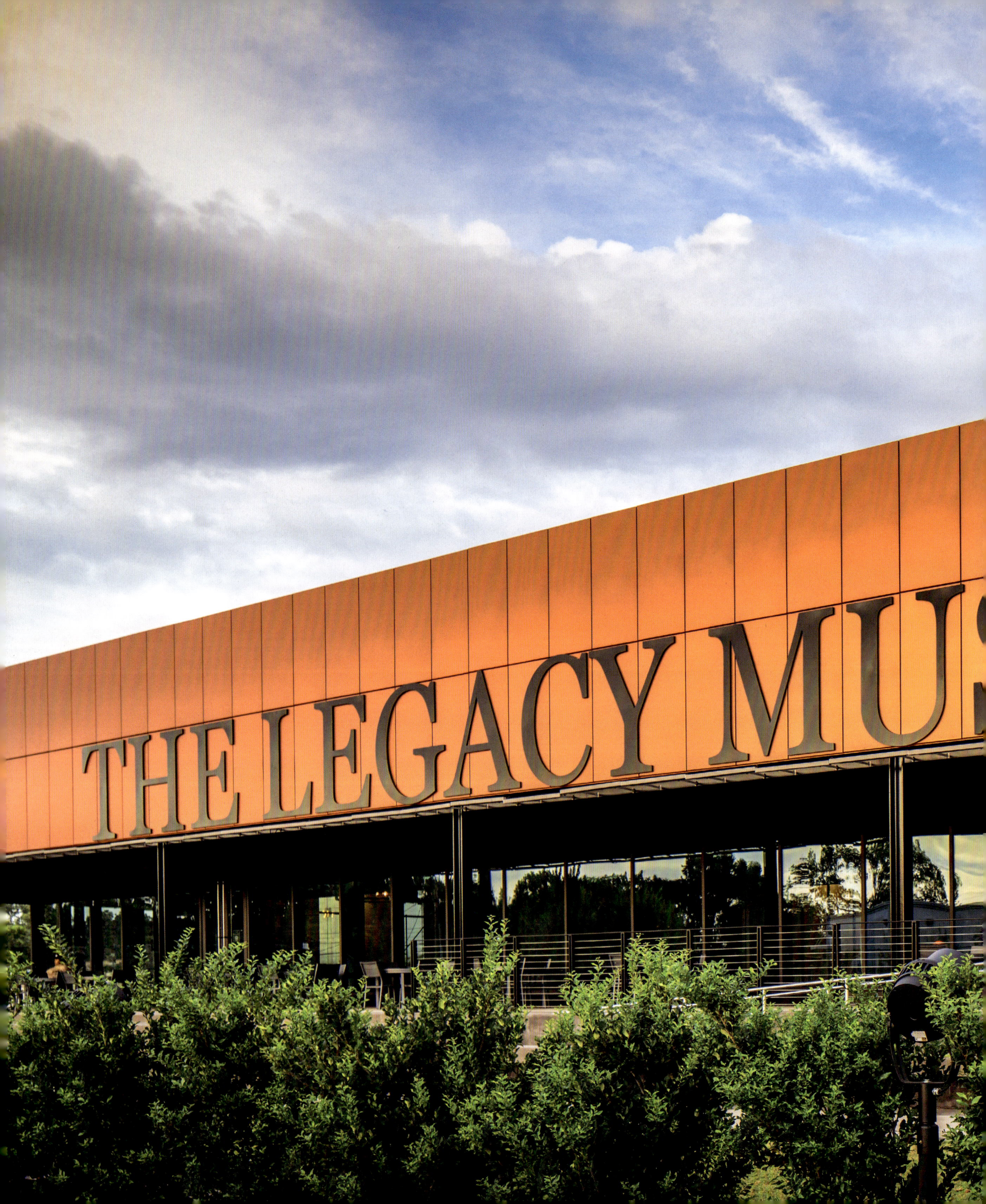
THE LEGACY MUS

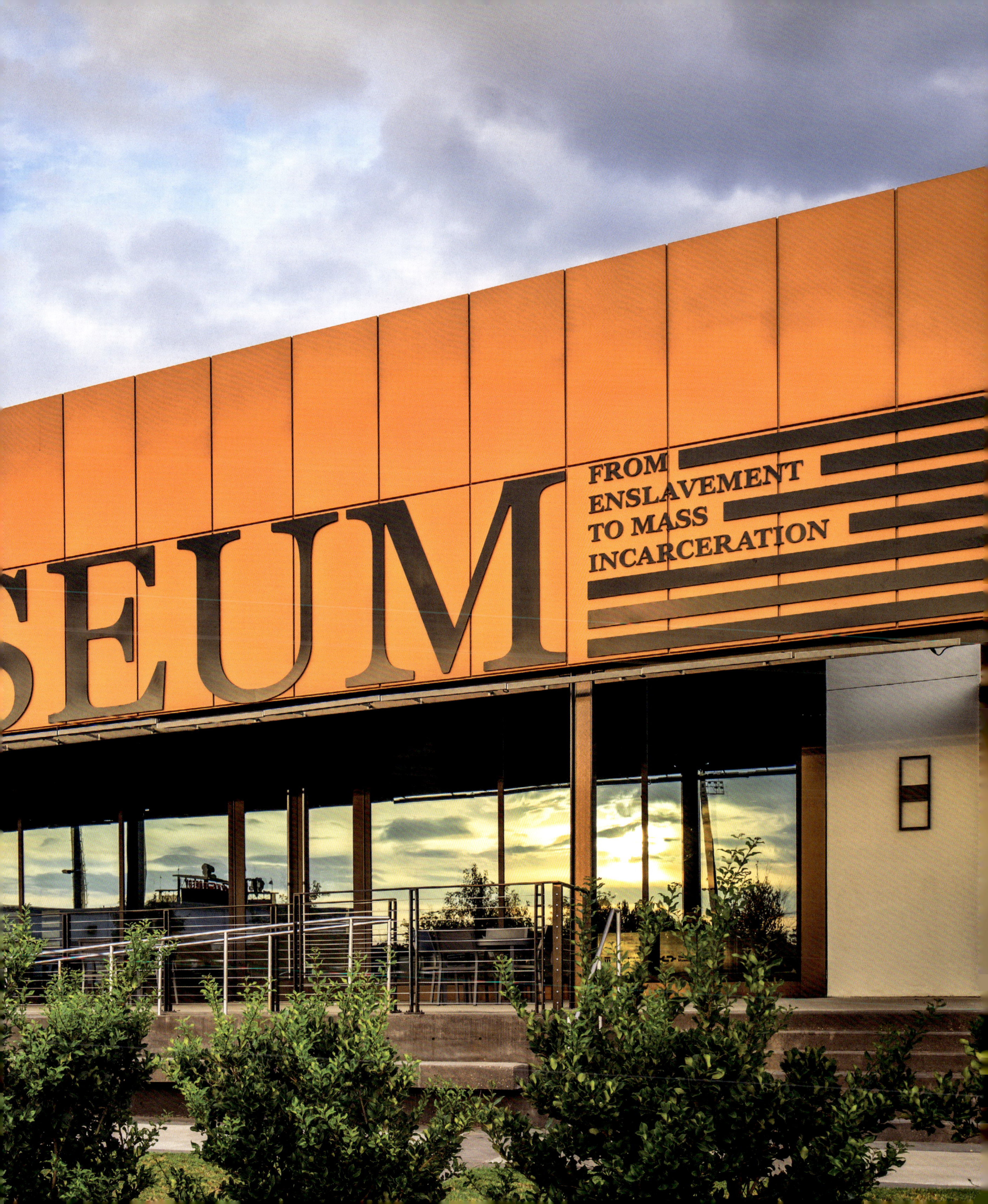
SEUM
FROM
ENSLAVEMENT
TO MASS
INCARCERATION

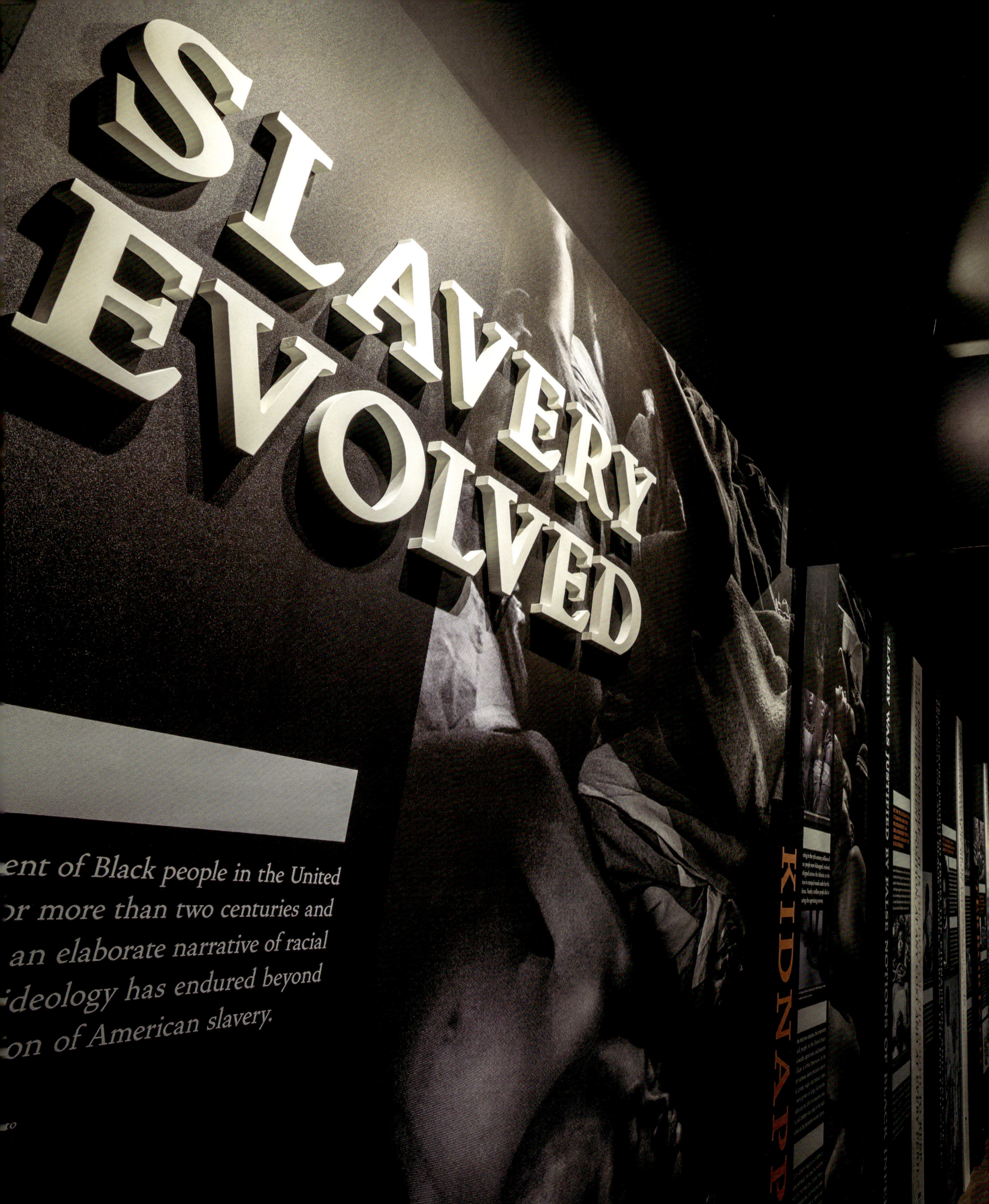
SLAVERY
EVOLVED
ent of Black people in the United
or more than two centuries and
an elaborate narrative of racial
ideology has endured beyond
on of American slavery.
KIDNAP
SLAVERY WAS JUSTIFIED BY FALSE NOTIONS OF BLACK IN

The Legacy Museum offers a powerful, immersive journey through America's history of racial injustice.

On the site of a cotton warehouse where enslaved Black people were forced to labor in bondage, the Legacy Museum tells the story of enslavement in America and its legacy through interactive media, first-person narratives, world-class art, and data-rich exhibits.

Visitors travel through a comprehensive history of America that details the role of racial bigotry and the legacy it creates, from the racialization of enslavement to the era of Jim Crow and racial terror lynchings to the current mass incarceration crisis—and find inspiration and hope in the soaring Reflection Space and world-class art gallery.

The Evolution of Slavery

More than 150 years after the formal abolition of slavery, and more than 50 years after violent opposition to the Civil Rights Movement captured national and international headlines, America seems at once a nation both changed and stuck. Social movements and legal reforms have achieved major advancement but failed to eradicate continuing inequality rooted in a history of racial injustice.

Slavery in the United States lasted for more than two centuries. It deprived enslaved Black people of all legal rights and autonomy and created a permanent racial hierarchy that grew from and reinforced an elaborate narrative of racial inferiority that denied Black people's humanity and endured long after slavery was officially abolished in 1865.

The legal instruments that abolished racialized chattel slavery in America did nothing to address the narrative of racial hierarchy that sustained enslavement, nor did they establish a national commitment to racial equality.

For that reason, we believe that slavery did not end; it evolved. In the era that followed, white Southerners who had once been supporters of slavery and defenders of the Confederacy reestablished the racial hierarchy of white supremacy through racial terror, lynching, and other brutal violence, while Northern officials and national leaders did little.

At the end of World War II, the United States was determined to portray itself as a model of democratic freedom on the global stage and the South came under new pressure to reform its Jim Crow segregation laws. In 1954, the Supreme Court's *Brown v. Board of Education* decision striking down segregated public schools foreshadowed the demise of legalized segregation. White political leaders and communities responded with massive resistance and violently defended racial inequality as their way of life. Through courageous activism and inspiring leadership, the Civil Rights Movement achieved the passage of federal laws and social shifts that inspired people throughout the world and fundamentally changed the lives of all Americans.

But the dehumanizing narrative of racial difference at the root of it all continued to survive and evolve, perpetuating racial inequality and giving rise to inhumane criminal justice policies.

We are now in an era of mass incarceration that is inextricably linked to our history of racial injustice. Despite its long use as a tool of racial control, criminal justice was the institutional system least targeted by civil rights reforms, and it now produces the most persistent racialized outcomes. With the world's highest incarceration rate, America's harsh and biased criminal policies maintain racialized barriers to

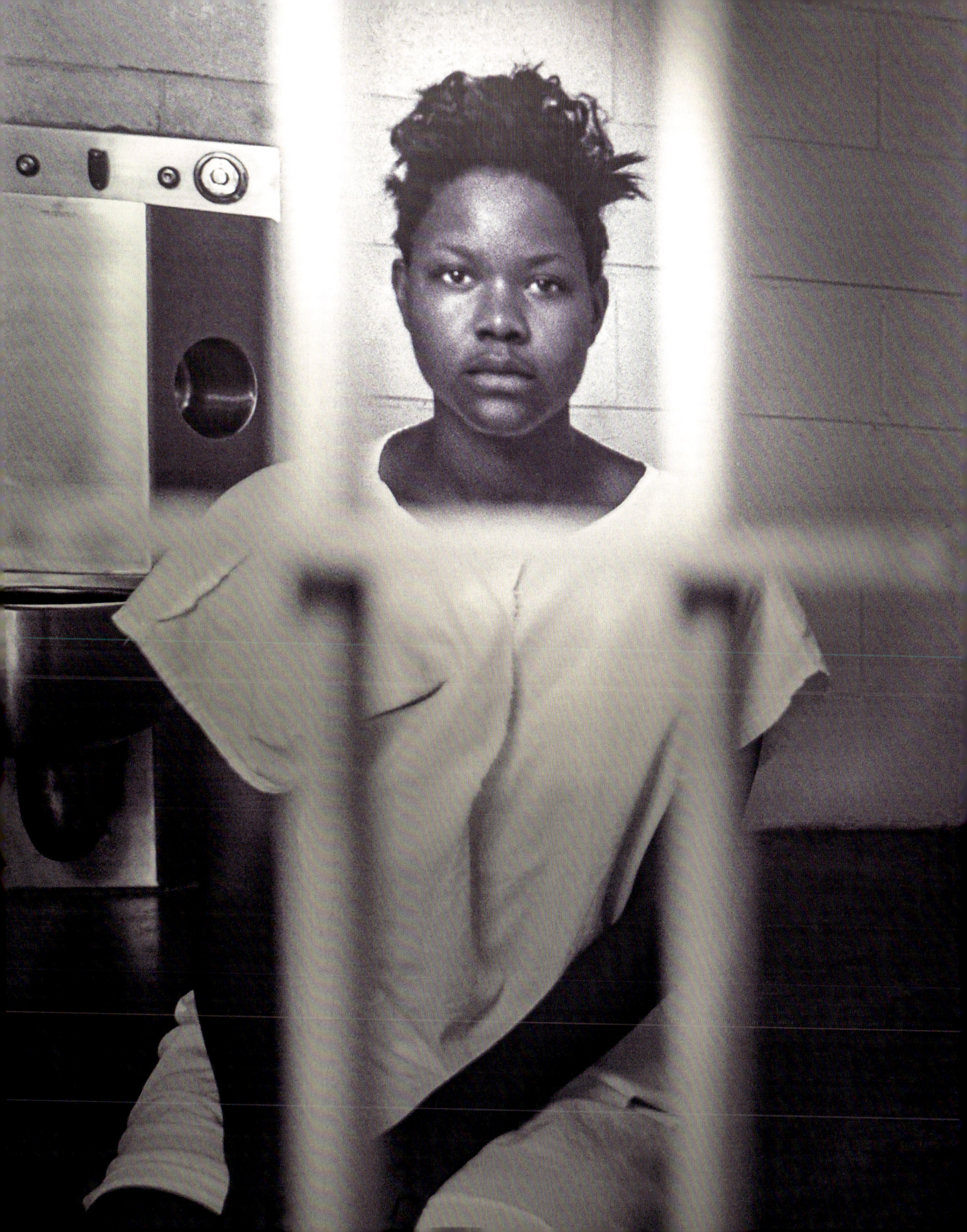

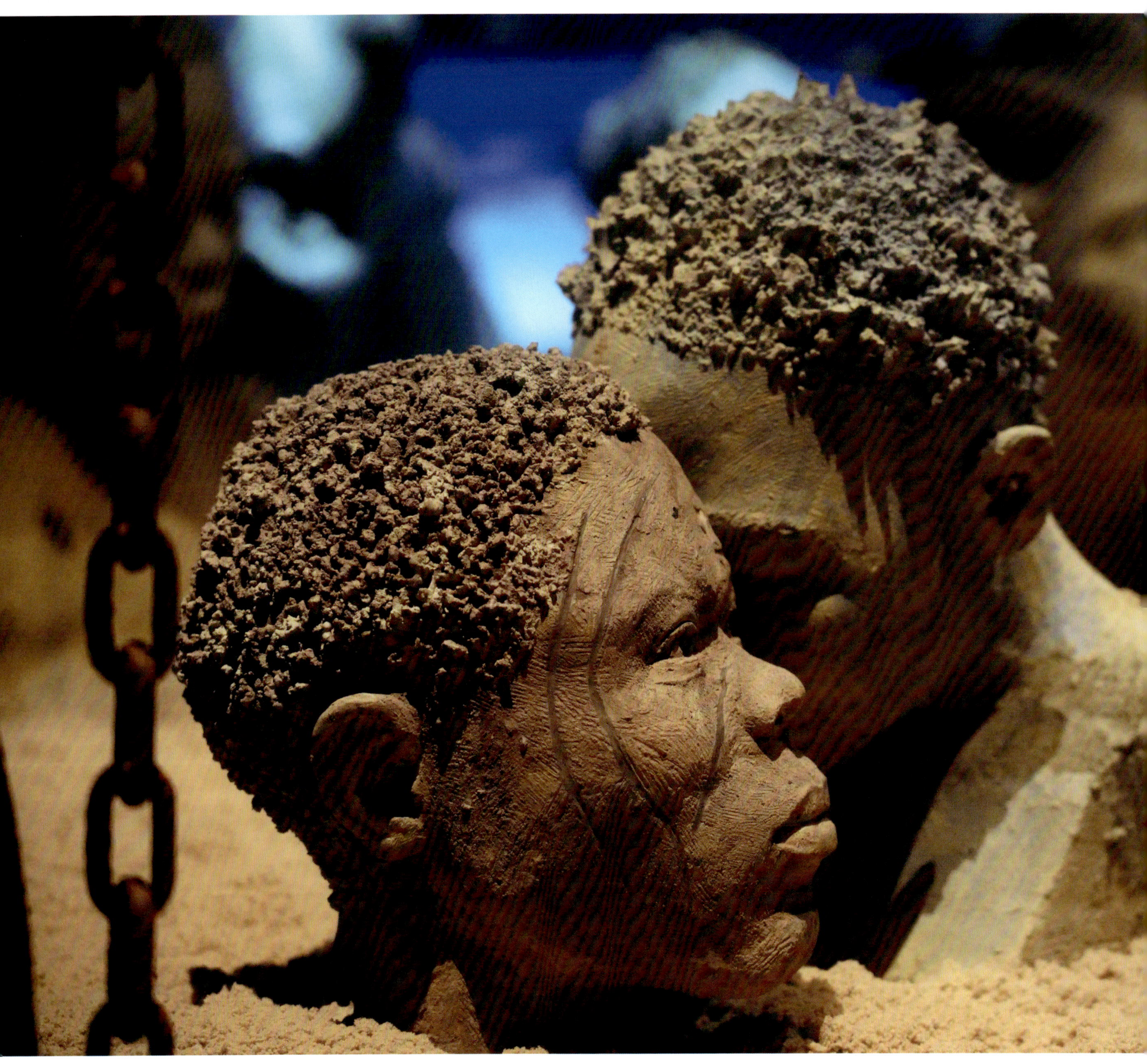

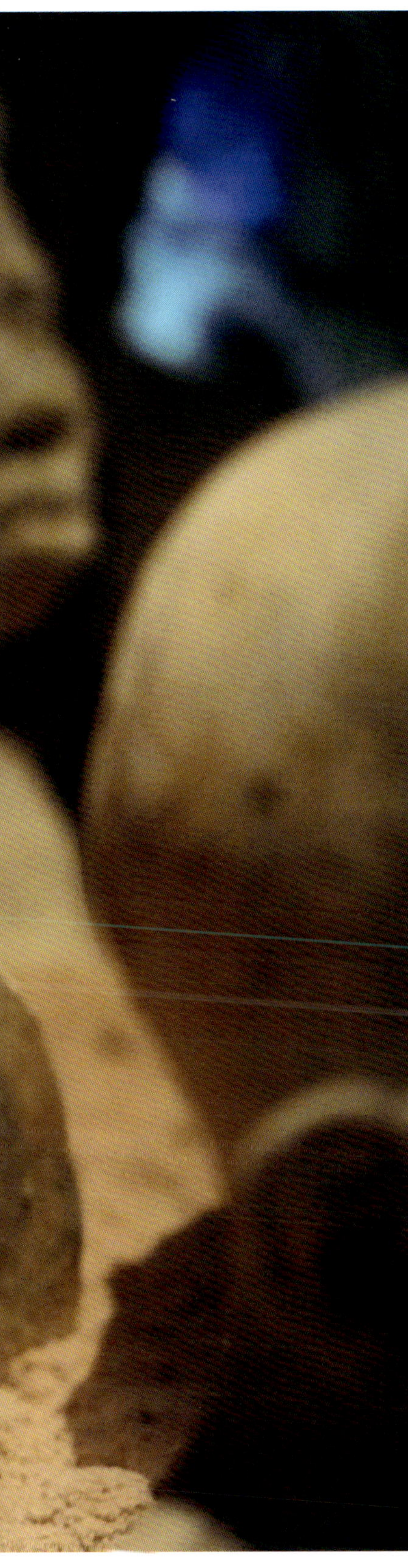

Above and pages 22–25:
Kwame Akoto-Bamfo
Nkyinkyim: Dirge Across the Atlantic / Nkyinkyim: Melancholic Lullabies, 2020, 2021
Concrete

equality. In the twenty-first century, one in three Black boys is projected to go to jail or prison in his lifetime.

The Supreme Court has signaled a willingness to recede from legal protections established during the civil rights era, while increasingly polarized political rhetoric impedes the kind of honest and open dialogue needed to move this country forward. Our national discourse does not sufficiently comprehend our history or its legacy of racial inequality. That lack of understanding enables inequality to persist. Only through grappling with this difficult past can our country move in a different direction.

Other nations that have suffered devastating human rights abuses demonstrate that healing must grow out of a common process. The communities that suffered the Rwandan genocide, the apartheid era in South Africa, and the Holocaust conducted by Nazi Germany recognized that reconciliation requires honestly facing the extent of the atrocity: Who benefited? Who suffered? What injuries are universal?

In the United States, we have not undertaken the work necessary to understand and acknowledge the full impact of more than two centuries of slavery, the post-Reconstruction era of racial terror and lynching, and the resulting mass migration of African Americans fleeing the South during the first half of the twentieth century.

Meanwhile, our history of racial inequality and economic injustice has created continuing challenges for all Americans. We rightly celebrate the proud and inspiring achievements of the Civil Rights Movement. But that story is incomplete, and the progress made then cannot advance now without telling the truth about our history of racial inequality.

Reshaping the national conversation on race is a difficult task that is long overdue. The Legacy Museum invites the entire nation to begin this journey by confronting America's history of racial injustice with honesty, courage, and hope for the future.

Tracing the Roots of Injustice: Origins of the Legacy Museum

The Equal Justice Initiative is a nonprofit law organization that has worked for more than thirty years to improve justice and fairness for the poor, disadvantaged, and incarcerated. Founded in 1989 to provide legal assistance to men and women on Alabama's death row, EJI has represented the condemned, wrongly convicted, unfairly sentenced, children in the criminal justice system, and the mentally ill and disabled facing imprisonment. We are actively working to end inhumane conditions

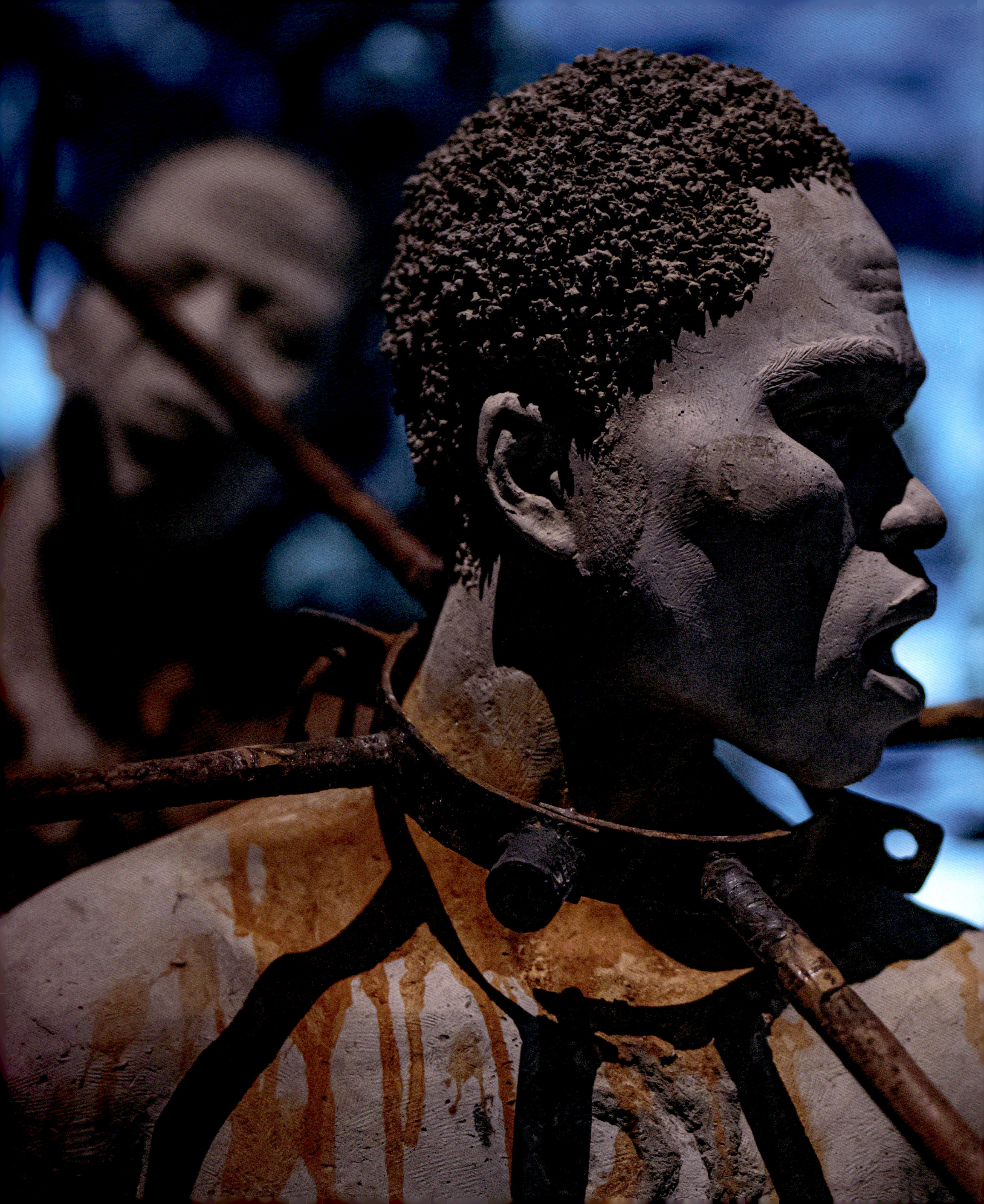

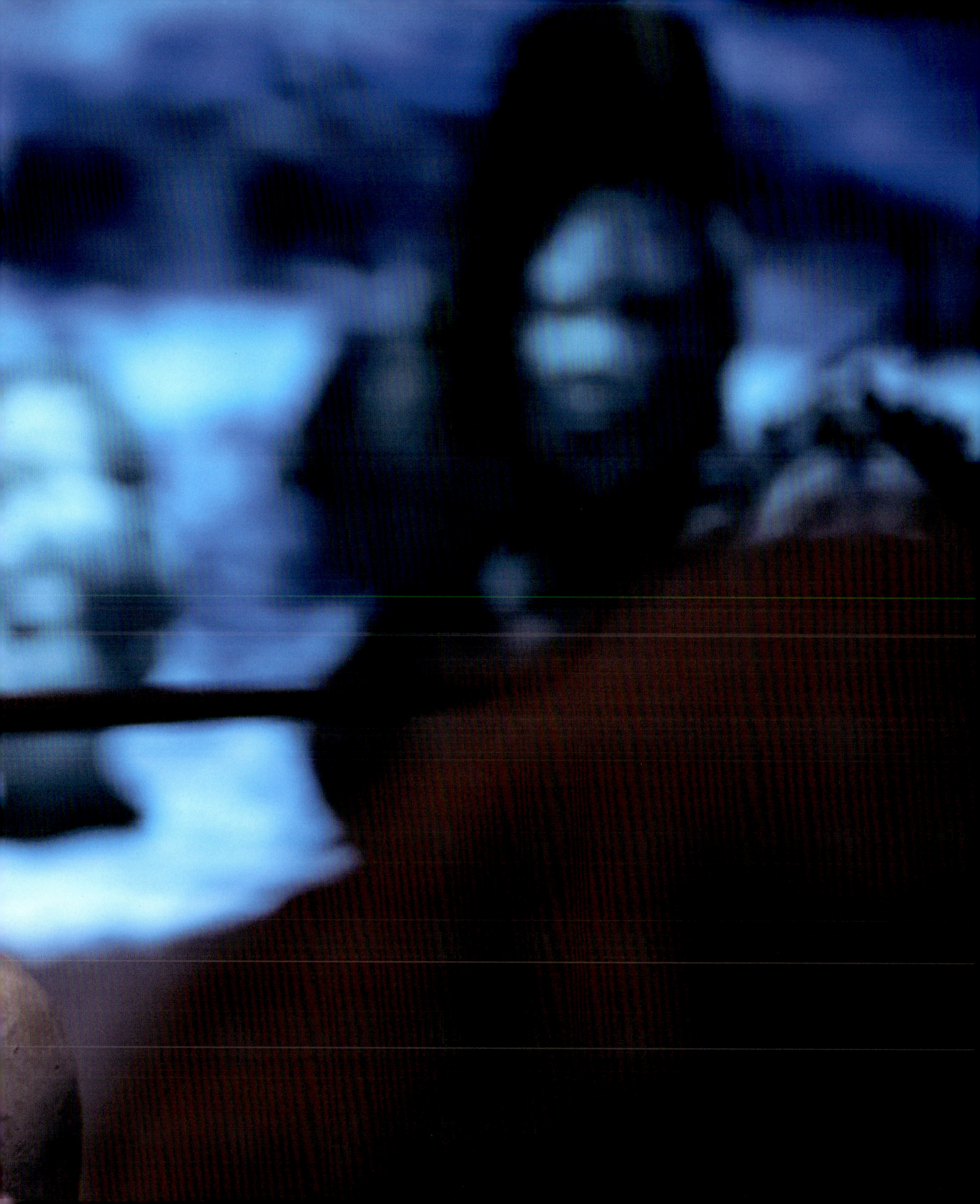

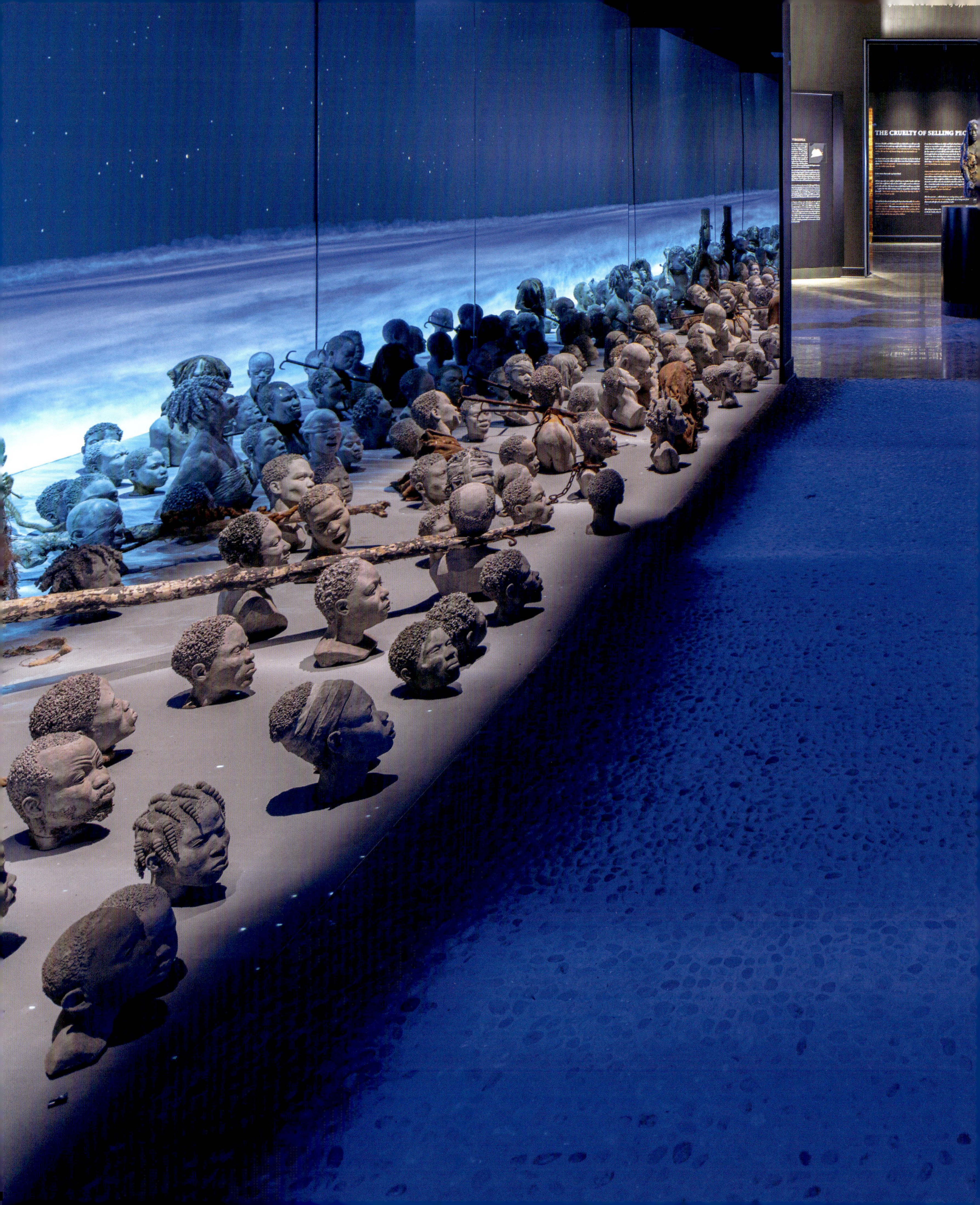
THE CRUELTY OF SELLING

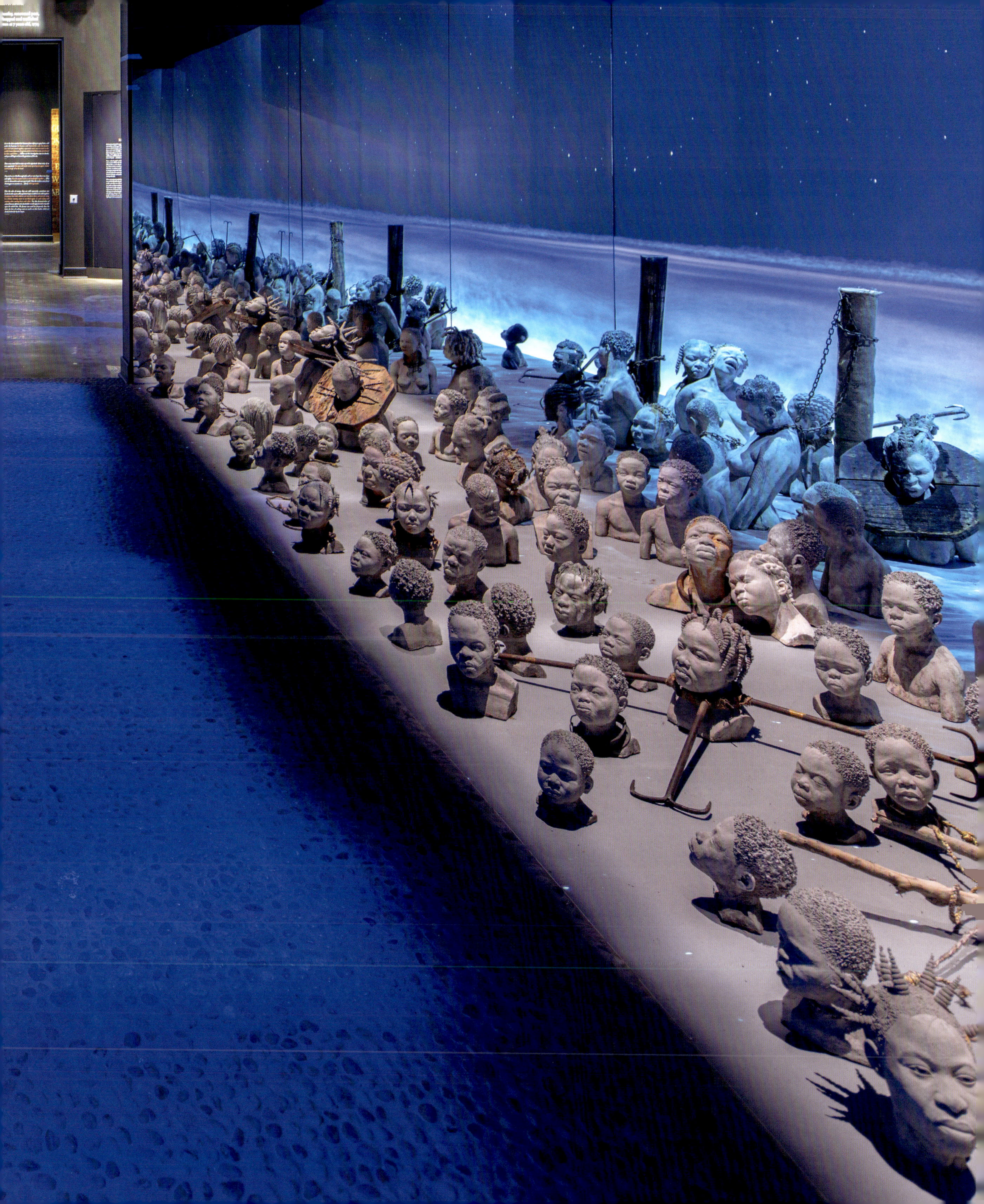

of confinement, improve reentry opportunities for the formerly incarcerated, and eliminate mass imprisonment, extreme punishments, and cruel sentencing practices.

So why has this law office opened a racial history museum?

Over decades of working to combat abuse and injustice within the criminal justice system, EJI advocates have witnessed firsthand the realities of racially biased mass incarceration and directly observed the connections between past and present. We have stood in countless courthouses with Confederate monuments on their front lawns and visited countless prisons where chained Black men labor in fields that were once plantations worked by enslaved people. We have also watched politicians endorse increasingly punitive, "tough-on-crime" policies.

From these observations, we learned that slavery, racial terror, and Jim Crow segregation are still palpable in the American South and discernible in federal lawmaking and national rhetoric. We learned that, to be effective, conversations about race and mass incarceration must include this historical perspective—a perspective that has always informed our work and inspired us to expand the conversation beyond the courtroom.

EJI's Race and Poverty Project, begun in 2008, includes a public education campaign to change the narrative about modern criminal justice issues by infusing it with racial history. A decade of educational exhibitions, community outreach, research, and publications showed us that people are interested in our message and encouraged us to expand its reach in 2018.

The Legacy Museum sits in the heart of one the most active and prominent sites of trafficking, selling, and abuse of enslaved Black people in America. A physical site and an outreach program, the museum is designed as an engine for education about the legacy of racial inequality. Exhibits feature narrative content and videography, the nation's most comprehensive collection of data on lynching, courageous testimonies from former and current EJI clients, and new technology that brings to life previously unseen archival information about the Domestic Trade of Enslaved People. Together, these materials and the visitors who engage with them will transform the site from a space of historical trauma to one of truth and healing.

We believe that telling the truth of enslavement, racial terror and lynching, Jim Crow segregation, and mass incarceration can free us from the division and conflict that has grown out of centuries of euphemism and avoidance. We believe that bravely committing to this effort can set our community on the path to the honest reflection that will uproot and cure these poisons for good. And we believe there is no more time to lose.

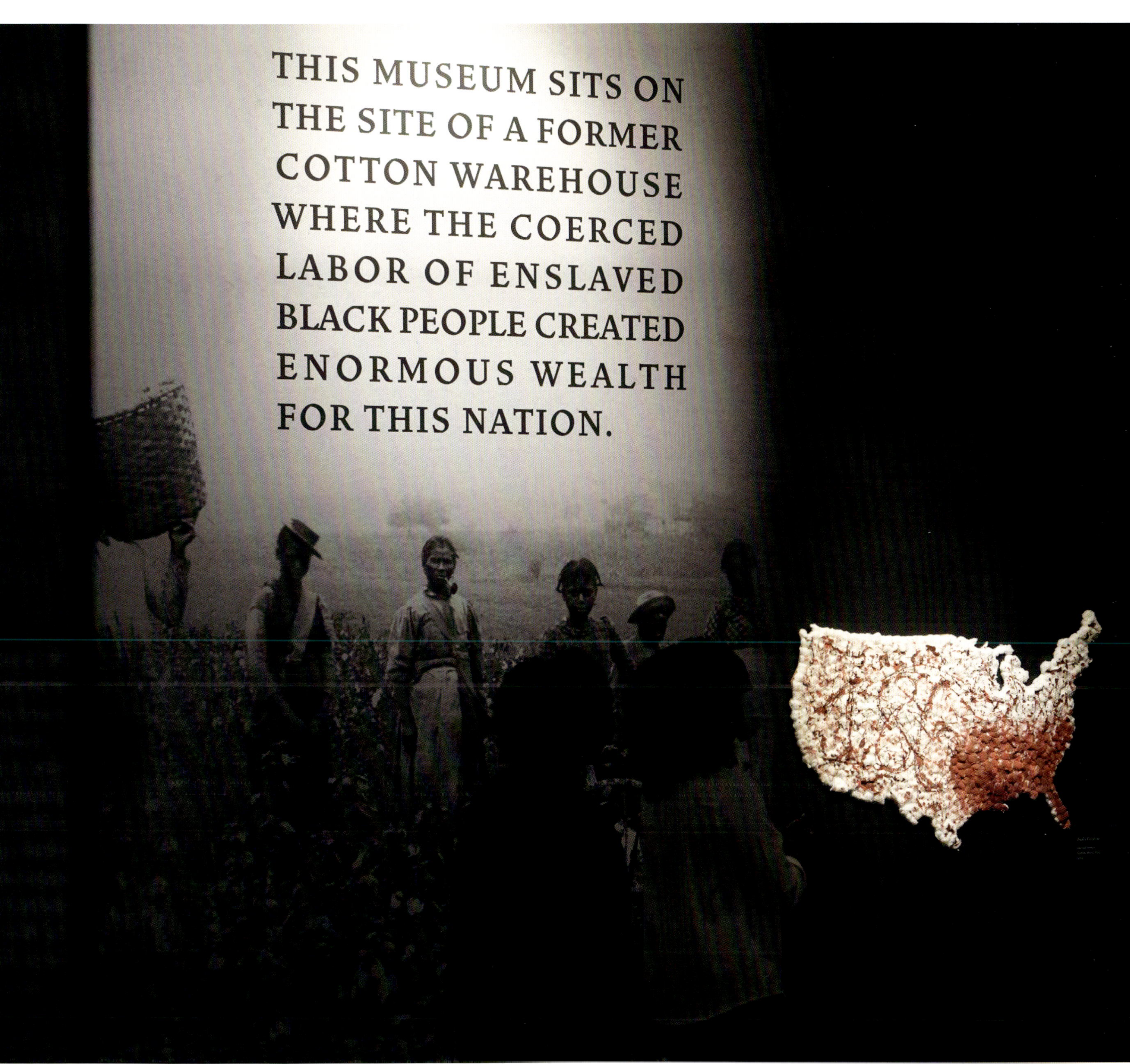

Artwork at bottom right:
Sharod Farmer
Fool's Freedom, 2019
Cotton, wood, glue, paint

The slave went free; stood a brief moment in the sun; then moved back again toward slavery.

—W. E. B. DU BOIS

“You Are Here”: Centering Racial History in Montgomery

In the late eighteenth and early nineteenth centuries, after the United States government used violence and coercion to seize land from the Indigenous Peoples who had inhabited the region for centuries, white people began moving to territories in the Lower South that would ultimately become the states of Alabama, Louisiana, Mississippi, and Florida. The invention of the cotton gin and the high price of cotton in the 1790s dramatically increased white settlers’ demand for enslaved Black labor in this region.

Congress abolished the Transatlantic Trade of Enslaved People in 1808, so the growing demand was met by the Domestic Trade of Enslaved People.

From 1810 to 1860, an estimated one million Black people were sold and forcibly moved from the Upper to the Lower South. Montgomery, Alabama, developed into one of the most active “slave trading” sites in the country. The city’s proximity to the Alabama River allowed “slave traders” to employ new methods of transportation, including the steamboat. In 1851, enslaved Black workers completed construction of a rail line linking Montgomery to Georgia and destinations farther north.

The number of enslaved people arriving in Montgomery reached hundreds per day. The city became one of the nation’s main “slave markets” and its citizens prospered from a growing agrarian economy fueled by “slave labor” and the widespread and profitable trafficking of enslaved people. By 1860, Alabama’s population included 400,000 enslaved Black people. Montgomery—where nearly two out of every three residents were enslaved—had a higher population of enslaved people than any other Alabama city.

Montgomery had more “slave trading” spaces than churches or hotels. The city’s commercial district and downtown center were the location of many “slave depots” and warehouses, and enslaved men, women, and children were bought and sold in auctions conducted at Court Square.

Today, Montgomery embraces a dual identity as the “Cradle of the Confederacy” and “Birthplace of the Civil Rights Movement.” The public landscape is littered with references to Confederate history, but the central role of slavery is nearly invisible. For generations, residents have traced paths once walked by Black people in chains and stood on sites that once held enslaved people awaiting auction with no knowledge of this forgotten and unmarked past.

Now, in Montgomery, the Legacy Museum will help us remember.

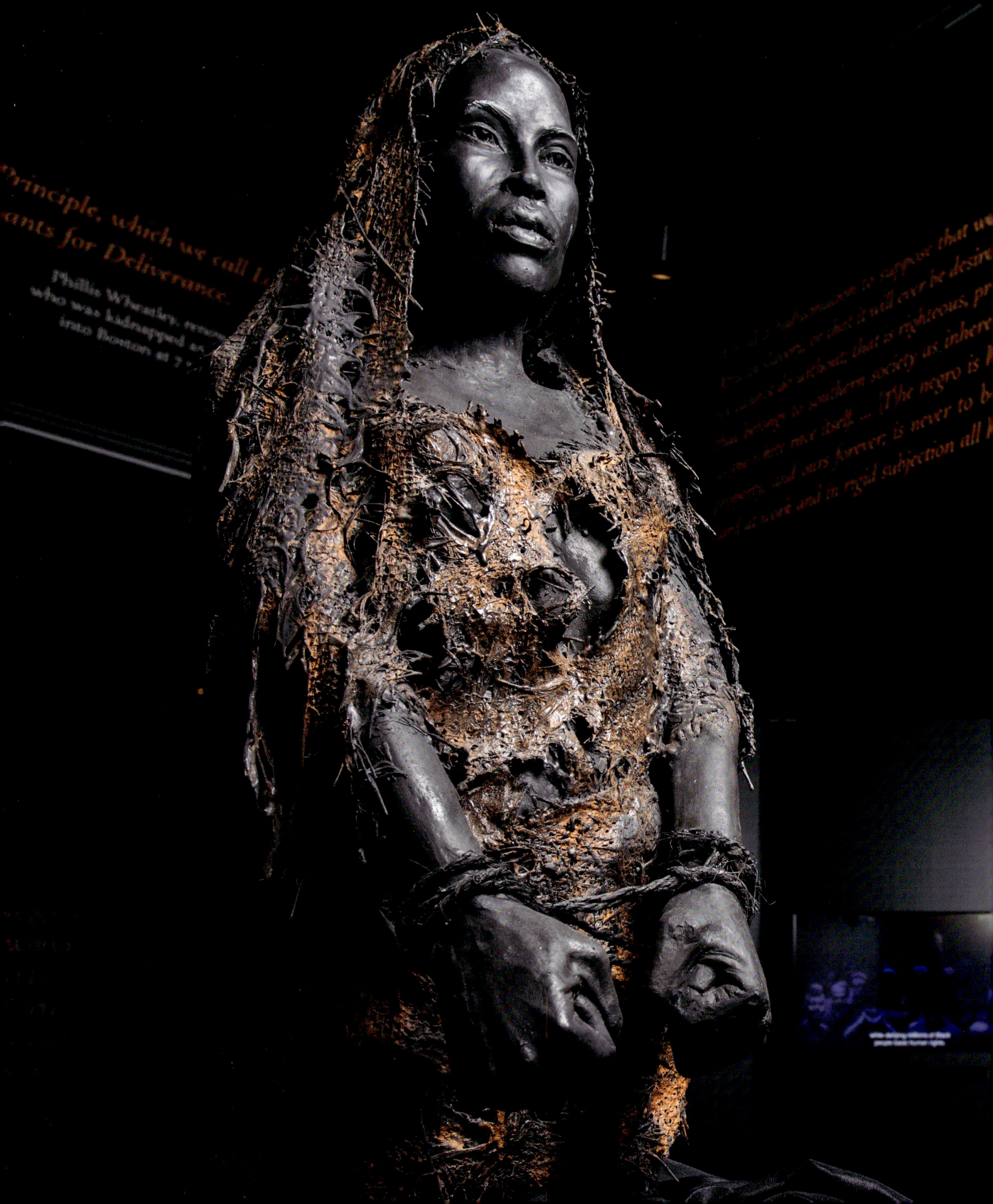

Principle, which we call
ants for Deliverance.
Phillis Wheatley,
who was kidnapped at
into Boston at 7
the negro is
subjection all

Transatlantic Trade of Enslaved People

Between 1501 and 1867, nearly 13 million African people were kidnapped, forced onto European and American ships, and trafficked across the Atlantic Ocean to the Americas, including the British, French, and Spanish colonies that would later comprise the United States.

Two million people died during the barbaric Middle Passage.

The global trafficking that separated millions of women, men, and children from their homes, families, and cultures destabilized African countries and left them vulnerable to conquest, colonization, and violence for centuries.

And in the Americas, a caste system based on race and color emerged in tandem with legal and political systems to codify white supremacy and enshrine enslavement as a permanent and hereditary status. That racial hierarchy continues to haunt our nation today.

Coastal communities across the U.S. were permanently shaped by the trafficking of African people. Local economies in New England, Boston, New York City, the Mid-Atlantic, Virginia, Richmond, the Carolinas, Charleston, Savannah, the Deep South, and New Orleans were built around the enslavement of Black people.

Kidnapping, trafficking, abusing, and dehumanizing African people and their descendants created generational wealth for Europeans and white Americans across occupations and industries, from early European colonists to priests and popes, shipbuilders to rum and textile producers, bankers to insurers.

The Transatlantic Trade of Enslaved People generated the capital that was used to build some of America's greatest cities and most successful companies. Many families, businesses, and institutions continue to benefit today from the enormous wealth produced by enslavement, but few have acknowledged or honestly confronted this history.

Sandrine Plante
Exode, No Home, 2019
Acrylic resin

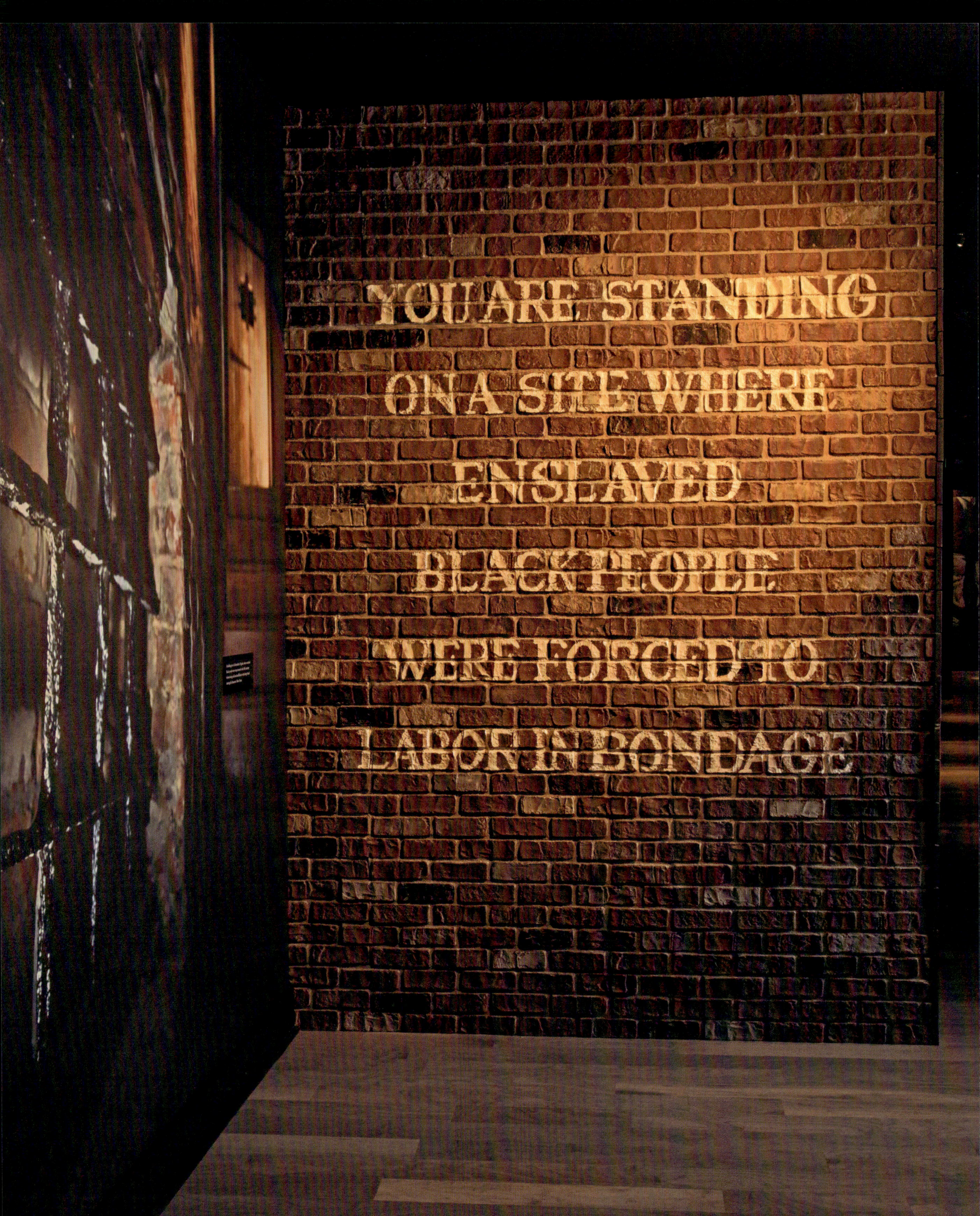
YOU ARE STANDING
ON A SITE WHERE
ENSLAVED
BLACK PEOPLE
WERE FORCED TO
LABOR IN BONDAGE

The Era of Enslavement in America

Beginning in the seventeenth century, millions of African people were kidnapped, enslaved, and shipped across the Atlantic to the Americas in cramped vessels and under horrific conditions. Nearly two million people died at sea during the agonizing journey. American slavery developed from a form of indentured servitude into a permanent, hereditary status centrally tied to race. After Congress abolished the International Trade of Enslaved People in 1808, more than one million enslaved men, women, and children were transported from the Upper South to the Deep South by boat, rail, and overland routes that they were forced to march in chained coffles.

Supporters of slavery created a narrative of racial inferiority to excuse the practice of owning and selling human beings. That narrative defined Black people as less human than white people, and it was used to justify laws and customs that deprived the enslaved of all legal rights and autonomy. Legal, political, religious, and scientific institutions defended Black people's lifelong and inescapable enslavement as permissible and necessary.

The system of enslavement was enforced through violence. Black people in bondage were forced to labor, often in brutal and inhumane conditions and for no pay. They also faced sexual exploitation, separation from loved ones, and violent, sometimes deadly punishments including whippings, beatings, and mutilation.

Despite the great risks, Black people sought and fought for freedom throughout the era of slavery. The Underground Railroad developed as a complex network stretching from the Deep South to the North and Canada. Managed by remarkable leaders like Harriet Tubman, it helped thousands of Black people escape enslavement.

Black people were also active in the struggle to legally end slavery once and for all. In some cases, enslaved people mounted armed revolts against white enslavers to disrupt the system of enslavement, and throughout the North and beyond, free Black people were influential writers, speakers, and thinkers in the abolitionist movement.

In 1865, after the Confederacy waged a war to save slavery and lost, the Thirteenth Amendment abolished chattel slavery. Federal forces occupied the South to enforce the formerly enslaved's new rights and citizenship in a period of Reconstruction, and newly freed Black Americans boldly hoped for real political and economic opportunity.

Instead, the abrupt end of Reconstruction in 1877 saw the withdrawal of federal troops, returned control of Southern state governments to former Confederates, and the narrative of racial inferiority was restored to justify the continued dehumanization of Black people.

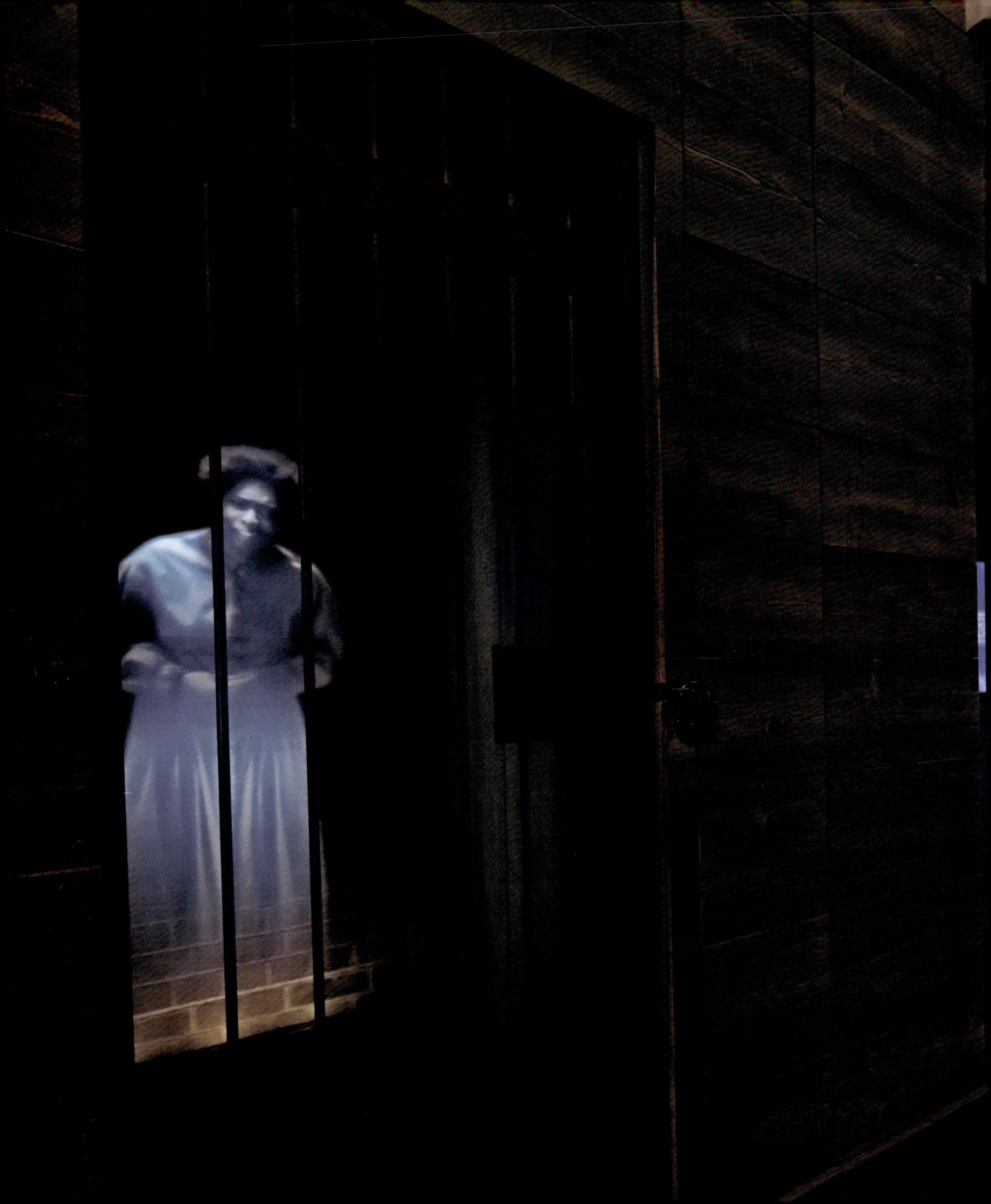

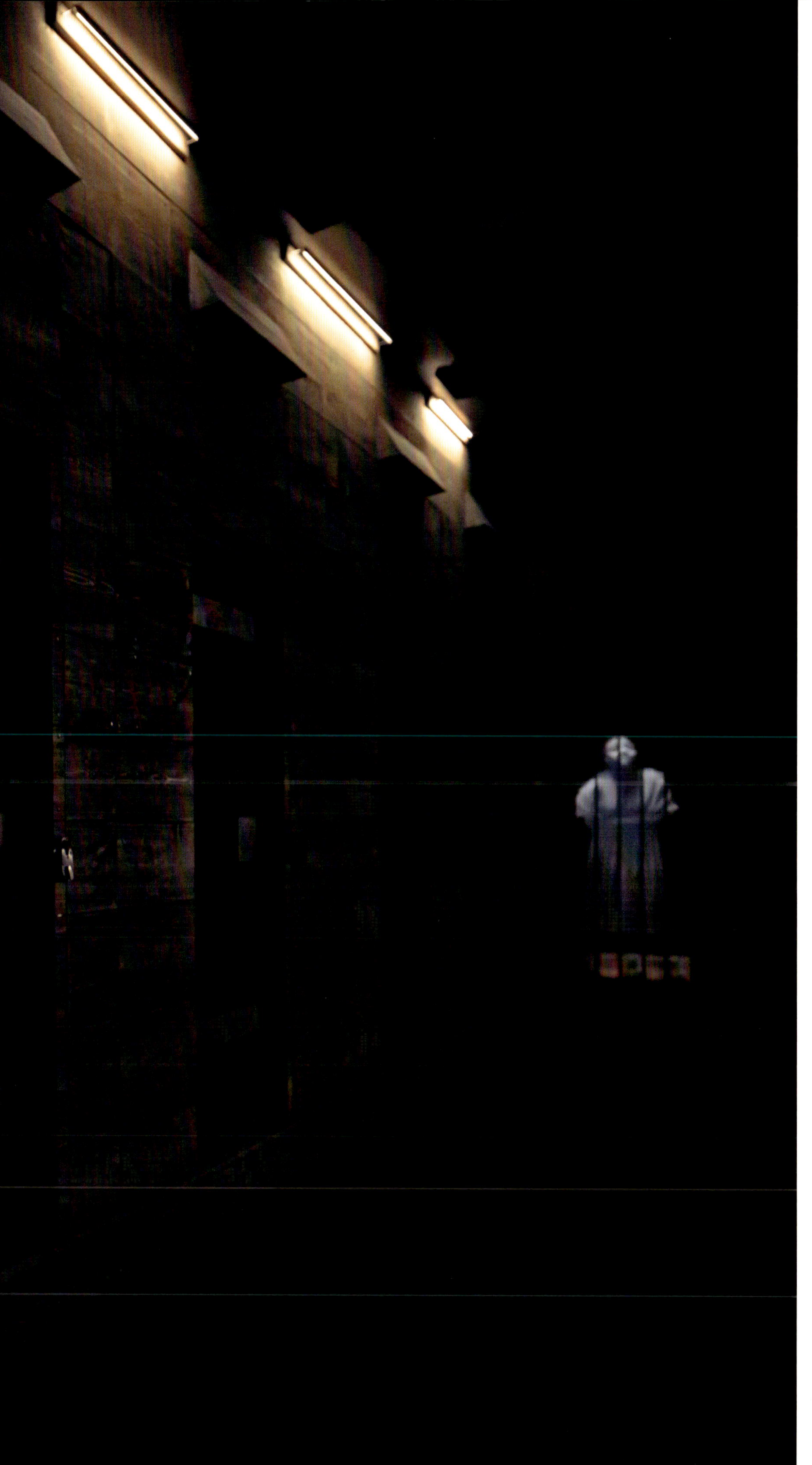

Holograms animate authentic, first-person narratives of enslaved people who were trafficked and sold away from loved ones.

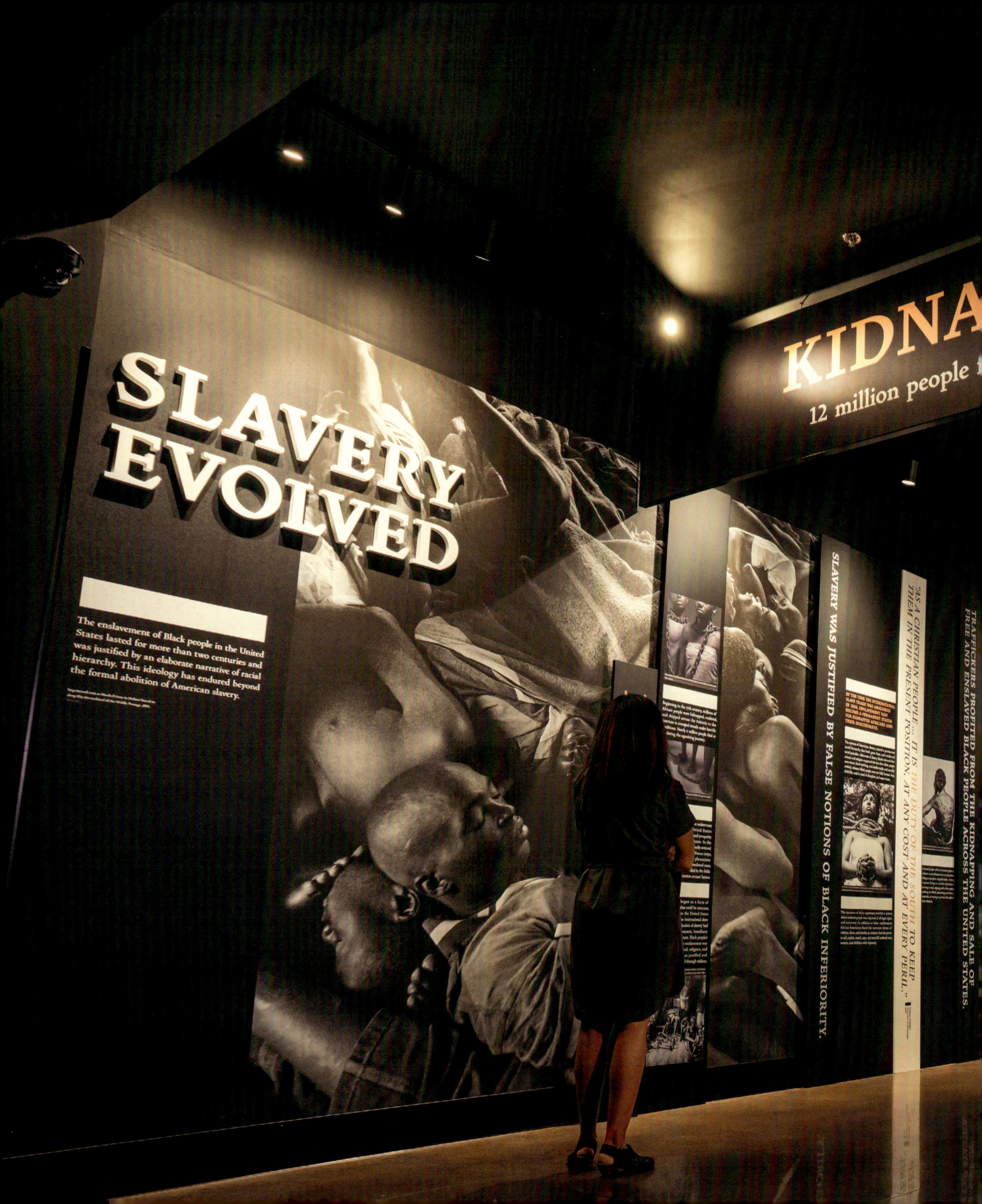

SLAVERY EVOLVED

The enslavement of Black people in the United States lasted for more than two centuries and was justified by an elaborate narrative of racial hierarchy. This ideology has endured beyond the formal abolition of American slavery.

KIDNA

12 million people

SLAVERY WAS JUSTIFIED BY FALSE NOTIONS OF BLACK INFERIORITY.

"AS A CHRISTIAN PEOPLE... IT IS THE DUTY OF THE SOUTH TO KEEP THEM IN THE PRESENT POSITION, AT ANY COST AND AT EVERY PERIL."

TRAFFICKERS PROFITED FROM THE KIDNAPPING AND SALE OF FREE AND ENSLAVED BLACK PEOPLE ACROSS THE UNITED STATES.

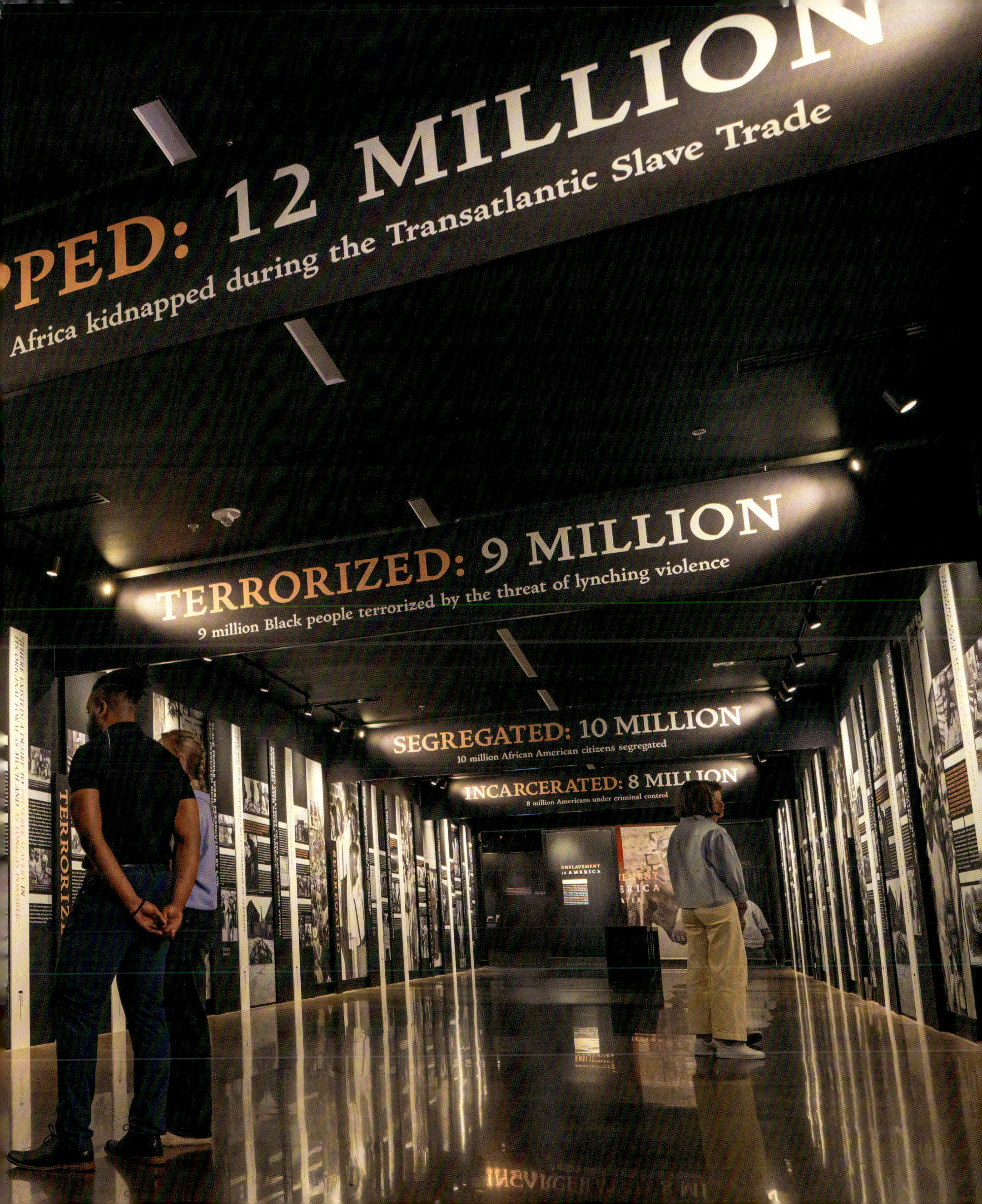

PED: 12 MILLION
Africa kidnapped during the Transatlantic Slave Trade

TERRORIZED: 9 MILLION
9 million Black people terrorized by the threat of lynching violence

SEGREGATED: 10 MILLION
10 million African American citizens segregated

INCARCERATED: 8 MILLION
8 million Americans under criminal control

ENSLAVEMENT IN AMERICA

TERRORIZ

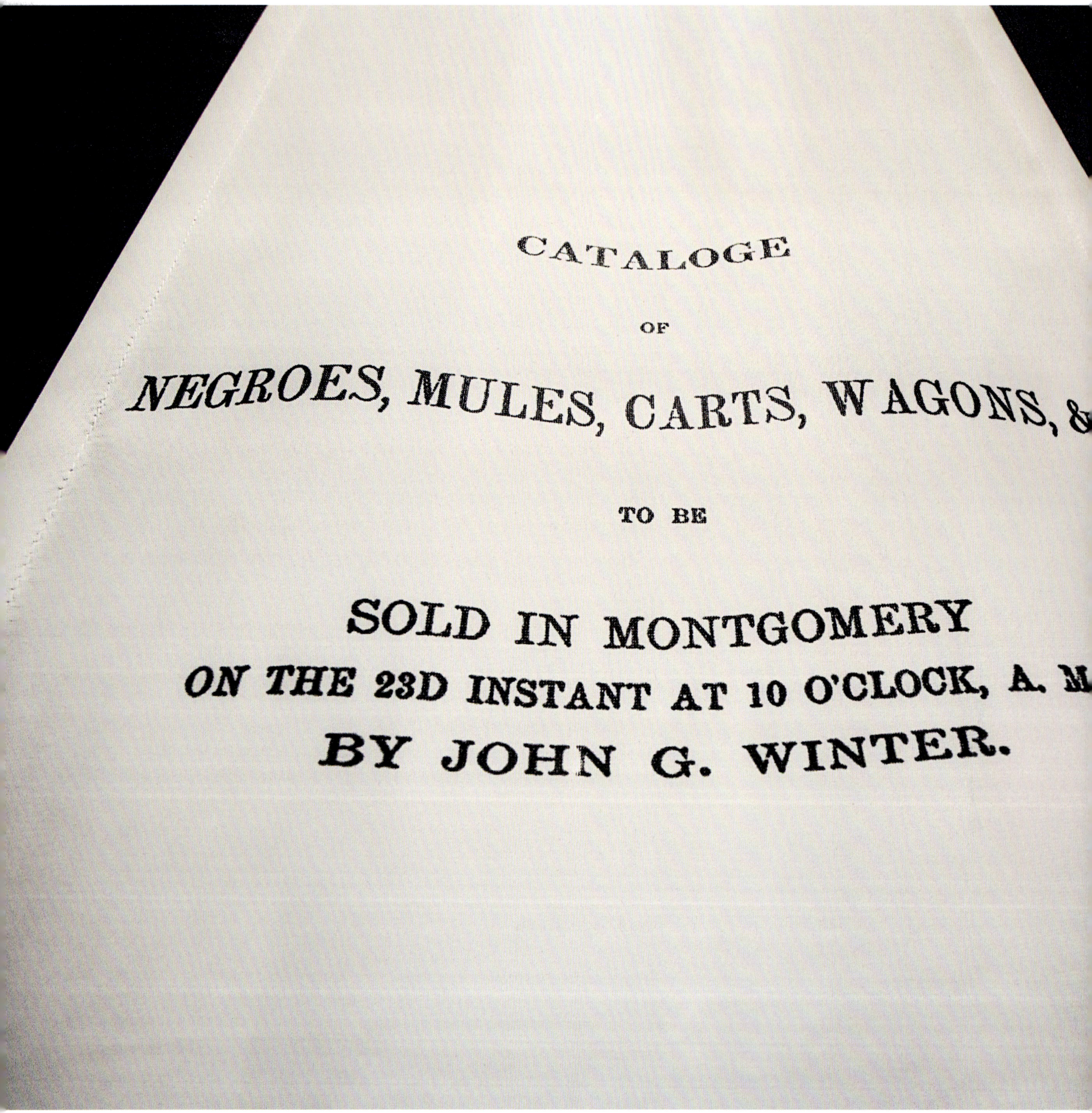

CATALOGE

OF

NEGROES, MULES, CARTS, WAGONS, &

TO BE

SOLD IN MONTGOMERY

ON THE 23D INSTANT AT 10 O'CLOCK, A. M

BY JOHN G. WINTER.

Warehouses, Depots, and "Slave Jails"

During the Domestic Trade of Enslaved People, enslaved people available for sale or scheduled for auction were sometimes confined in pens or cells in "slave depots," jails, and warehouses.

Formerly enslaved Black men and women later described this period as the most agonizing and torturous time of their lives, as they waited to meet an unknown fate while dreading possible separation from family and loved ones. For many, the psychological trauma was too much to bear.

In warehouses throughout downtown Montgomery, enslaved people were imprisoned alongside horses, pigs, cattle, and bales of cotton. Through imagery, narrative, and song, the Warehouse Exhibit gives voice to the memories of those who suffered and survived slavery in America.

The Paper Trail: Catalog, Auctions, and Runaway Notices

The business of slavery dominated Southern cities like Montgomery during the nineteenth century. Traders posted "slave auction" and sale notices on street corners, on buildings, and in newspapers, making the commercial trade of enslaved people impossible to ignore.

In 1854, wealthy Montgomery merchant John G. Winter prepared to sell 117 enslaved Black men, women, and children from his estate by producing an advertisement catalog that listed each person for sale by first name, age, and physical attributes.

When the horrors of the Domestic Trade of Enslaved People caused enslaved people to flee north, enslavers posted notices, posters, and bounties to entice "slave catchers" and law enforcement officers to capture and return "fugitive slaves."

These publications compose a documentary history of "slave trafficking" and illustrate the way enslavement permeated American life.

Seeking Family

American slavery devalued Black families, ignored their human dignity, and offered no protection under the law.

Roughly half of all enslaved people were separated from a spouse or parent due to sale—as many as 150,000 people in Alabama alone—and about one in four of those sold were children.

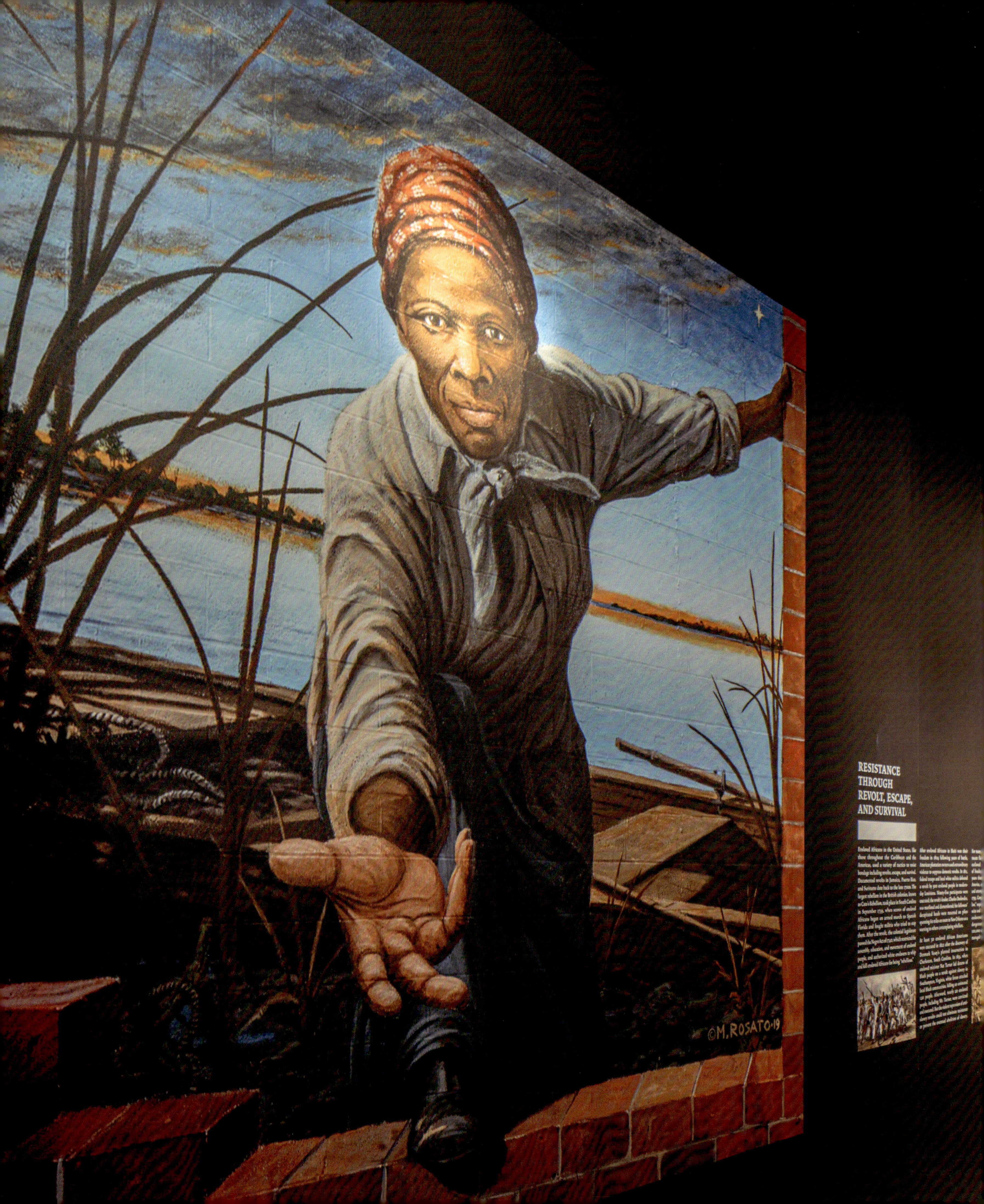

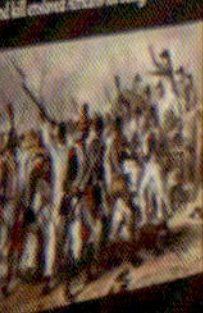
©M.ROSATO·19
RESISTANCE THROUGH REVOLT, ESCAPE, AND SURVIVAL

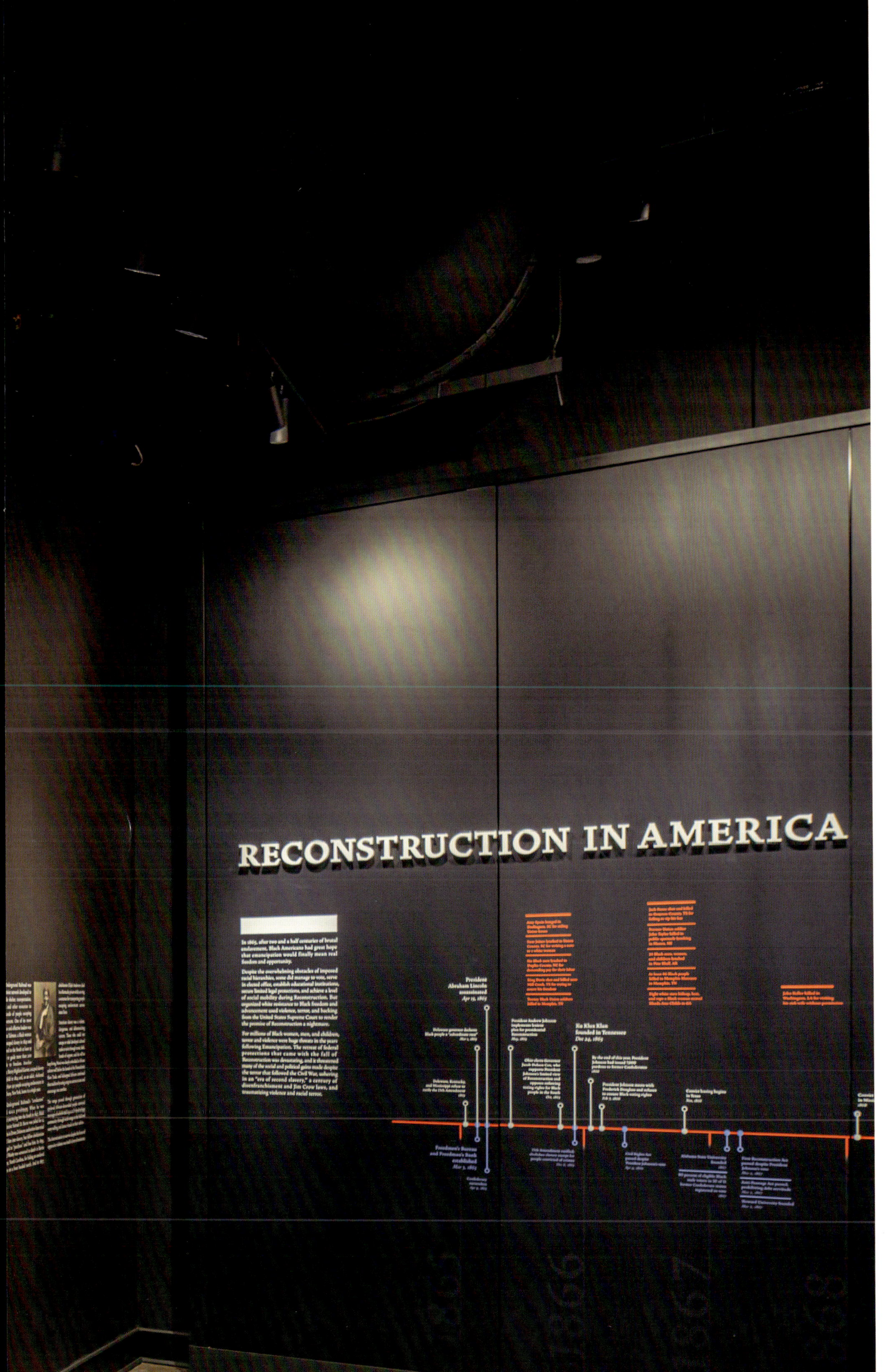

Artwork at left: Michael Rosato
Take My Hand, 2019
Mural

After the Civil War, formerly enslaved people posted desperate notices in newspapers seeking information about family members sold away during the Domestic Trade of Enslaved People. The United States did very little to help formerly enslaved families reunite after Emancipation, and most formerly enslaved people never found their children, siblings, or spouses.

These notices reveal that the horrors of enslavement continued into freedom and illustrate the deep bonds of family and enduring pain of separation.

Recalling Bondage

In the decades leading up to the Civil War, white Southerners defended slavery as a benevolent system that benefited enslaved Black people. Some still echo those sentiments even today.

The written accounts of Black people who lived the reality of slavery paint a different picture. Many formerly enslaved people documented their lives in bondage by writing first-person accounts of backbreaking labor, sexual abuse, physical punishment, separation from loved ones, and daring escape. Invaluable fuel for the abolitionist movement when published, these priceless narratives illustrate the truth of American slavery's brutal inhumanity.

The Era of Racial Terror

After Emancipation, Black people were legally free from involuntary labor, but Southern whites—who soon regained economic and political control of the region—still refused to recognize them as equals or even fully human.

The Civil Rights Act of 1866 and the Fourteenth Amendment gave African Americans full citizenship and equal rights, but the federal government's lackluster enforcement undermined the laws' impact and ended altogether with the premature withdrawal of federal troops from the South. White Southern identity remained grounded in a belief that white people were inherently superior to African Americans.

African Americans' rights were widely violated. Without a path to landownership or economic advancement, African Americans across the South were forced into sharecropping: working on white-owned land; dependent on food, shelter, tools, and seed advanced by the landowner; and trapped in a cycle of debt and poverty that lasted generations.

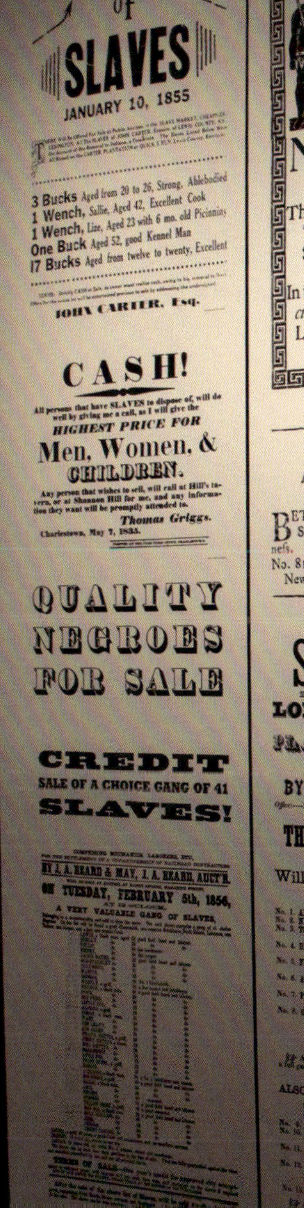

GREAT SALE of SLAVES
JANUARY 10, 1855
3 Bucks Aged from 20 to 26, Strong, Ablebodied
1 Wench, Sallie, Aged 42, Excellent Cook
1 Wench, Lize, Aged 23 with 6 mo. old Picinniny
One Buck Aged 52, good Kennel Man
17 Bucks Aged from twelve to twenty, Excellent
JOHN CARTER, Esq.
CASH!
HIGHEST PRICE FOR
Men, Women, & CHILDREN.
Thomas Griggs.
QUALITY NEGROES FOR SALE
CREDIT
SALE OF A CHOICE GANG OF 41
SLAVES!

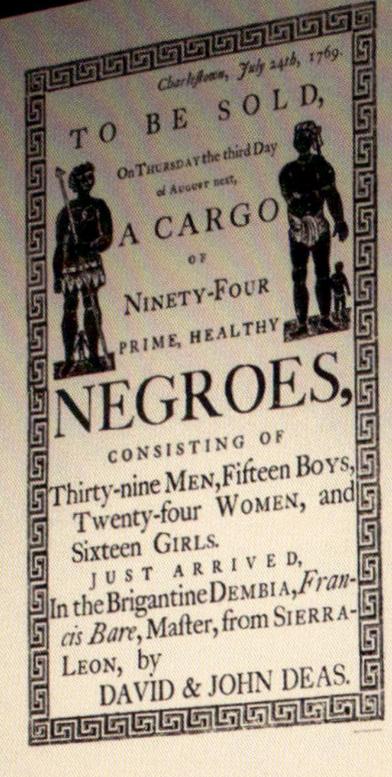

Charlestown, July 24th, 1769.
TO BE SOLD,
On THURSDAY the third Day of AUGUST next,
A CARGO
OF
NINETY-FOUR
PRIME, HEALTHY
NEGROES,
CONSISTING OF
Thirty-nine MEN, Fifteen BOYS,
Twenty-four WOMEN, and
Sixteen GIRLS.
JUST ARRIVED,
In the Brigantine DEMBIA, Francis Bare, Master, from SIERRA-LEON, by
DAVID & JOHN DEAS.
For Sale,
A LIKELY, HEALTHY, YOUNG
NEGRO WENCH,
BETWEEN fifteen and fixteen Years old: She has been ufed to the Farming Bufinefs. Sold for want of Employ.—Enquire at No. 81, William-ftreet.
New-York, March 30, 1789.
SLAVES!
LONG CREDIT SALE
OF
PLANTATION HANDS
FROM ALABAMA, WITHOUT RESERVE.
BY N. VIGNIÉ, AUCTIONEER,
THURSDAY, MARCH 25, 1858,
AT 12 O'CLOCK, M.
Will be sold in the Rotunda of the
ST. LOUIS HOTEL,
HEWLETT & BRIGHT.
SALE OF
VALUABLE
SLAVES,
(On account of departure)
NEGRO CATALOG
LIST OF A GANG
—OF—
Forty-Four Negroes
ACCUSTOMED TO THE CULTURE OF COTTON AND PROVISIONS,
IN ST. JOHNS, BERCKLY.
By P. J. PORCHER & BAYA.
On TUESDAY, 8th Inst,
MART, CHALMERS STREET,
CITY OF CHARLESTON,
NEGROES FOR SALE
BY
Brown & Hulger.
MONTGOMERY, ALABAMA.
RAFFLE
DARK BAY HORSE, "STAR,"
MULATTO GIRL, "SARAH,"
Will be Raffled for
CHANCES AT ONE DOLLAR EACH.
JOSEPH JENNINGS.
Will be Sold,
Before the door of the Eagle Tavern.
At 12 o'clock, on Monday the 24th instant,
A NUMBER OF
VALUABLE
SLAVES;
CONSISTING OF
An excellent Carpenter, a Brick Moulder,
A Tanner, a good Crop Hand,
2 Women, and 5 children.
The Women are excellent House Servants and young, the Men too are mostly young.
Thomas Taylor.
ESTATE SALE!
BY ORDER OF EXECUTOR.
By LOUIS D. DeSAUSSURE.
On Wednesday, 19th Inst.
CHARLESTON, SO. CAROLINA.
MESSRS. RYAN & SON'S MART,
IN CHALMERS STREET,
A PRIME GANG OF
67 NEGROES,
HOUSE SERVANTS.
Sheriff sale of likely Negroes.
HENRY M'GHEE,
Sheriff of Lawrence County.

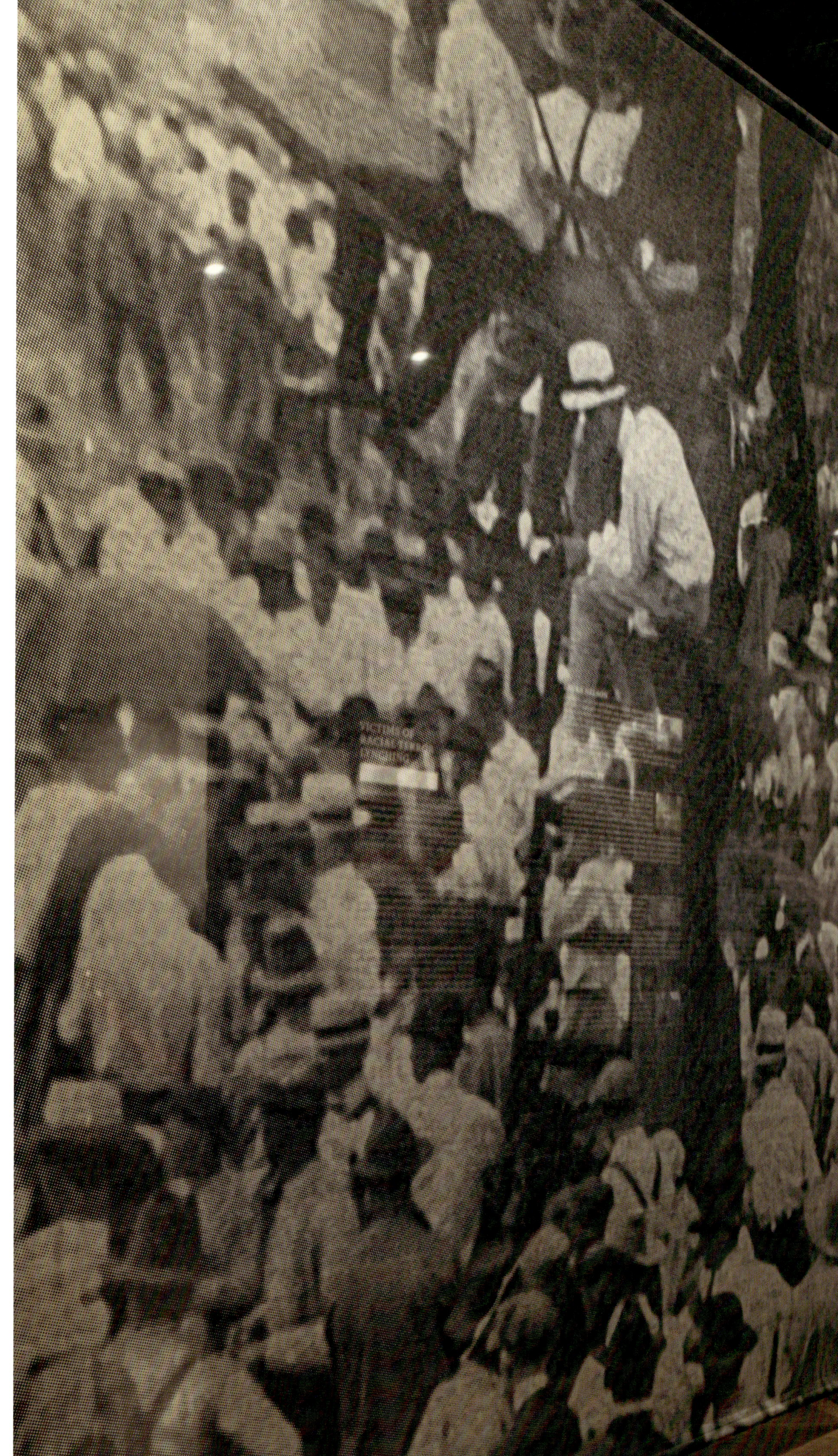

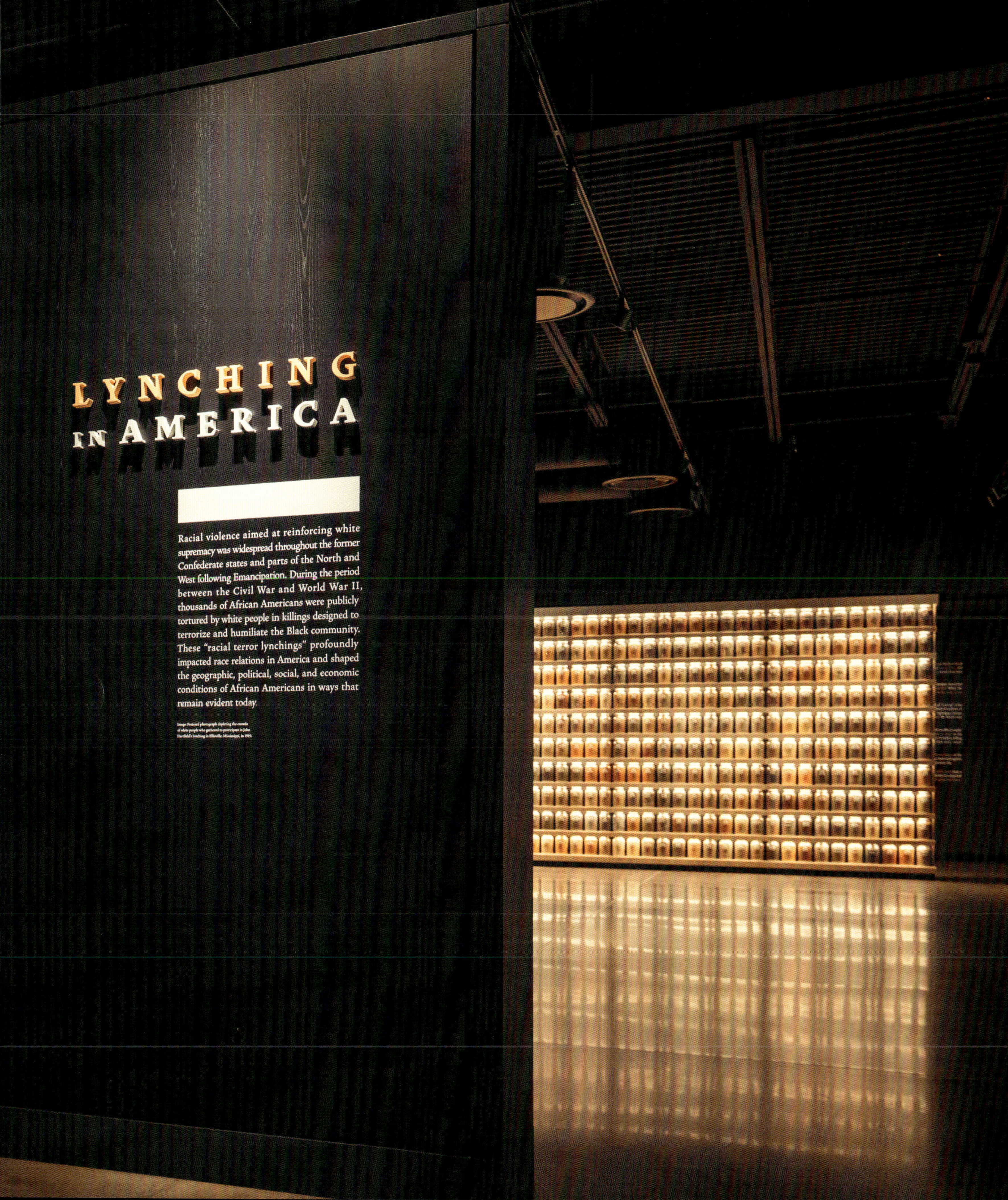
LYNCHING
IN AMERICA
Racial violence aimed at reinforcing white supremacy was widespread throughout the former Confederate states and parts of the North and West following Emancipation. During the period between the Civil War and World War II, thousands of African Americans were publicly tortured by white people in killings designed to terrorize and humiliate the Black community. These "racial terror lynchings" profoundly impacted race relations in America and shaped the geographic, political, social, and economic conditions of African Americans in ways that remain evident today.

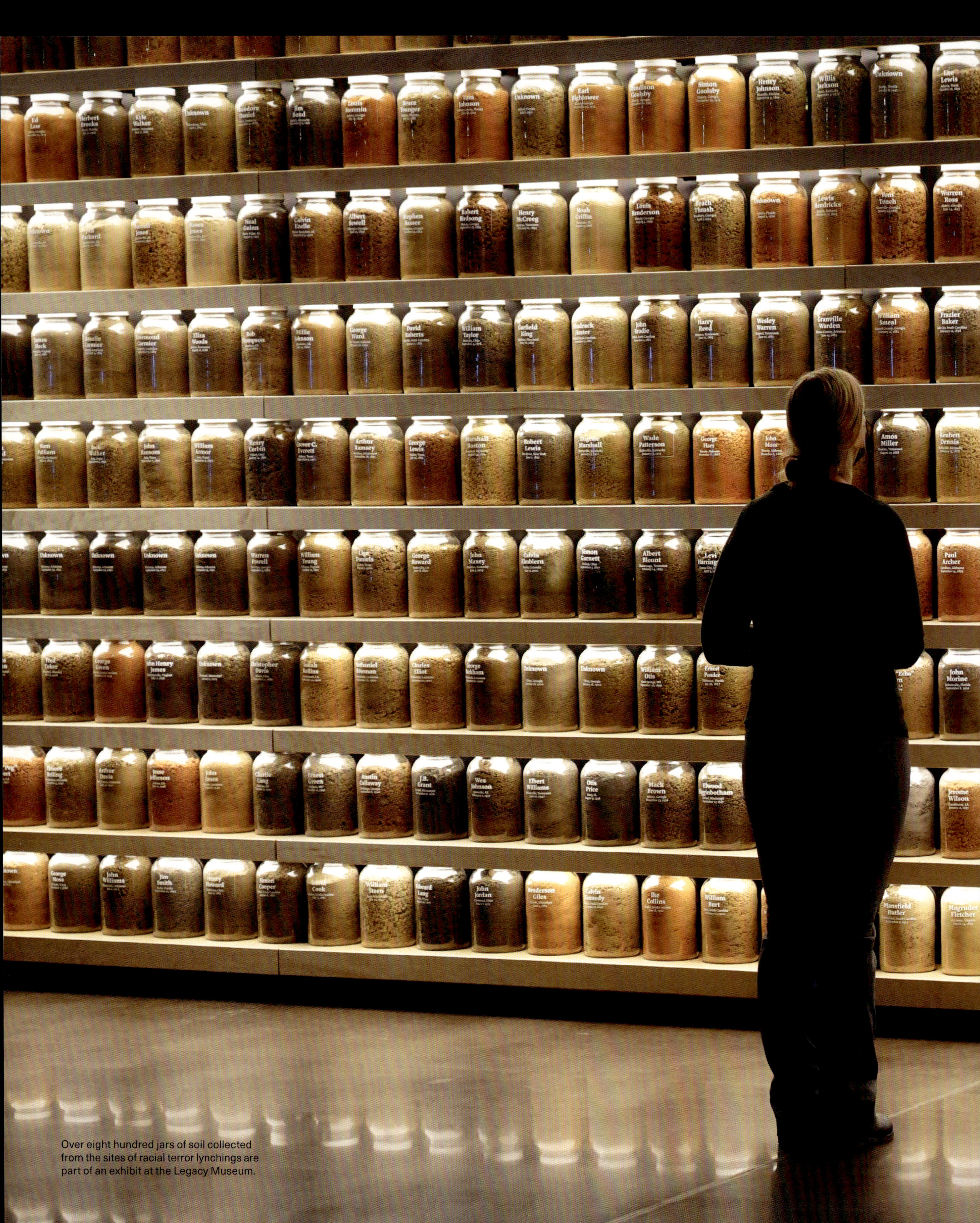

Over eight hundred jars of soil collected from the sites of racial terror lynchings are part of an exhibit at the Legacy Museum.

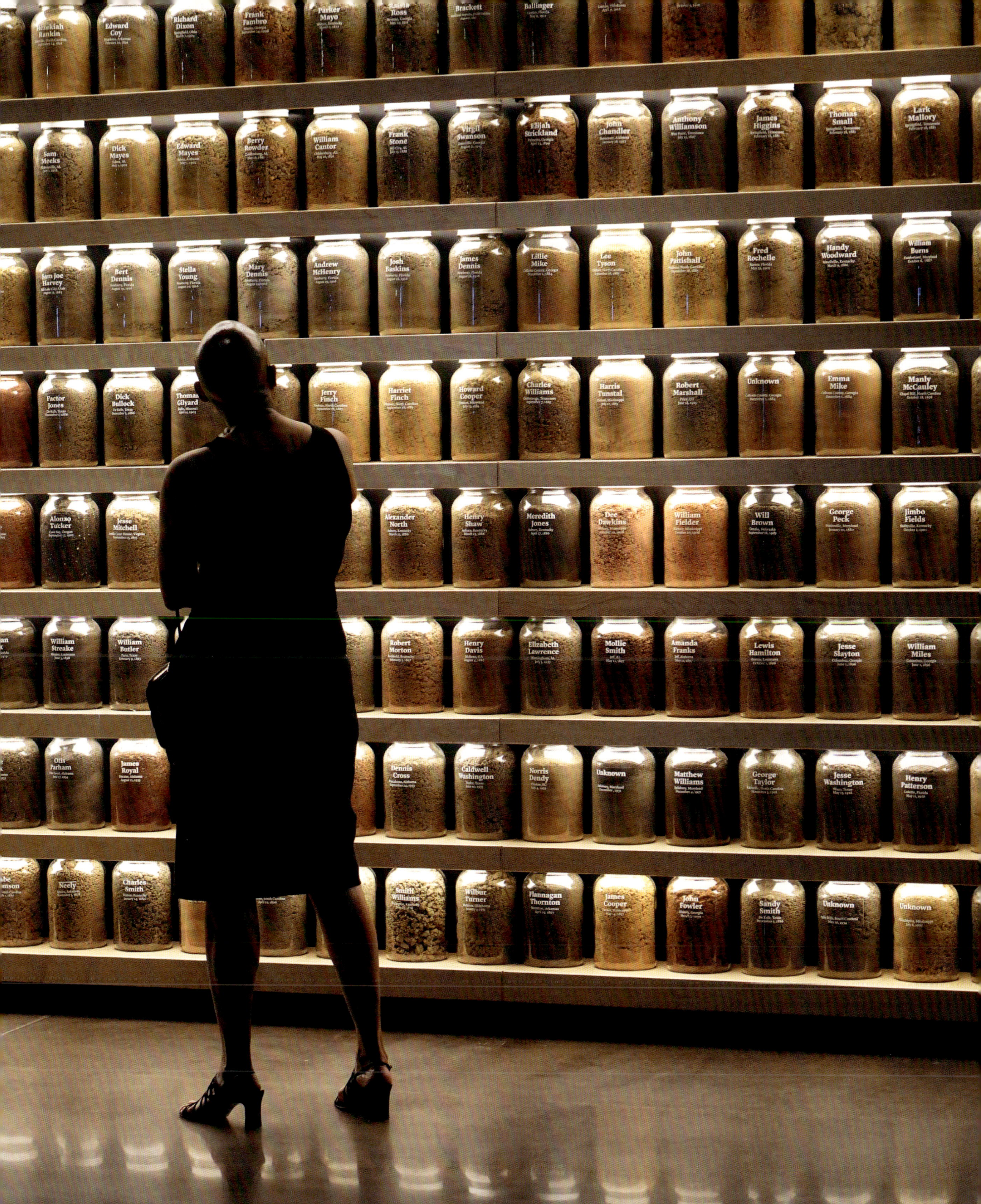

Hezekiah Rankin
Edward Coy
Richard Dixon
Frank Fambro
Parker Mayo
Sam Meeks
Dick Mayes
Edward Mayes
Berry Rowder
William Cantor
Frank Stone
Virgil Swanson
Elijah Strickland
John Chandler
Anthony Williamson
James Higgins
Thomas Small
Lark Mallory
Sam Joe Harvey
Bert Dennis
Stella Young
Mary Dennis
Andrew McHenry
Josh Baskins
James Dennis
Lillie Mike
Lee Tyson
John Pattishall
Fred Rochelle
Handy Woodward
William Burns
Factor Jones
Dick Bullock
Thomas Gilyard
Jerry Finch
Harriet Finch
Howard Cooper
Charles Williams
Harris Tunstal
Robert Marshall
Unknown
Emma Mike
Manly McCauley
Alonzo Tucker
Jesse Mitchell
Alexander North
Henry Shaw
Meredith Jones
Dee Dawkins
William Fielder
Will Brown
George Peck
Jimbo Fields
William Streake
William Butler
Robert Morton
Henry Davis
Elizabeth Lawrence
Mollie Smith
Amanda Franks
Lewis Hamilton
Jesse Slayton
William Miles
Otis Parham
James Royal
Dennis Cross
Caldwell Washington
Norris Dendy
Unknown
Matthew Williams
George Taylor
Jesse Washington
Henry Patterson
Neely
Charles Smith
Wilbur Turner
Flannagan Thornton
James Cooper
John Fowler
Sandy Smith
Unknown
Unknown

FORMER COLORED SOLDIER IS LYNCHED FOR HAVING A WHITE SWEETHEART

BUTCHERED IN JAIL.

An Alabama Mob Kills Five Prisoners in Their Cells.

Note Written to White Girl Costs Young Negro His Life

Youth

INSULTING TALK OVER A PHONE GETS NEGRO LYNCHED

Farmersville, Tex., Aug. 12.—Commodore Jones, a negro, who it is alleged

LYNCHERS THANKED BY JUDGE

Lynched for Writing a Note.

APALACHICOLA, Fla., August 20.—A lynching took place at Ochelhes, Calhoun

MOB LYNCHES A NEGRO BOY

Wrote Insulting Notes to Two White Ladies and Was Publicly Whipped.

OIL SOAKED NEGROES BURNED

SHE ELOPED WITH A NEGRO,

And a Mob Pursued, Killing the Negro and Returning the Girl to Her Home.

FATALLY FLOGGE

Negro Terribly Beaten by W for Violating a Farming Contract.

Negro Drowned by Florida Mob After Hands Are Severed

Lynched Because He Didn't Say 'Mr.'

MISSOURIANS ADOPT NEW METHOD OF LYNCHING

Negro Taken From Constable, Big Rock Is Tied to Feet and Body Thrown Into River.

A NEGRO HANGE

Because He Would N Work for a Farme in Georgia.

HEMPSTEAD MOB LYNCHES NEGRO NEAR GUERNSEY

Riddles Body With Bullets After Taking Him From Train

BURNED AT THE STAKE

Leavenworth, Kansas, the Scene of the Latest Lynching Atrocity.

NEGRO PROTESTED INNOCENCE

Nearly 8,000 People Witnessed the Lynching and Hundreds Scrambled For Relics of Burning.

NEGRO LYNCHED BY BOOTLEGGERS

Officers Believe They Suspected Him Of Telling Location Of Stills

FIND HEADLESS BODY

Police Blame Death On Moonshiners—Corpse Thrown In Creek

STORM JAIL AS BULLETS FLY AND HANG NEGRO

Florida Black Was Accused of Making Insulting Proposal to Woman.

SAY CHICAGO MOB LYNCHED WRONG MAN

Girls Unable to Recognize Body as That of Their Assailant in Ghetto Riot

NEGRO LYNCHED.

Robert Morton Hanged for Writing a Note to a White Woman.

A COUPLE OF INDIANS MURDERED.

An Unconfirmed Report That the Sac and Fox Indian Agency Has Been Raided by Outlaws—A Wife Sold for Twenty-Five Dollars.

NEGRO FINGERS FOR SOUVENIR

Mob Which Lynched Lee Hall, Mu derer of a Sheriff.

NEGRESS HANGS.

Found Suspended From Limb of Tree. No Clew to Cause of Hanging.

Saturday Was a Good Day for Lynching.

MOB LYNCHES A PREACHER.

He Had Shielded a Colored Lad Who Was Accused of Assault.

NEGRO IS LYNCHED FO SUING SLAYER OF

Louisiana Mob Hangs Com ant Against White Ma

MOB IN TEXAS LYNCHES 15-YEAR-OLD NEGRO BOY

FLORIDA MOB KILLS NEGRO

Bullet-Riddled Body Found in Ditch.

OFFICERS THINK HIM INNOCENT OF CHARGE

Taken from Log Cutters' Camp. Accused of Peeping Through Window.

MOB REALIZES ITS MISTAKE.

Hanged Wrong Negro, So Pursues Chase of the Right One.

MOB LYNCHED WRONG MAN

PAID PENALTY FOR CRIME OF HIS BROTHER.

THE REVOLVER IS MISSING

WHOLESALE LYNCHIN

Nine Men Taken By a From a Georgia Jail.

EIGHT SHOT TO DEA

SKINNED HIM ALIVE.

A Negro Literally Flayed and Burned in Kentucky.

KILL NEGRO, BURN HOUSE AND CHURCH

Armed Men Wreak Vengeance on Negro Settlement in Garland County.

BURNED AT THE STAKE

Citizens of Corsicana Savagely Tortured John Henderson.

NEGRO FIEND BURNED ALIVE.

Tied to a Stake on the Scaffold in the Square at Tyler, Tex.

12,000 PEOPLE WITNESSED IT

The Mob's Victim Had Assaulted, Murdered and Mutilated the 19-Year-Old Wife of a White Man.

NEGRO IS KILLED FOR REMARKS TO WOMAN

Preacher Shot to Death by Band of Whites.

TWO WOMEN LYNCHED BY MISSISSIPPI MOB

Mother, Son, and Daughter Put to Death.

FREED BY JURY, LYNCHED BY M

Mississippi Negro Declared Guilty of Murder

KILLED BY VOLLEY OF BO

B LYNCHES NEGRO AND CROPS HIS EARS

Thousands Witness Burning of Negro

DEATH SILENCED HIS TONGUE.

John Lee Killed for Talking Too Much.

Banned from voting through law and violence, the formerly enslaved were governed by all-white legislatures that passed "Black Codes" and authorized convict leasing. African Americans were criminalized, imprisoned, or fined, and then sold to private citizens or companies to work off their "debts" for state profit. Thousands of prisoners were reenslaved in mines, on farms, and on plantations, where conditions were horrific and many died.

Racial violence aimed at reestablishing white supremacy was widespread throughout the former Confederate states following Emancipation. In the eight decades between the end of the Civil War and the end of World War II, white people publicly tortured thousands of African Americans in "racial terror lynchings" designed to terrorize and intimidate the Black community.

In this environment of terror, many African Americans became refugees in their own country as they fled the violence and persecution so prevalent in the South. Between 1910 and 1940, nearly six million refugees fled the South for urban ghettos in the North and West. This massive, forced exodus, known as the Great Migration, forever altered the demographic landscape of America.

Racial Terror Lynching

After Emancipation and Reconstruction, lynching became a vicious tool of racial control, especially in the South, where the vast majority of African Americans lived.

Between 1880 and 1940, more than four thousand African American men, women, and children were killed by white mobs in racial terror lynchings: public acts of violence and torture that traumatized Black communities.

These gruesome and ritualistic killings sometimes targeted Black people who were accused of committing a crime and, because of their race, deemed unworthy of an investigation or trial.

Violating the racial hierarchy could also lead to lynching. Many victims were killed for "offenses" like arguing with a white person, writing a note to a white woman, scolding white children, failing to call a white man "mister," and not yielding the road to a white driver. Still others were targeted for challenging white supremacy through activism, such as organizing sharecroppers unions, registering Black voters, or simply refusing to submit to white control.

In Rosewood, Florida; Tulsa, Oklahoma; and Elaine, Arkansas, the violence of lynch mobs grew to target entire Black communities, resulting in deadly massacres that killed residents, destroyed property, and forced survivors to flee.

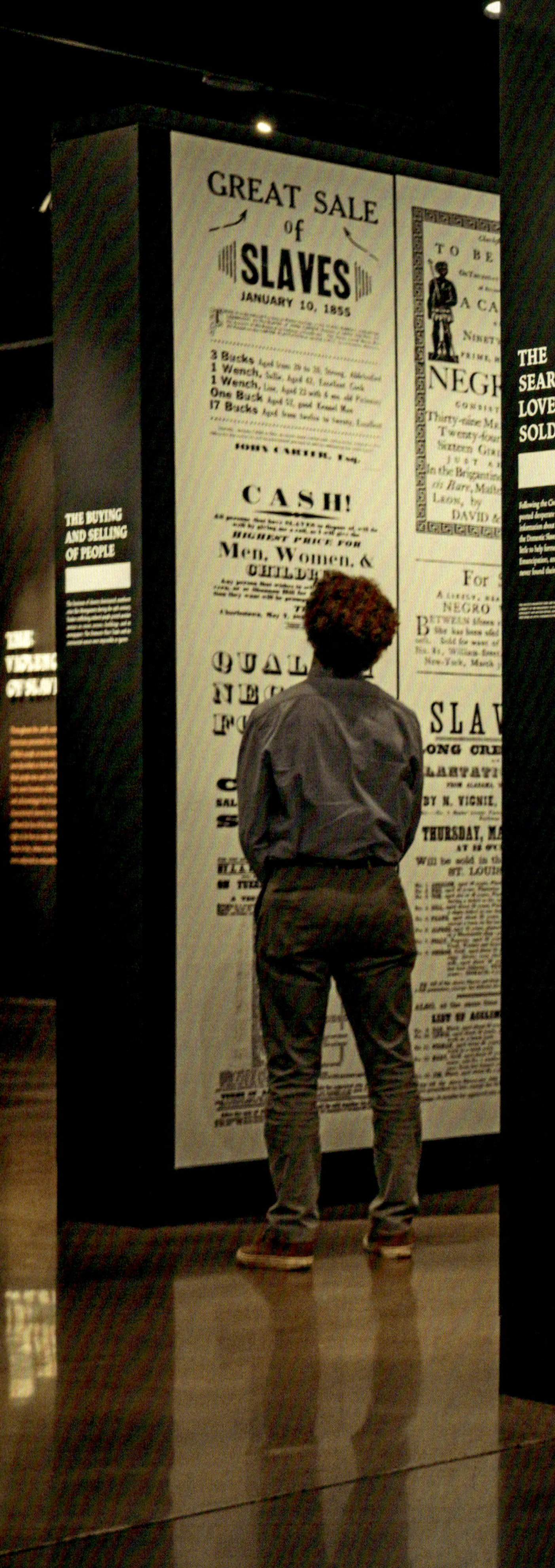
GREAT SALE of SLAVES
JANUARY 10, 1855
CASH!
THE BUYING AND SELLING OF PEOPLE
THE SEARCH FOR LOVED ONES SOLD AWAY
...and Clarisa Lampkins, my brother Cyrus Brown was sold to old John Brown. When I left my mother I was only twelve years of age. I am now in San Antonio, Texas. Any information will be gladly received by Celia Lampkine, now Martha Brown.
Information Wanted.
Of Moses Lumly, who was raised near Oxford, N. C., by Dr. John Hicks, and sold to Wm. Lumly, of Rome, Ga., at which place he was living when Sherman's army reached there in the Spring of 1864. Also, of Polly Noel, who lived in Vicksburg, Miss., up to the time the law was passed in that State prohibiting persons of color living there. She then moved to Nashville, since which time nothing has been heard of her by her relatives. Address,
RICHARD GRAY,
my12-3m Box 74, Macon, Miss.
MISS FRANCIS POVLER INQURIES for relatives, all of whom, a mother, Mrs Jennie, two brothers, Benjamin and Soloman and a sister, Mary Esther, once belonged to James Meaders, Chambers county, Ala. Address me care John S. Taylor, South Norwalk, Conn.
MR. EDITOR—I wish to inquire by the help of your paper for some of my people. I got a letter from Brother Stephen Toliver, in Texas stating that our Brother Frank and Sister Mary Toliver have never been seen nor heard from since they were sold, and I wish to inquire for them. He states that they were sold in New Orleans, and the man that bought them took them up the Mississippi river, but he did not know his name. Names as follows: Our first owner, who raised us, was Mr. Louis Toliver, who lived in Mississippi. I have got one sister I left in Alabama in 1860, but I don't think that Brother Frank and Sister Mary can recollect her, as she was taken from them when they were small, and I have never heard from her nor any of the children yet. Her name is Pininie Green. Her husband was Robin Green. Her sons Stephen and one Richard. She had a large family but I cannot recollect all of the children's names. They belonged to Joe Green, who lives near Montgomery, Ala. Address Valentine Toliver, Shreveport, La.
MR. EDITOR—I wish to find my sister Francis. We all belonged to the Austins, at Chillicote, Missouri. My mother was Cloa, she came to her death by hanging herself. There were three children of us, brother Amos, sister Francis and myself, Caroline. Sister Francis was sold about 26 or 27 years ago to a speculator by the name of Bess. She had one child when sold. She was a bright mulatto. I was sold to the same speculator a short time after she was and brought South. Address me at Muskogee, Indian Territory, box 156. CAROLINE HOLLOWAY.
Information Wanted.
JOHN WILSON, a colored man, formerly a slave belonging to James Denton, of Colbert County Maryland, desires to find his five children, named respectively: George, Dennis, Sarah Jane, Nat and Lethe. They were all carried to Richmond, the first year of the war, by James Borne, or Maryland, and sold, to whom it is not known. The object of this notice is to discover their whereabouts. Information addressed to me at Mocksville, N.C., will be thankfully received.
March 18, 1867. JOHN WILSON.
Of my two sonss, Sidney and Harrison who belonged to Clem. Cannon, who formerly lived in Shelbyville, Bedford county Tenn, and were sold to Goodbar. A trader, and when last heard from were in Montgomery, Ala. The oldest one is about 26 years of age. My name is Sidney. When they left I belonged to a man by the name of Elliott. Information of them will be thankfully received by myself or their mother, whose name is Eliza Cannon. Please address Colored Tennessean, Box 1150
Jan13-lm SYDNEY ELLIOTT.
INFORMATION WANTED
OF MY SON WM. PASCAL McGEE, and two daughters, Isabella and Easter Fanny McGee. My son was in the 2d Kansas Colored Infantry, Company H. Any information concerning either of them will be thankfully received. I was formerly a servant of Mrs. Jane Gillespie, of Louisville, Tenn, Address JANE McGEE
mar20-1m Box 227, Knoxville, Tenn.
INFORMATION WANTED.—I was born in Virginia. My mother's name was Rebecca (called Becky), father's name Billy, brother's name Washington and sister's name Sady. I was sold to a slave trader named Billy Hunter, when I was about four or five years old, or perhaps younger, and brought to South Carolina, where I now reside. I know nothing of my relatives. My name is Martha. Any information of the above named parties will be gladly received by Martha Kennedy. Address C. G. Garrett, Laurens C. H., S. C.
INFORMATION WANTED.—In the year 1844, three of my children were sold, SARAH, WILLIAM and PRISCILLA, from the estate of Mr. Lucius Dixon, of Fauquier county, Va. They were small children at the time.—Since then I have never heard of them. Should this advertisement reach them, write to me of their whereabouts. Direct to the care of Captain Murray Mason, Haymarket, Prince William county, Va. MIMEY GRIGSBY.
Haymarket, Prince Wm. co., ap 25-3t*
[Southern papers please copy.]
I will be thankful for information concerning my wife, named Matilda, and daughter named Sally. They belonged to Bob. McCallop, in Alabama. On the approach of the Federal forces he left with them saying he was going to Texas, and I have ne er been able to get any word from them since. Address, Squire Norman, care of St. Paul's Church, Shreveport, La.
Information Desired.
Mrs. Eliza Stewart, nee Eliza Robinson, wife of Henry Stewart, of this city, is anxious to learn the whereabouts of her brother, who was known as Richard Peeke, when sold by his master, Wm. Holliday, of Hagerstown, Md., long before the late rebellion. He is supposed to be in Alabama or Georgia, engaged in raising cotton. Any information about Mr. Peeker will be thankfully received by his anxious sister, residing at 108 Cherry avenue, Harrisburg, Pa. Southern papers please copy.
Information Wanted.
INFORMATION wanted of my brother Lewis Burris sold from Hatteras Island N. C. His owner Edmund Burris sold him from his wife and two children, to Wm. Howard who took him to Silver Springs Florida. At the time he was sold the writer was about five years old. Our mother Hester Burris is still living and is very anxious to hear from him.
Address Joanna Burris
care Christian Recorder,
5m.11-4t. 631 Pine St. Philadelphia.
Do You Know Him?
I would like to know the whereabouts of Benjamin Curry to whom I was married long before John Brown's Insurrection. We had two children. He being a slave was sold away from me to Richmond, Va., and I have not heard from him since. His master's name was Isaac Foulk of Harper's Ferry, Va.
Any information will be glad received. Address,
Mrs. ANNE MATTHEWS,
No. 9 Linton St.,
Pittsburg, Allegheny Co., Pa.
WANTS TO FIND HER RELATIVES.
Mrs Sarah Daniels of DeFuniak Springs, Fla., writes: "At the time of the war Ihad three brothers and a sister who were carried from South Carolina to Alabama by a white Methodist preacher by the name of Ledbetter. They were named respectively, Hezekiah, William Capers, Robert and Laura. I shall be very garteful for any information of them.
Address, Mrs Sarah Daniels.
De Funiak Springs, Fla.

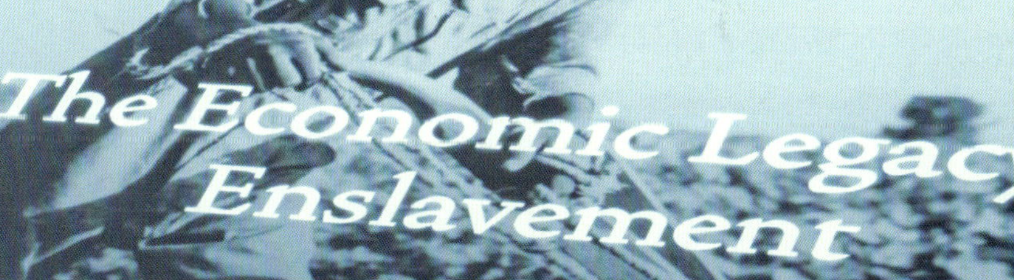
The Economic Legacy
Enslavement
Scroll for more

State and federal officials turned a blind eye to this carnage, and in some cases endorsed it as justified and necessary. Not surprisingly, virtually all racial terror lynchings were committed with impunity by mobs that proudly mailed photograph postcards of hanging corpses and sometimes kept gruesome souvenirs of their crimes with no fear of prosecution. Countless lynching victims were issued death certificates declaring that they were killed "at the hands of persons unknown."

Lynching Research and Data

For more than five years, Equal Justice Initiative researchers scoured books, journals, archival collections, and newspaper records; visited lynching sites; and interviewed community members to document the history of racial terror lynching in the United States.

The resulting data revealed more than 4,000 African Americans lynched in Alabama, Arkansas, Georgia, Florida, Kentucky, Louisiana, Mississippi, North Carolina, South Carolina, Tennessee, Texas, and Virginia between 1877 and 1950, and hundreds more killed in other states throughout the country.

Visitors to the Legacy Museum have full access to that data through a digital terminal featuring an interactive map and descriptions of select lynchings.

In Remembrance

Beginning in 2015, EJI initiated a campaign to recognize the victims of lynching. Volunteers throughout the country gathered at mostly unmarked lynching sites to reflect on the legacy of lynching and gather soil in remembrance. The gathered soil forms an exhibit within the Legacy Museum that powerfully and tangibly represents the history of racial terror.

The project aims to transcend time and altered terrain to bear witness to the devastation these murders wrought upon individuals, families, communities, and our nation as a whole. The Legacy Museum's soil exhibit contains over eight hundred jars of soil representing lynching victims killed throughout the South and beyond.

We remember them by telling their stories.

Opposite and page 54:
Jars of soil collected from around the country as part of EJI's Community Remembrance Project.

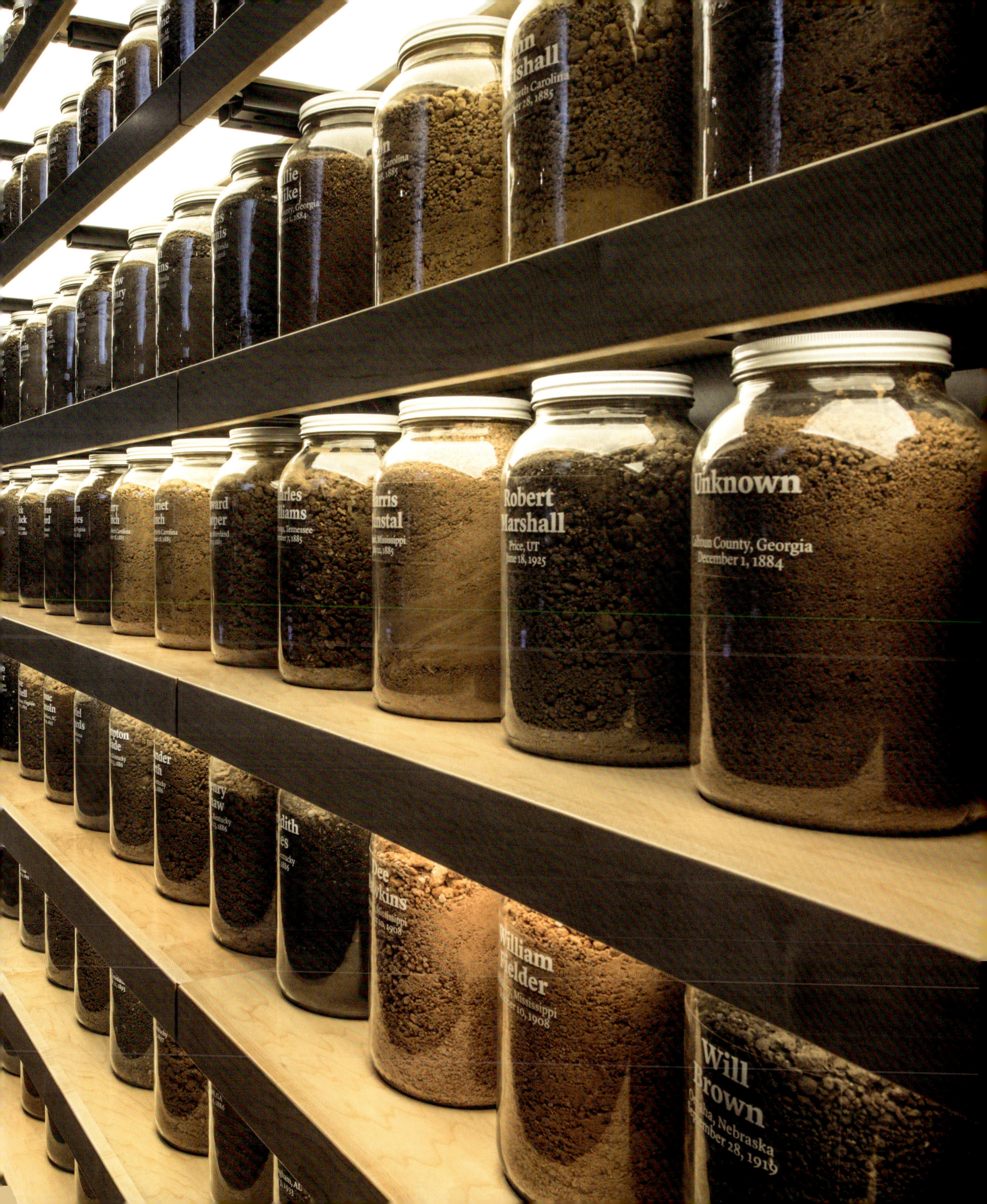
Unknown
County, Georgia
December 1, 1884
Robert
Price, UT
Dee
William
Fielder
Will
Brown
Nebraska

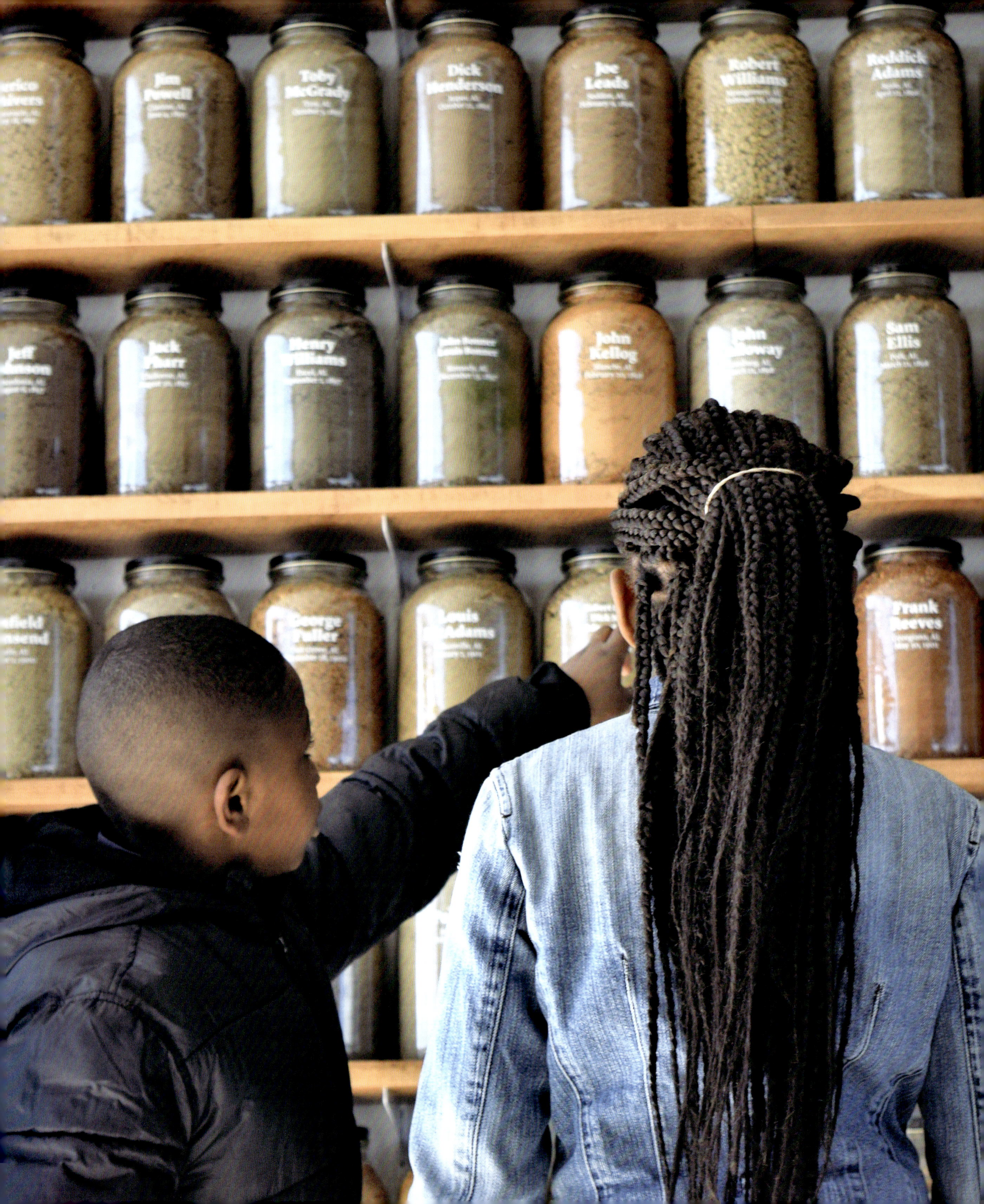
Jim Powell
Toby McGrady
Dick Henderson
Joe Leads
Robert Williams
Reddick Adams
Jack Pharr
Henry Williams
John Kellog
Sam Ellis
George Fuller
Louis Adams
Frank Reeves

The Era of Segregation

Black Southerners who survived racial terror remained subject to Jim Crow, a humiliating and rigid racial caste system that cemented African Americans' status as second-class citizens by sharply restricting their rights, movement, and opportunities.

Southern elected officials used the law to preserve racial segregation and maintain white supremacy, while law enforcement officers regularly refused to protect civil rights activists from violence.

When federal courts began to strike down segregation laws for the first time in generations, white communities organized massive resistance. The courage of civil rights activists and the lingering legacy of segregation today cannot be understood without examining the widespread white opposition to racial equality during this era.

After the Supreme Court's 1954 decision in *Brown v. Board of Education* outlawed racial segregation in public schools, the backlash was immediate: many school districts closed rather than accept Black children; local White Citizens' Councils and a resurgent Ku Klux Klan used economic intimidation, threats, and violence to target Black parents and children who tried to enroll in white schools; and politicians vowed to resist the ruling at any cost. Many Southern states passed laws to evade and delay federal orders to integrate.

Civil rights victories mounted, leading to federal court orders striking down racial segregation in parks, pools, buses, restaurants, and neighborhoods. Violent opposition became frequent and deadly. In 1963, four young Black girls were killed when a bomb exploded in the 16th Street Baptist Church in Birmingham, Alabama. That year, military veteran and NAACP field secretary Medgar Evers was shot and killed in his own Jackson, Mississippi, driveway by a white man who had previously declared, "I believe in segregation like I believe in God."

The criminal justice system emerged as an effective tool for suppressing the Civil Rights Movement. Activists regularly faced arrest and prosecution.

Between his emergence as a leader of the Montgomery Bus Boycott in 1955 and his assassination in 1968, Dr. Martin Luther King Jr. was arrested more than a dozen times for leading nonviolent civil rights demonstrations; repeatedly threatened with violence and hanged in effigy; and covertly targeted by FBI officials who labeled him "the most dangerous and effective Negro leader in the country."

Against overwhelming odds, the Civil Rights Movement successfully disrupted the legal architecture that had sustained Jim Crow. But the narrative of white supremacy that fueled segregation and white opposition to racial equality persisted.

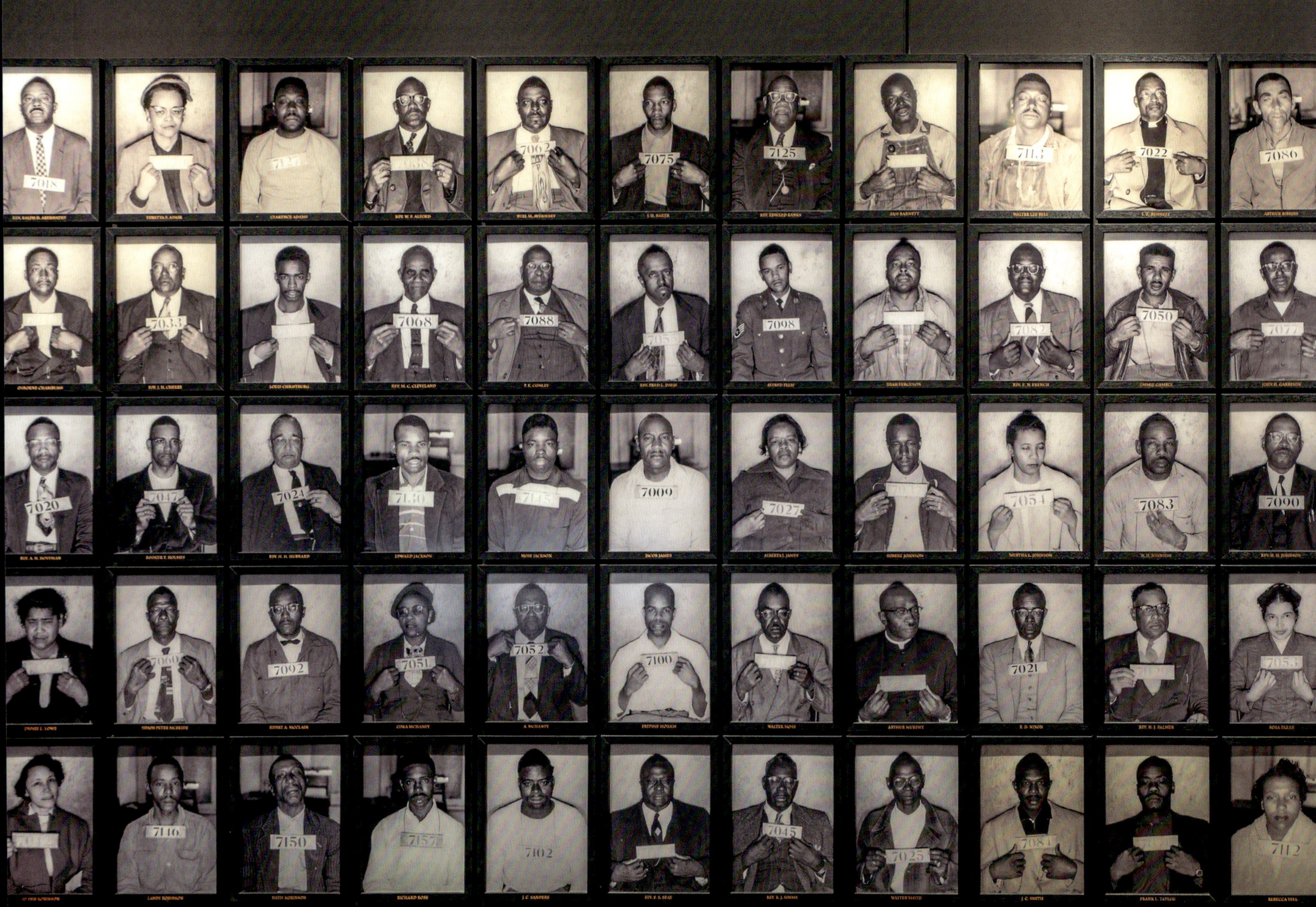
THE MONTGOME

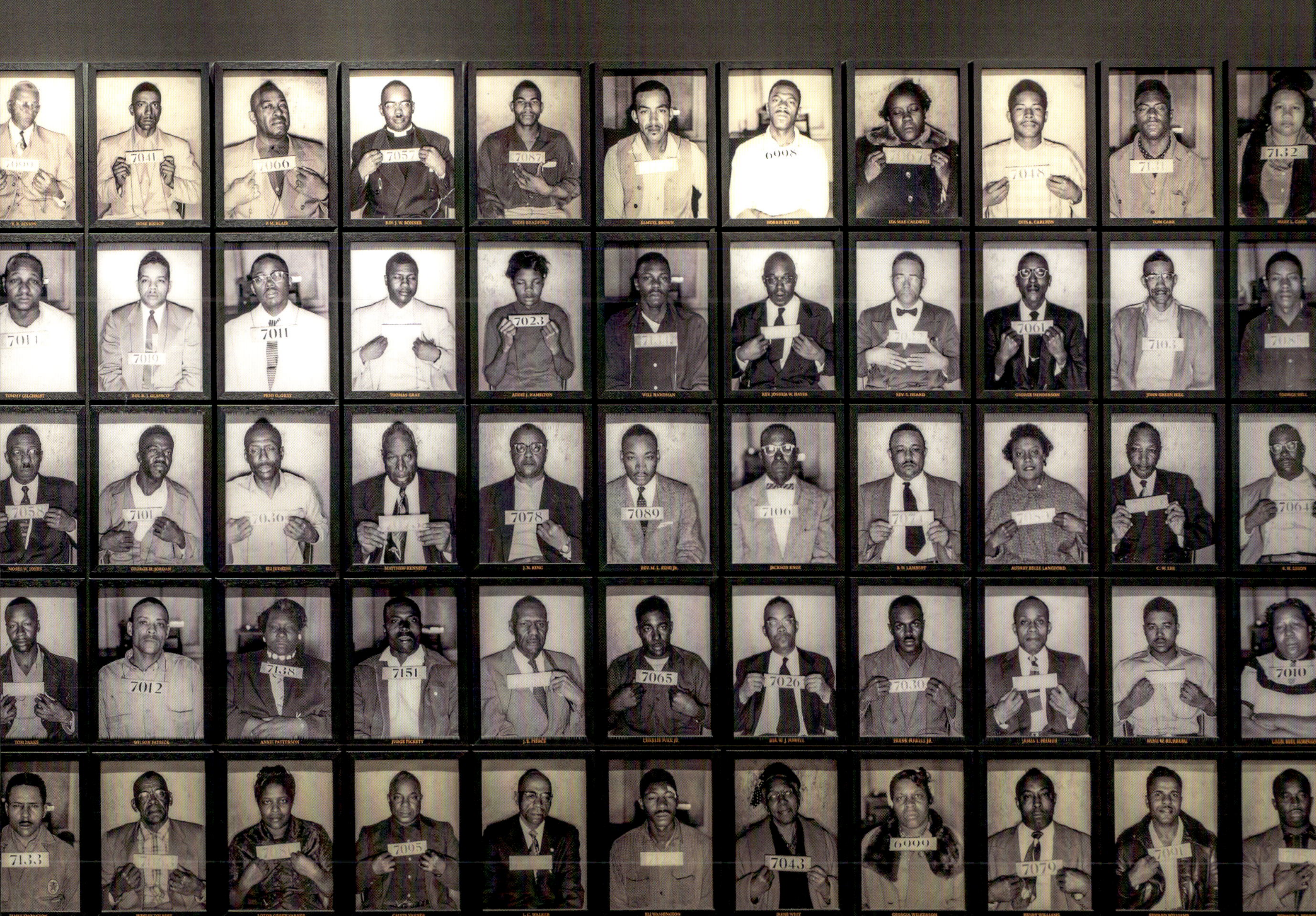
RY BUS BOYCOTT

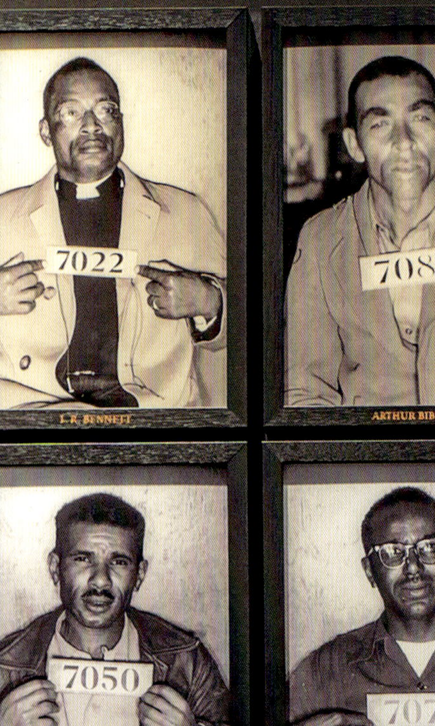
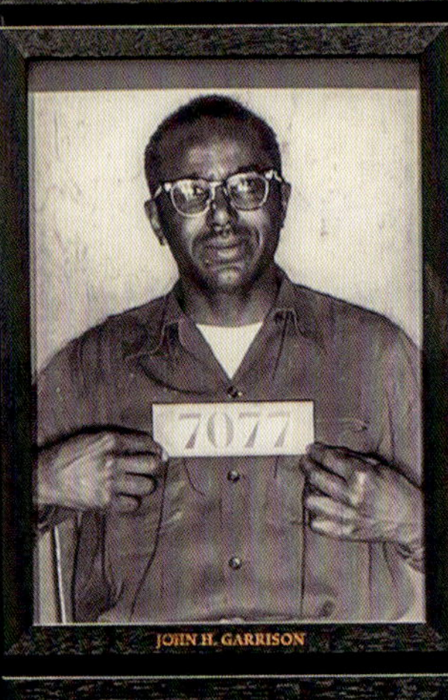
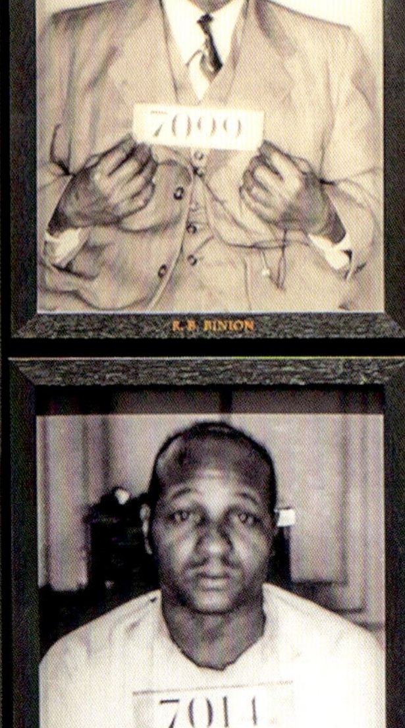
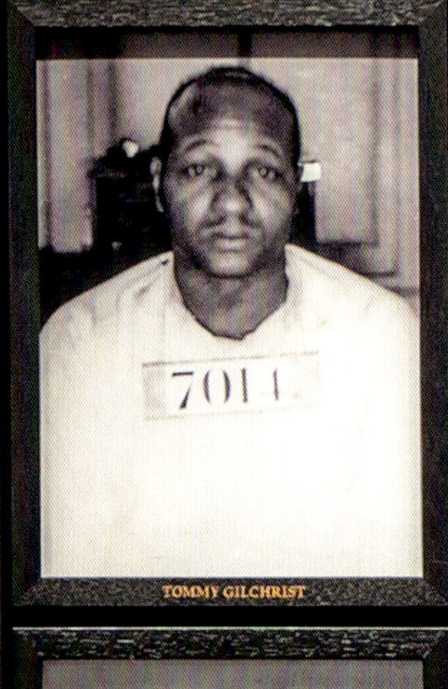
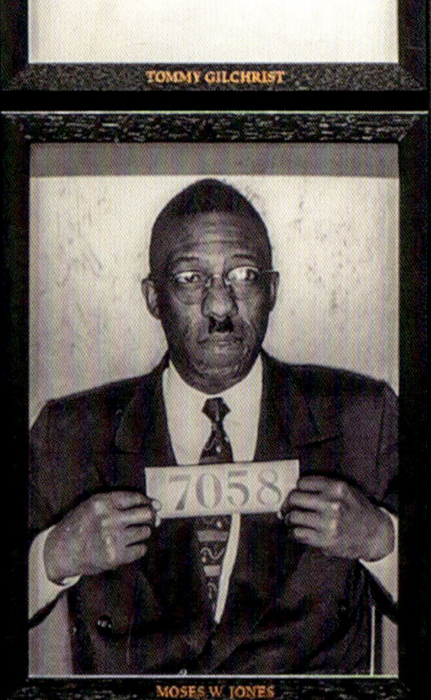
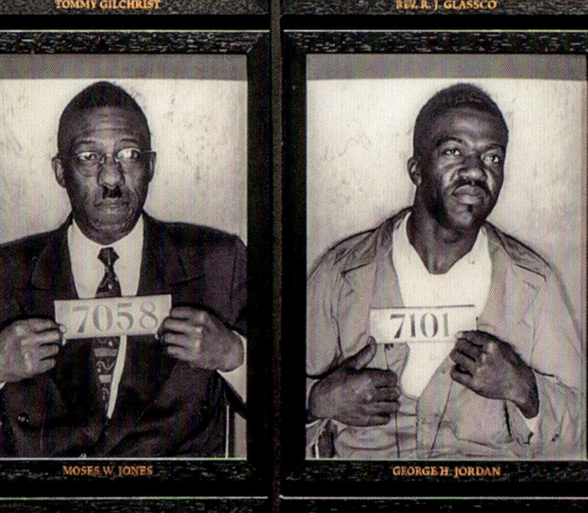
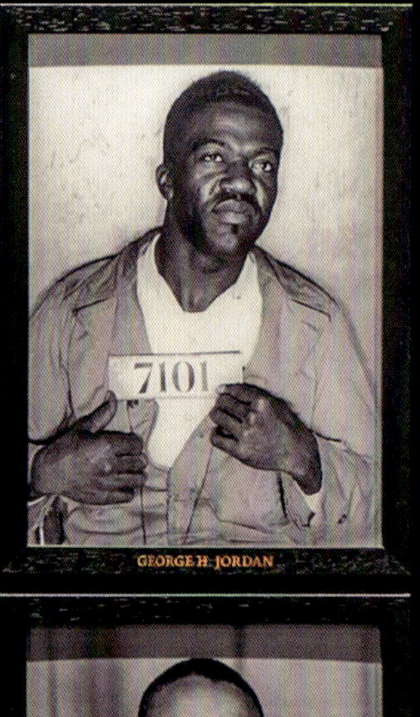
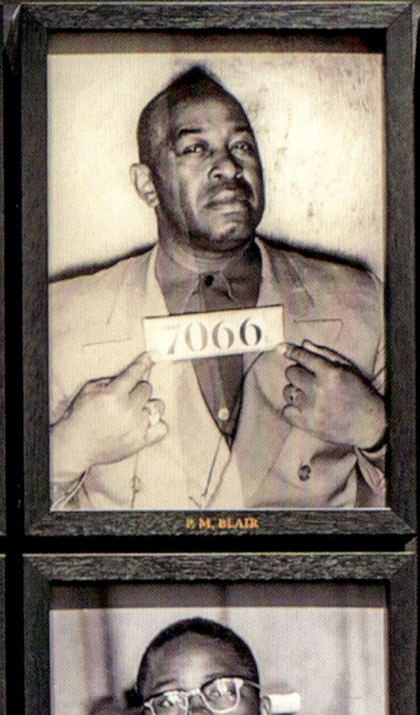
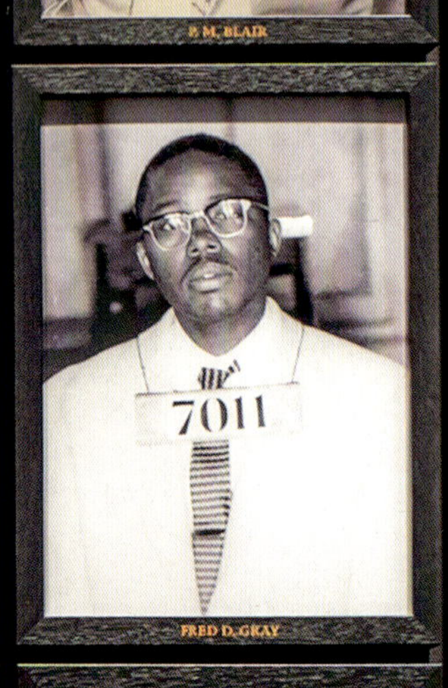
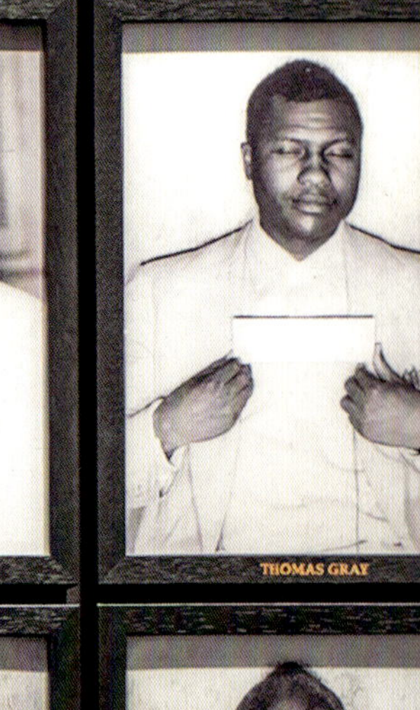
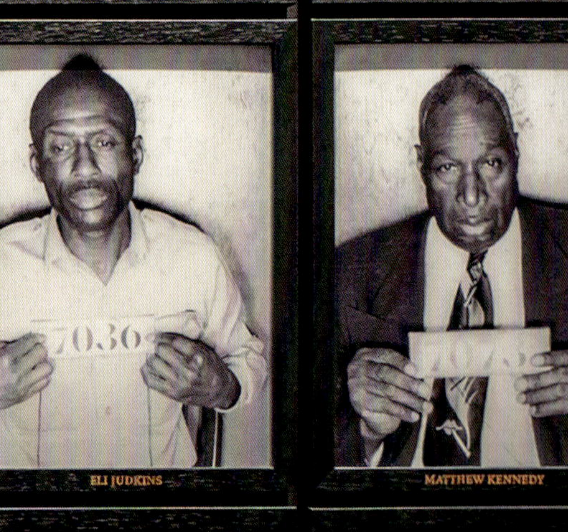
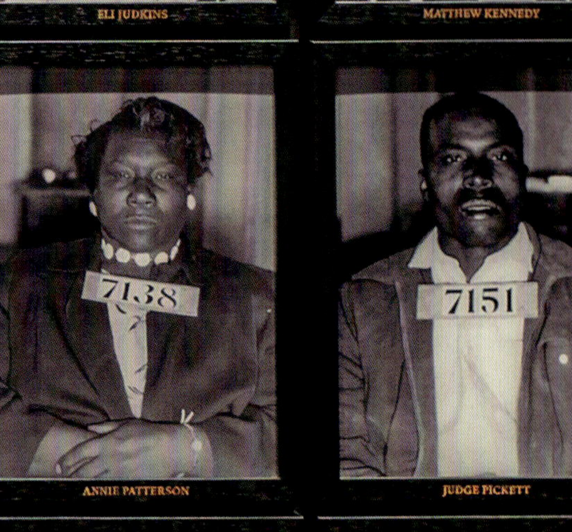
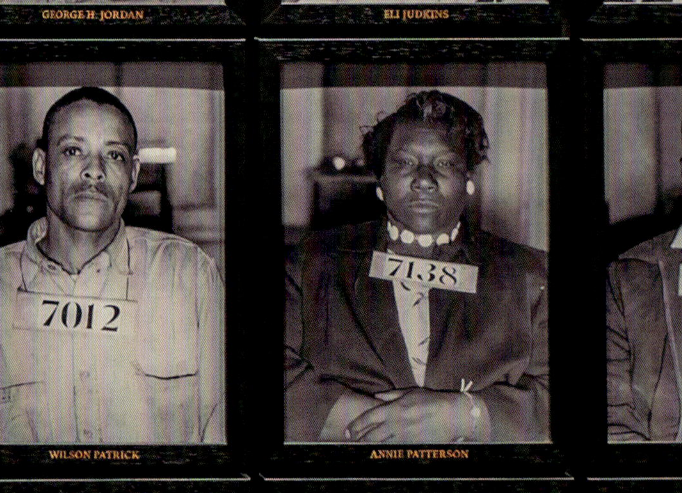
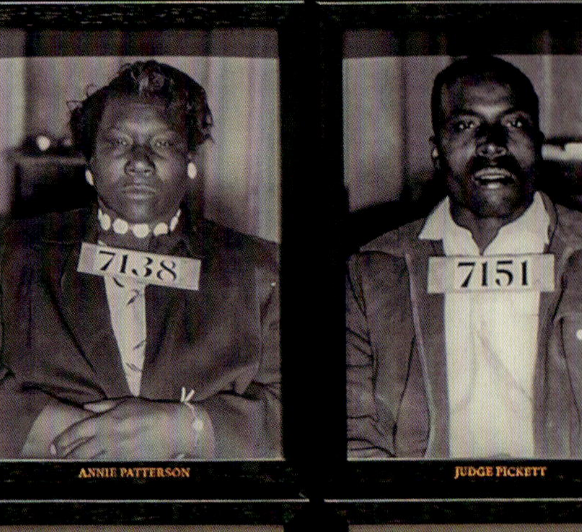
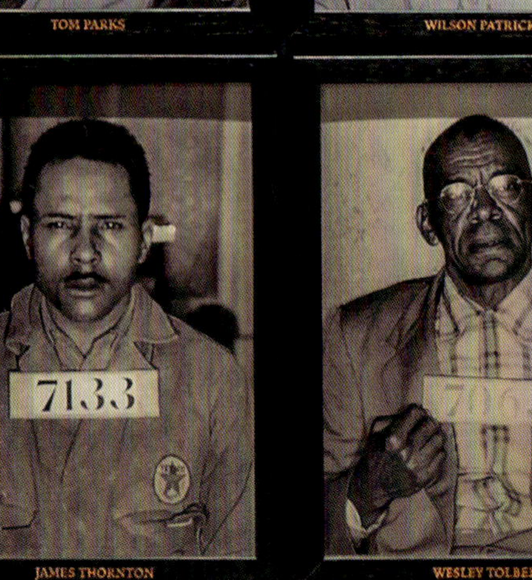
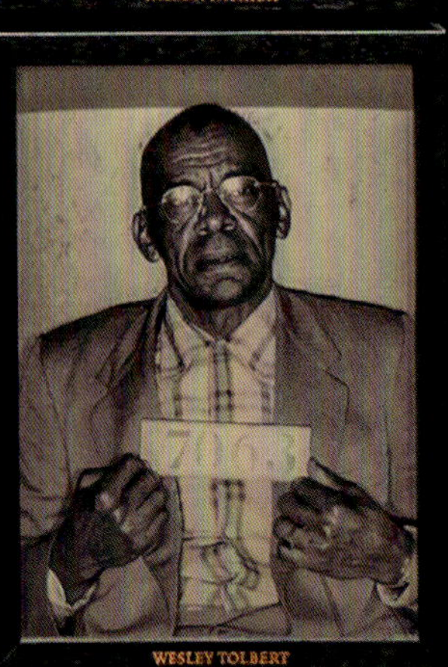
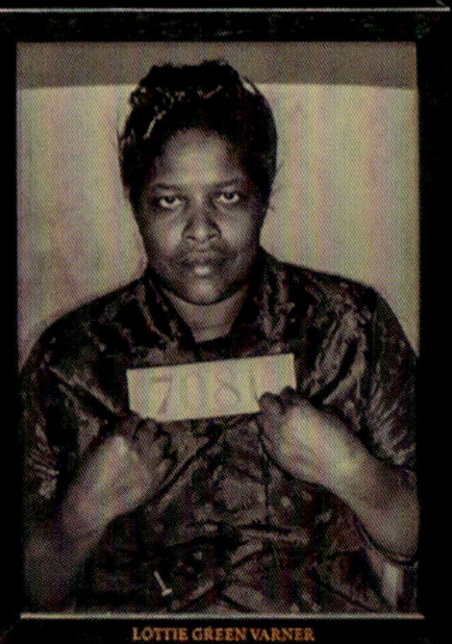
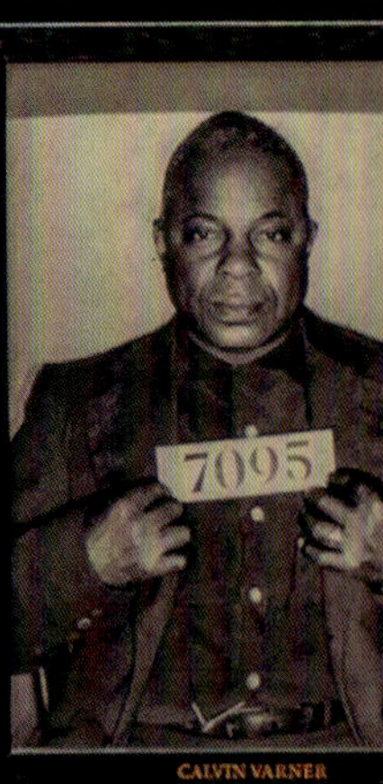
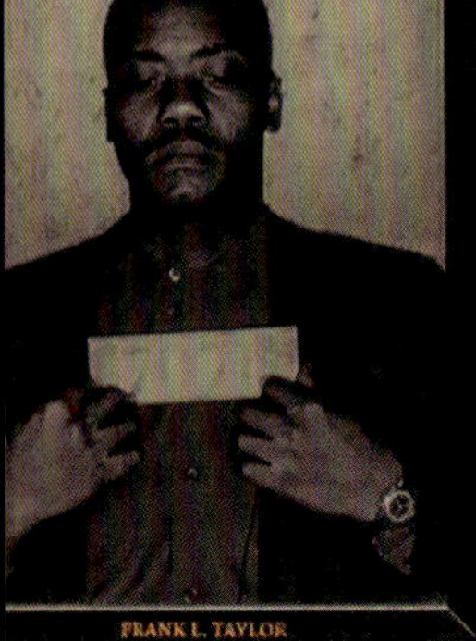
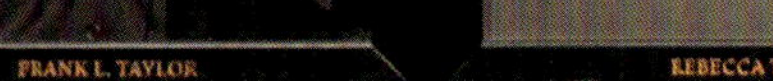

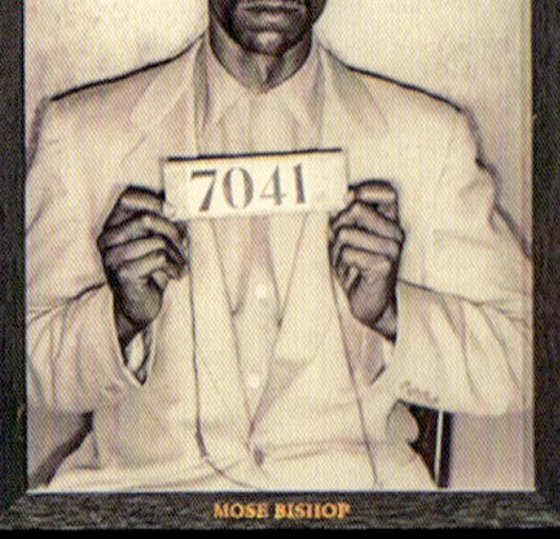
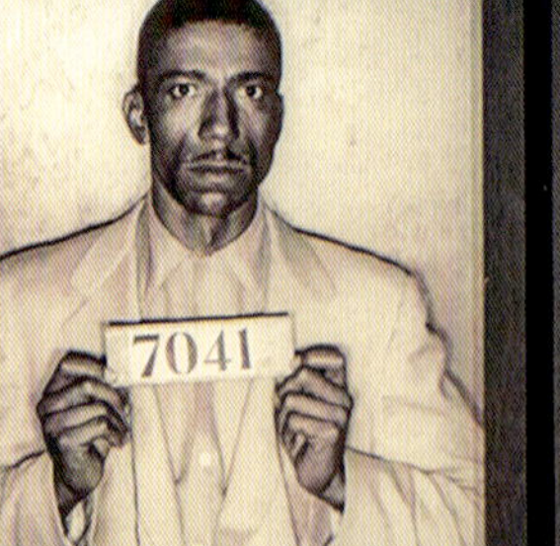
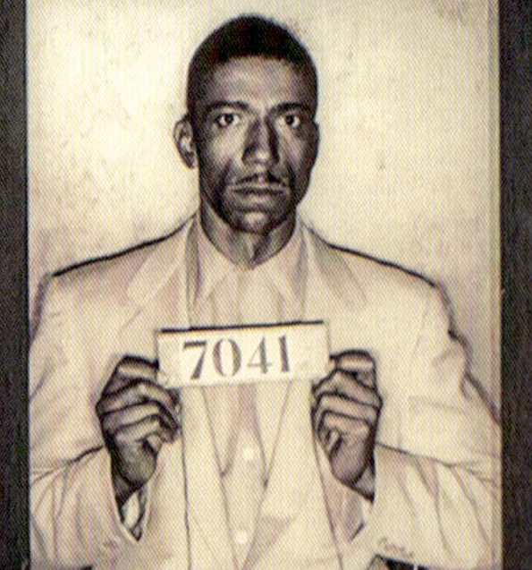
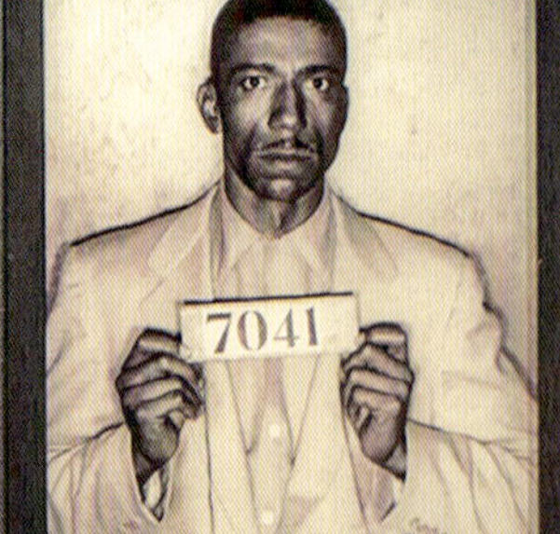
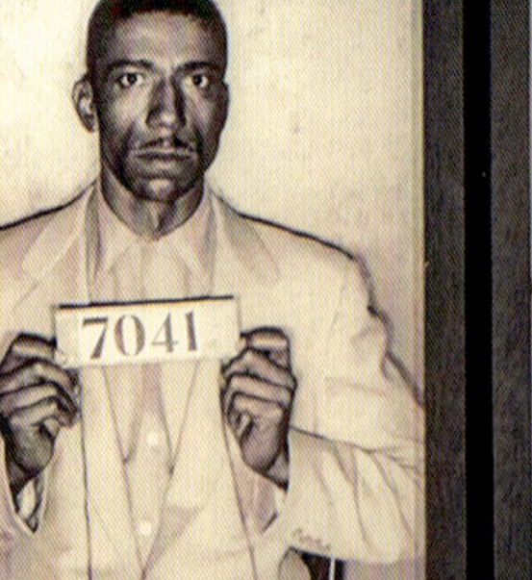
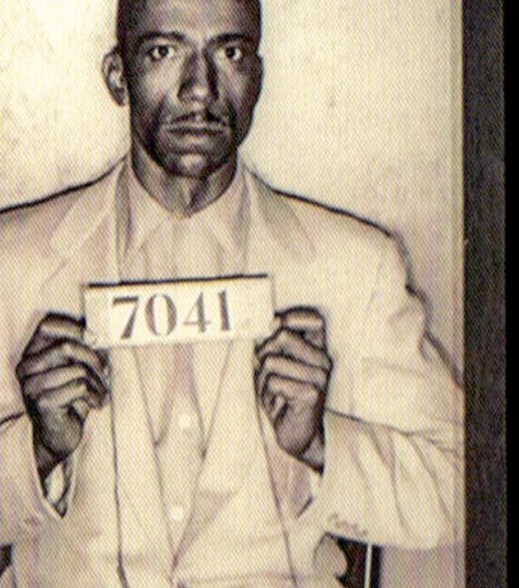
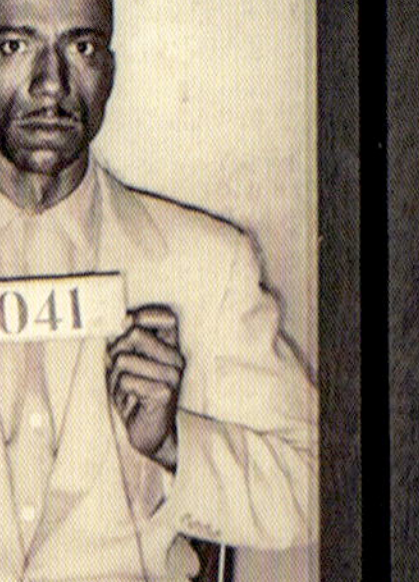
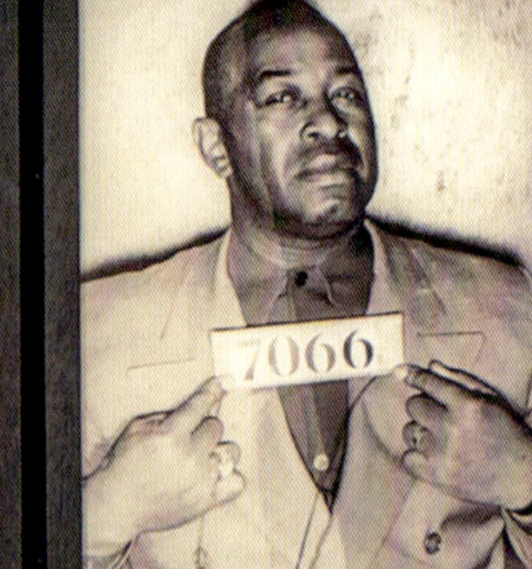
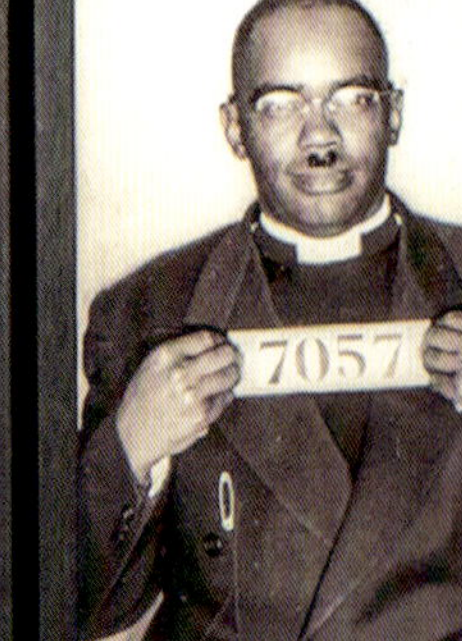
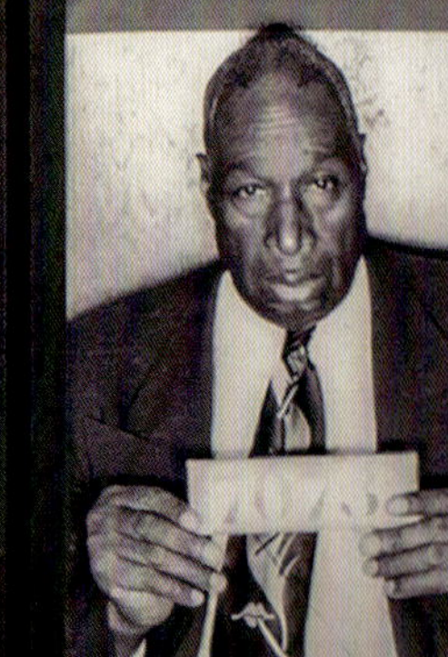
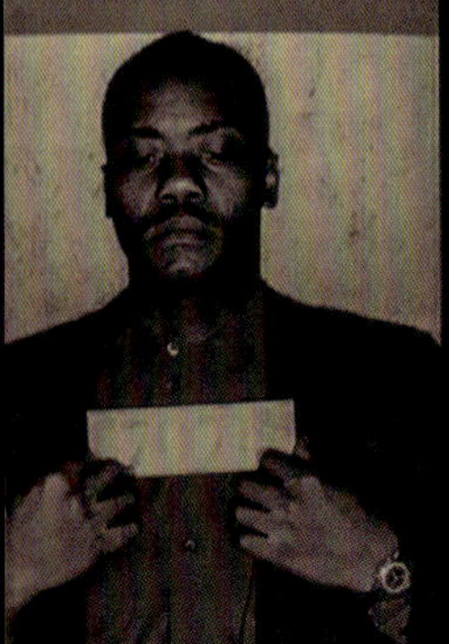
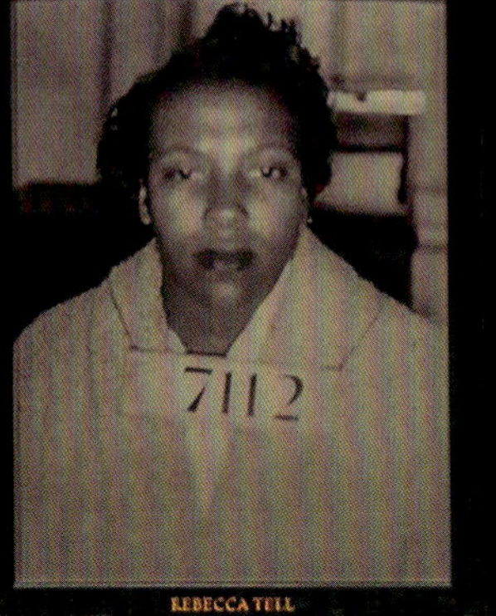
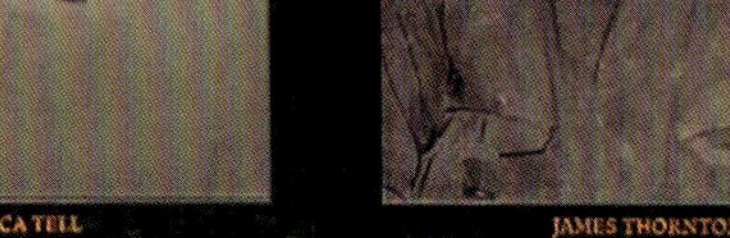
7022
L. R. BENNETT
7086
ARTHUR BIBBINS
7099
R. B. BINION
7041
MOSE BISHOP
7066
P. M. BLAIR
7057
REV. J. W. BONNER
7050
JIMMIE GAMBLE
7077
JOHN H. GARRISON
7014
TOMMY GILCHRIST
7019
REV. R. J. GLASSCO
7011
FRED D. GRAY
THOMAS GRAY
7083
W. H. JOHNSON
7090
REV. H. H. JOHNSON
7058
MOSES W. JONES
7101
GEORGE H. JORDAN
7036
ELI JUDKINS
MATTHEW KENNEDY
REV. H. J. PALMER
7053
ROSA PARKS
TOM PARKS
7012
WILSON PATRICK
7138
ANNIE PATTERSON
7151
JUDGE PICKETT
FRANK L. TAYLOR
7112
REBECCA TELL
7133
JAMES THORNTON
WESLEY TOLBERT
LOTTIE GREEN VARNER
7095
CALVIN VARNER

Montgomery Bus Boycott

African Americans in Montgomery, Alabama, began boycotting city buses in December 1955 to protest the poor treatment Black passengers received on the segregated vehicles. The segregated buses reinforced the myth of racial hierarchy; Black passengers were required by law to give up their seats to white passengers and were only allowed to sit or stand at the back of the buses, which also made far fewer stops in Black residential communities than in white ones.

On February 20, 1956, local officials issued warrants for the arrests of civil rights activists, including Dr. Martin Luther King Jr., Jo Ann Robinson, Rosa Parks, and the Reverend Ralph Abernathy, for organizing the Montgomery Bus Boycott. The following day, a grand jury indicted eighty-nine of the leaders of the boycott, accusing them of violating a 1921 statute forbidding boycotts without "just cause."

In the grand jury report that accompanied the indictment, the grand jurors repudiated anti-segregation efforts. "In this state we are committed to segregation by custom and law; we intend to maintain it," they wrote. "The settlement of differences over school attendance, public transportation and other facilities must be made within those laws which reflect our way of life."

As the indicted boycott leaders surrendered themselves into custody at the police station, hundreds of African Americans gathered outside in a show of support for their efforts to challenge racial discrimination and fight segregation in Alabama.

Of those indicted, only Dr. King was prosecuted. Despite defense evidence that the boycott was peaceful and that discriminatory bus service inflicted harm on the Black community, Dr. King was quickly convicted, fined $1,000, and given a suspended jail sentence of one year of hard labor.

The indictment, along with Dr. King's conviction, strengthened local African Americans' resolve to fight segregation and attracted national attention to the growing Civil Rights Movement.

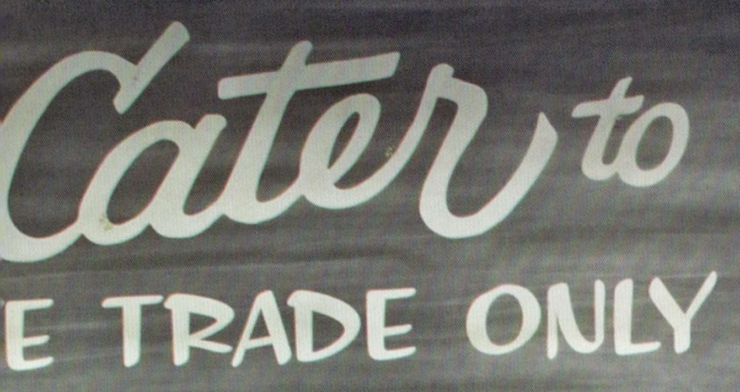

Attention White Home Buyers!

The Largest Restricted White Community in Washington

Buy or Rent in the section known as

Eckington High Veiw
BloomingDale Edgewood

IMPERIAL LAUNDRY

WE WASH FOR WHITE PEOPLE ONLY

WHITE ONLY

MAIDS IN UNIFORM ACCEPTED

WAITING ROOM FOR WHITE ONLY

BY ORDER POLICE DEPT.

WE SERVE WHITE'S only

NO SPANISH or MEXICANS

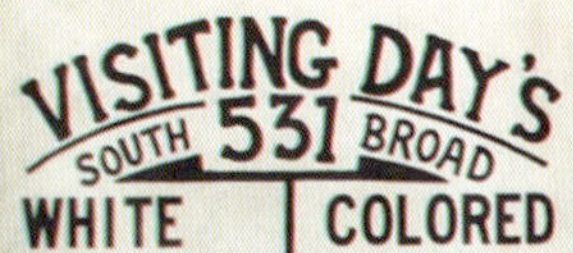

WHITE | COLORED

SUNDAY & WEDNESDAY | MONDAY & FRIDAY

MORNINGS 10:00 AM TO 11:45 AM

AFTERNOONS 1:00 PM TO 2:45 PM

PACKAGES RECEIVED TIL 12-NOON ONLY

CLOTHES PACKAGES ONLY ALLOWED

ICE-WATER WHITE-PEOPLE

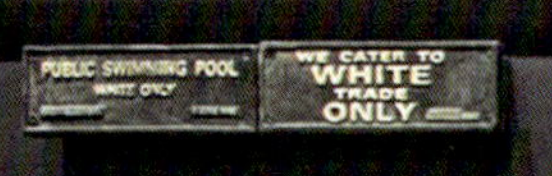

NO NEGROES OR ANIMALS!

VIRGINIA STATE LAW REQUIRES ALL COLORED PASSENGERS TO RIDE IN REAR OF BUS

CITIZENS RAPID TRANSIT CO.

RENTALS

NO NEGROES
NO DOGS
NO WHORES

TEXAS 1949

WE CATER TO WHITE TRADE ONLY

Clark's Cafe

ALL WHITE HELP

A good place to eat

WHITE ONLY

NO NIGGER OR NEGRO ALLOWED INSIDE BUILDING

NO COLORED ALLOWED

BY ORDER OF MANAGER SEPTEMBER 12, 1952

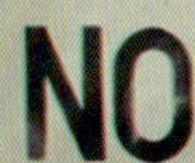

NO NEGROES OR APES ALLOWED

TEXAS S&P 1951

WHITE WOMEN

SENORAS BLANCAS

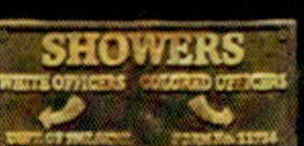

PONCE DE LEON IS A PRIVATE PARK

UNDER CITY POLICE REGULATIONS.
NO DISORDERLY CHARACTERS TOLERATED.
COLORED PERSONS ADMITTED AS SERVANTS ONLY.

white Only

S · MEXICAN

RTO RICANS

Not Allowed

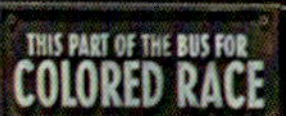

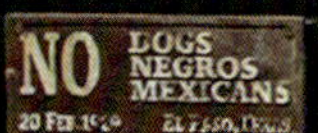

WE WANT WHITE TENANTS IN OUR WHITE COMMUNITY

NO NEGRO OR APE ALLOWED IN BUILDING

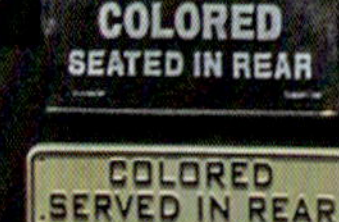

NEGROES MUST MOVE TO THE BACK OF THE BUS

SPARTA, MISS. TRANSIT

ALL COLORED-TRAD MUST, TAKE THEIR EAT'S AND DRINKS OUTSIDE

NO NEGROES ALLOWED AFTER SUNDOWN

NEGROS NOT WANTED IN THE NORTH OR SOUTH SEND THEM BACK TO AFRICA WHERE GOD ALMIGHTY PUT THEM TO BEGIN WITH THAT IS THEIR HOME

WHITE ONLY NO NEGROES

White Only Beck's CABS

THIS PART OF BUS FOR WHITE PEOPLE

SHOWERS

MEALS AT ALL HOURS
RESTAURANT.
ALL WHITE HELP.

UNION PACIFIC RAILROAD
WHITES ONLY

WHITE
ONLY!

VER HEARD
OF MENA
E CITY OF THE OZARK MOUNTAINS
ELEVATION 1200 FEET
No Mosquitoes
No Blizzards
No Malaria
No Drouth
No Negroes
Schools and Churches
Lodges and Societies
Parks and Driveways
Fruits and Flowers
Health and Happiness
ADDRESS
CRETARY MENA COMMERCIAL CLUB
MENA, ARKANSAS

NO
NEGROS OR
APES
·JULY 1951·

THE BLACKEST LAND
GREENVILLE
WELCOME
THE WHITEST PEOPLE

FOR
WHITE PASSENGERS

ELK WALLOW
PICNIC
GROUNDS
FOR
WHITE
ONLY

WHITES ONLY
WITHIN CITY LIMITS
AFTER DARK

Whites Only
Telephone Booth
Lincoln Telephone & Telegraph

NO NIGGERS
NO JEWS
NO DOGS

WHITE WAITING
— ROOM —
ntrastate Passengers

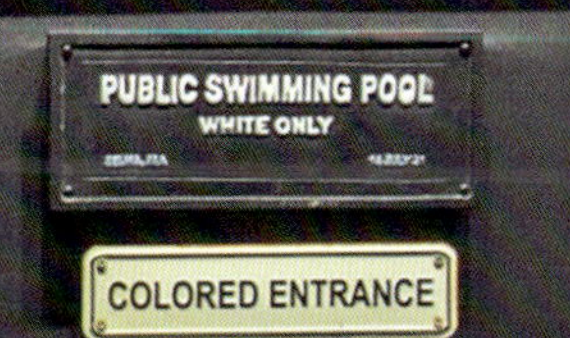

LOOK LADIES
SEGREGATED REST ROOMS
Full Length Mirrows
JUMPER'S GOOD GULF

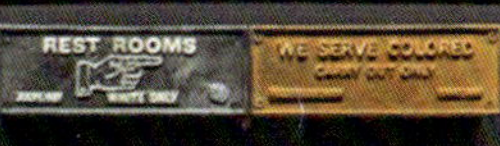

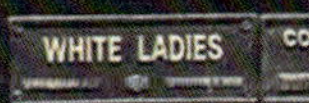

WHITE ONLY

NOTICE
IT IS REQUIRED BY LAW UNDER
PENALTY OF FINE OF $5.00 TO $25.00
THAT WHITE AND NEGRO PASSENGERS MUST
OCCUPY THE RESPECTIVE SPACE OR SEATS
INDICATED BY SIGNS IN THIS VEHICLE.
TEXAS PENAL CODE: ARTICLE 1659, SEC.4
DALLAS CITY ORDINANCE: NO.2904

TOILETS
VHITE'S ONLY

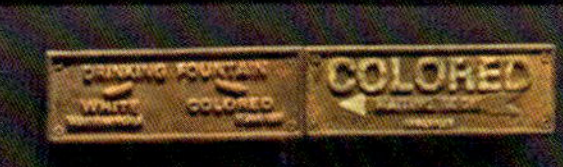

NORTH CAROLINA LAW
White Patrons Please Seat From Front
Colored Patrons Please Seat From Rear
NO SMOKING

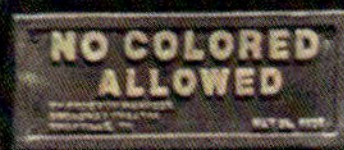

POSITIVELY
NO BEER SOLD
TO INDIANS

· NO ·
NIGGERS
PUERTORICAN
MEXICANS
ALLOWED

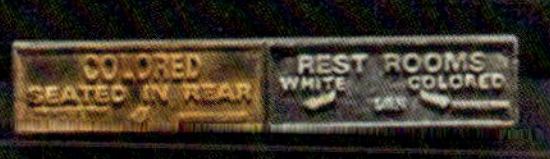

HIS PARK WAS GIVEN FOR
HITE PEOPLE ONLY.
MEXICANS AND
EGROES STAY OUT.
ORDER OF PARK BOARD.

THIS PARK
FOR
WHITE PEOPLE ONLY

WHITE
CUSTOMERS
Only!
6¢

COLORED
GO TO BACK OF BUS

MOTEL ROOM
POLICY
NO NEGROES
NO DOGS
NO MEXICANS

FOR
RENT
NO NEGROES
NO SPANISH

We Employ
WHITE HELP
And Cater To
WHITE PEOPLE

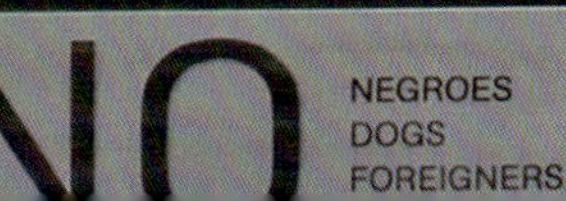

REST ROOMS

White Supremacy by Law

In cities and states throughout the country, elected officials passed laws that ordered racial separation in major and mundane segments of everyday life, from segregated seating on public buses to banning interracial romance and marriage.

In Montgomery, Alabama, Black and white people were prohibited from playing cards, dominoes, or checkers together. Birmingham, Alabama, barred white nurses from treating Black male patients. Circuses in Louisiana were required to have separate entrances and ticket booths for Black and white patrons. And the state of North Carolina required white and Black children's public school textbooks to be stored separately.

Dozens of Jim Crow laws throughout the nation codified white supremacy and trapped African Americans behind a wall of inequality.

Bigotry and Humiliation

The enforcement of racial segregation laws routinely humiliated the non-white people targeted for exclusion.

Public and private establishments, especially in the South, promoted racial hierarchy through posted placards and race-conscious policies and practices. Signs declaring that certain facilities and services were available only to whites normalized racial bigotry and bombarded African Americans with the constant message of their perceived inferiority.

The Role of the Court

The Supreme Court advanced racial equality during the Civil Rights Movement through decisions like *Brown v. Board of Education*, but this was a shift in the Court's historical record on race.

After the Civil War, when the nation adopted constitutional amendments designed to promote racial equality and protect Black voting rights, the Court issued rulings that blocked efforts to protect non-white citizens from violence and discrimination and allowed states and private companies to create and maintain Jim Crow laws that reinforced white supremacy.

The system of inequality that civil rights activists courageously organized to challenge was not created and sustained merely by individual prejudice and extremist vigilantes. For nearly a century after Emancipation, racial inequality was enforced by the nation's most powerful institutions, including its highest court.

We are committed to segregation by custom and law; we intend to maintain it.

— GRAND JURY INDICTMENT OF 89 MONTGOMERY BUS BOYCOTT LEADERS, 1956

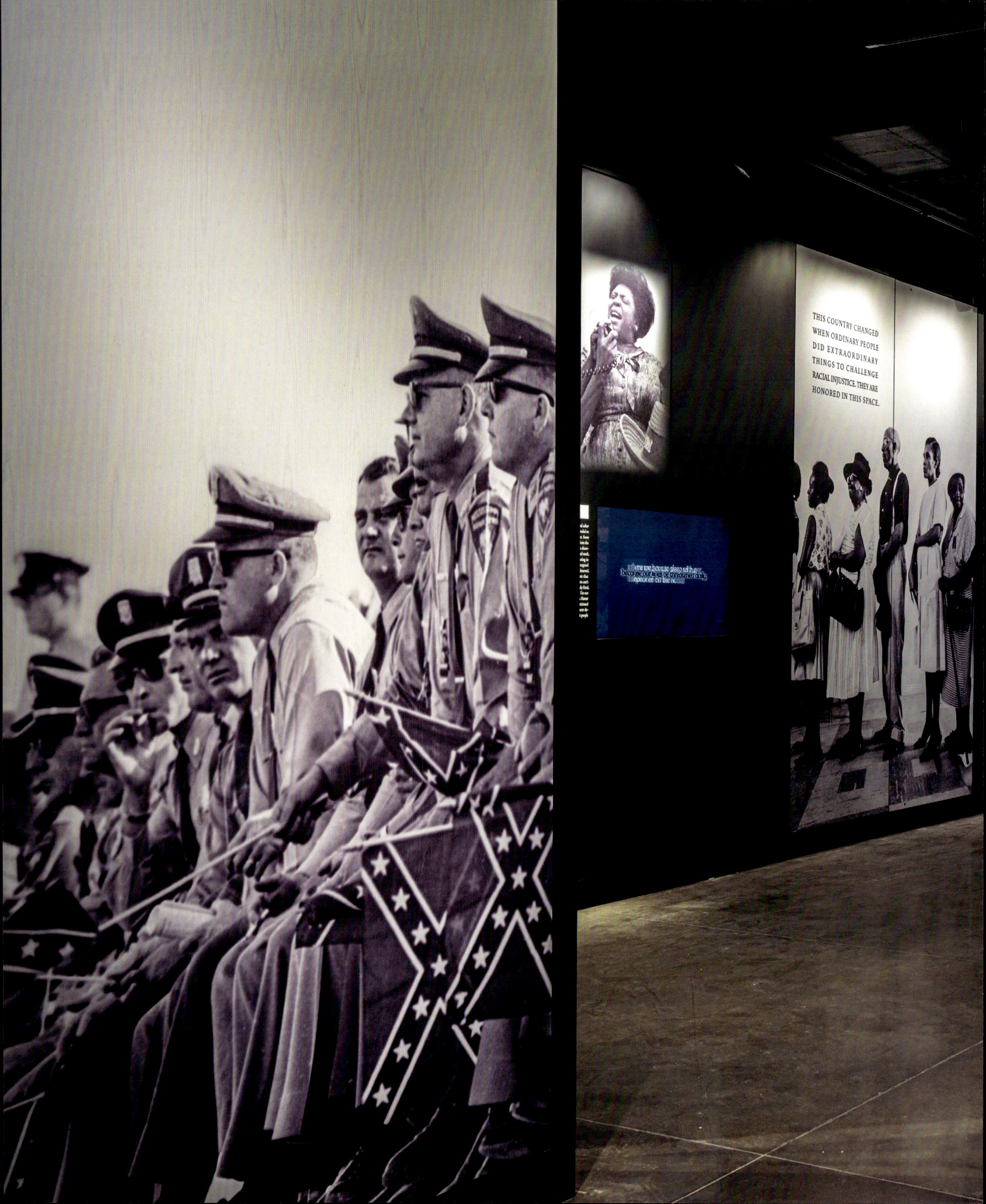
THIS COUNTRY CHANGED
WHEN ORDINARY PEOPLE
DID EXTRAORDINARY
THINGS TO CHALLENGE
RACIAL INJUSTICE. THEY ARE
HONORED IN THIS SPACE.

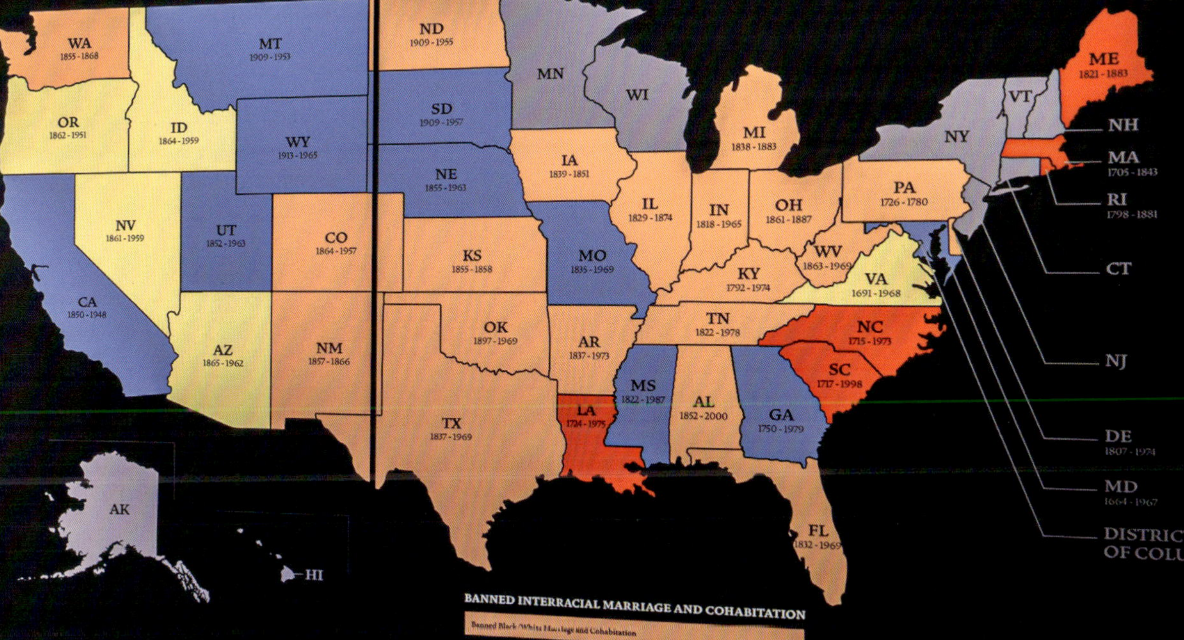
SEGREGATING LOVE
RACIAL RESTRICTIONS ON ROMANCE
Most states in America have adopted laws that ban or criminalize romance, marriage, or cohabitation between people who are Black with people who are white. These laws were adopted to preserve racial hierarchy and white supremacy and have existed throughout most of our nation's history. Every state that banned interracial romance prohibited cohabitation or marriage between a Black person and a white person. Some states banned relations between people who are white with people who are Asian or Native. These "crimes" could result in years of imprisonment for offenders, and some states did not eliminate these laws until the late 20th century.
WA 1855 - 1868
MT 1909 - 1953
ND 1909 - 1955
MN
WI
MI 1838 - 1883
NY
VT
ME 1821 - 1883
NH
MA 1705 - 1843
RI 1798 - 1881
CT
OR 1862 - 1951
ID 1864 - 1959
WY 1913 - 1965
SD 1909 - 1957
IA 1839 - 1851
NE 1855 - 1963
PA 1726 - 1780
IL 1829 - 1874
IN 1818 - 1965
OH 1861 - 1887
NV 1861 - 1959
UT 1852 - 1963
CO 1864 - 1957
KS 1855 - 1858
MO 1835 - 1969
WV 1863 - 1969
VA 1691 - 1968
KY 1792 - 1974
CA 1850 - 1948
NJ
TN 1822 - 1978
NC 1715 - 1973
OK 1897 - 1969
AR 1837 - 1973
AZ 1865 - 1962
NM 1857 - 1866
SC 1717 - 1998
MS 1822 - 1987
AL 1852 - 2000
GA 1750 - 1979
TX 1837 - 1969
LA 1724 - 1975
DE 1807 - 1974
MD 1664 - 1967
DISTRICT OF COLU
AK
HI
FL 1832 - 1969
BANNED INTERRACIAL MARRIAGE AND COHABITATION
Banned Black/White Marriage and Cohabitation
Banned Black/White and Asian/White Marriage and Cohabitation
Banned Black/White and Native/White Marriage and Cohabitation
Banned Black/White, Native/White, and Asian/White Marriage and Cohabitation
None

The narrative of racial difference, developed as a defense for slavery, persisted after Emancipation through evolving systems of inequality. Today that narrative has become a justification for inhumane treatment of "criminals" that is directly rooted in the dehumanizing rhetoric of enslavement, racial terror, and Jim Crow.

The Era of Mass Incarceration

The era of racial terror fostered the racialization of criminality. Whites claimed that lynching was necessary to protect their property, lives, and lifestyles from Black "criminals." This presumption of guilt and dangerousness has burdened African Americans for generations.

The Civil Rights Movement addressed discrimination in voting, education, employment, housing, and public accommodations but left criminal justice largely untouched.

At the close of the civil rights era, politicians seized on "law and order" as a winning campaign platform and used thinly veiled racial appeals to win elections. Since the start of President Richard Nixon's racially biased war on drugs in 1971, the American prison population has increased from three hundred thousand to more than 2.3 million.

> ***Did we know we were lying about the drugs? Of course we did.***
> —John Ehrlichman, President Richard Nixon's domestic policy chief

America's harsh, inhumane, and biased system of criminal justice ensnares poor people of all races and disproportionately impacts non-white people. African Americans are saddled with a presumption of guilt and dangerousness that makes them vulnerable to biased policing and wrongful arrest and conviction.

In many states, the majority of imprisoned people are Black or brown, and the impact of race on the death penalty is well documented. People of color are vastly more likely to be killed by law enforcement officers while unarmed and to be unjustly convicted of crimes. Children of color suffer higher rates of suspension, expulsion, and arrest at school and have disproportionate contact with the juvenile justice system. These devastating disparities are rooted in America's history of racial injustice.

Excessive punishment is widespread in our legal system, where children are sentenced to imprisonment until death and prison conditions are often abusive and deadly.

Even after serving their sentences, millions of Americans face significant collateral consequences that bar them from voting and serving on juries; restrict their access to public housing, food stamps, and other social services; subject them to discrimination in the search for employment; and impact nearly every other facet of daily life.

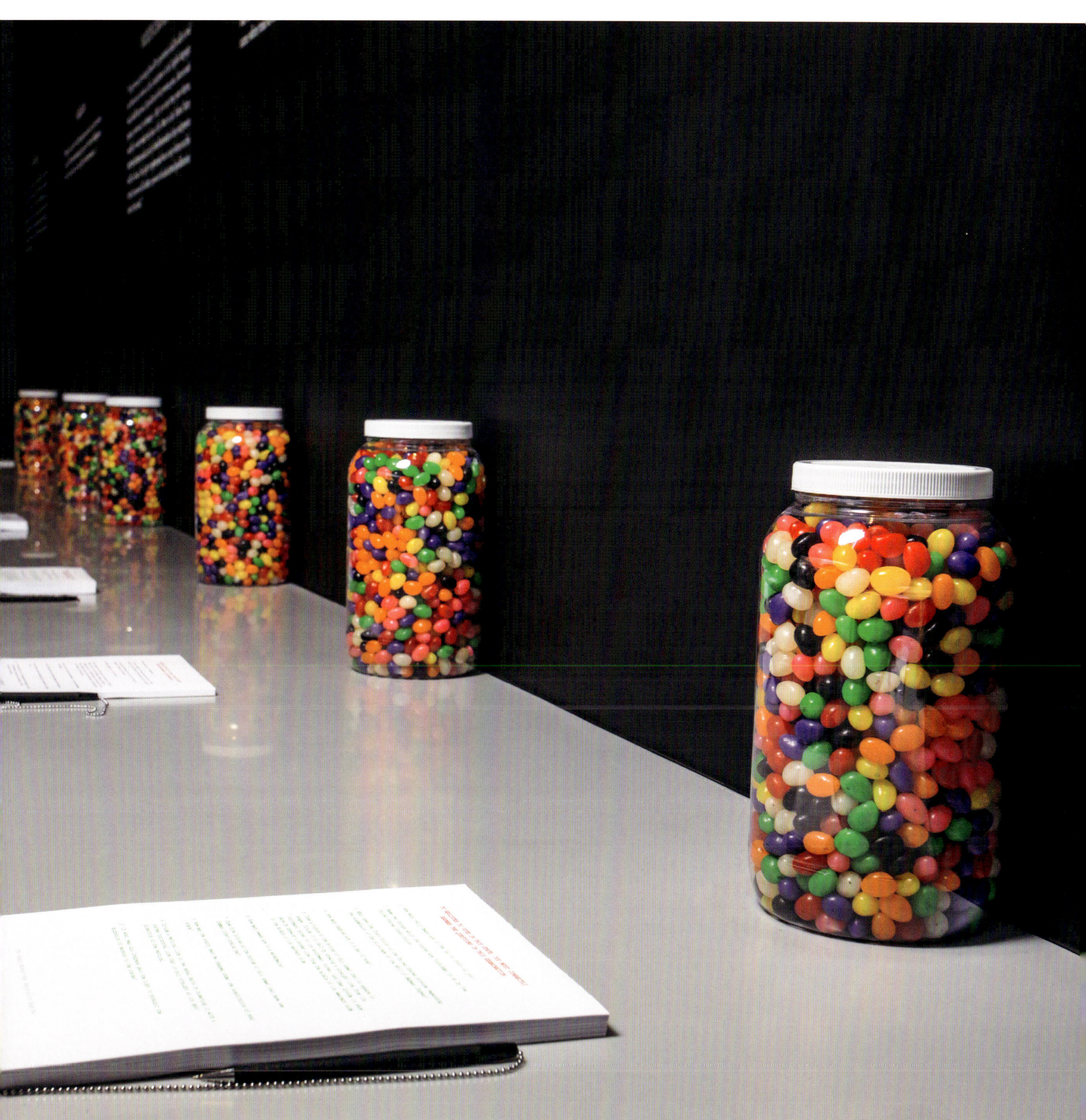

Visitors can take a poll test and experience how arbitrary and humiliating tests were used to disenfranchise Black people and create barriers to voting.

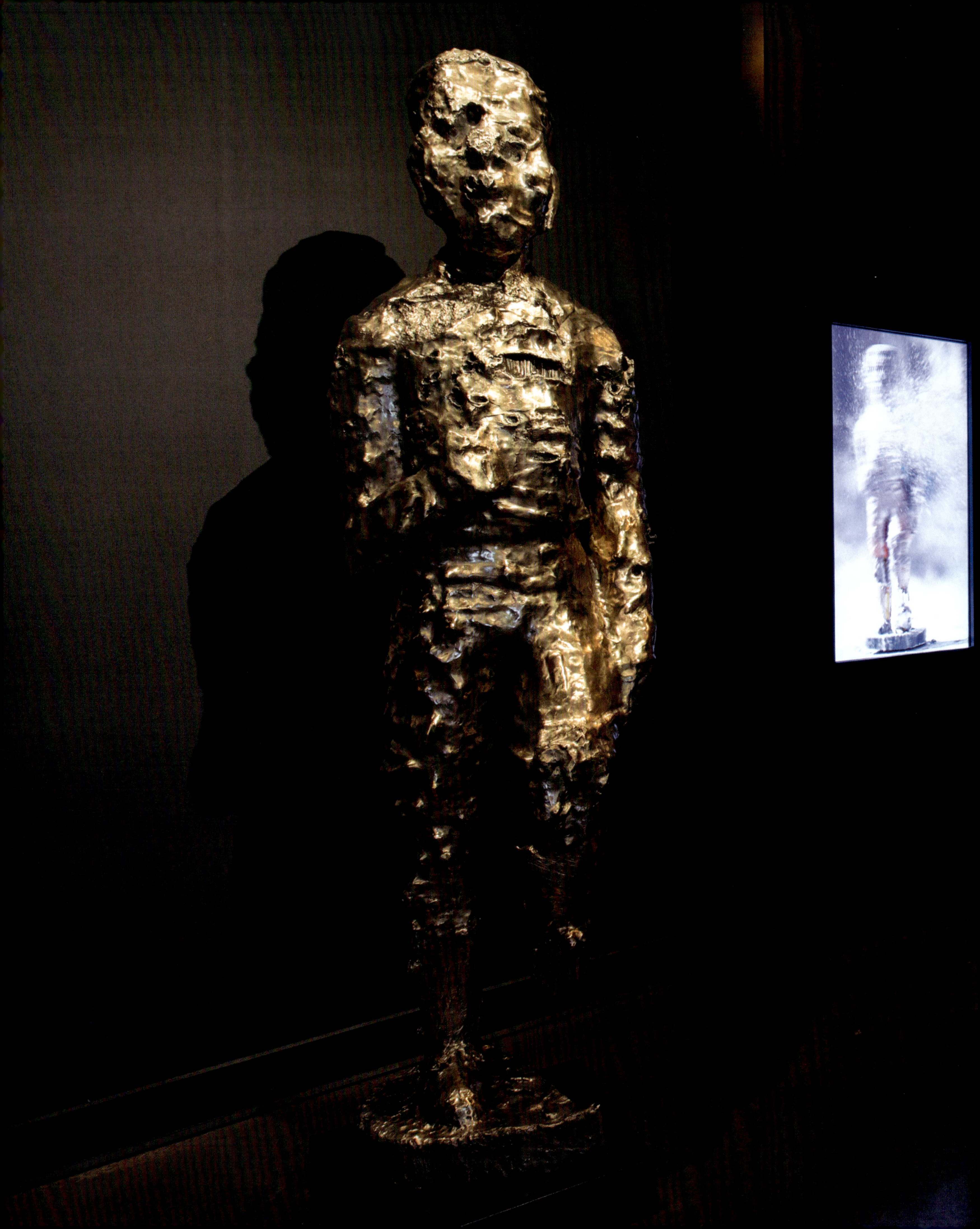

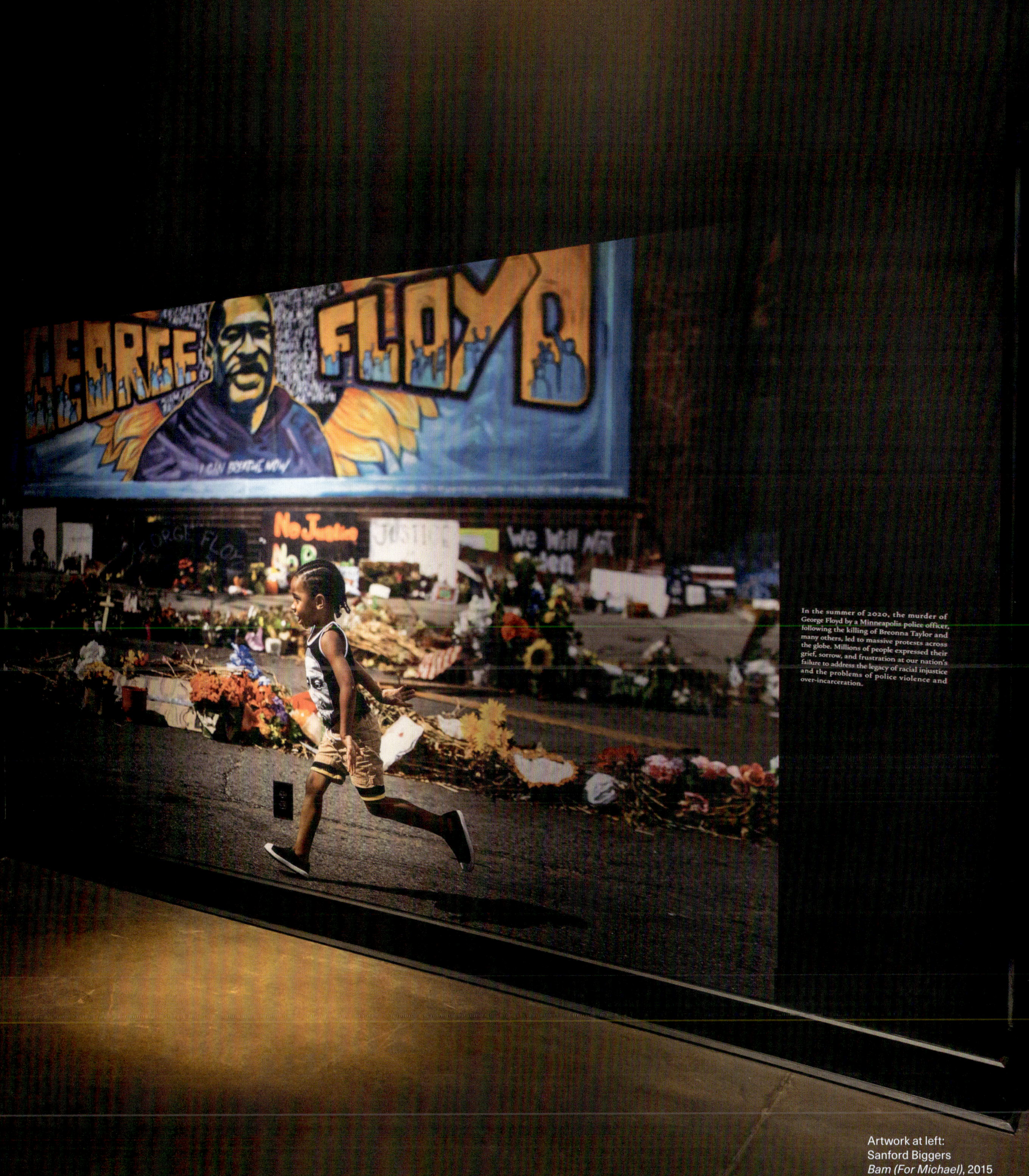

Artwork at left:
Sanford Biggers
Bam (For Michael), 2015
Bronze

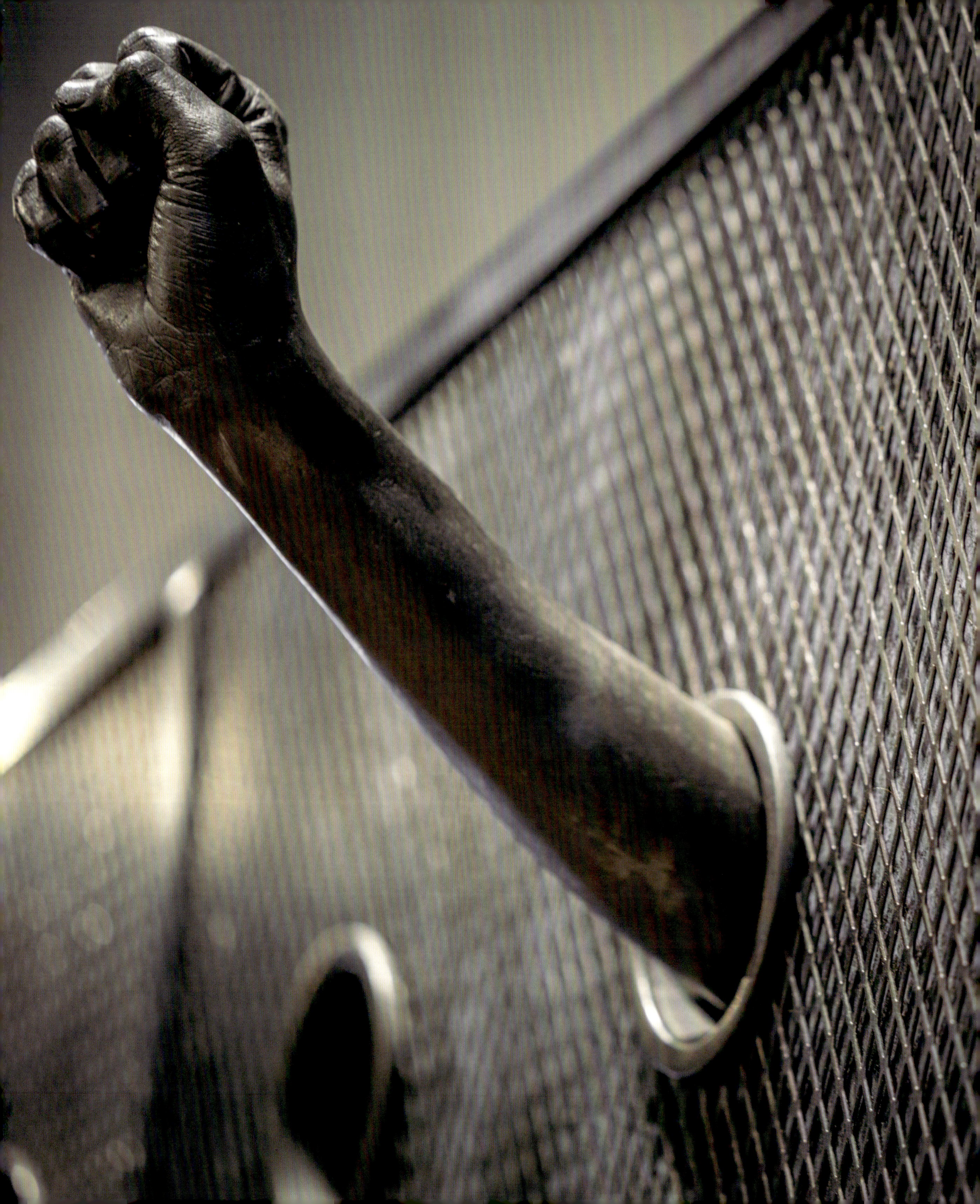

The Death Penalty

The death penalty in America is a direct descendant of lynching. More than eight in ten American lynchings between 1889 and 1918 occurred in the South, and more than eight in ten of the more than 1,400 executions carried out in this country since 1976 have been in the South.

The modern death penalty continues to value white life and devalue Black life. A crime is much more likely to result in a death sentence if the victim is white. African Americans—who comprise less than 13 percent of the country's population—make up 42 percent of people sentenced to death nationwide, and 34 percent of those executed since 1976.

The death penalty is an expensive policy defined by bias and error. More than 200 people have been exonerated and released from death row since executions resumed in the late 1970s. For every eight people executed in this country, one innocent person on death row has been identified and exonerated.

While some states have suspended, repealed, or reduced their use of the death penalty in response to growing concerns about reliability, Southern states continue to condemn and execute people in large numbers, disproportionately targeting the poor and people of color.

Anthony Ray Hinton spent nearly thirty years on Alabama's death row for a crime he did not commit. Since his release, he has dedicated himself to sharing his story as a testimony, urging Americans and people around the globe to end the death penalty. The Legacy Museum prison visitation booths feature his story.

The criminal justice system's endorsement of racially biased narratives has never been meaningfully confronted. Understanding the current system's roots in our history of racial injustice requires truthful engagement with that history and its legacy.

Sentencing Children to Die in Prison

The punitive trend in American criminal justice has led to excessive punishments imposed on some of the most vulnerable defendants imaginable.

Many young children in America are imperiled by abuse, neglect, domestic and community violence, and poverty. Without effective intervention and help, these children suffer, struggle, and fall into despair and hopelessness. Some young teens cannot manage the emotional, social, and psychological challenges of adolescence and eventually engage in destructive and violent behavior.

Hank Willis Thomas
A Luta Continua (detail), 2013
Aluminum

Many states have ignored the crisis and dysfunction that creates child delinquency and instead chosen to subject kids to further victimization and abuse in the adult criminal justice system.

Children as young as eight have been prosecuted as adults, and thousands of children across the United States have been sentenced as adults and sent to adult prisons. About ten thousand children are housed in adult jails and prisons on any given day in America, where they are five times more likely to be sexually assaulted and face increased risk of suicide.

Some three thousand children nationwide have been sentenced to life imprisonment without the possibility of parole, some as young as thirteen years old.

Conditions of Confinement

After several decades of "tough on crime" lawmaking, the American prison system confines one in one hundred Americans and has grown into a costly, overcrowded, dangerous, and inhumane mess.

In 2011, conditions became so extreme in California—where harsh Three Strikes, You're Out policies inflated prison populations and budgets—that the Supreme Court found them "incompatible with the concept of human dignity" and ordered the state to release 46,000 incarcerated people. California passed its Three Strikes law in 1994. It requires that a person convicted of a felony who has two or more prior convictions for certain offenses must be sentenced to at least twenty-five years to life in state prison, even if the third offense is nonviolent. People have been sentenced to life in prison for shoplifting a pair of socks or stealing bread, according to the Committee for Three Strikes Reform.

In many cases, prison conditions impede rehabilitation and compound the trauma and disadvantages that incarcerated men, women, and children bring with them.

Despite evidence that long-term solitary confinement leads to anxiety, paranoia, hallucinations, deep depression, and a heightened risk of suicide, an estimated 75,000 people are held in isolation currently, according to a recent study.

Physical and sexual abuse are rampant in many prison systems, where incarcerated men and women have limited recourse when they are victimized by other incarcerated people or prison staff. Some of the nation's most dangerous, abusive, and deadly prisons are located in Alabama.

Deborah Roberts
Nessun Dorma: None Shall Sleep, 2018
Mixed media collage on canvas

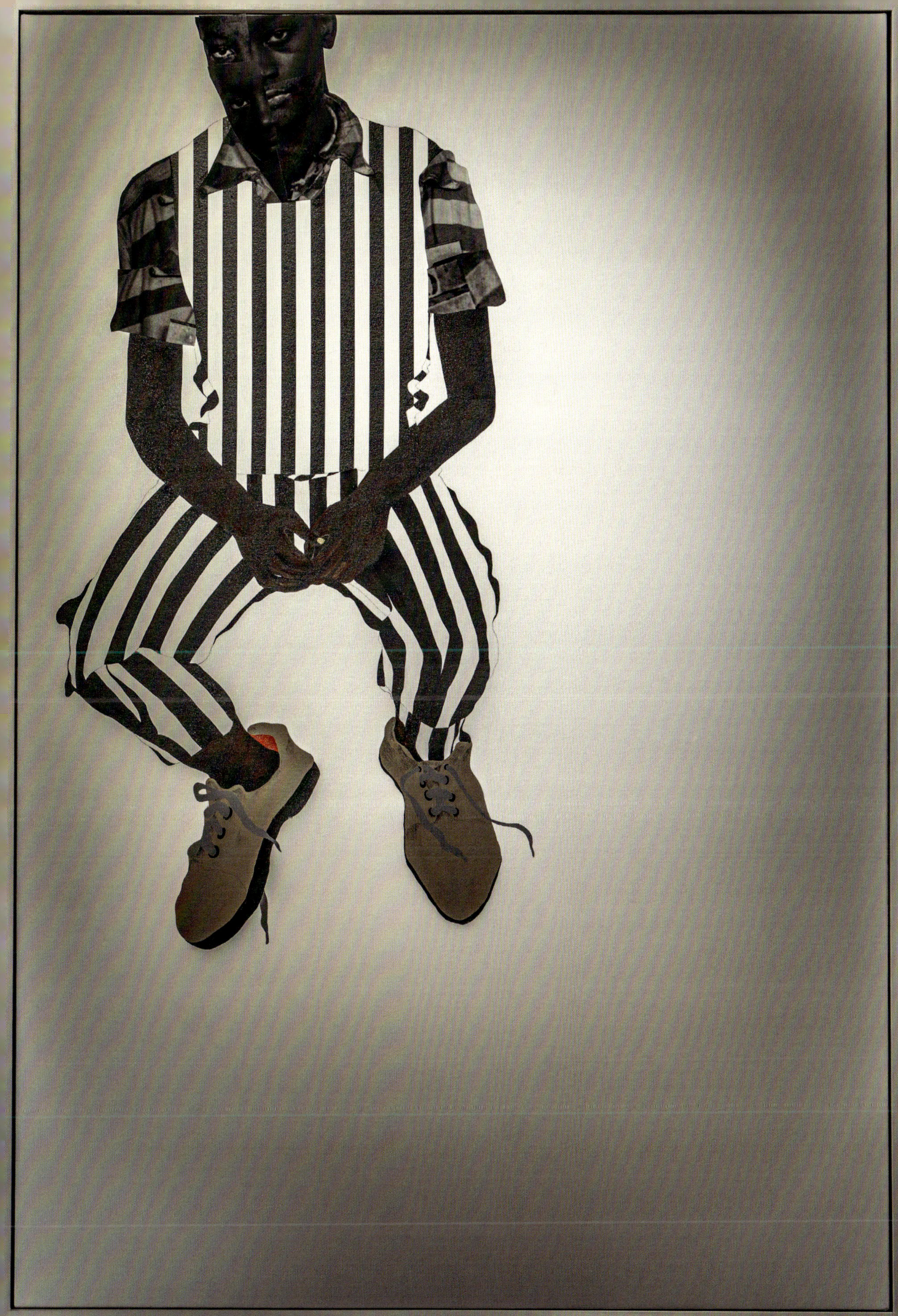

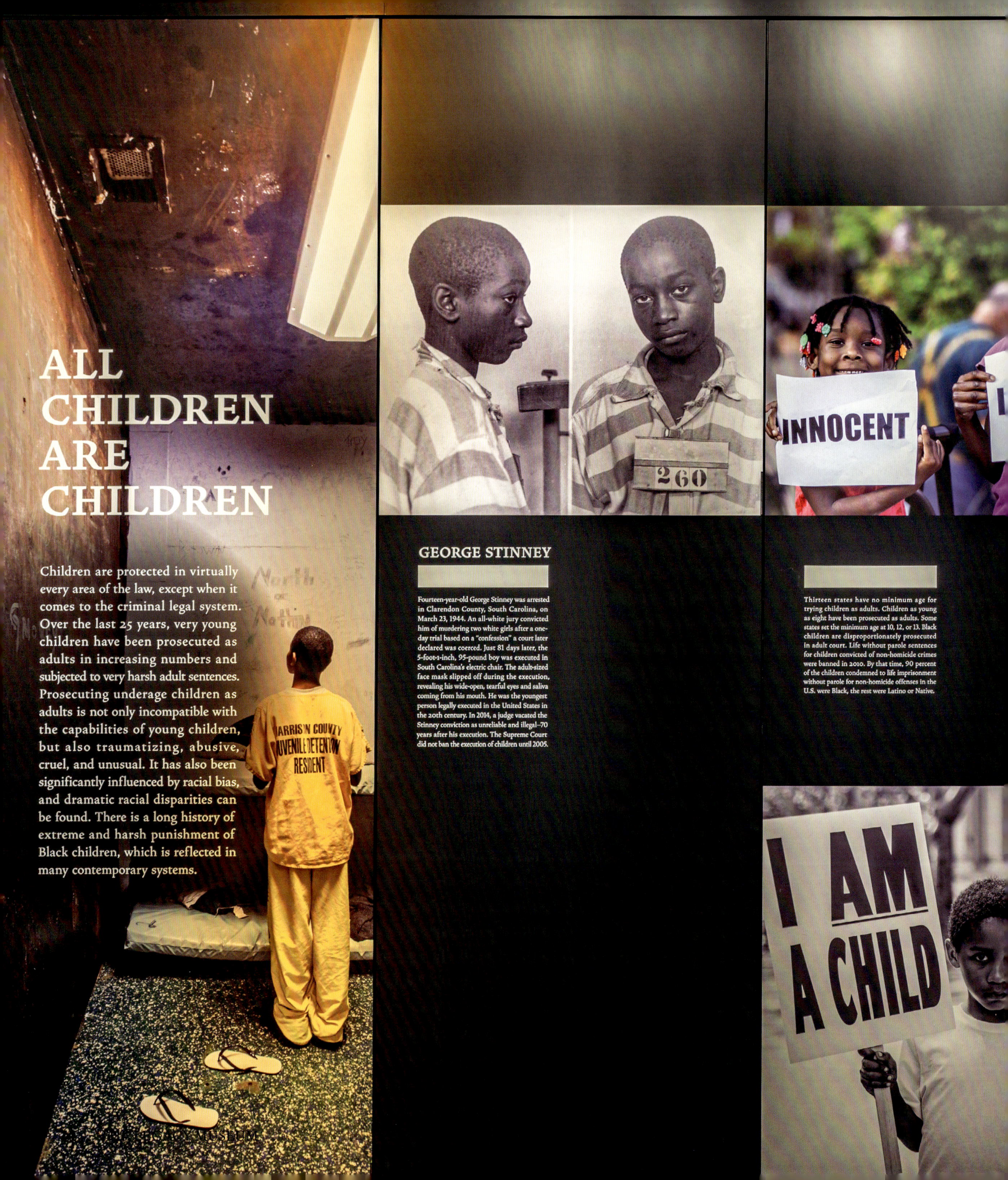

ALL CHILDREN ARE CHILDREN

Children are protected in virtually every area of the law, except when it comes to the criminal legal system. Over the last 25 years, very young children have been prosecuted as adults in increasing numbers and subjected to very harsh adult sentences. Prosecuting underage children as adults is not only incompatible with the capabilities of young children, but also traumatizing, abusive, cruel, and unusual. It has also been significantly influenced by racial bias, and dramatic racial disparities can be found. There is a long history of extreme and harsh punishment of Black children, which is reflected in many contemporary systems.

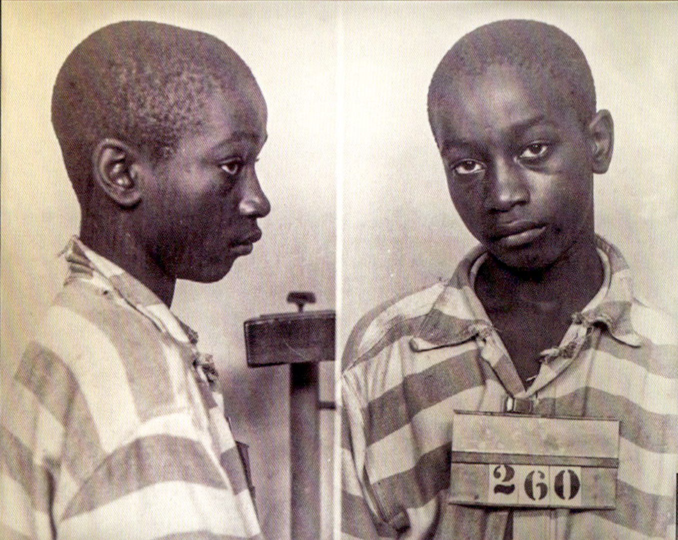

GEORGE STINNEY

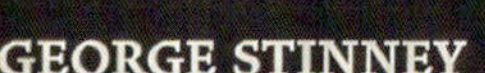

Fourteen-year-old George Stinney was arrested in Clarendon County, South Carolina, on March 23, 1944. An all-white jury convicted him of murdering two white girls after a one-day trial based on a "confession" a court later declared was coerced. Just 81 days later, the 5-foot-1-inch, 95-pound boy was executed in South Carolina's electric chair. The adult-sized face mask slipped off during the execution, revealing his wide-open, tearful eyes and saliva coming from his mouth. He was the youngest person legally executed in the United States in the 20th century. In 2014, a judge vacated the Stinney conviction as unreliable and illegal–70 years after his execution. The Supreme Court did not ban the execution of children until 2005.

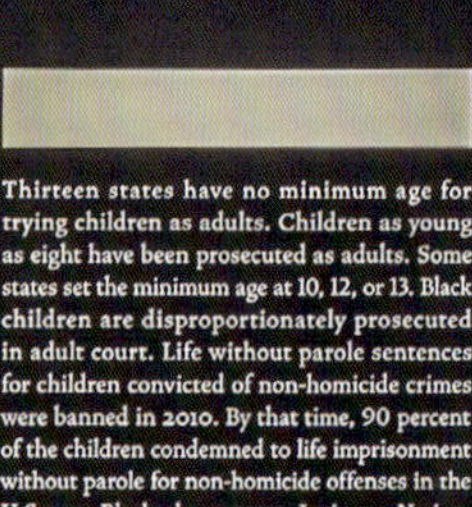

Thirteen states have no minimum age for trying children as adults. Children as young as eight have been prosecuted as adults. Some states set the minimum age at 10, 12, or 13. Black children are disproportionately prosecuted in adult court. Life without parole sentences for children convicted of non-homicide crimes were banned in 2010. By that time, 90 percent of the children condemned to life imprisonment without parole for non-homicide offenses in the U.S. were Black, the rest were Latino or Native.

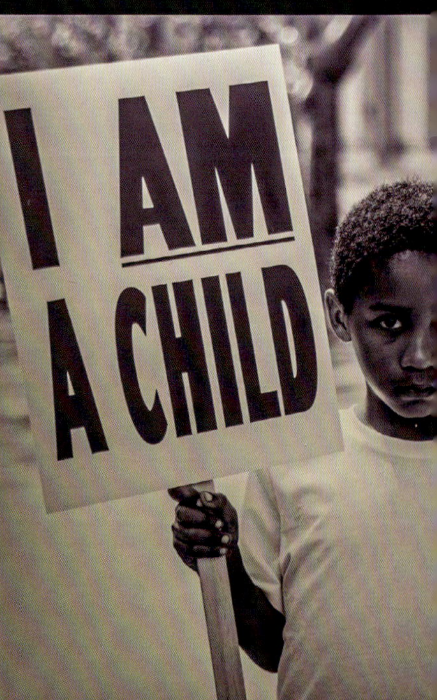

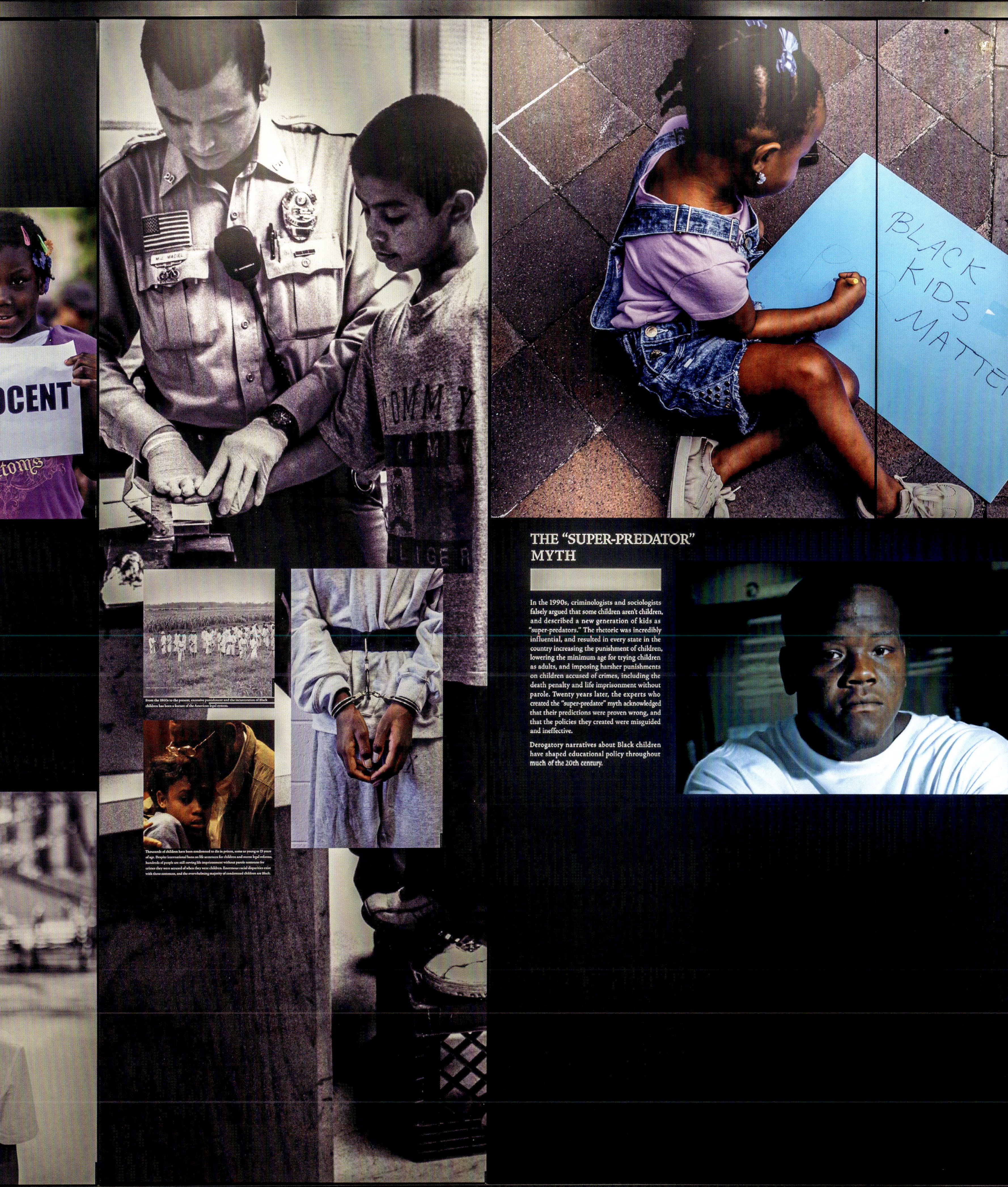

From the 1860s to the present, excessive punishment and the incarceration of Black children has been a feature of the American legal system.

Thousands of children have been condemned to die in prison, some as young as 13 years of age. Despite international bans on life sentences for children and recent legal reforms, hundreds of people are still serving life imprisonment without parole sentences for crimes they were accused of when they were children. Enormous racial disparities exist with these sentences, and the overwhelming majority of condemned children are Black.

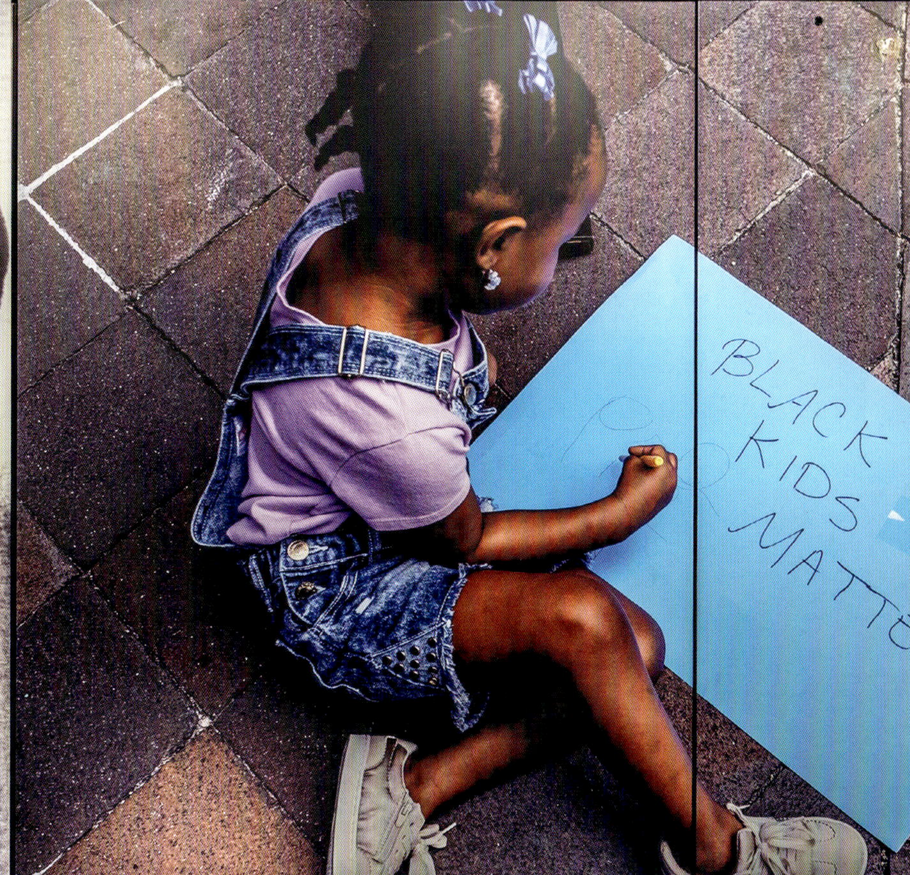

THE "SUPER-PREDATOR" MYTH

In the 1990s, criminologists and sociologists falsely argued that some children aren't children, and described a new generation of kids as "super-predators." The rhetoric was incredibly influential, and resulted in every state in the country increasing the punishment of children, lowering the minimum age for trying children as adults, and imposing harsher punishments on children accused of crimes, including the death penalty and life imprisonment without parole. Twenty years later, the experts who created the "super-predator" myth acknowledged that their predictions were proven wrong, and that the policies they created were misguided and ineffective.

Derogatory narratives about Black children have shaped educational policy throughout much of the 20th century.

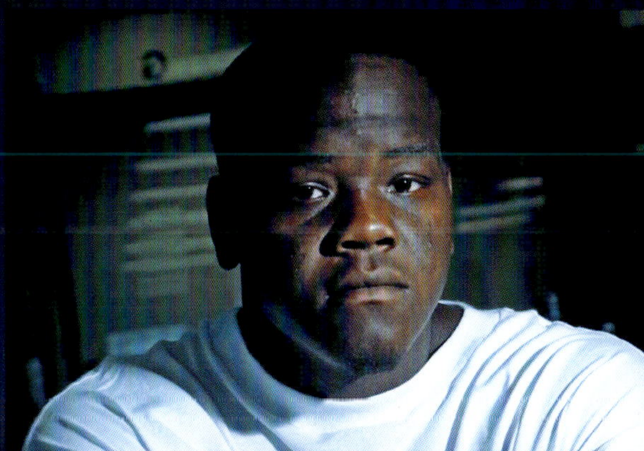

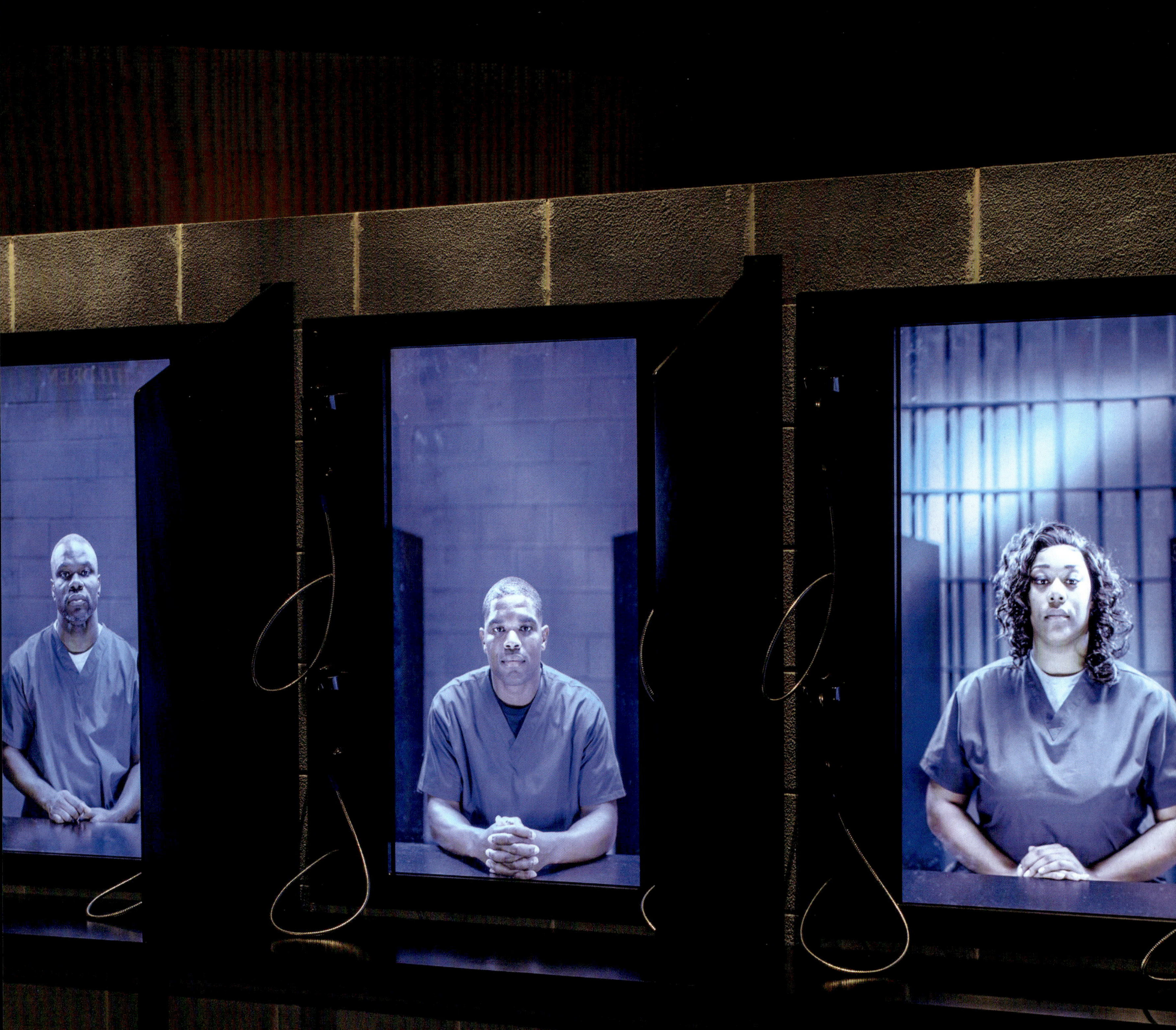

Voices from Inside

It is impossible to understand mass incarceration without listening to the voices of the incarcerated. Every day, EJI receives scores of letters from incarcerated men, women, and children who need assistance. We also maintain relationships with formerly incarcerated clients who are navigating the challenges of reentry to life outside the prison system.

Visitors to the Legacy Museum are invited to bear witness by reading letters from incarcerated people and by hearing directly from courageous EJI clients in simulated prison visits.

Anthony Ray Hinton spent thirty years on Alabama's death row for a crime he did not commit before being released in 2015.

Monica Washington was raped by a prison guard in 2010 while confined in the Alabama prison with the highest rate of sexual assaults of any women's facility in the nation.

Ian Manuel was sentenced to life without parole at age thirteen and served twenty-six years, including twenty in solitary confinement, before Supreme Court decisions led to his resentencing and release.

Robert Caston, who was sentenced to die in prison in Louisiana at age seventeen, served more than forty-five years before the same Supreme Court rulings enabled his release in 2012 at age sixty-four.

Diane Jones was sentenced to life without parole in 2000 when Alabama's Habitual Felony Offender Act forced a judge to sentence her based on a seventeen-year-old conviction for forging checks to buy groceries. Ms. Jones served more than five years before EJI was able to secure her release in 2006.

Kuntrell Jackson, age fourteen, was sentenced to life without parole in Arkansas. He served more than seventeen years in prison and was paroled in 2017 after EJI won his case at the Supreme Court.

Ronald Elston was sentenced to life imprisonment without parole under Alabama's harsh mandatory sentencing laws and spent thirty-three years in prison before EJI successfully challenged his sentence and helped him secure release on parole in 2015.

If we have the courage and tenacity of our forebears, who stood firmly like a rock against the lash of slavery, we shall find a way to do for our day what they did for theirs.

—MARY MCLEOD BETHUNE

Reflection Space

From the first abolitionists fighting to end American slavery to the youth activists of today, thousands have led the fight against racial injustice in this country.

People of faith, elected officials, community leaders, legal advocates and other professionals, activists, writers, musicians, and artists have achieved major victories in the ongoing movement for equality, and have inspired many more to resist injustice.

The Legacy Museum's Reflection Space honors these individuals while providing visitors a place to pause and reflect on their museum experience.

Resistance Through Art

The arts have played a critical role in documenting and challenging racial injustice in America. The Legacy Museum's dedicated fine arts space exhibits the work of visionary painters, sculptors, photographers, writers, musicians, and visual artists engaged in the struggle to overcome racial inequality.

The Legacy Museum includes a world-class art gallery with major works from some of the most celebrated Black artists, including Glenn Ligon, Kehinde Wiley, Elizabeth Catlett, Sanford Biggers, Betye Saar, Alison Saar, Gordon Parks, Faith Ringgold, Hank Willis Thomas, Kerry James Marshall, Deborah Roberts, Willie Birch, Nelson Makamo, Whitfield Lovell, Kwame Akoto-Bamfo, Sandrine Plante, Paul S. Briggs, Titus Kaphar, Romare Bearden, John Biggers, Yvette Cole, Kay Brown, Simone Leigh, and the extraordinary vernacular artist Winfred Rembert.

The gallery includes pieces created specifically for the Legacy Museum, and its entire collection is curated in dialogue with the museum's historical narrative. Collaborations with Wynton Marsalis, Jon Boogz, Lil Buck, the Aeolians from Oakwood University (an HBCU in Alabama), Chrystal Rucker, and Brandie Sutton explore the role of music and dance in understanding our nation's history and the role of the arts.

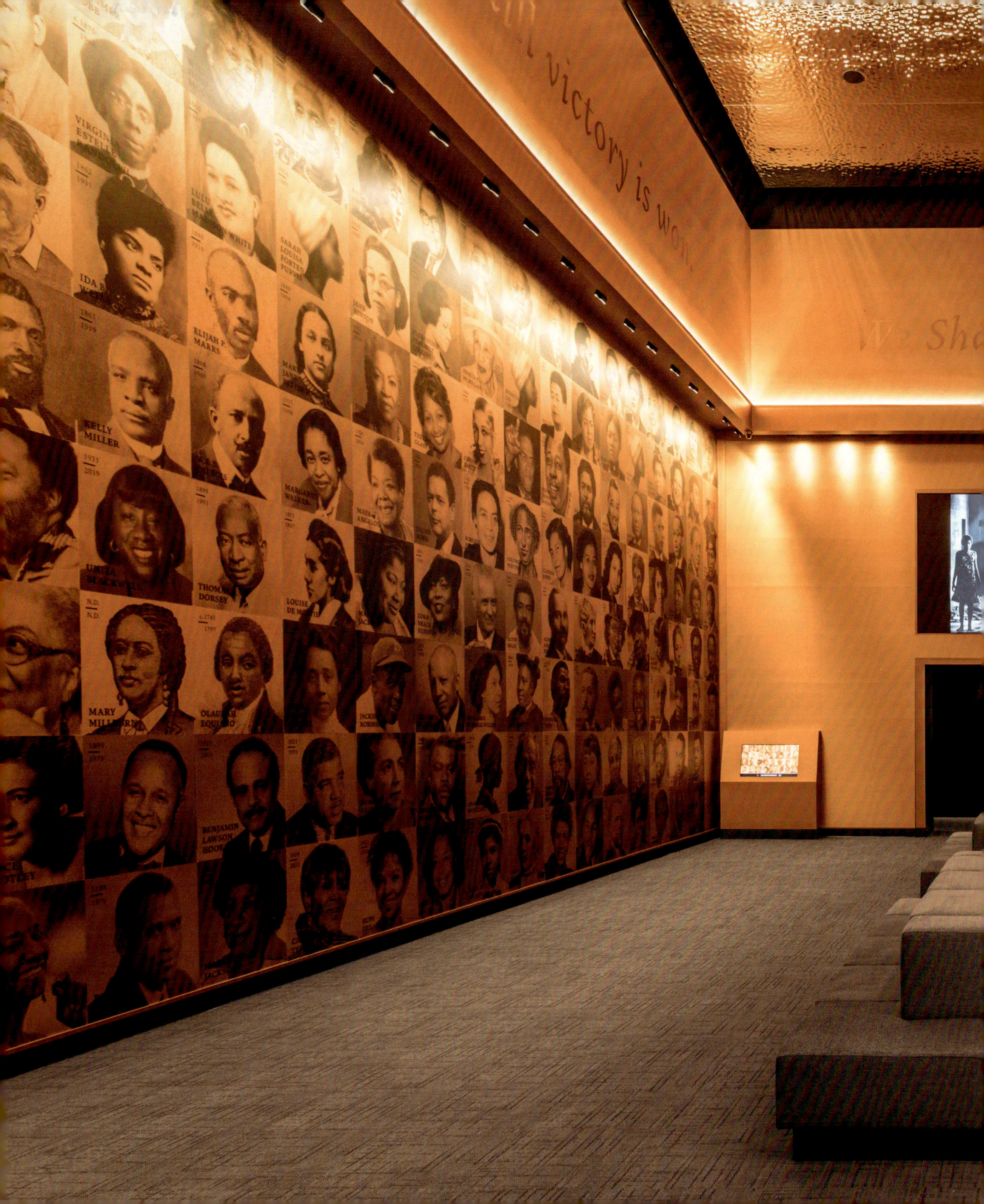
victory is won.
KELLY MILLER
ELIJAH P. MARRS
MARGARET WALKER
BENJAMIN LAWSON HOOKS

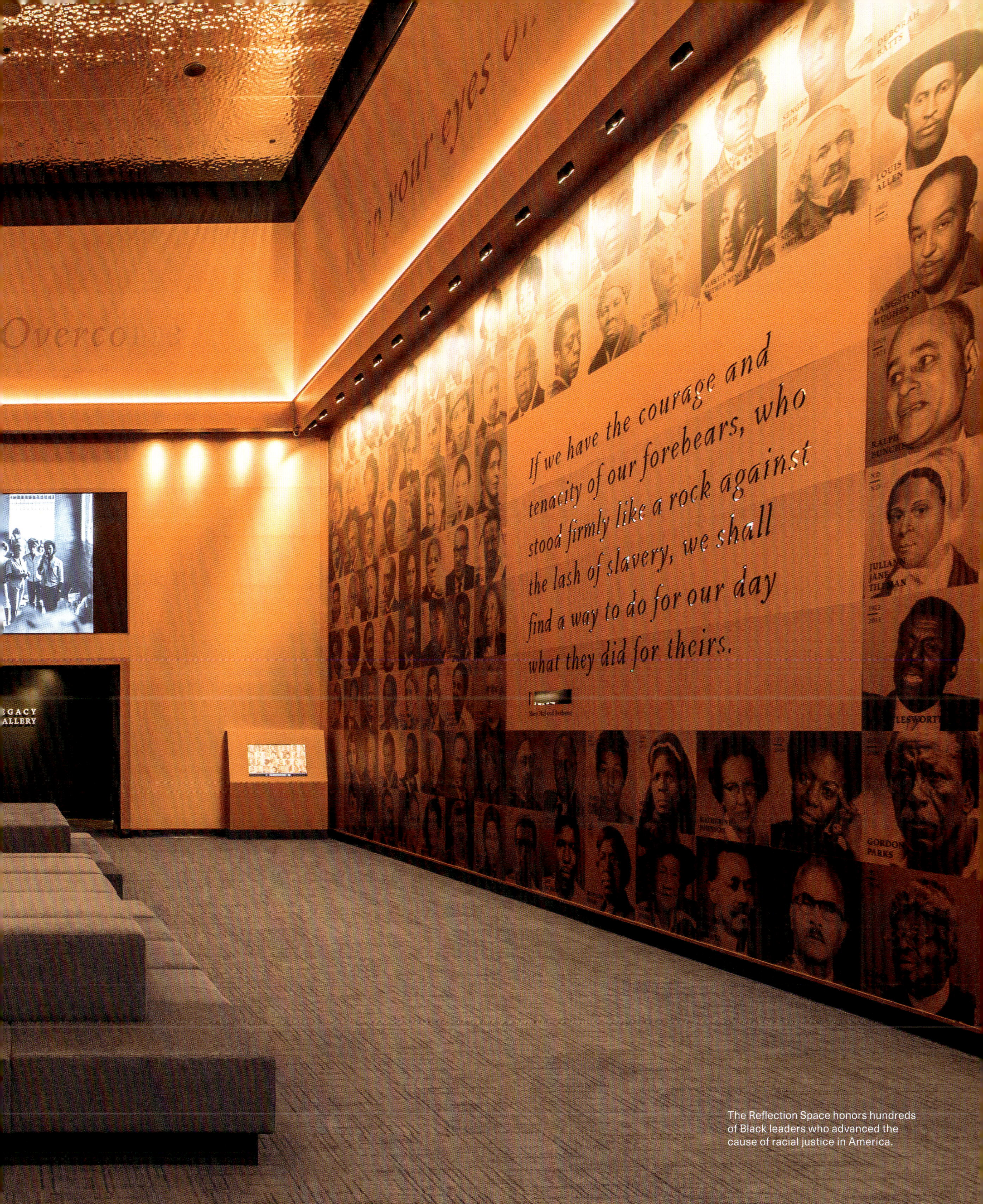

The Reflection Space honors hundreds of Black leaders who advanced the cause of racial justice in America.

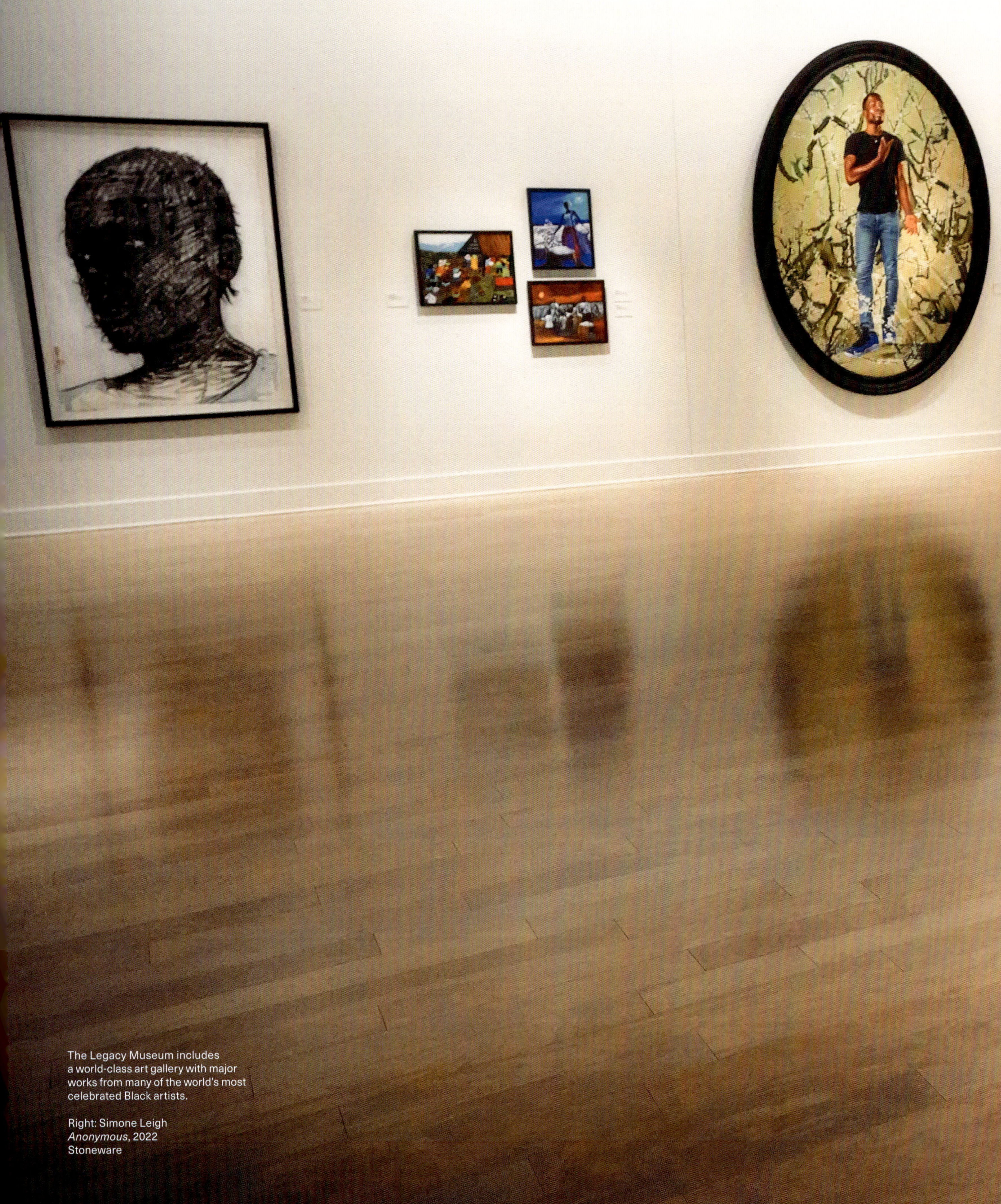

The Legacy Museum includes a world-class art gallery with major works from many of the world's most celebrated Black artists.

Right: Simone Leigh
Anonymous, 2022
Stoneware

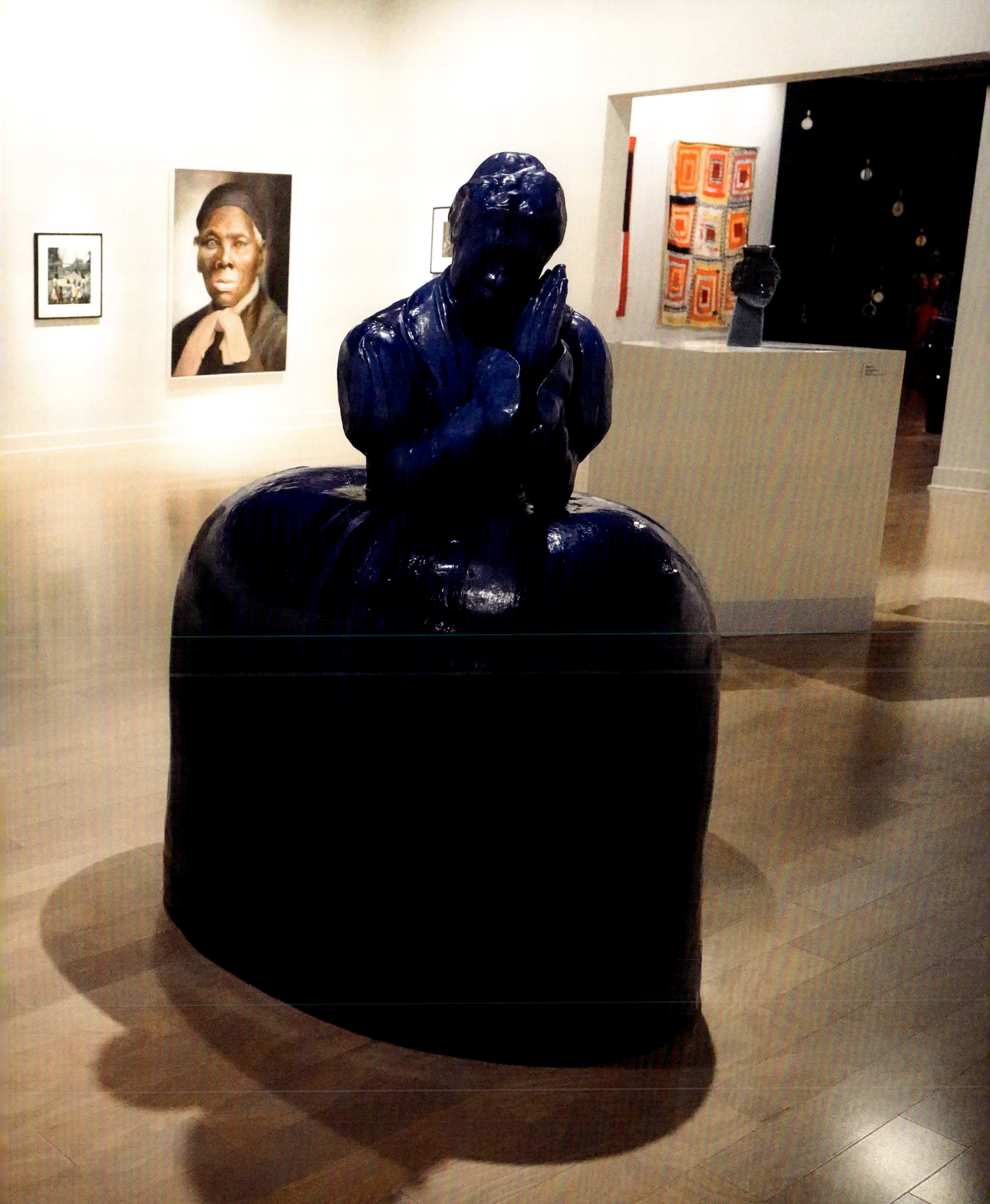

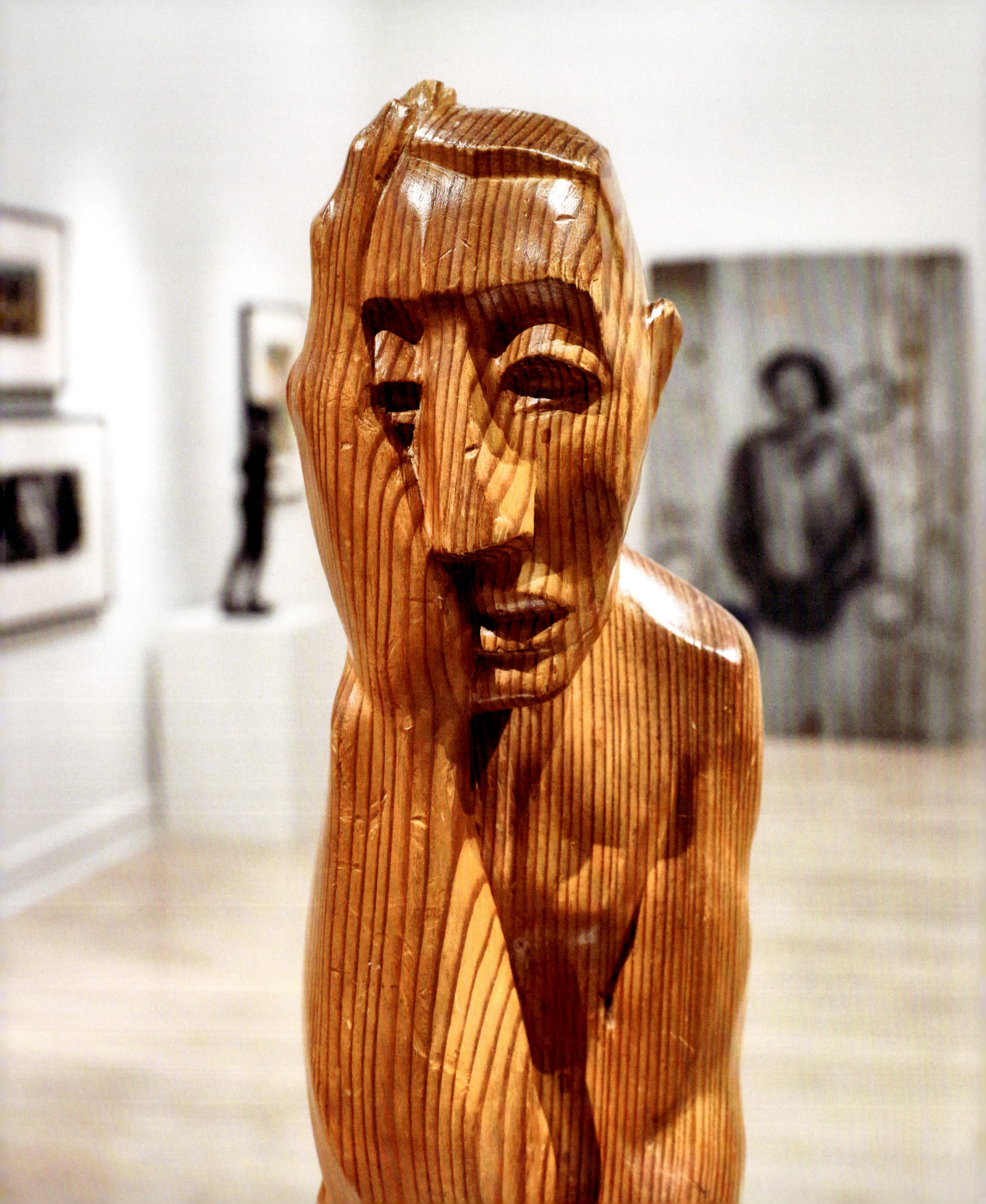

James C. McMillan
Afro-Thinker (detail), 1953–56
Carved wood

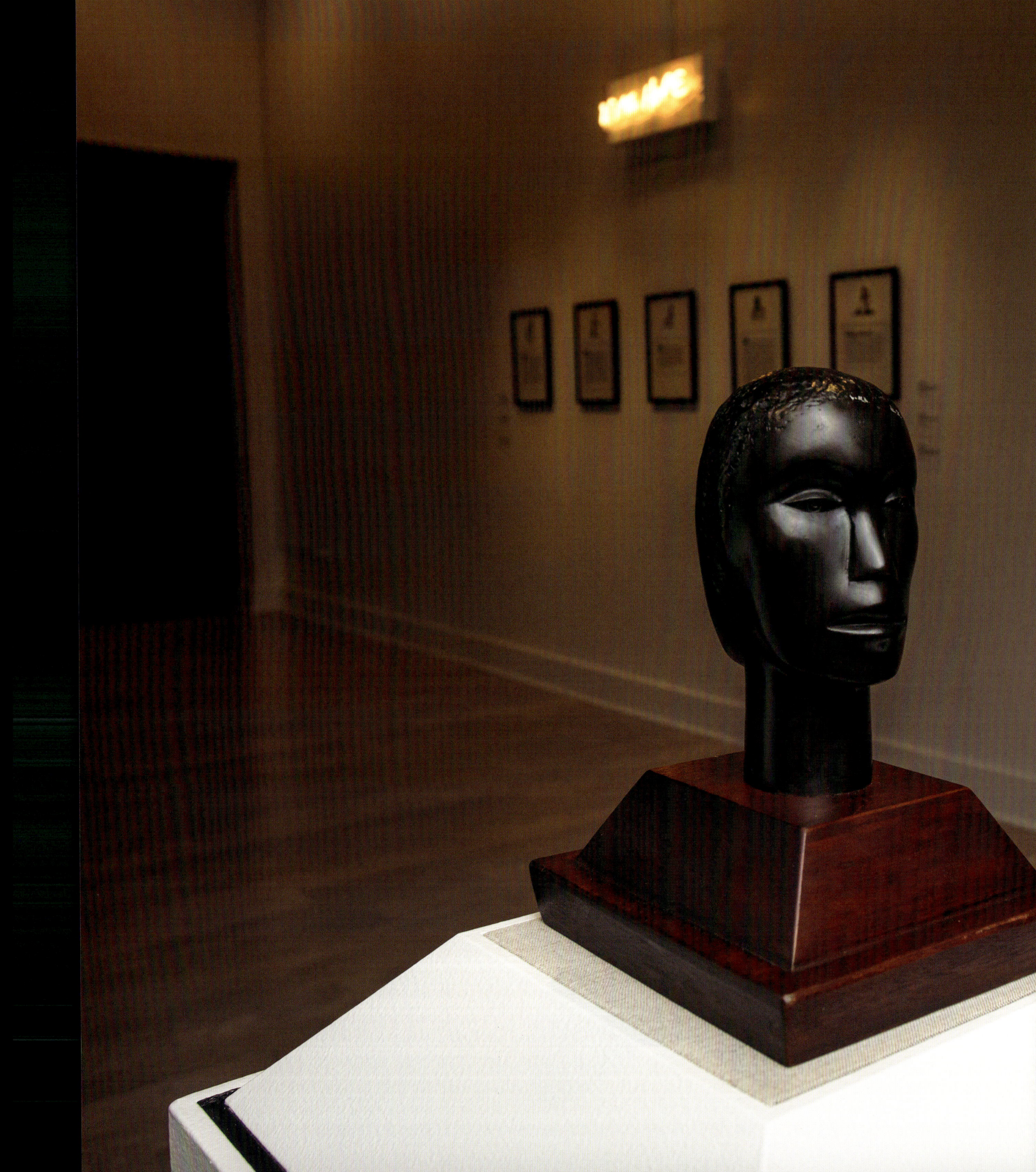

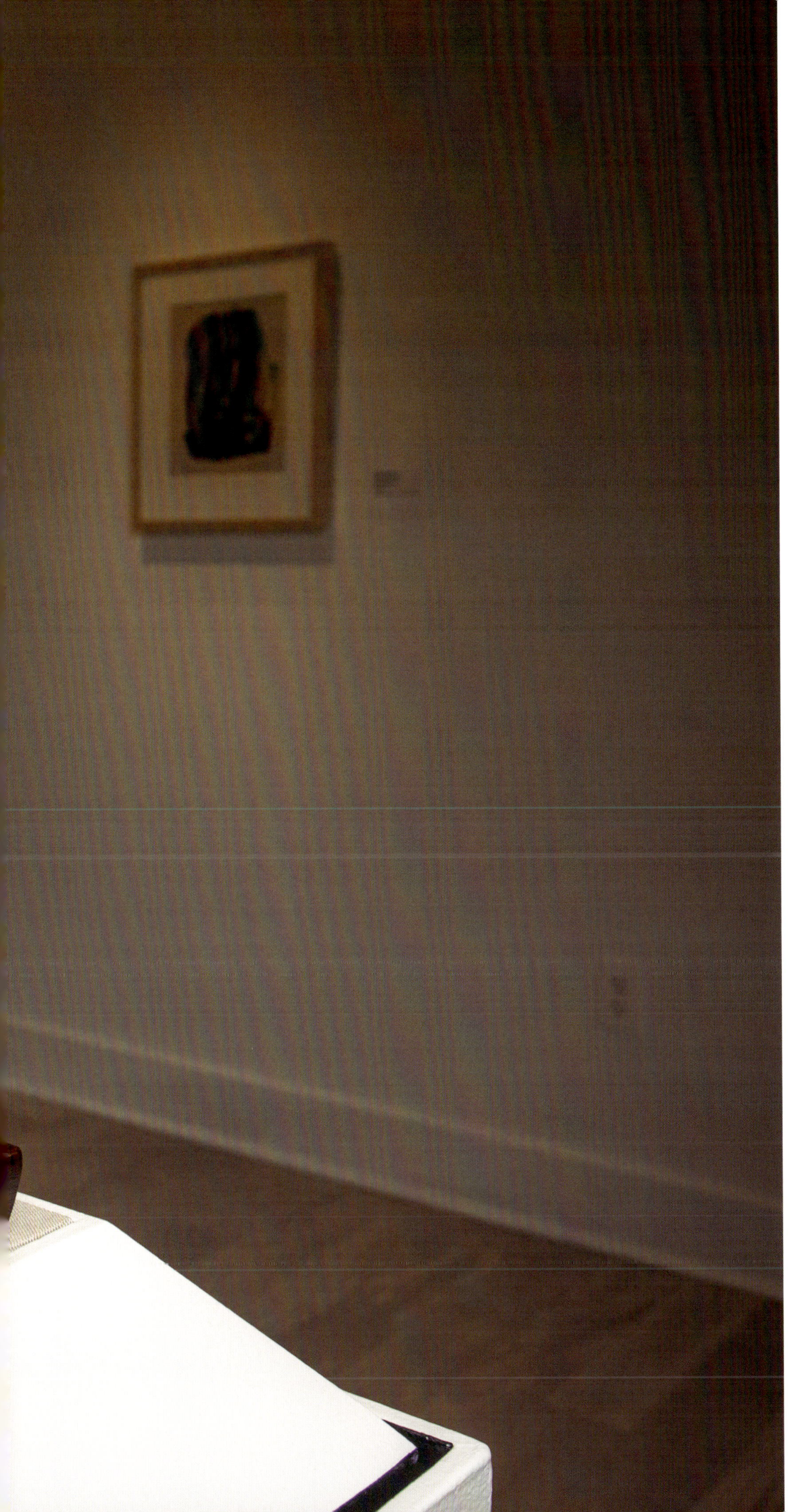

Elizabeth Catlett
Faces for Two Worlds, 1980
Bronze cast on wood base

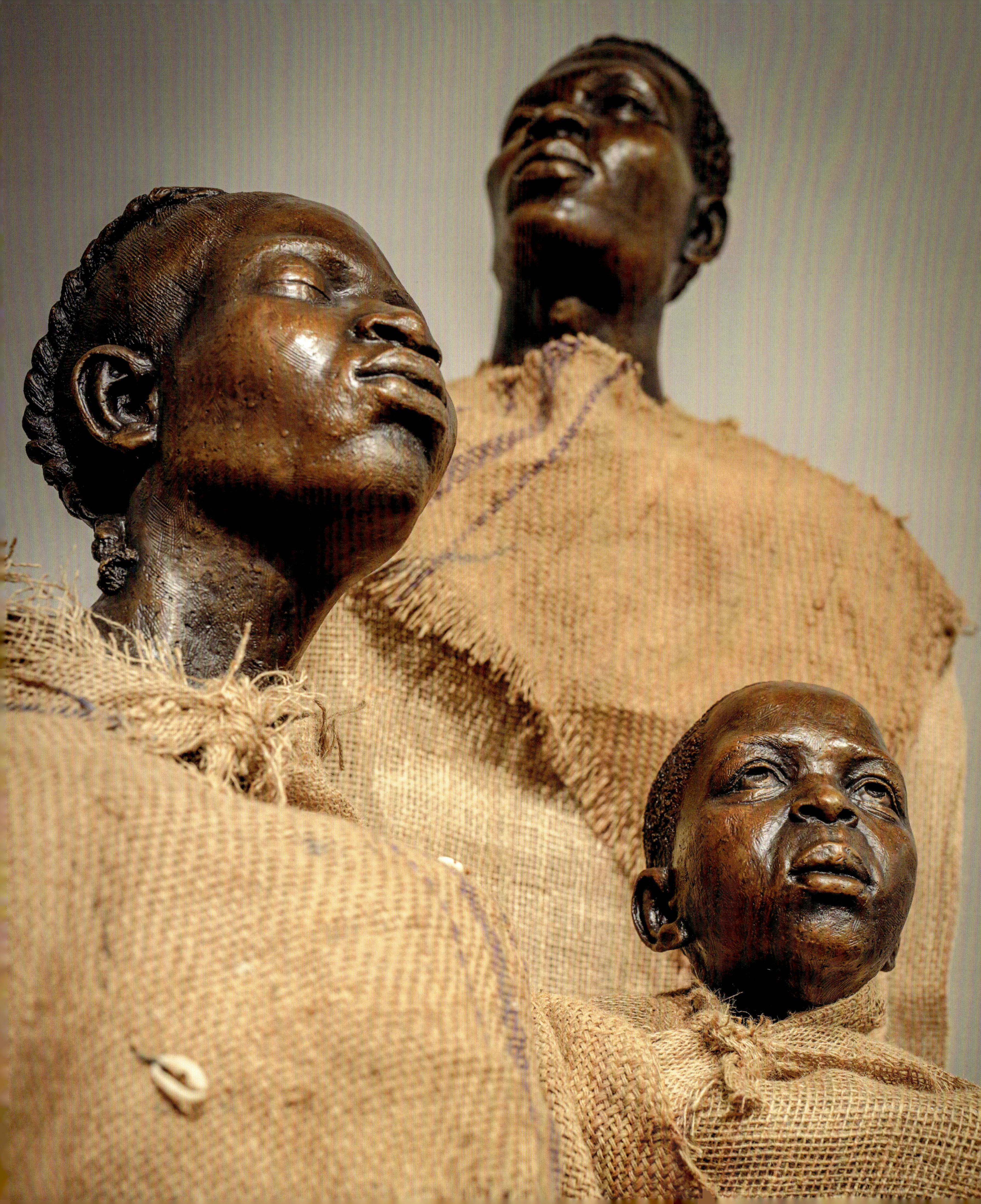

Kwame Akoto-Bamfo
untitled

Simone Leigh
Titi (Cobalt), 2021
Glazed stoneware

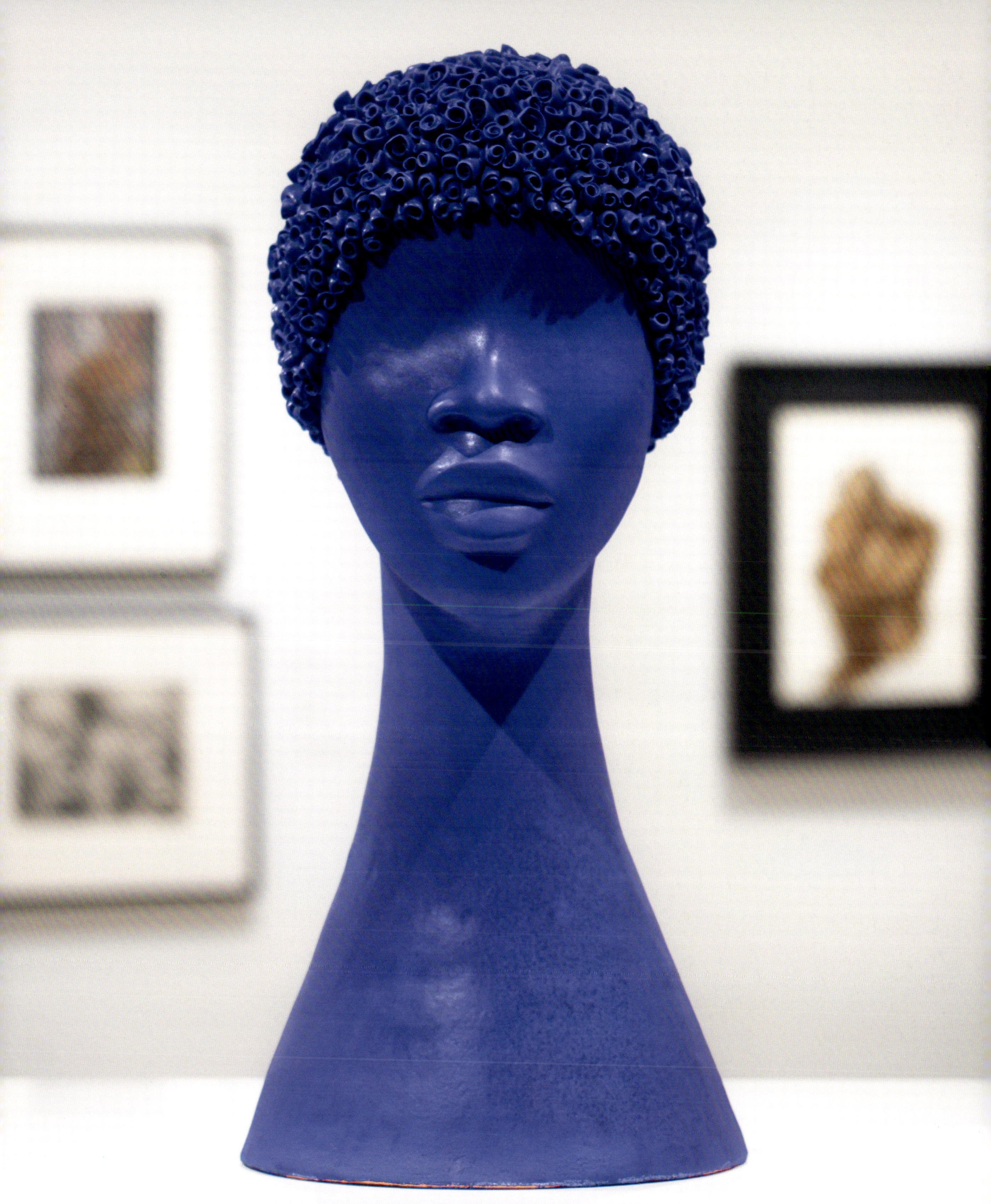

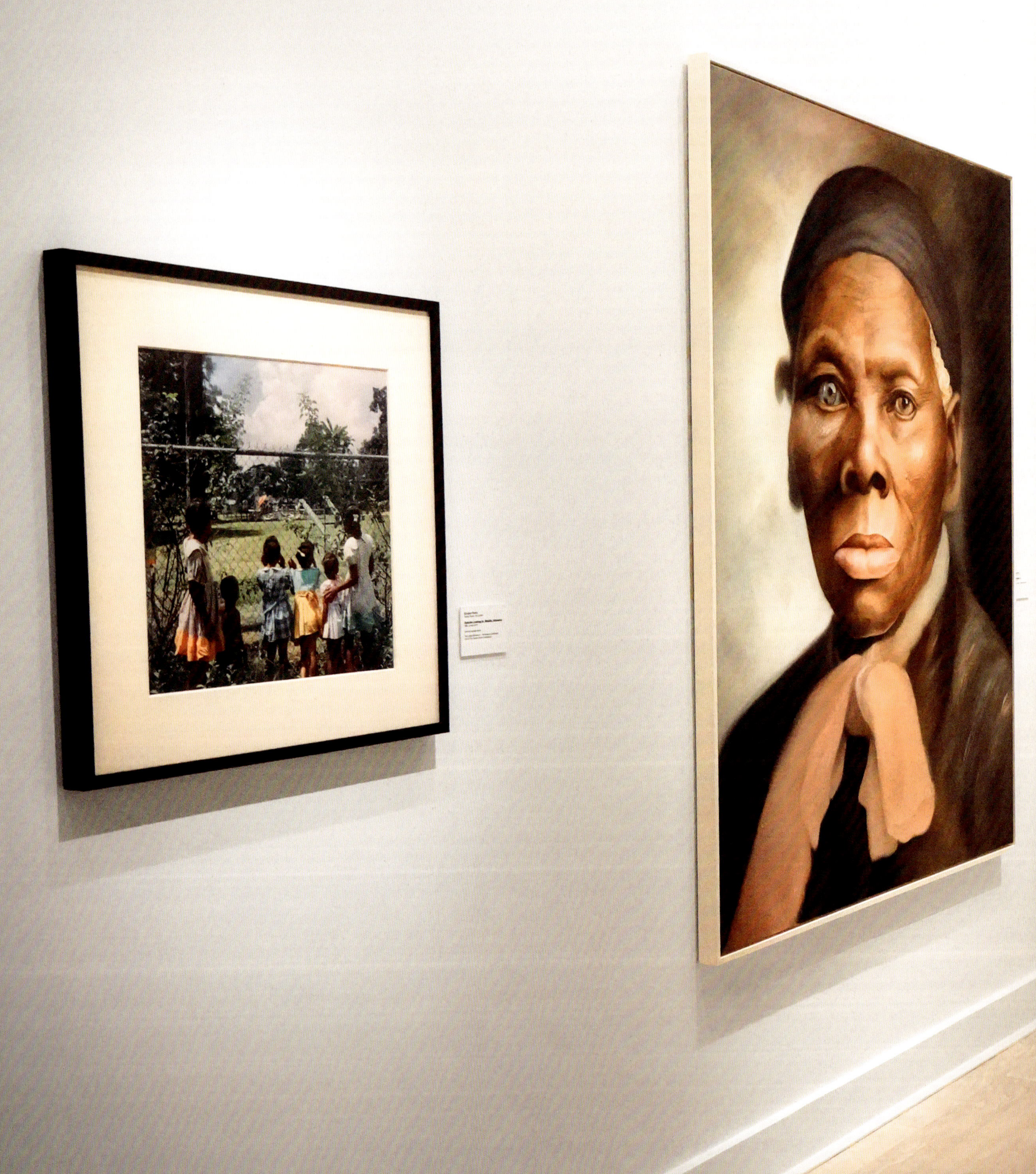

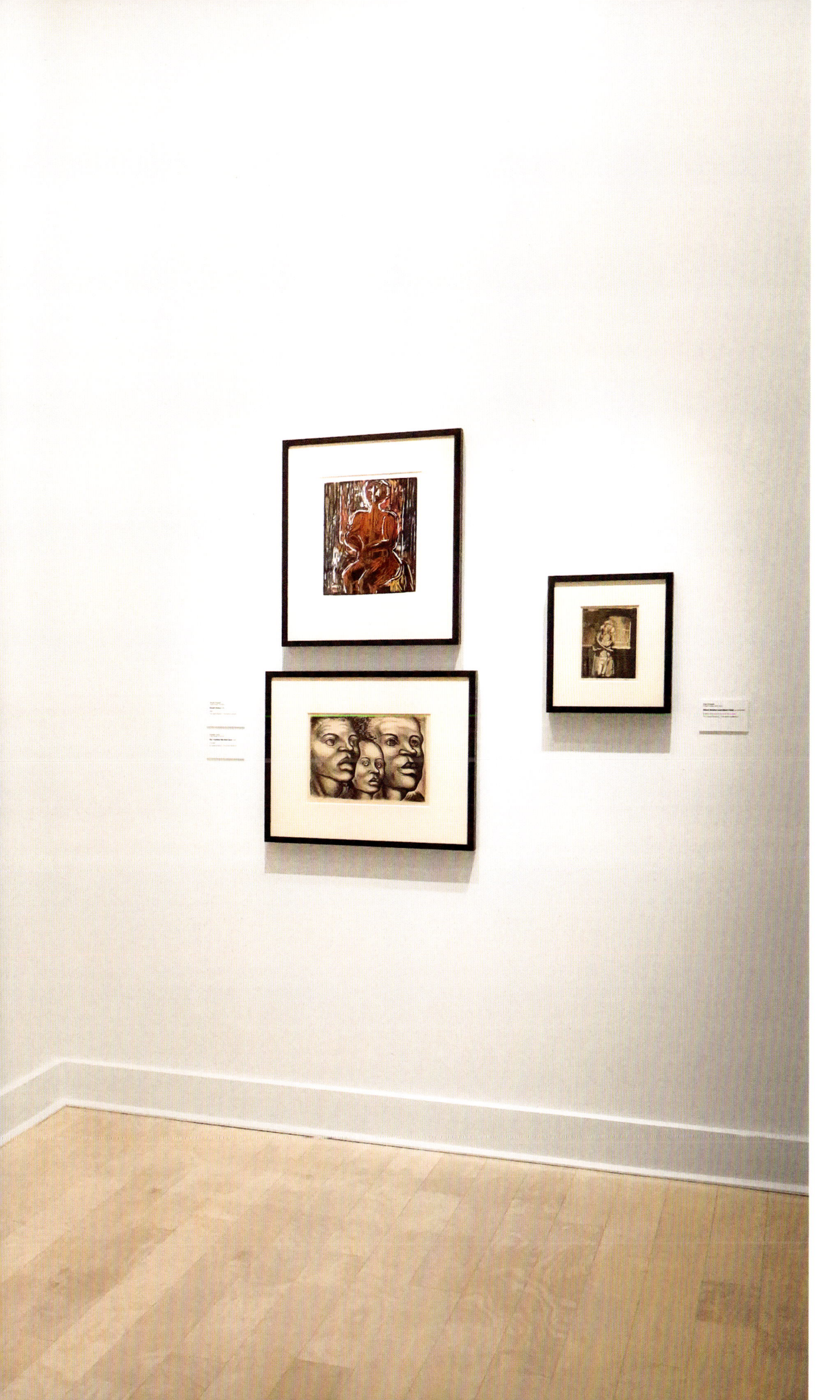

From left to right:

Gordon Parks
Outside Looking In, Mobile, Alabama, 1956, printed 2012
Archival pigment print

Jade Yasmeen
The Pain Below, 2021
Oil on canvas

Top: David Driskell
Brown Venus, 2016
Relief print

Bottom: Claude Clark
The Troubles We Have Seen, 1940
Lithograph

Kay Brown
Black Mother and Male Child, ca. 1974–75
Etching and aquatint on cream wove paper

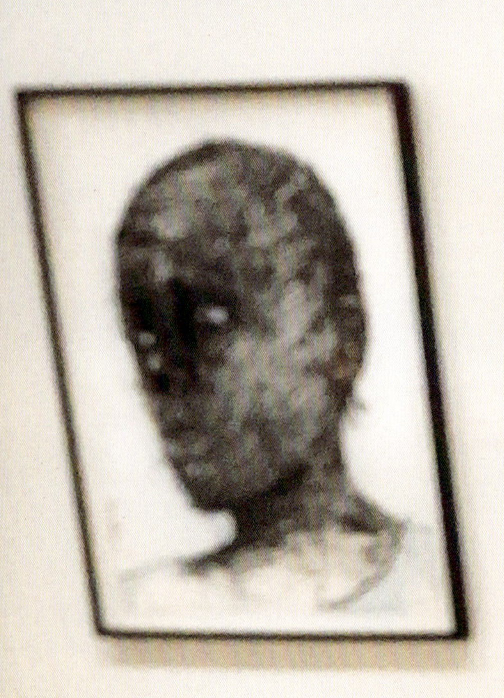

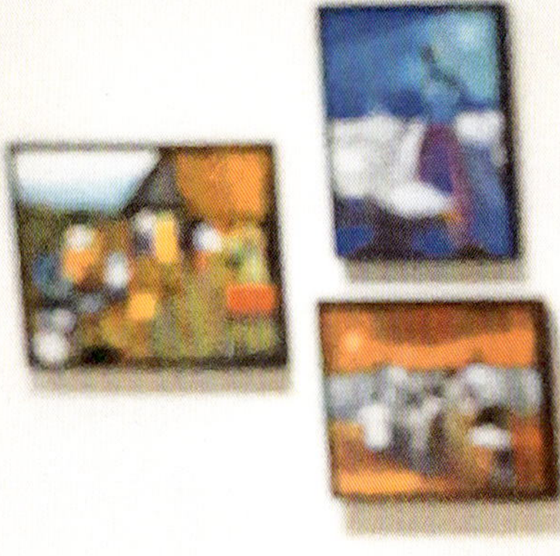

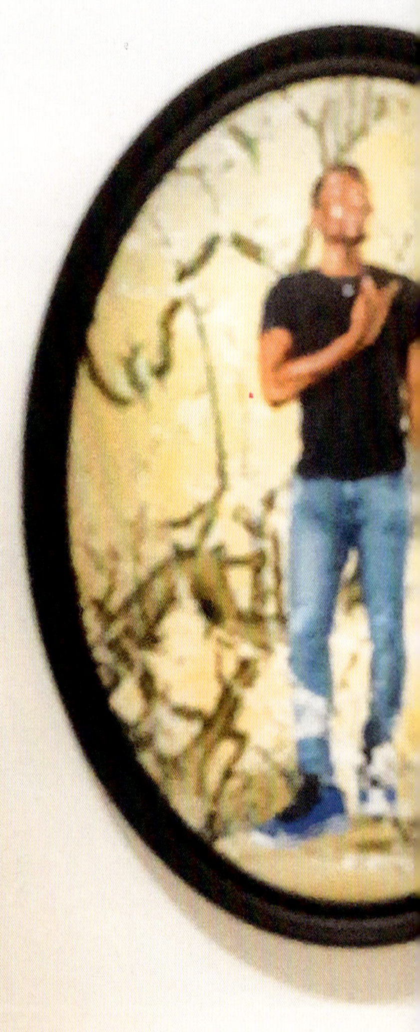

Right: Simone Leigh
109 (Face Jug Series), 2021
Salt-fired porcelain

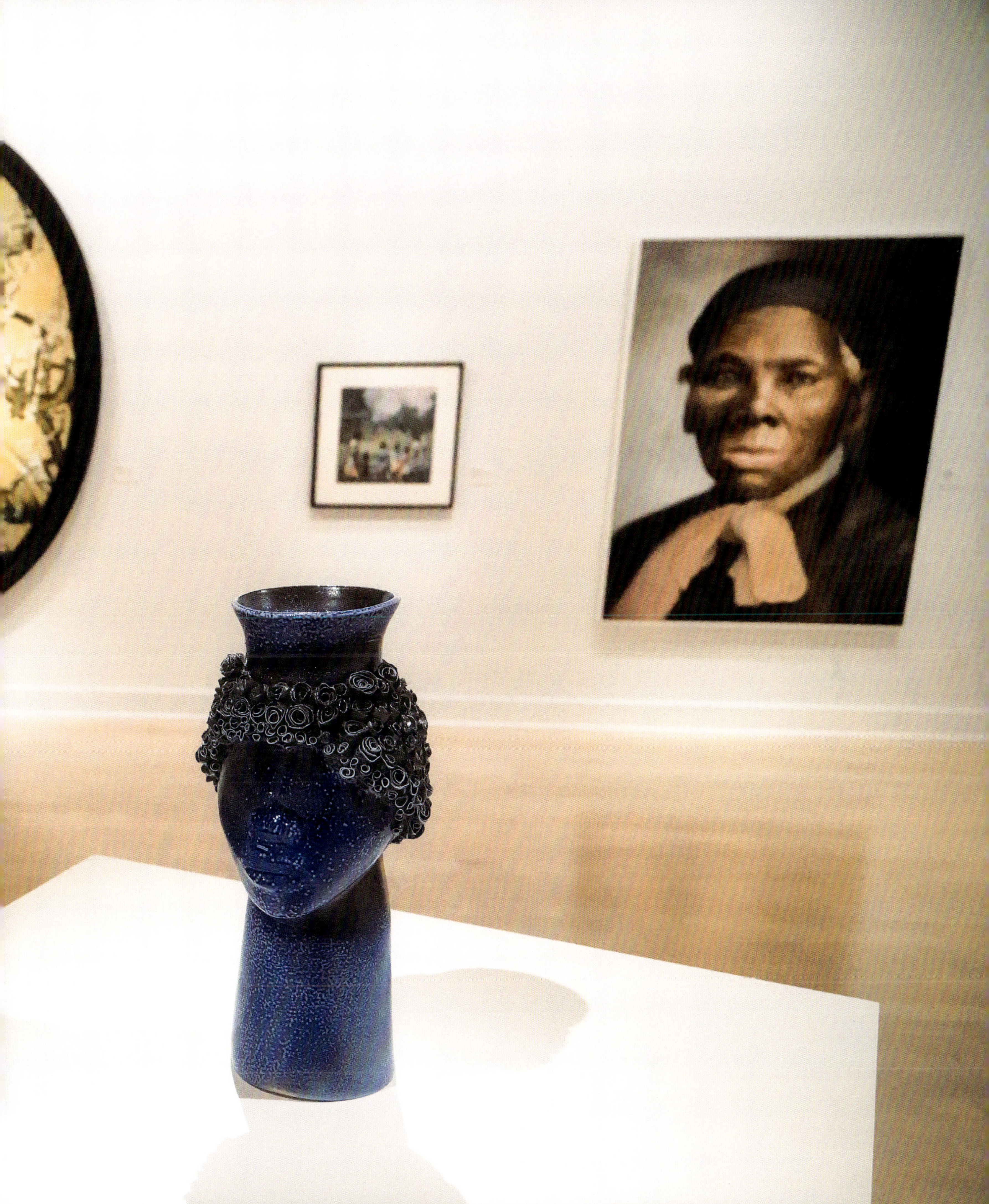

John Biggers
Freedom March (detail), 1952
Terra-cotta

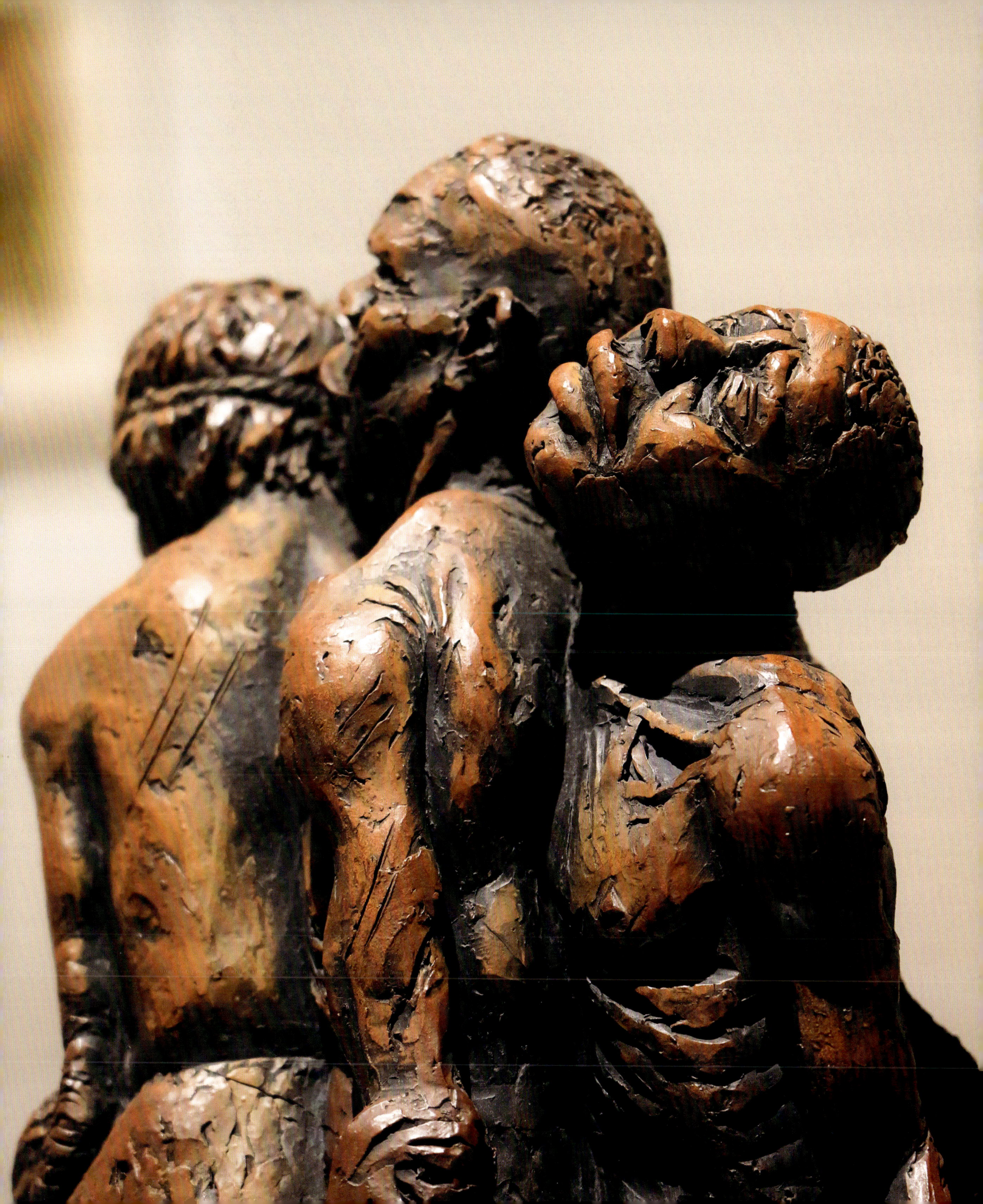

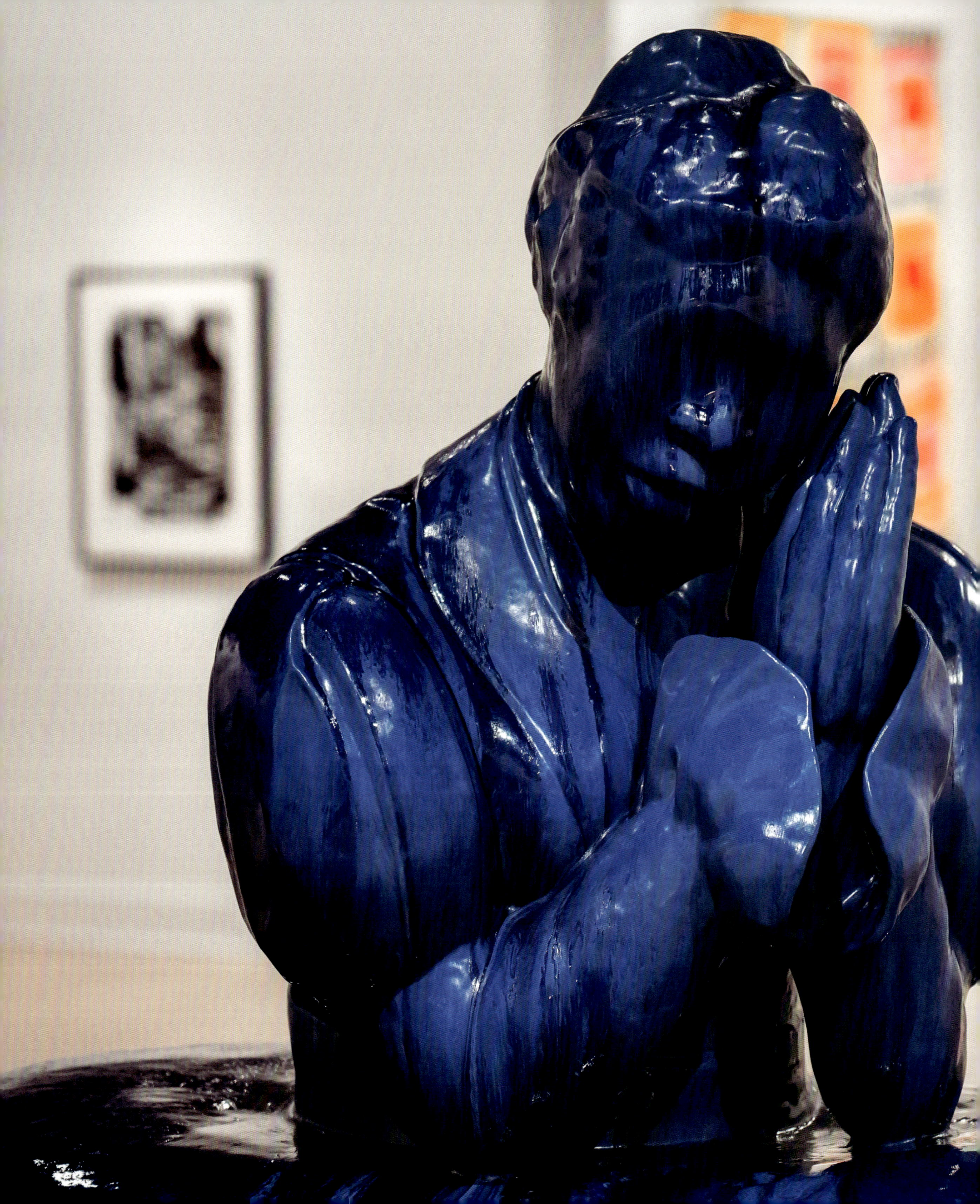

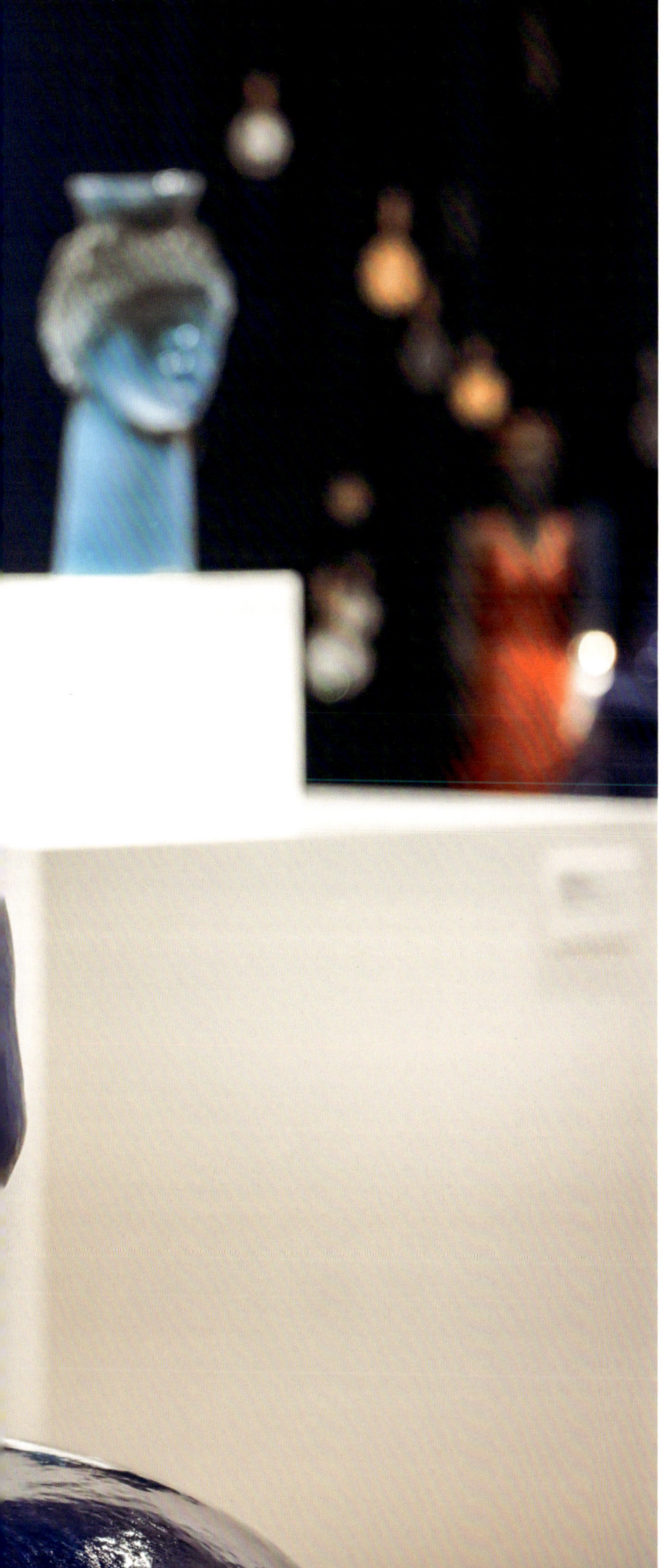

Simone Leigh
Anonymous (detail)

Alison Saar
The Beckoning (detail), 2021
Copper, wood, ceiling tin, fabric, paint, light bulbs, found vintage bottles, celluloid mirrors, and light sockets

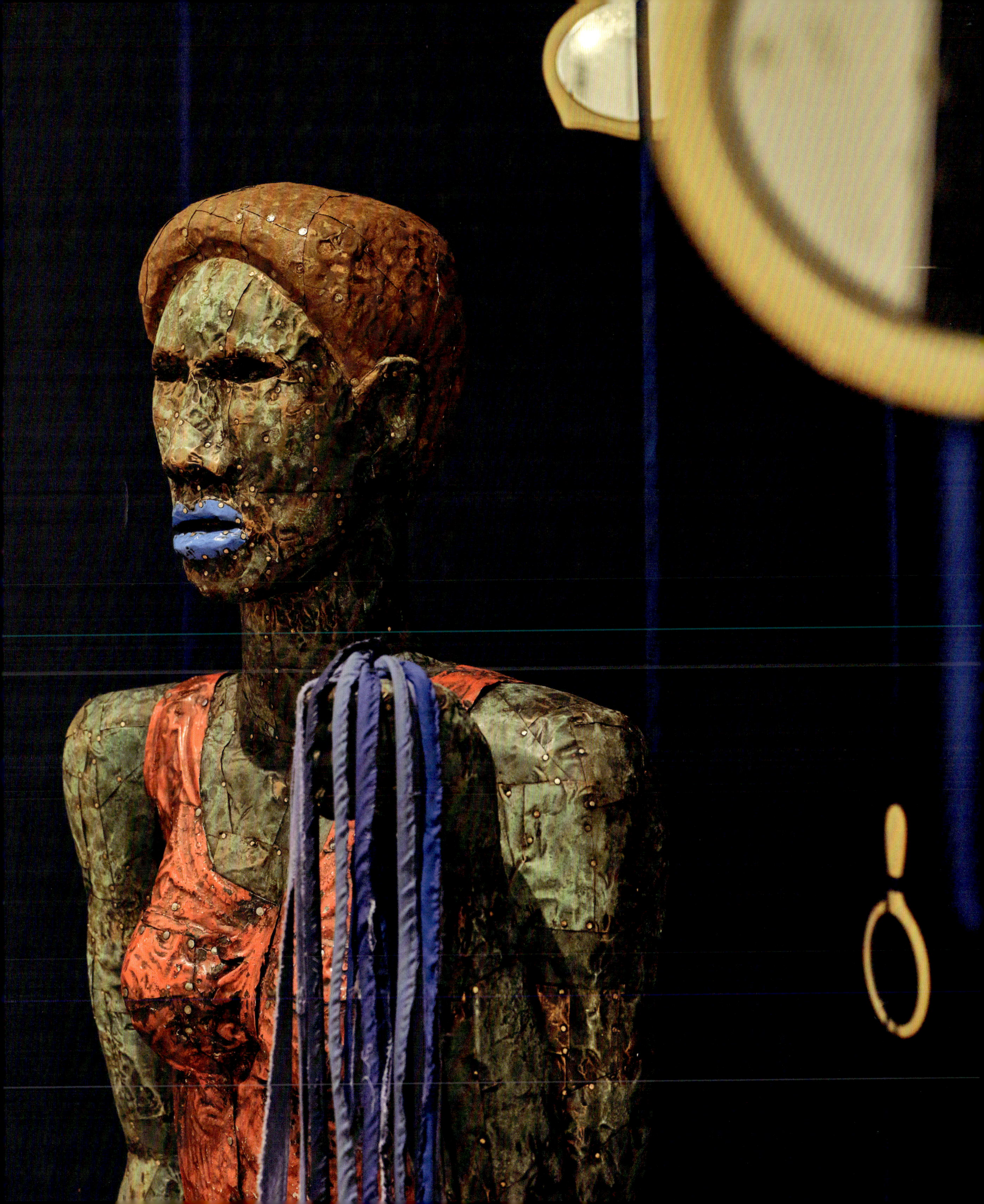

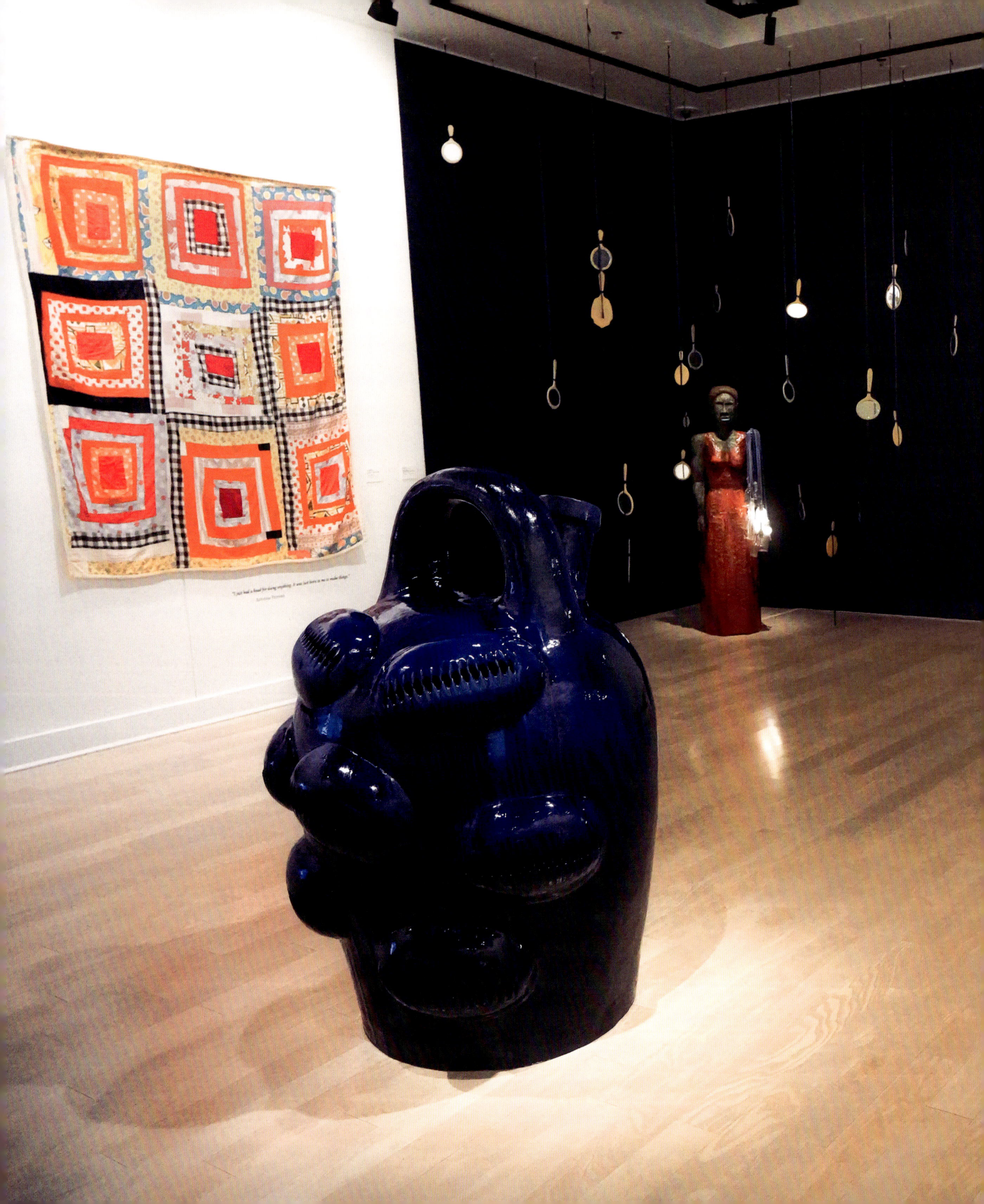

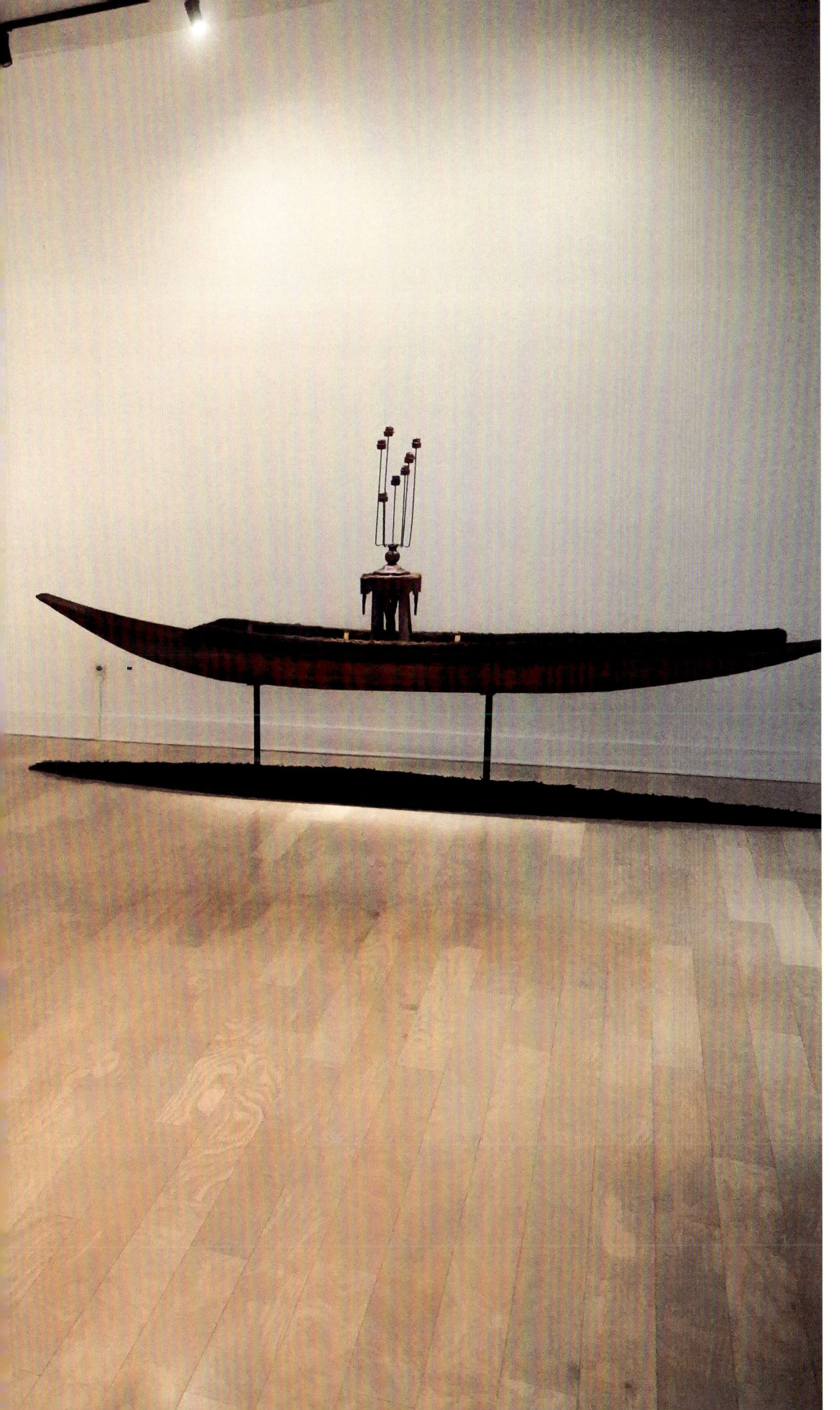

From left to right:

Arlonzia Pettway
“Housetop” – Nine Block Variation, 1982
Printed cotton and corduroy

Simone Leigh
Jug, 2022
Stoneware

The Beckoning

Betye Saar
Seeking Secrets of Destiny, 2024
Mixed media

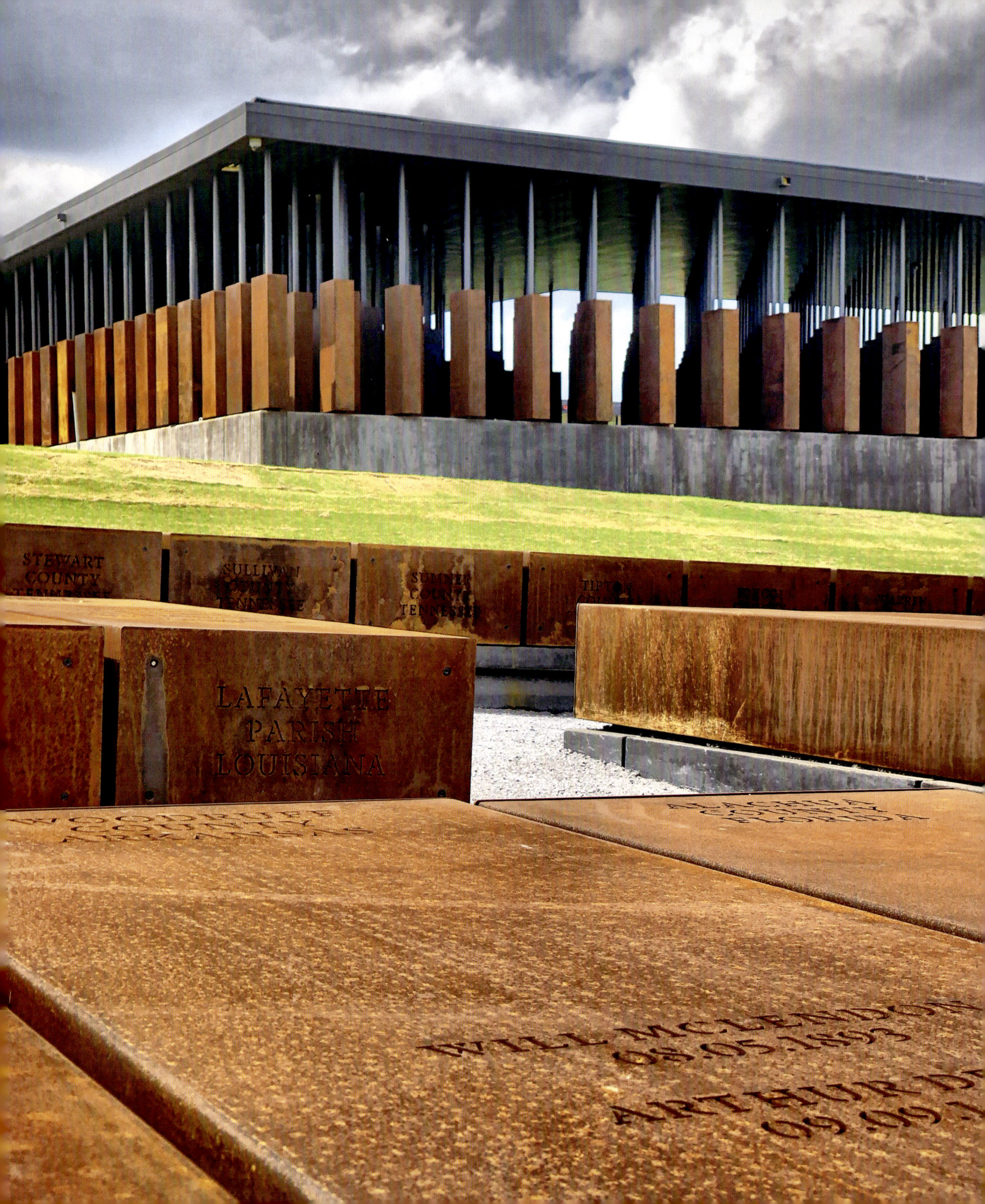
STEWART
COUNTY
LAFAYETTE
PARISH
LOUISIANA
WILL MCLENDON

THE NATIONAL MEMORIAL FOR PEACE AND JUSTICE

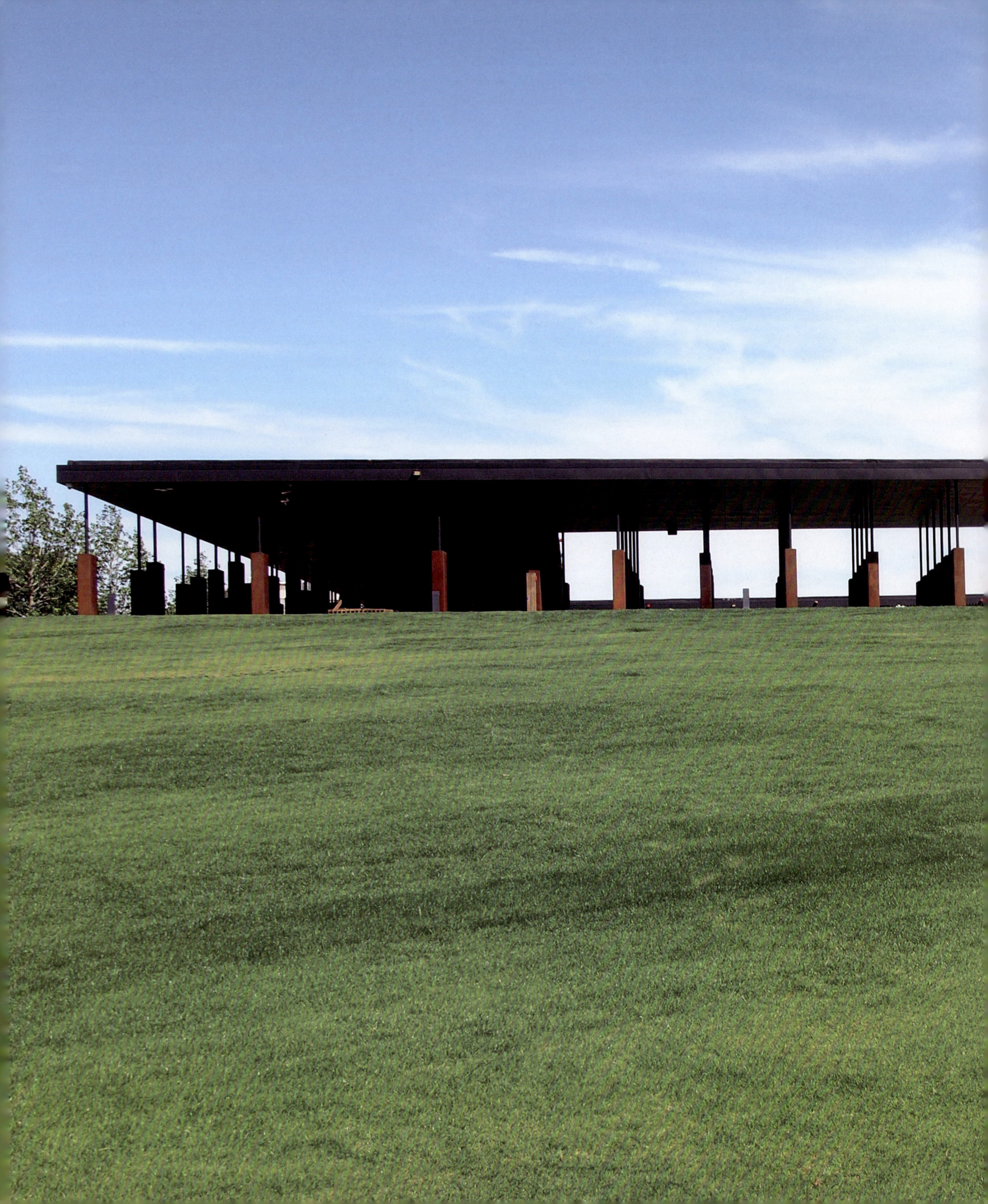

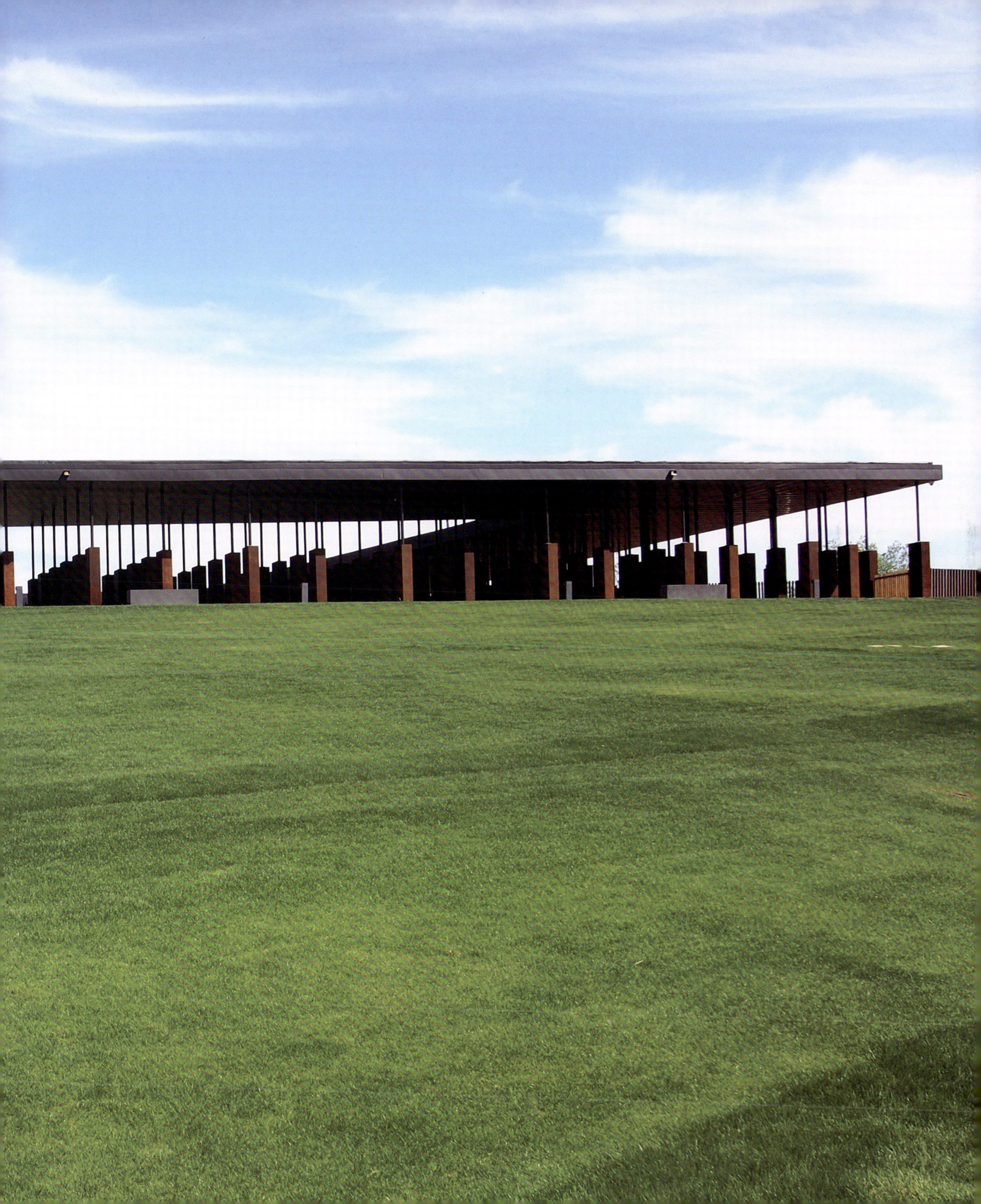

The National Memorial for Peace and Justice is the nation's first comprehensive memorial dedicated to thousands of African American victims of racial terror lynchings between 1877 and 1950. The Memorial opened in April 2018 in Montgomery, Alabama.

The Memorial is dedicated to educating visitors about how two centuries of enslavement of Black people evolved into decades of terror and violence following the collapse of Reconstruction. It details the violence and terror that forced millions of African Americans to flee the South, and the continuing legacy of that terror through the twentieth century until today.

Using investigative research, sculpture, art, design, literature, and poetry, the Memorial is a space for everyone to confront our nation's history of racial inequality with hope that a future of peace and justice can be achieved. The Memorial is a beginning—an opportunity for communities across the country to confront the past with courage and begin a hopeful future in which truth leads to repair, restoration, and reconciliation.

Opposite and pages 110, 112–13, 115:
Kwame Akoto-Bamfo
Nkyinkyim Installation, 2018
Concrete

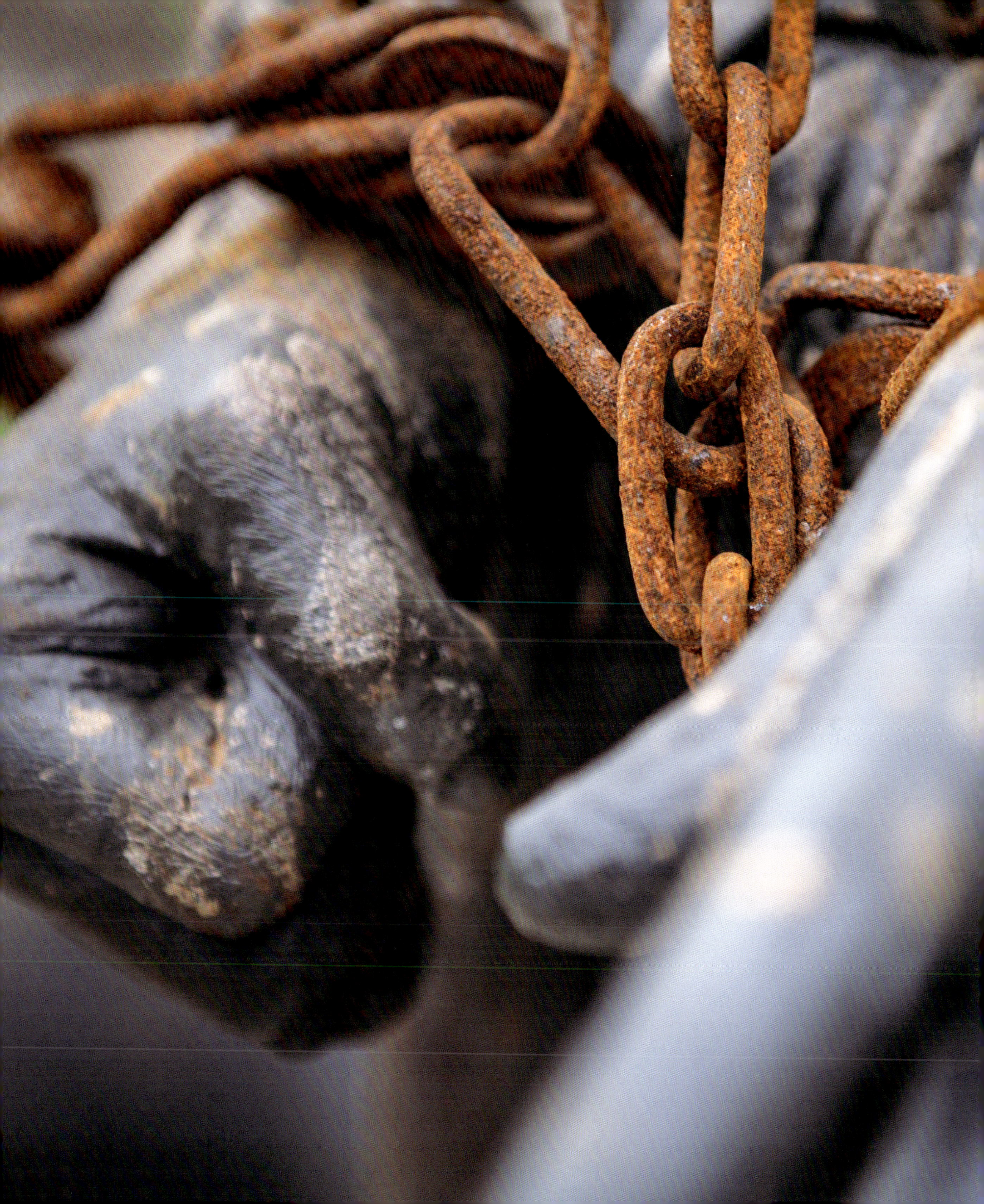

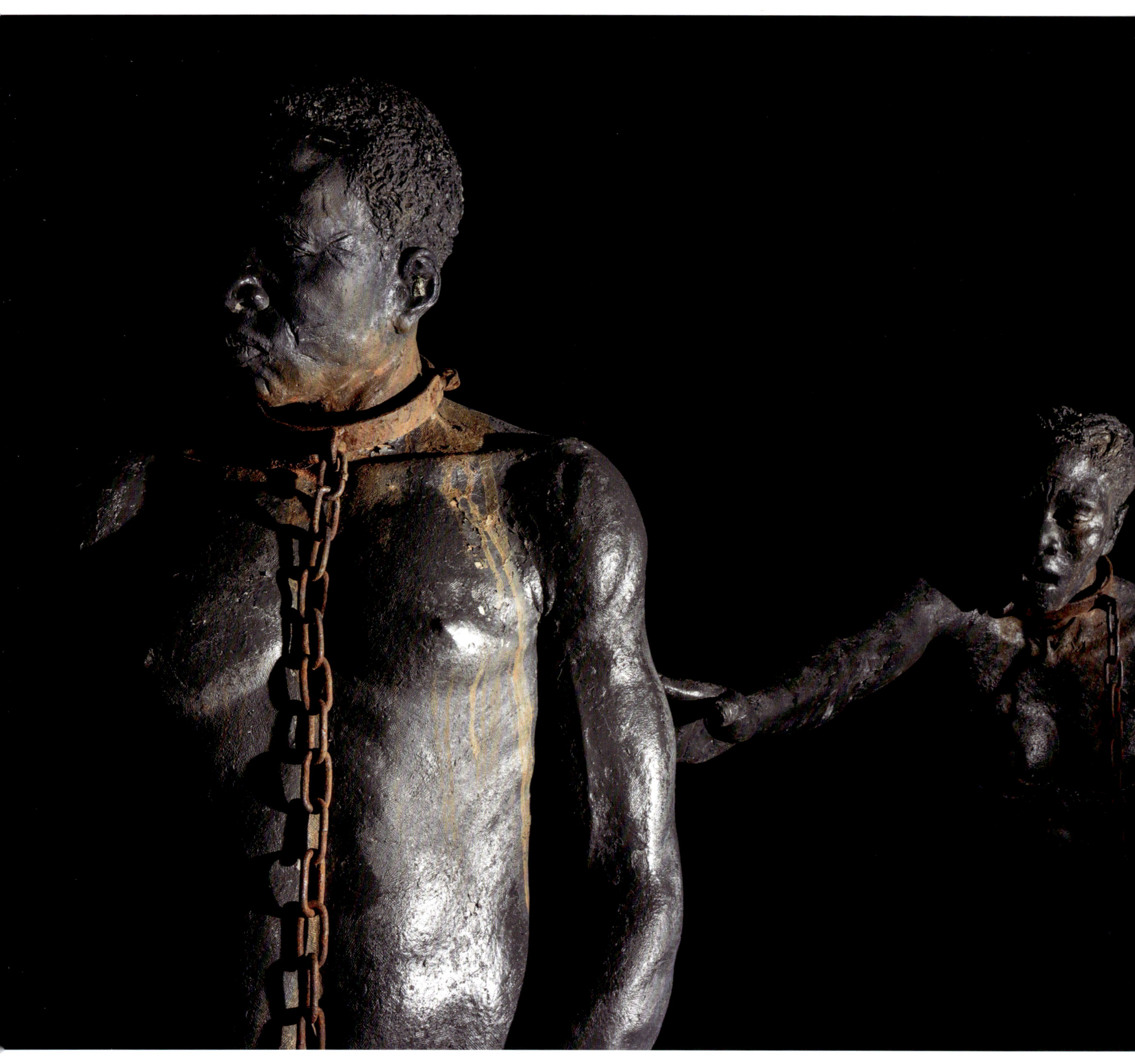

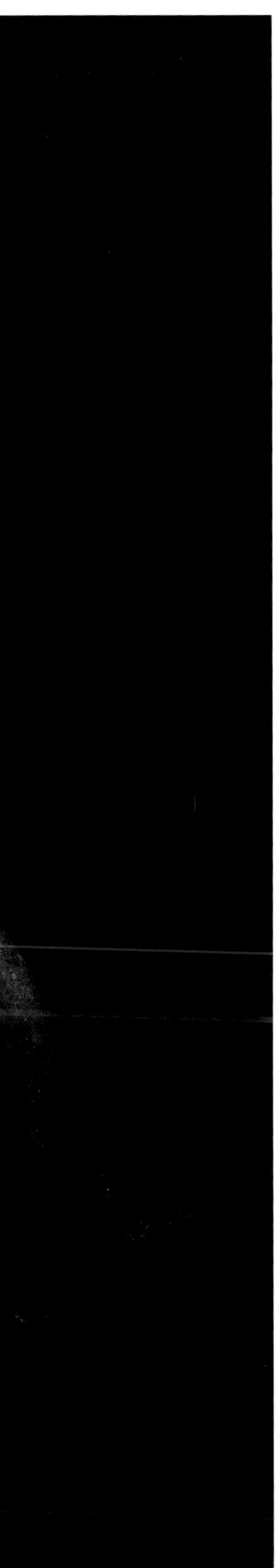

The Journey

Over more than twenty-five years, the staff of the Equal Justice Initiative witnessed the connections between Southern racial history and the modern injustice of mass incarceration, as well as the palpable links between lynching and the death penalty. In 2010, EJI staff began investigating thousands of racial terror lynchings in the American South, many of which had never been documented.

Believing that a more productive conversation about justice requires knowledge of historic injustice, EJI attorneys and researchers spent more than five years combing through newspaper archives, visiting communities to interview residents and survivors, and compiling a list of confirmed racial terror lynchings. Beyond counting the number of African American lynching victims, the project aimed to document the terror and trauma this sanctioned violence against the Black community created, and to identify the remnants of that history still impacting America today.

In February 2015, EJI released a report, “Lynching in America: Confronting the Legacy of Racial Terror,” which documented more than four thousand victims of racial terror lynching killed in twelve Southern states between 1877 and 1950. EJI later supplemented that research with more than three hundred additional racial terror lynchings committed in states outside the Deep South during the same period.

The era of racial terror was largely characterized by fear and silence. Black communities forced to witness brutal killings of friends or relatives by bold, undisguised white mobs were warned that the same fate awaited them if they protested, sought justice, or even openly discussed lynchings. This trauma endured for generations. For many, the history of lynching was discussed only in hushed whispers between elderly relatives, if at all.

After the report’s release, EJI received phone calls, letters, and emails from hundreds of people sharing information, describing oral histories that had survived in their families and neighborhoods, and inquiring about lynchings they had never known took place in their own backyards. Inspired by the energetic public response to the report, EJI set out to create opportunities to connect individuals and communities more broadly and deeply with this history.

Through its Community Remembrance Project, EJI began working with volunteers, local coalitions, and surviving descendants of racial terror to memorialize this era by collecting soil at lynching sites and erecting historical markers to truthfully and publicly reflect this history. In partnership with Google, EJI also launched an online portal with a digital version of the report, an interactive map of EJI’s lynching data, and video and audio interviews with people who reveal the impact of racial terror on their own families.

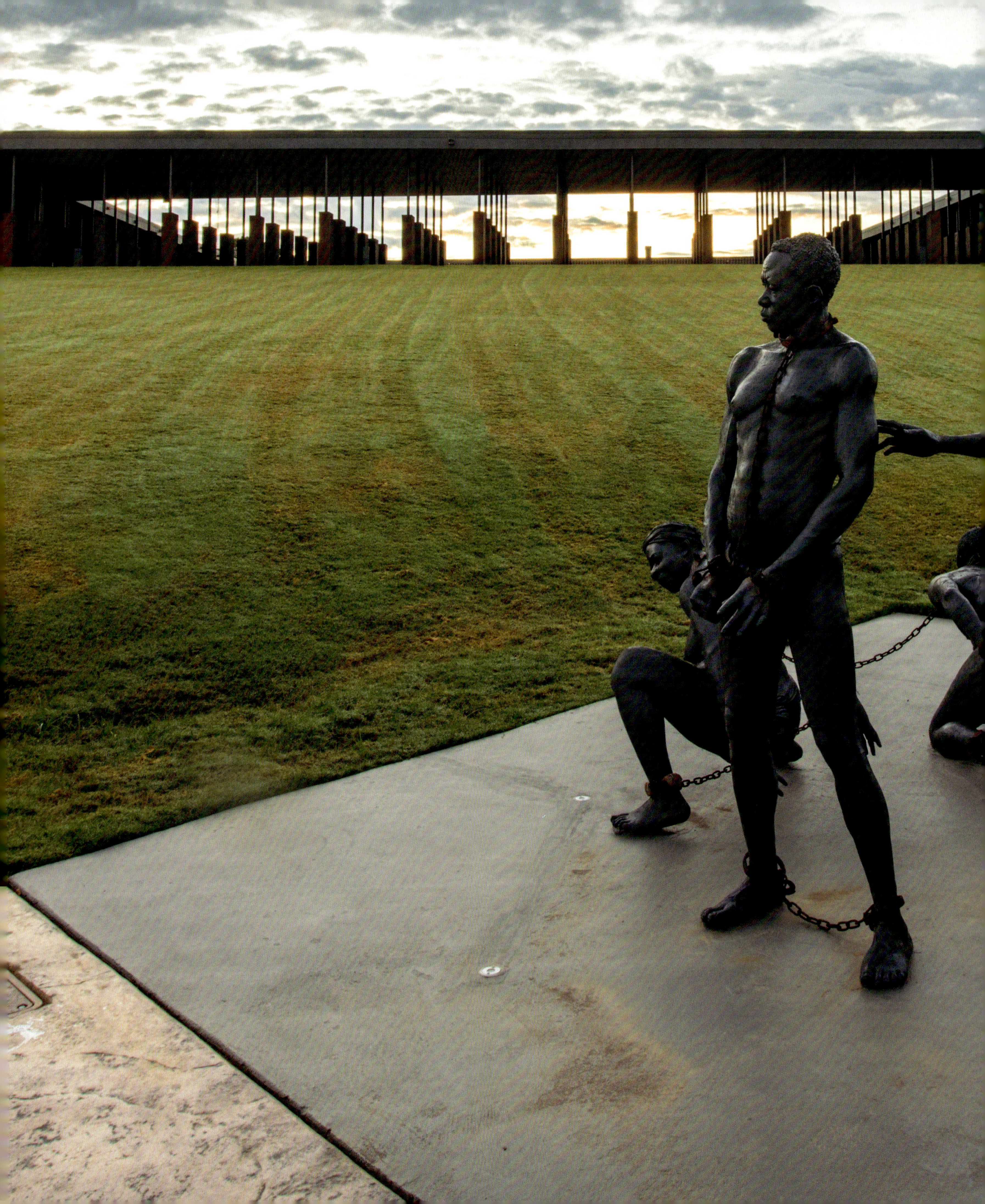

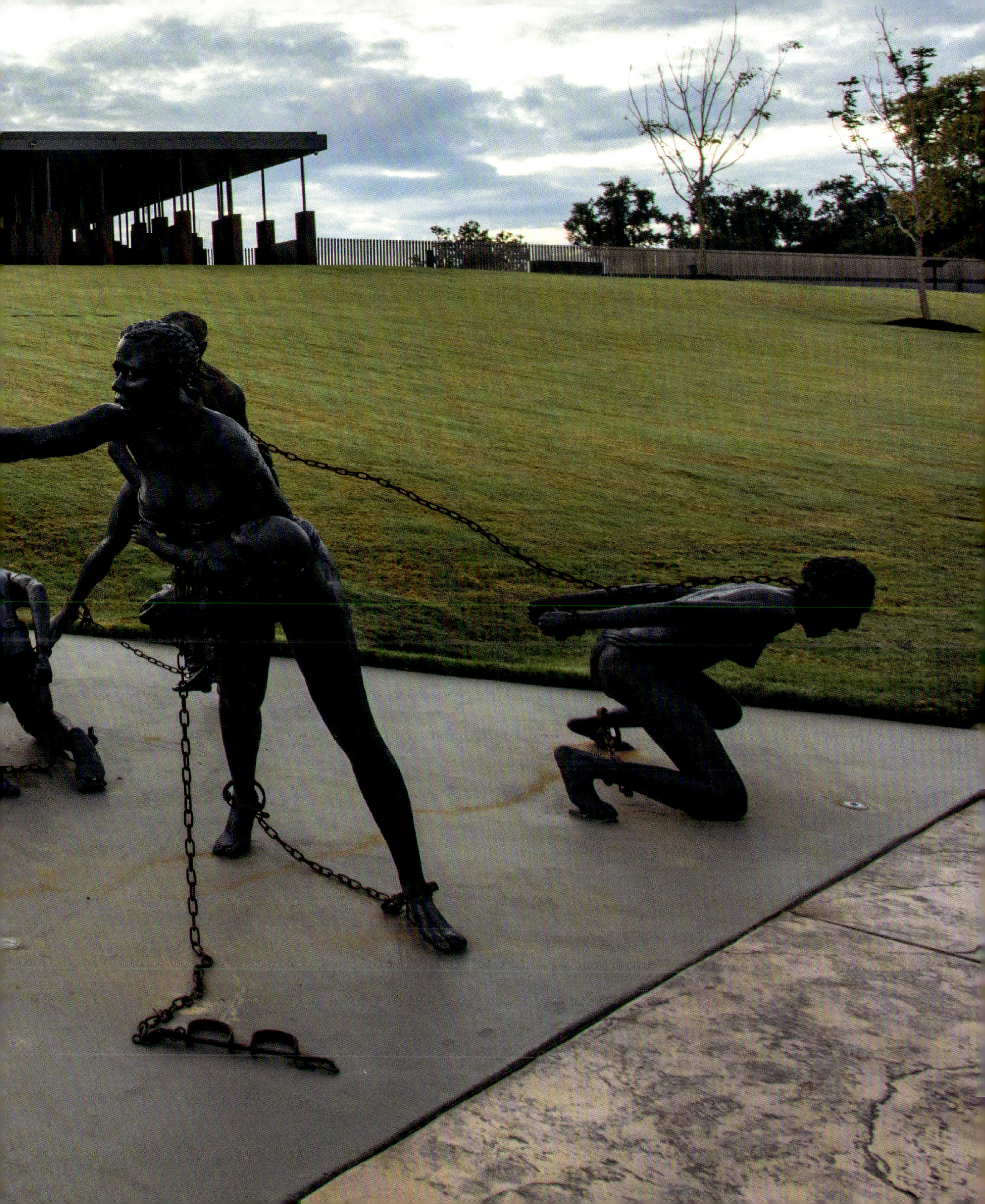

During the era of racial terror, Black activists like Ida B. Wells, researchers like Tuskegee University's Monroe Work, and organizations like the NAACP risked lethal violence to denounce lynching, demand justice, and document racial violence for future generations.

The memorial exists today both in memory of the many lives lost to racial terror and in honor of those whose work built the foundation on which we stand.

The Memorial

On April 26, 2018, the National Memorial for Peace and Justice opened as the nation's first memorial dedicated to the legacy of enslaved Black people, people terrorized by lynching, African Americans humiliated by racial segregation and Jim Crow, and people of color burdened with contemporary presumptions of guilt and police violence. Set on a six-acre elevated site with views of downtown Montgomery and the Alabama State Capitol, the memorial employs sculpture, prose, poetry, and architectural design to contextualize racial terror.

The Memorial is designed to take visitors on a journey from enslavement, to lynching and racial terror, through the fight for civil rights, and on to modern America's struggle with mass incarceration.

Upon entering the site, Ghanaian artist Kwame Akoto-Bamfo's sculpture *Nkyinkyim Installation*, depicting enslaved African men, women, and an infant, confronts visitors with striking beauty and wrenching pain. Near the end of the memorial, Dana King's *Guided by Justice* honors the women who sustained the Montgomery Bus Boycott, and Hank Willis Thomas's *Raise Up* dramatizes contemporary issues of police violence and racially biased criminal laws.

A pathway leads into a structure made of more than eight hundred six-foot corten steel monuments, each one representing a location in the United States where a racial terror lynching took place. The names of the lynching victims and the dates when these lynchings occurred are engraved on the monuments.

Visitors first encounter monuments at eye level. In the second corridor, the monuments slowly begin to rise overhead, where they evoke the violence we have gathered to remember. As the steel monuments oxidize at their own rates and patterns, they take on colors and textures as varied as the individual men, women, and children they memorialize.

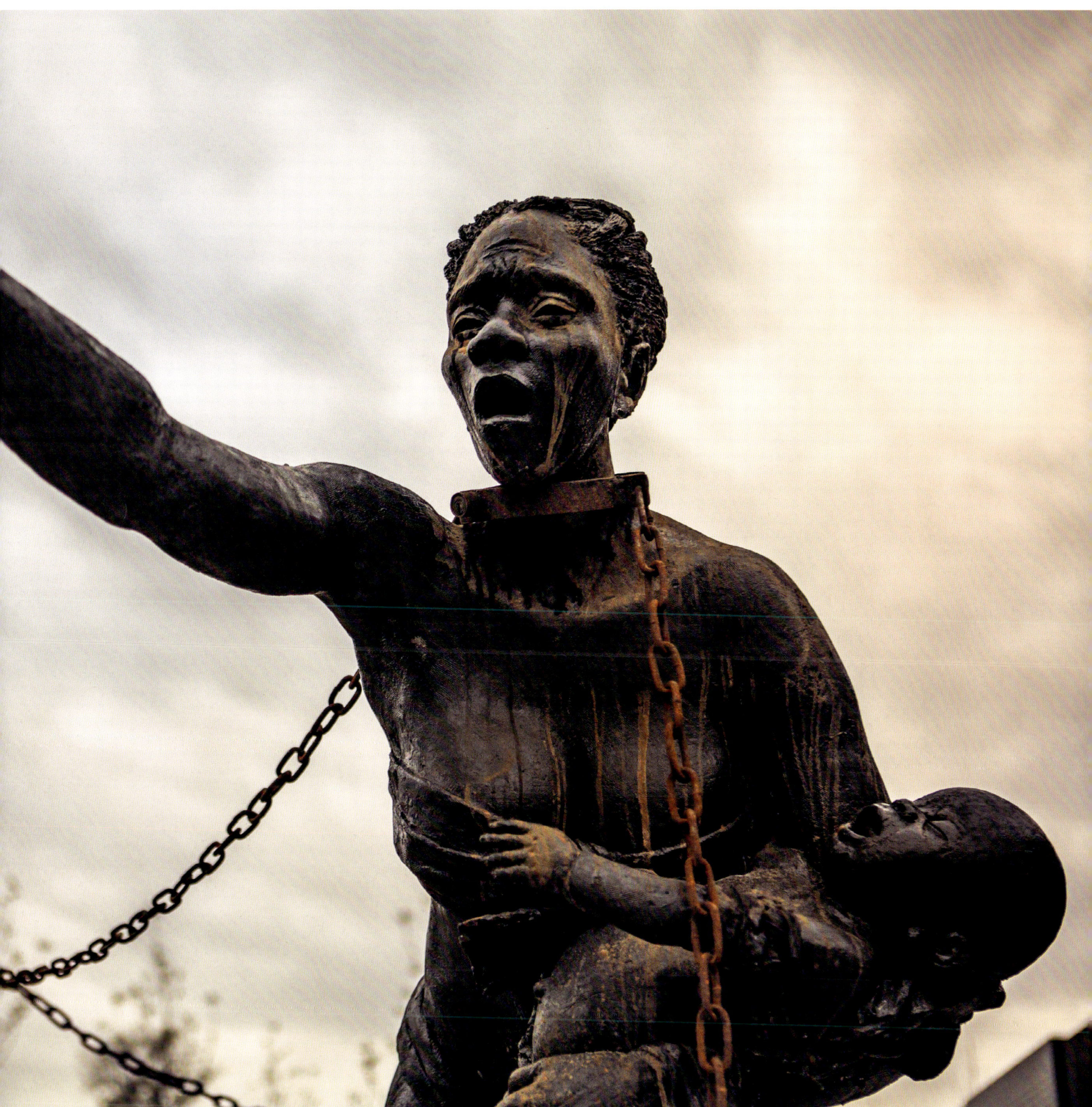

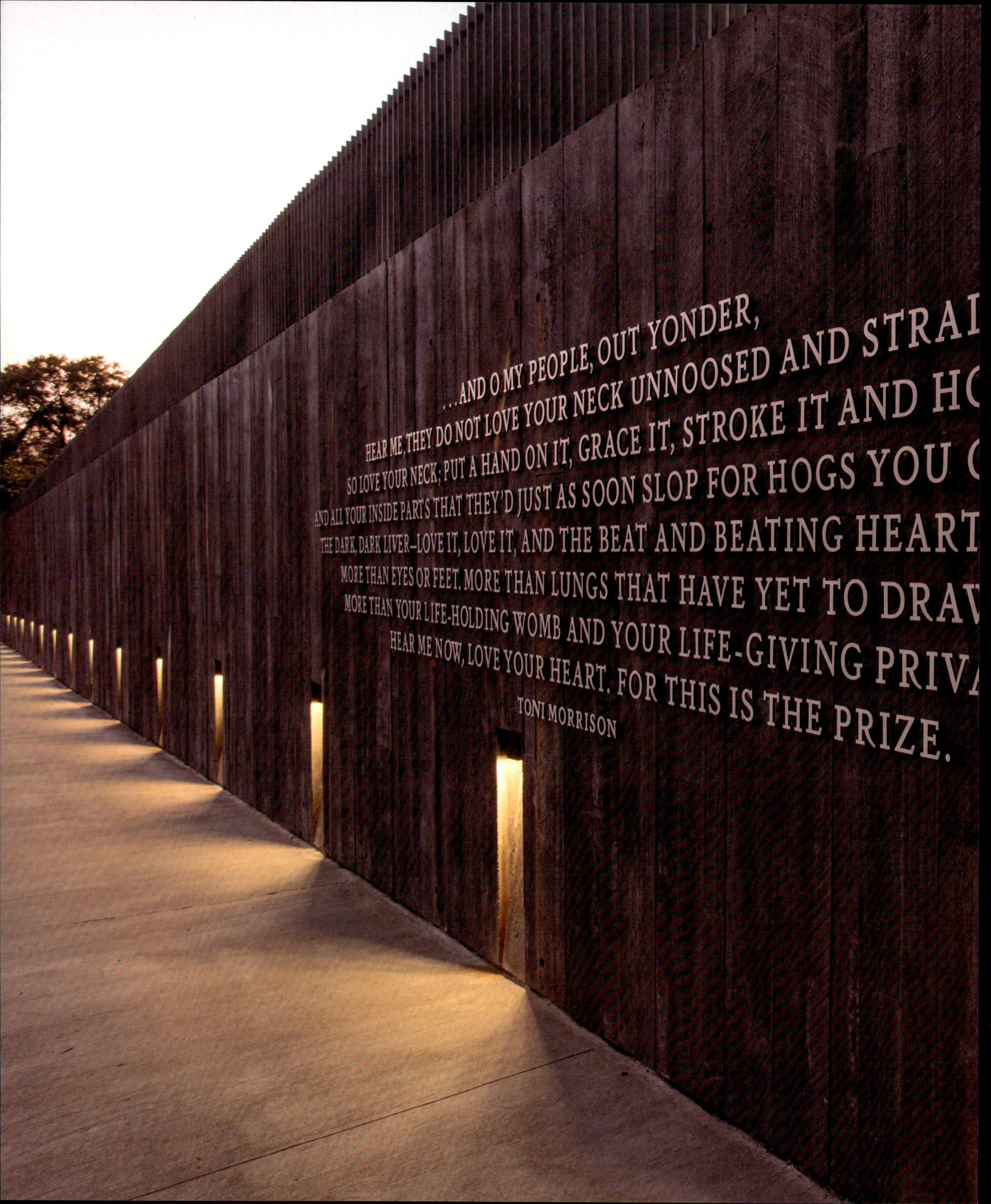
…AND O MY PEOPLE, OUT YONDER,
HEAR ME, THEY DO NOT LOVE YOUR NECK UNNOOSED AND
SO LOVE YOUR NECK; PUT A HAND ON IT, GRACE IT, STROKE IT AND
AND ALL YOUR INSIDE PARTS THAT THEY'D JUST AS SOON SLOP FOR HOGS YOU
THE DARK, DARK LIVER—LOVE IT, LOVE IT, AND THE BEAT AND BEATING HEART
MORE THAN EYES OR FEET. MORE THAN LUNGS THAT HAVE YET TO
MORE THAN YOUR LIFE-HOLDING WOMB AND YOUR LIFE-GIVING
HEAR ME NOW, LOVE YOUR HEART. FOR THIS IS THE PRIZE.
TONI MORRISON

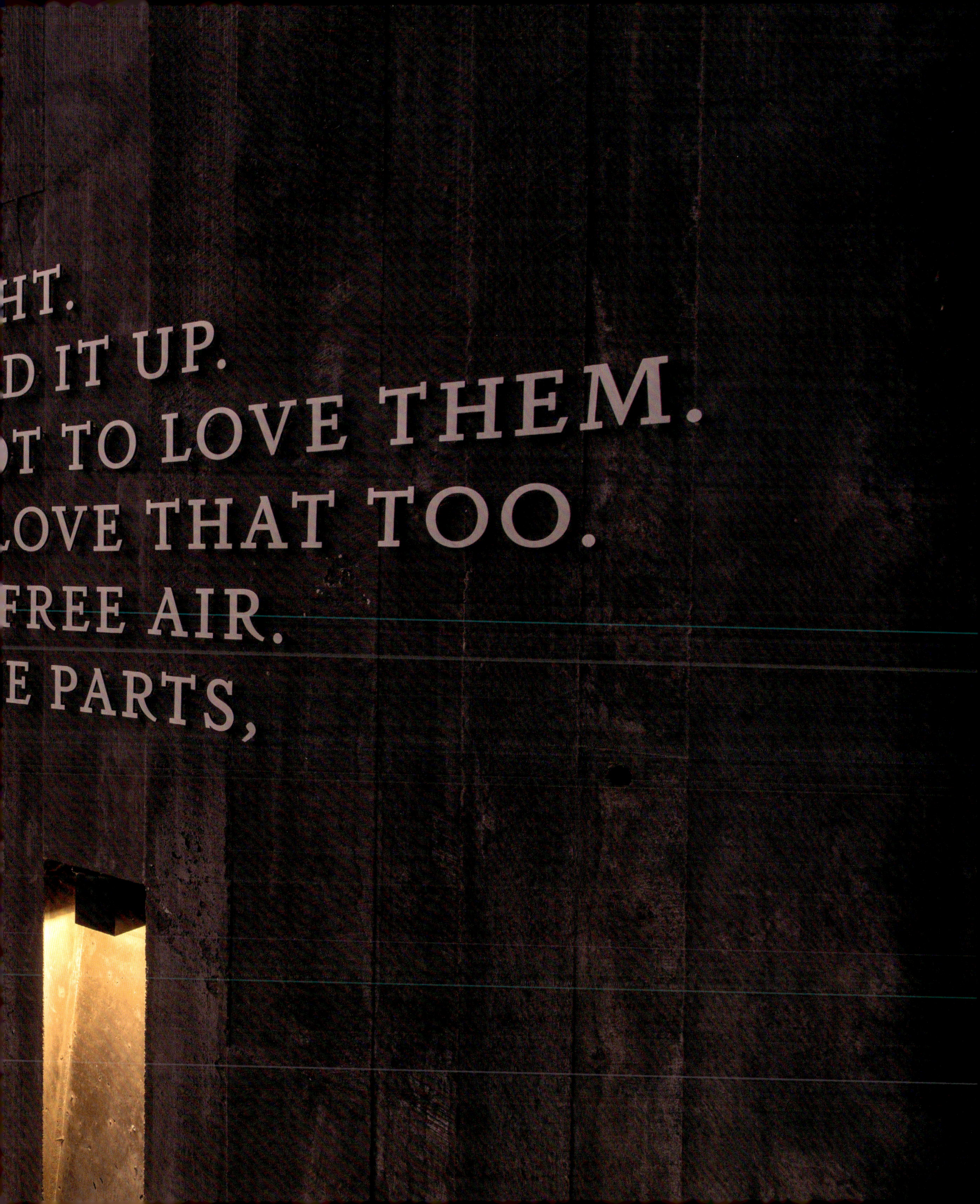

HT.
D IT UP.
T TO LOVE THEM.
LOVE THAT TOO.
FREE AIR.
E PARTS,

The third corridor tells the stories of more than ninety Black men, women, and children who were lynched, many for mere social transgressions. A water wall bears an inscription that invites visitors to remember the thousands of victims of lynchings whose names will never be known.

The memorial site features the literary talents of Toni Morrison, the poetry of Elizabeth Alexander, timeless words from Dr. Martin Luther King Jr., and a reflection space dedicated to anti-lynching crusader and journalist Ida B. Wells.

More than a static site for mourning and reflection, the National Memorial for Peace and Justice is a dynamic space for confronting and acknowledging the truth of racial terror. Visitors emerge into the monument park, which holds a duplicate of each of the corten steel monuments, but this time laying horizontal on the ground. The positioning allows for greater inspection and reckoning. Many visitors investigate their local community's history of racial terror violence. Some search for family members known to have been lynched decades ago.

The space summons all to appreciate the destruction caused by nearly a century of mob violence and lawlessness designed to maintain racial hierarchy in America.

The Historical Context

In the seventeenth and eighteenth centuries, twelve million African people were kidnapped, chained, and brought to the Americas after a torturous journey across the Atlantic Ocean. Nearly two million people died during the voyage. The labor of enslaved Black people fueled economic growth in the United States, where an ideology of white supremacy and racial difference was created to justify slavery and make it morally acceptable.

In the nineteenth century, a thriving plantation economy in the United States and the forcible taking of land from Indigenous People increased the demand for enslaved labor as calls to end the International Trade of Enslaved People gained traction. As a result, the Domestic Trade of Enslaved People escalated. More than a million enslaved people in the North were trafficked to the South, where the population of enslaved people grew dramatically.

. . . And O my people out yonder,
hear me, they do not love your
neck unnoosed and straight.
So love your neck; put a hand on it,
grace it, stroke it and hold it up.
And all your inside parts that
they'd just as soon slop for hogs
you got to love them. The dark,
dark liver – love it, love it, and
the beat and beating heart, love
that too. More than eyes or feet.
More than lungs that have yet to
draw free air. More than your life-
holding womb and your life-giving
private parts, hear me now, love
your heart. For this is the prize.

—TONI MORRISON, *BELOVED*

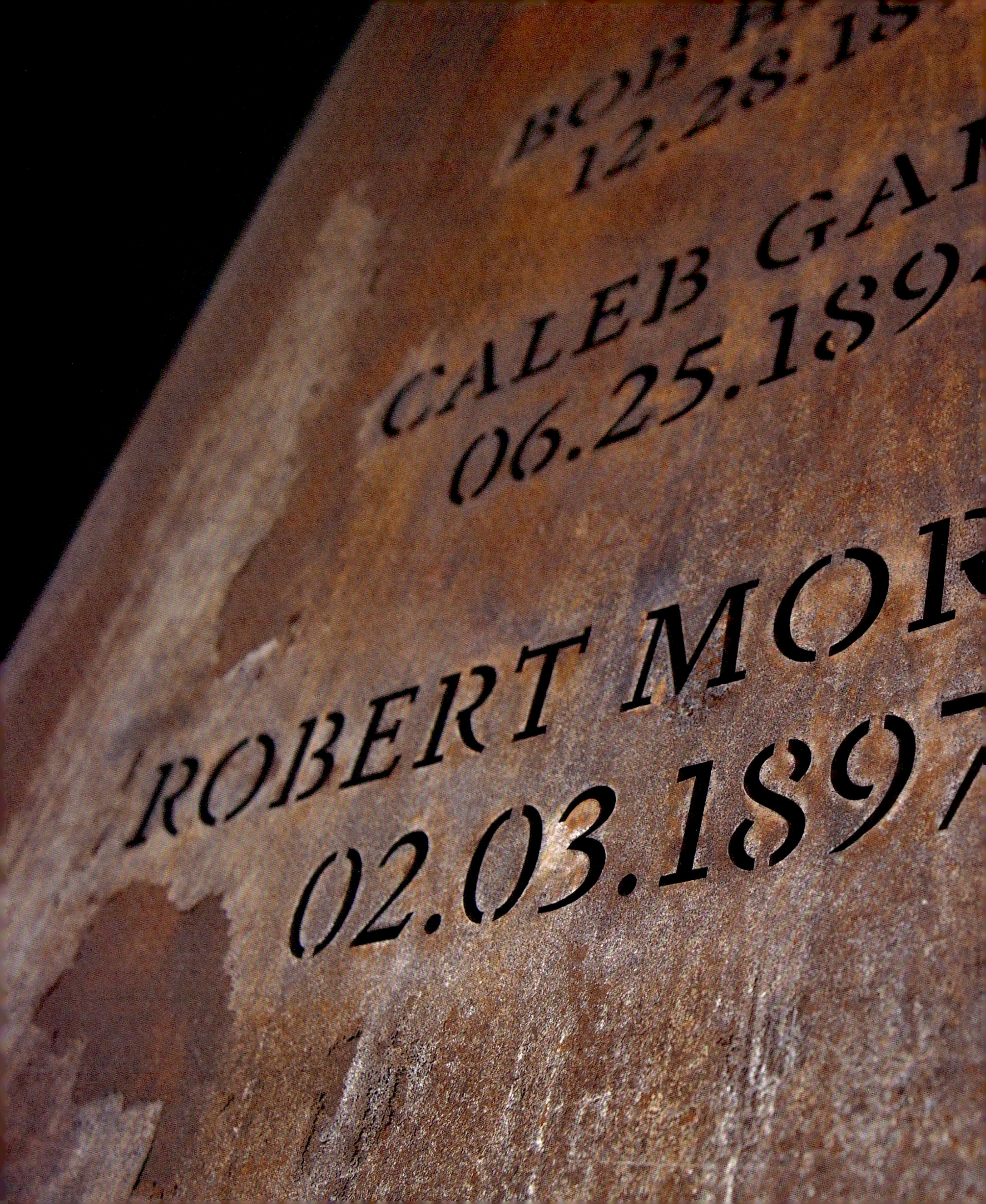
CALEB GA
06.25.189
ROBERT MOR
02.03.189

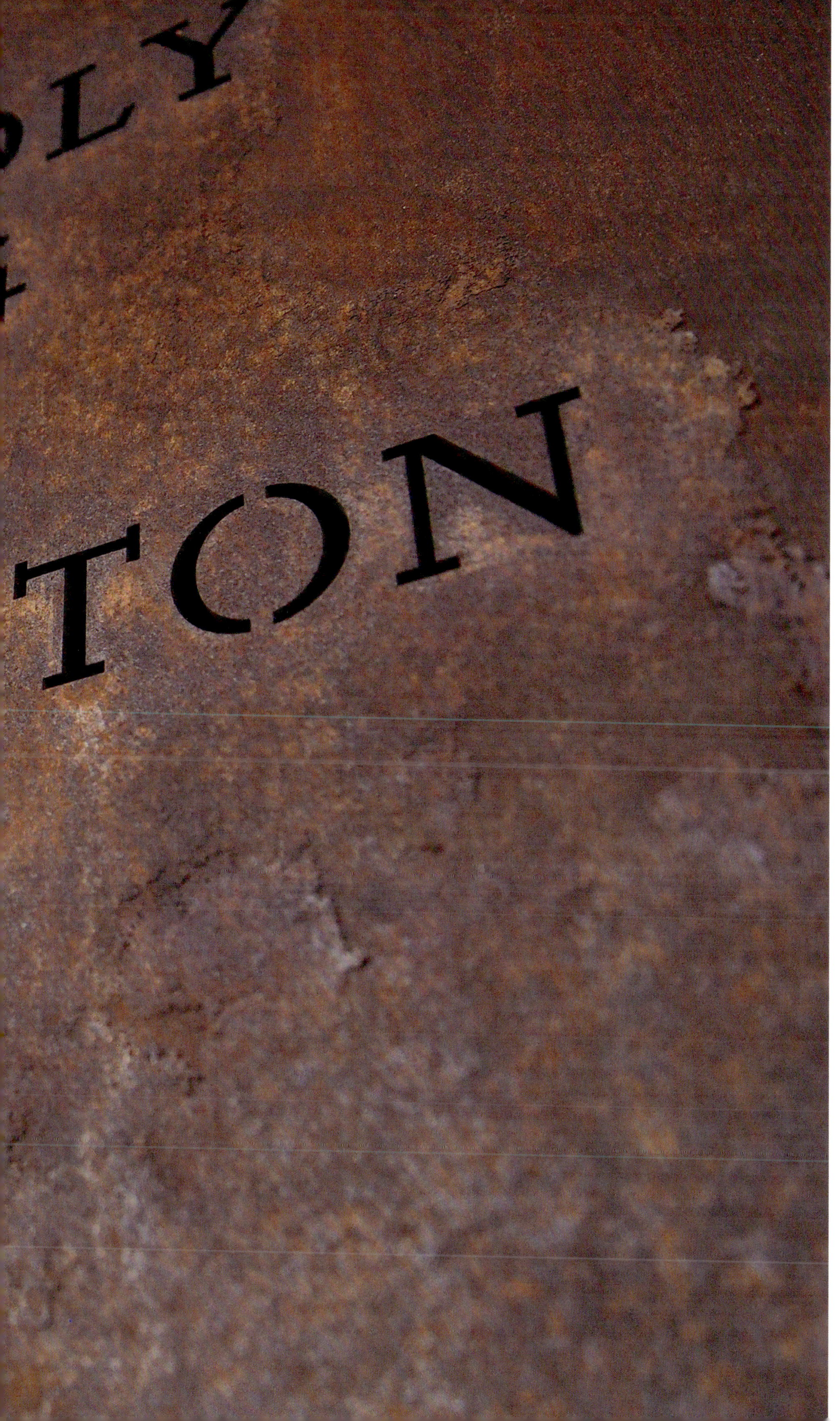

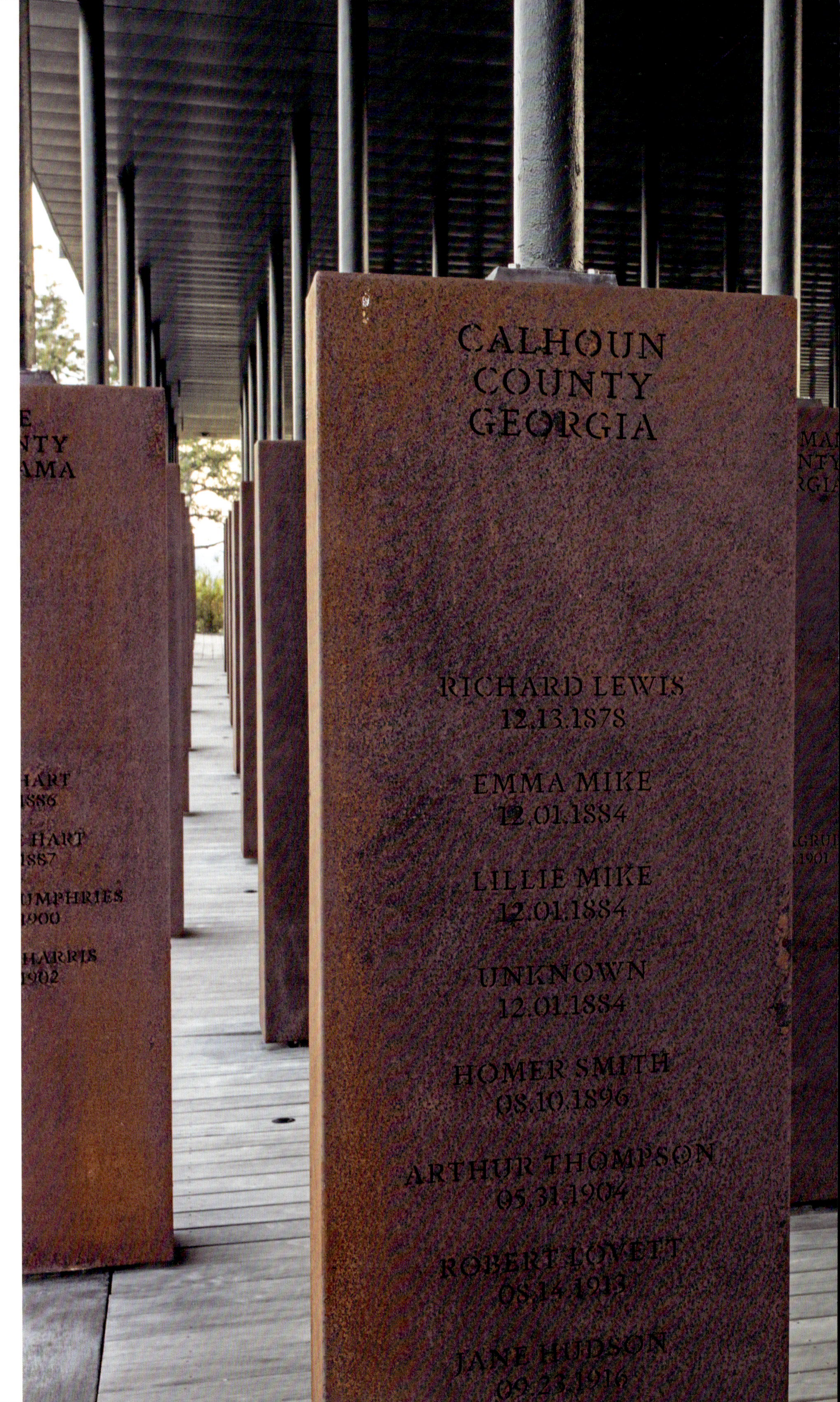
CALHOUN
COUNTY
GEORGIA
RICHARD LEWIS
12.13.1878
EMMA MIKE
12.01.1884
LILLIE MIKE
12.01.1884
UNKNOWN
12.01.1884
HOMER SMITH
08.10.1896
ARTHUR THOMPSON
05.31.1904
ROBERT LOVETT
08.14.1913
JANE HUDSON

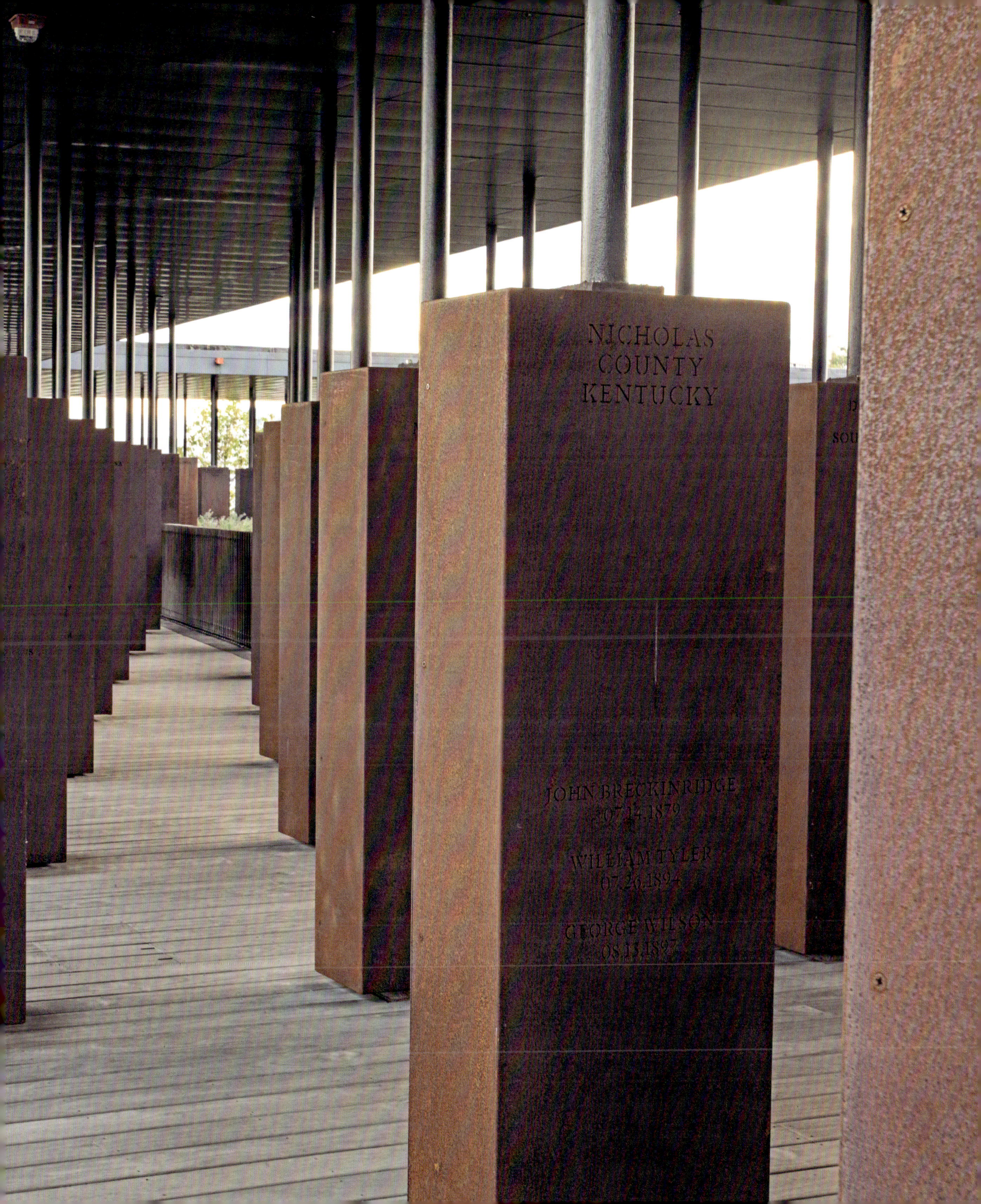
NICHOLAS
COUNTY
KENTUCKY
JOHN BRECKINRIDGE
07.14.1879
WILLIAM TYLER
07.26.1894
GEORGE WILSON
08.15.1897

Black people suffered brutal abuse and mistreatment throughout this region. Nearly half of all enslaved people were separated from their children, spouses, parents, or siblings during the Domestic Trade of Enslaved People.

After the South's defeat in the bloody Civil War, the Thirteenth Amendment was ratified. It prohibited involuntary servitude and forced labor "except as punishment for crime" but left intact a bitter resistance to racial equality.

The identities of many white Americans, especially in the South, were grounded in the belief that they were inherently superior to African Americans. Many white people reacted violently to the requirement to treat their former "human property" as equals and pay for their labor. In the first two years after the war, thousands of Black people were murdered for asserting their freedom or basic rights and entire Black communities were attacked by white mobs in cities like Memphis and New Orleans.

Federal efforts to protect formerly enslaved people were undermined by the United States Supreme Court, which overturned laws that provided remedies to Black people facing violent intimidation. Between 1868 and 1871, a wave of terror swept across the South, resulting in the deaths of thousands of African Americans, many of whom were killed merely for failing to obey a white person. Northern politicians retreated from a commitment to protect Black people, and in 1877, federal troops left the South. Racial terror and violence directed at Black people intensified. White Southerners barred Black people from voting, trapped them in exploitative sharecropping and tenant farming systems that would keep them indentured and poor for generations, and made racial segregation the law of the land.

Convict leasing—a horrific system in which Black people, convicted of largely social crimes that applied only to them, were leased to private businesses which forced them to work under inhuman conditions—was "worse than slavery." Racial integrity laws prohibited social interactions between people of different races, especially Black men and white women.

Racial terror lynching emerged as a primary tool to uphold racial hierarchy by forcing Black people to accept abusive mistreatment and subordination. Federal, state, and local governments largely tolerated these terrorist acts, which claimed the lives of thousands of African Americans, including many whose identities will never be known.

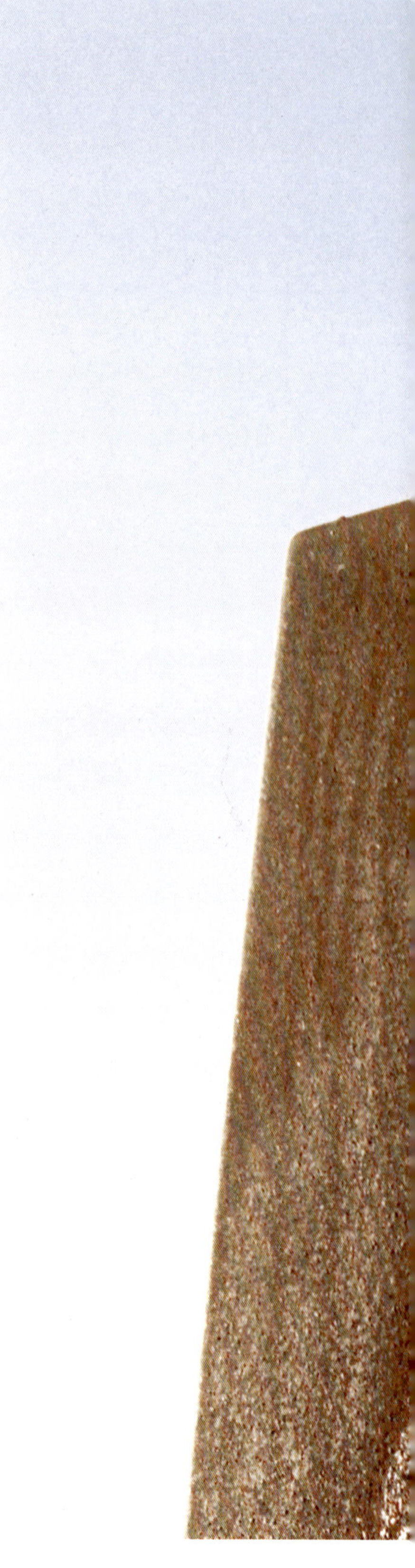

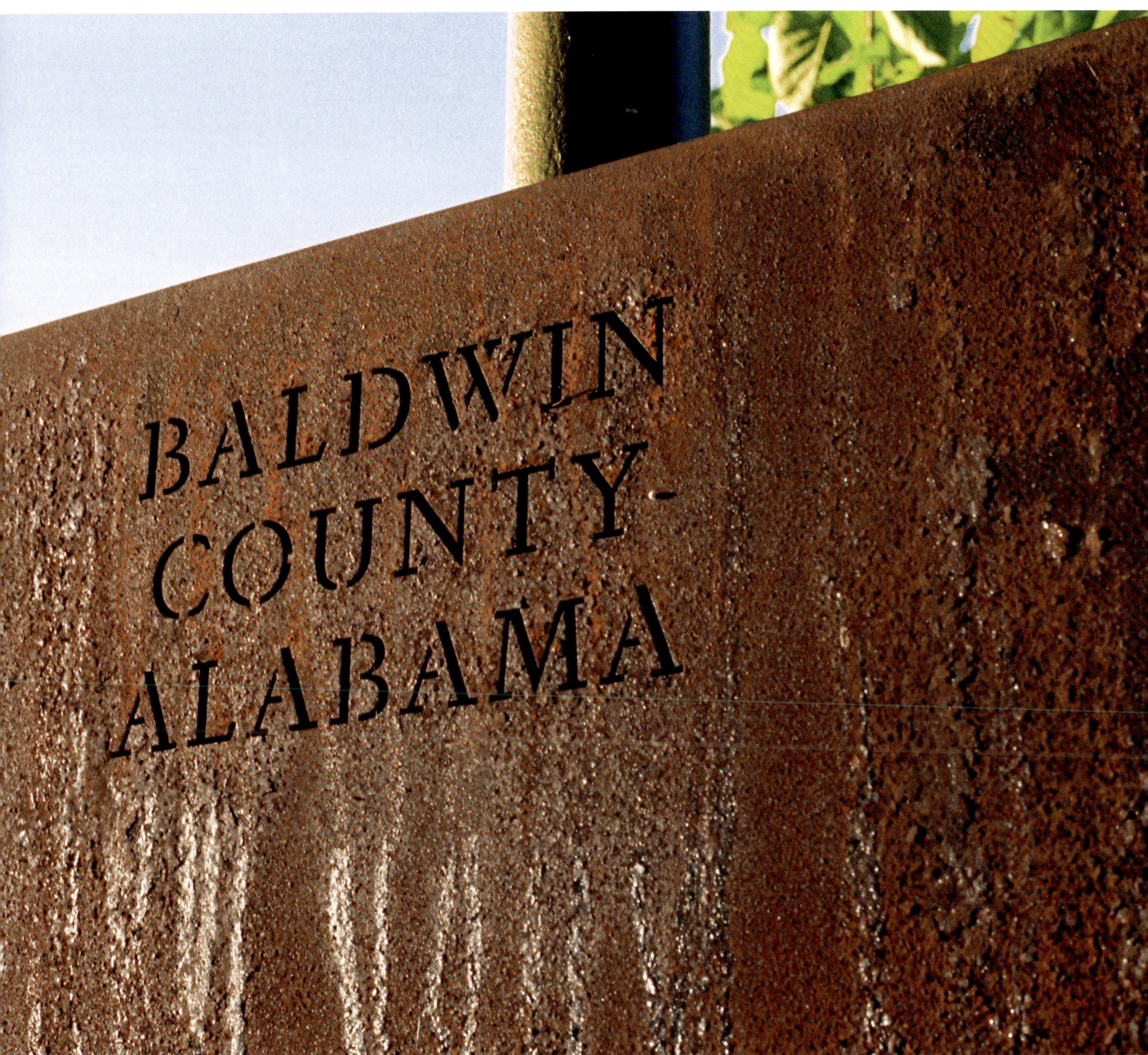
BALDWIN
COUNTY-
ALABAMA

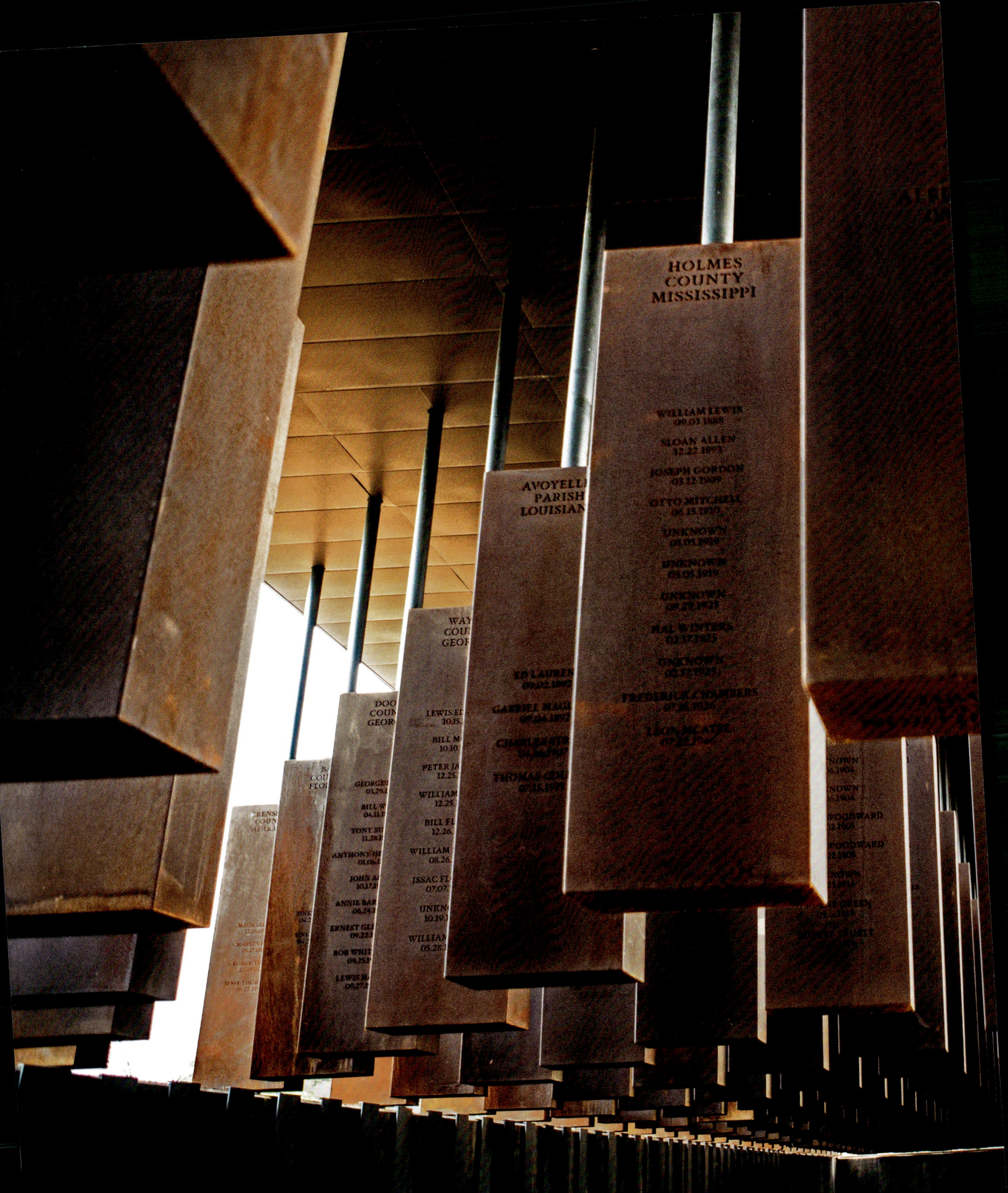

HOLMES
COUNTY
MISSISSIPPI

WILLIAM LEWIS

SLOAN ALLEN

JOSEPH GORDON

UNKNOWN

UNKNOWN

UNKNOWN

HAL WINTERS

UNKNOWN

FREDERICK CHAMBERS

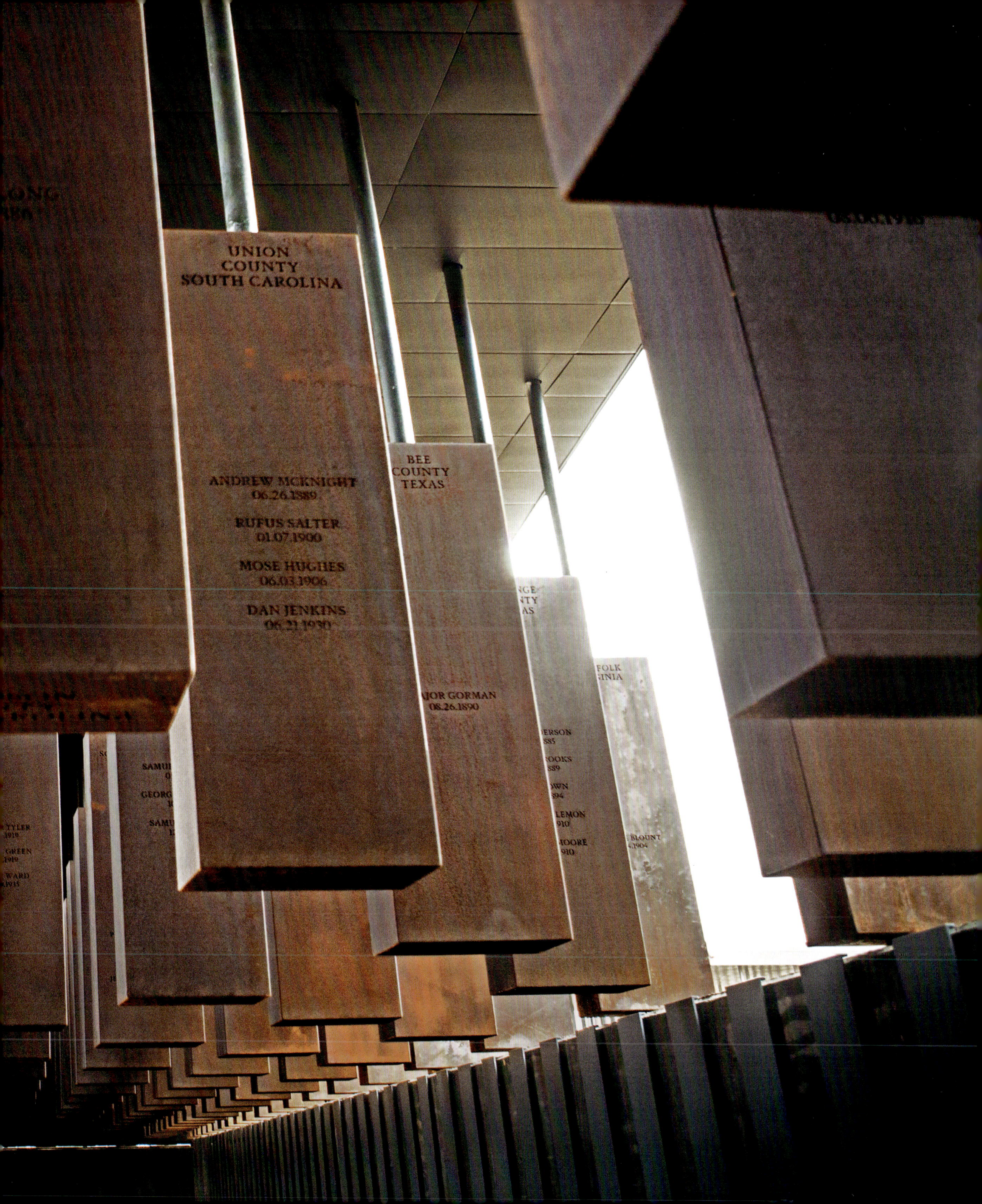

UNION
COUNTY
SOUTH CAROLINA

ANDREW MCKNIGHT
06.26.1889

RUFUS SALTER
01.07.1900

MOSE HUGHES
06.03.1906

DAN JENKINS
06.21.1930

BEE
COUNTY
TEXAS

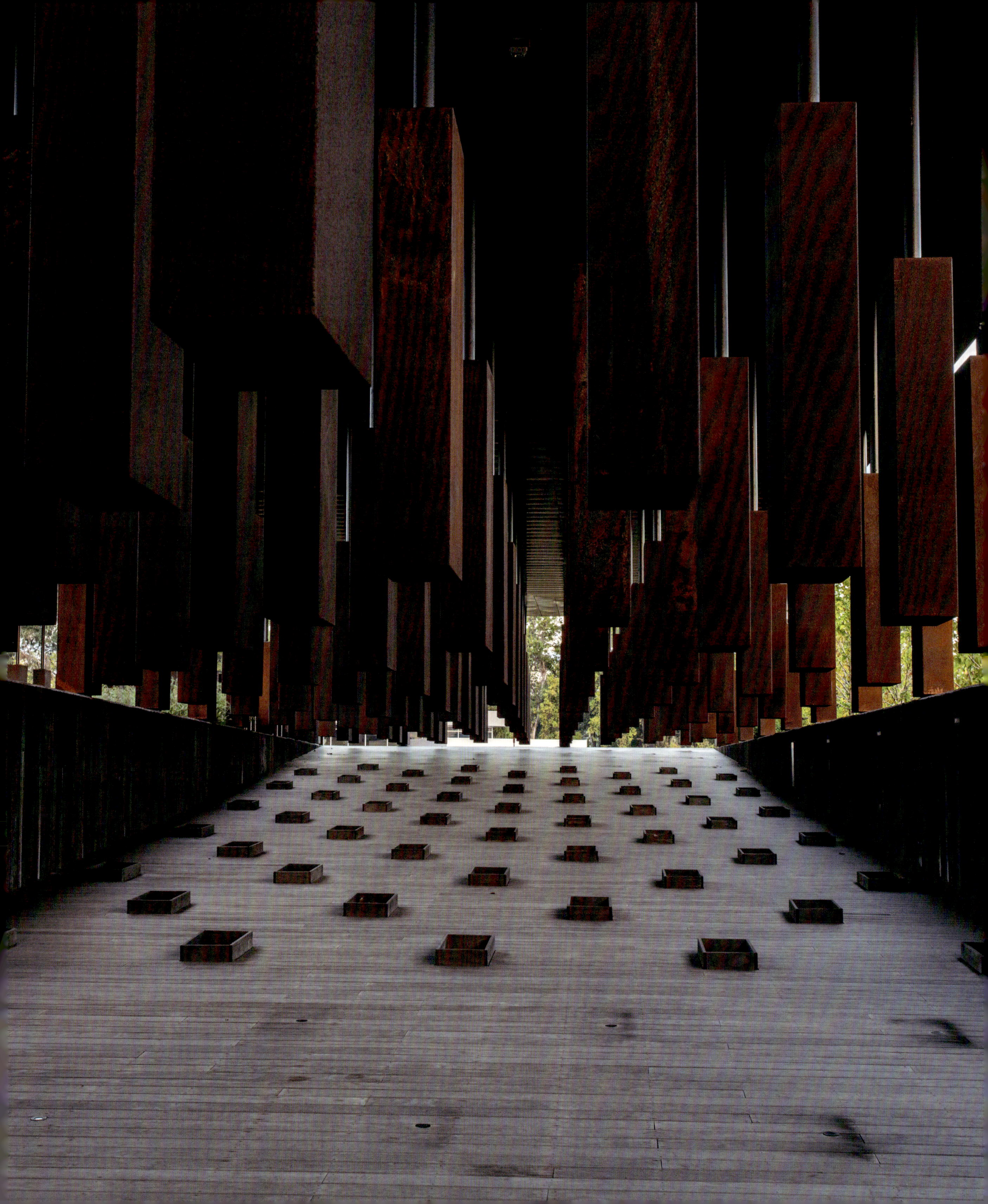

Arthur St. Clair, a minister, was lynched in Hernando County, Florida, in 1877 for performing the wedding of a Black man and white woman.

Charlotte Harris was lynched in Rockingham County, Virginia, in 1878 after a white man's barn burned down.

Jack Turner was lynched in Butler, Alabama, in 1882 for organizing Black voters in Choctaw County.

Sampson Harris was lynched in Bienville Parish, Louisiana, in 1885 after threatening to report white men for whipping his neighbors.

Dozens of Black sugarcane workers were lynched in Thibodaux, Louisiana, in 1887 for striking to protest low wages.

Seven Black people were lynched near Screamer, Alabama, in 1888 for drinking from a white man's well.

Warren Powell, fourteen, was lynched in East Point, Georgia, in 1889 for "frightening" a white girl.

A Black man was lynched in Millersburg, Ohio, in 1892 for "standing around" in a white neighborhood.

Henry Smith, seventeen, was lynched in Paris, Texas, in 1893 before a mob of ten thousand people.

Jack Brownlee was lynched in 1894 in Oxford, Alabama, for having a white man who attempted to assault his daughter arrested.

William Stephens and **Jefferson Cole** were lynched in Delta County, Texas, in 1895 after they refused to abandon their land to white people.

William Wardley was lynched in Irondale, Alabama, in 1896 because local white merchants wrongly thought his money was counterfeit.

Amanda Franks, **Mollie Smith**, and **James Nance** were lynched in Jeff, Alabama, in 1897 after their white employers claimed they had been poisoned.

Private James Neely was lynched in Hampton, Georgia, in 1898 for complaining when a white storeowner refused to serve him.

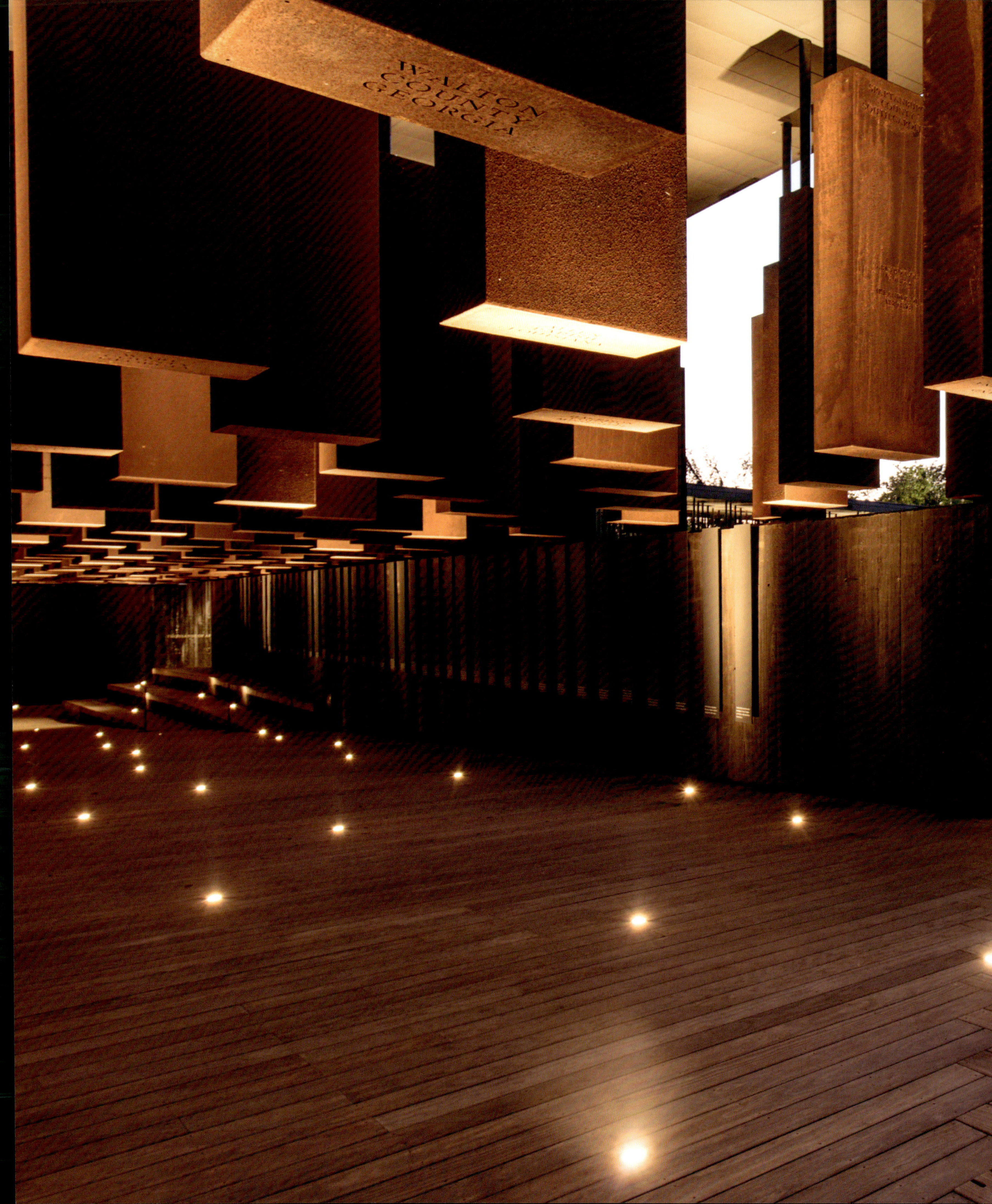
WALTON
COUNTY
GEORGIA

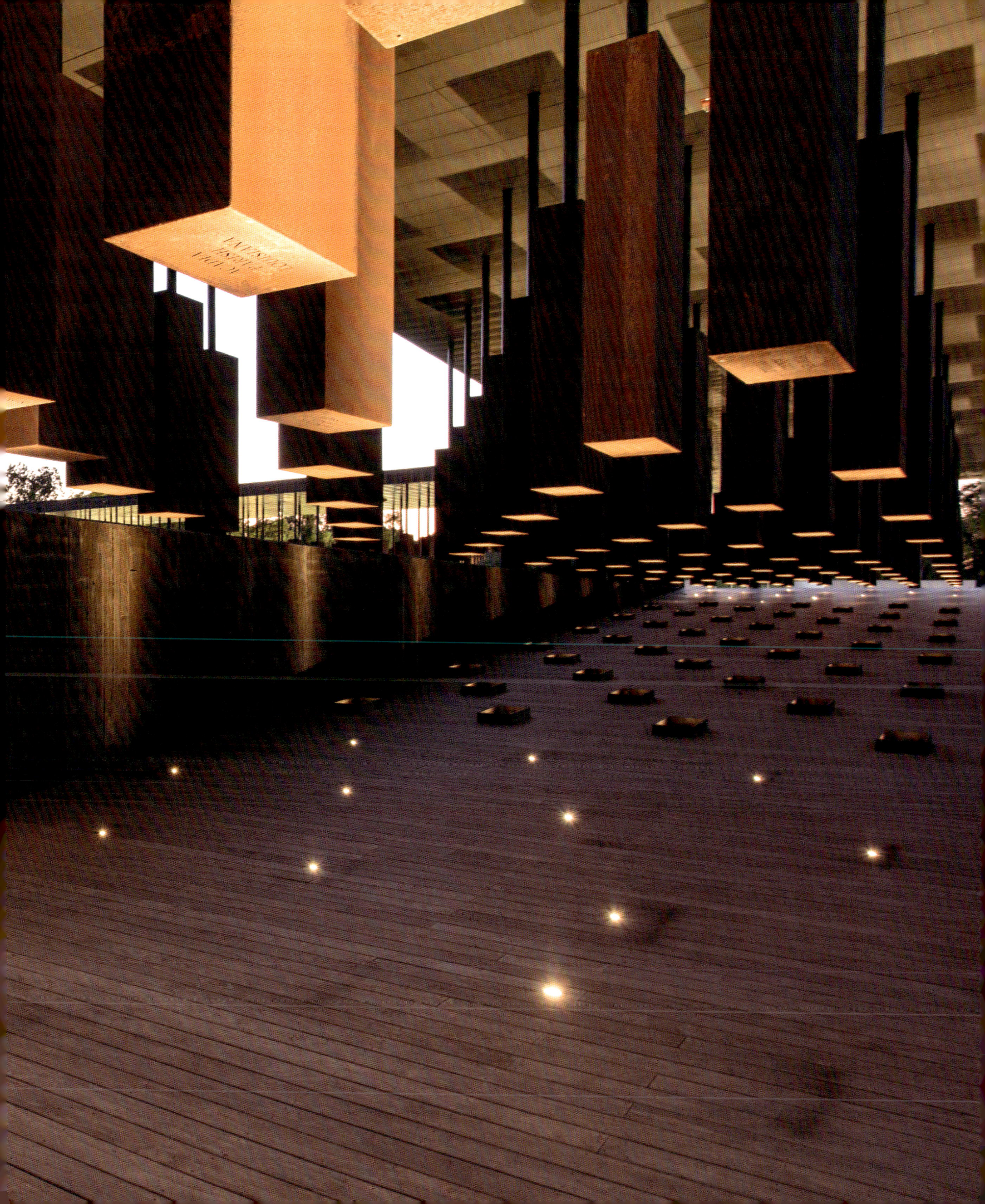

From 1865 to 1950, millions of Black Americans were targeted by racial terror lynchings. EJI has documented nearly 6,500 lynchings of African Americans by groups ranging from two to more than ten thousand white people. These lynchings—often in broad daylight and always with impunity—were vicious acts of murder.

Black people were lynched by hanging, burning, shooting, drowning, stabbing, and beating. Some were falsely accused of rape or murder, presumed guilty, and killed without investigation or trial. Others were lynched for political activism or economic success, slaughtered in widespread attacks on Black communities, killed in place of a friend or relative whom the mob could not locate, or targeted for violating social rules of racial hierarchy.

Racial terror lynchings were distinct from hangings and mob violence committed against white people and other groups because they were intended to terrorize Black Americans and enforce racial hierarchy. Unlike frontier justice in the West, racial terror lynchings generally took place in communities with functioning criminal courts that were viewed as too good for African Americans. Despite its lawlessness and terrifying unpredictability, lynching was sanctioned by law enforcement and elected officials.

Racial terror lynching was characterized by extreme violence: victims were tortured for hours before their brutalized bodies were displayed to traumatize other Black people. Members of the mob frequently documented their atrocities by posing for photographs with a dangling, bloodied, or burnt corpse.

Black lynching victims killed between 1877 and 1950 primarily died in the eleven former Confederate states, with Mississippi, Georgia, and Louisiana among the deadliest. Several hundred racial terror lynchings happened in other regions, with the highest numbers in Kentucky, Oklahoma, Missouri, Illinois, and West Virginia.

History, despite its wrenching pain, cannot be unlived, but if faced with courage, need not be lived again.

— MAYA ANGELOU

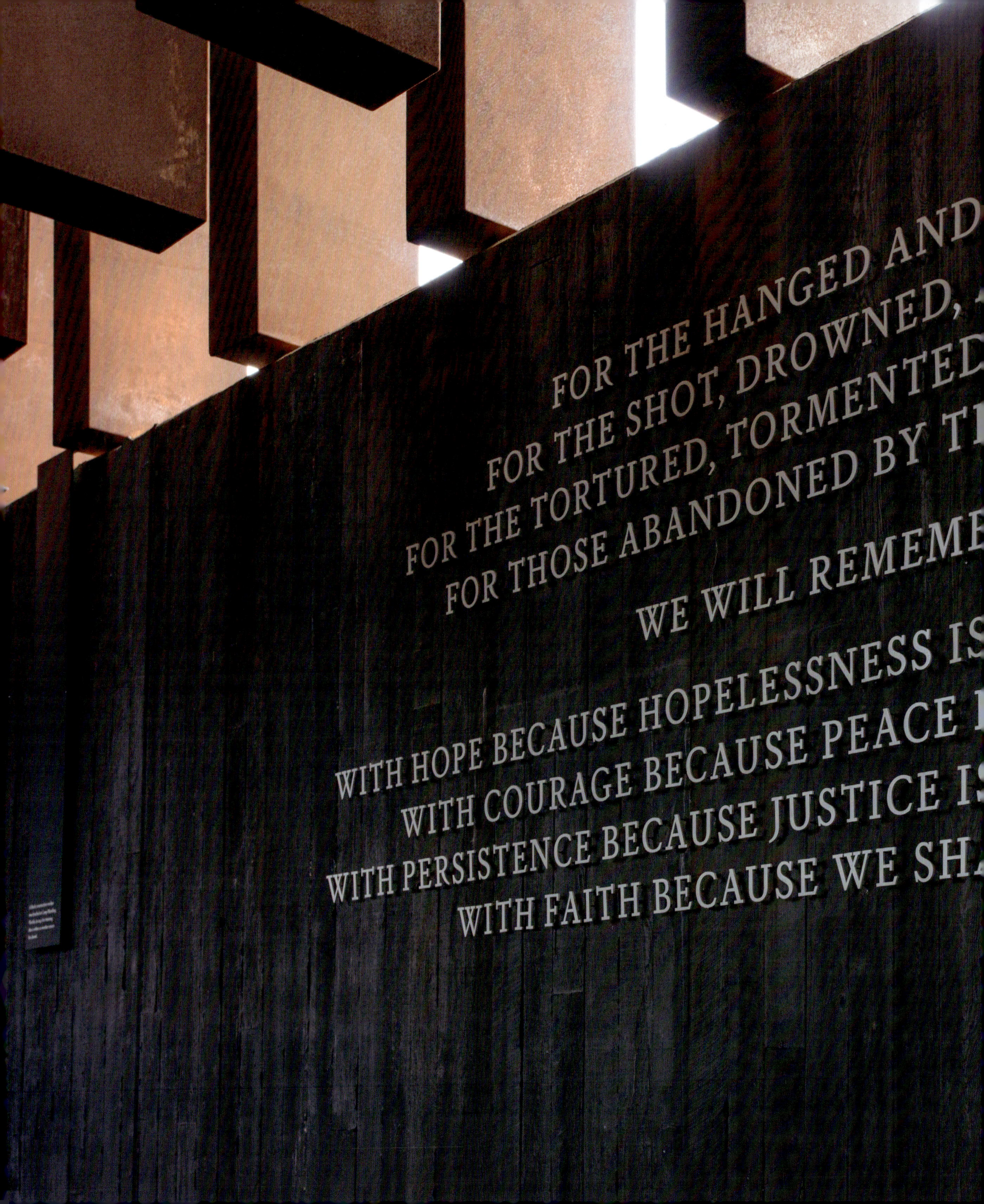

FOR THE HANGED AND

FOR THE SHOT, DROWNED,

FOR THE TORTURED, TORMENTED

FOR THOSE ABANDONED BY T

WE WILL REMEMB

WITH HOPE BECAUSE HOPELESSNESS IS

WITH COURAGE BECAUSE PEACE

WITH PERSISTENCE BECAUSE JUSTICE IS

WITH FAITH BECAUSE WE SH

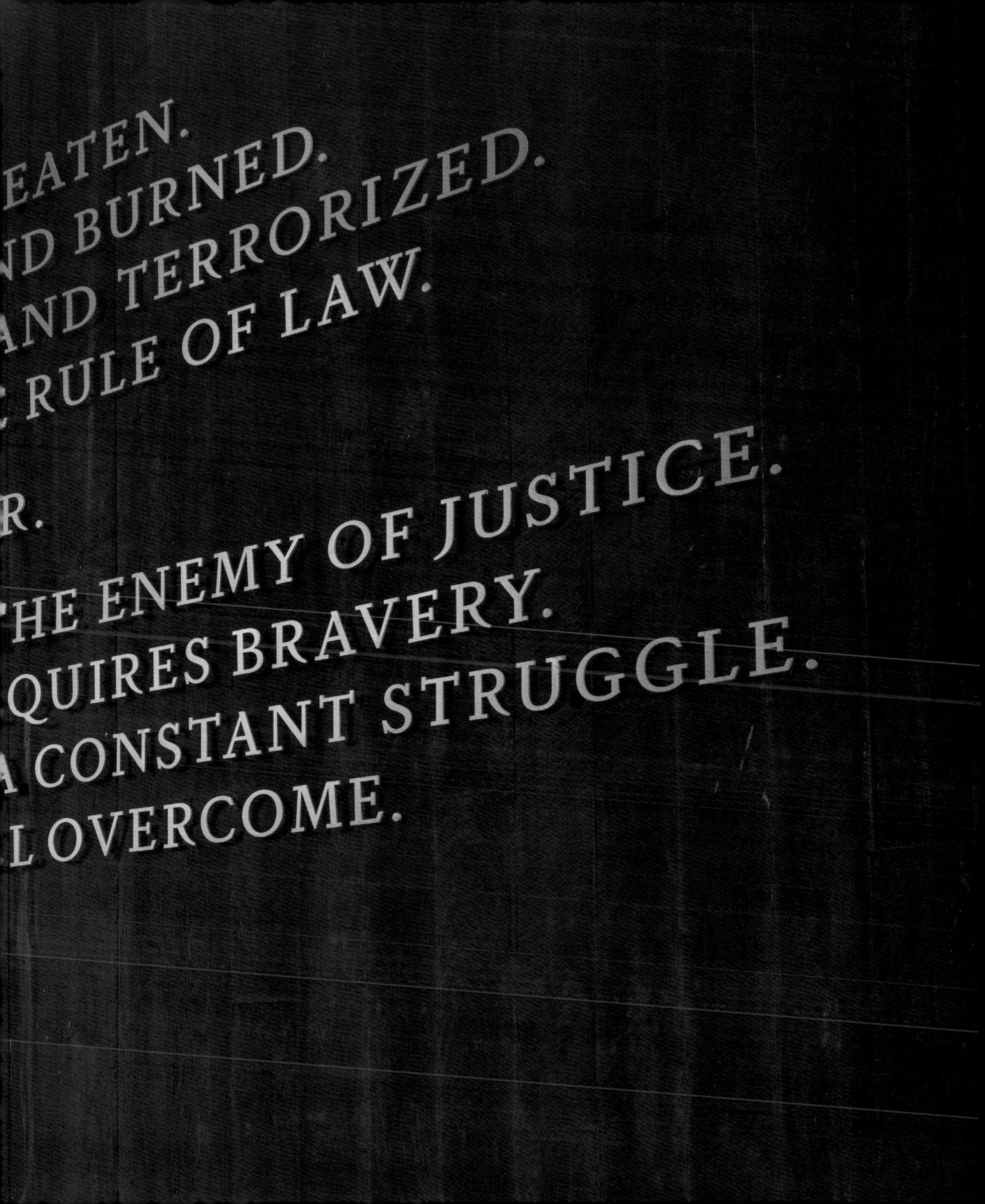

EATEN.
ND BURNED.
AND TERRORIZED.
RULE OF LAW.

R.

THE ENEMY OF JUSTICE.
QUIRES BRAVERY.
A CONSTANT STRUGGLE.
L OVERCOME.

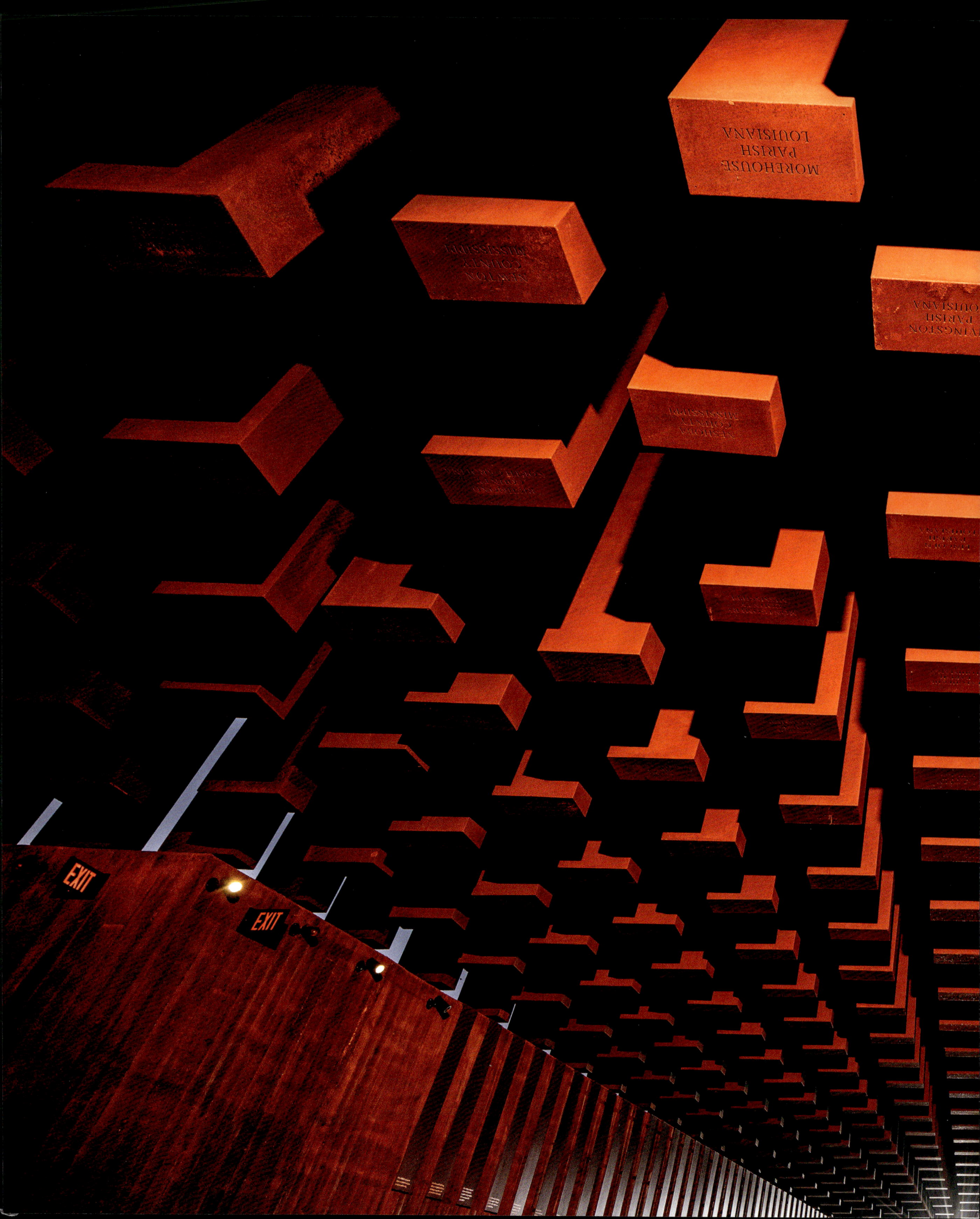
MOREHOUSE
PARISH
LOUISIANA
NEWTON
COUNTY
MISSISSIPPI
EXIT
EXIT

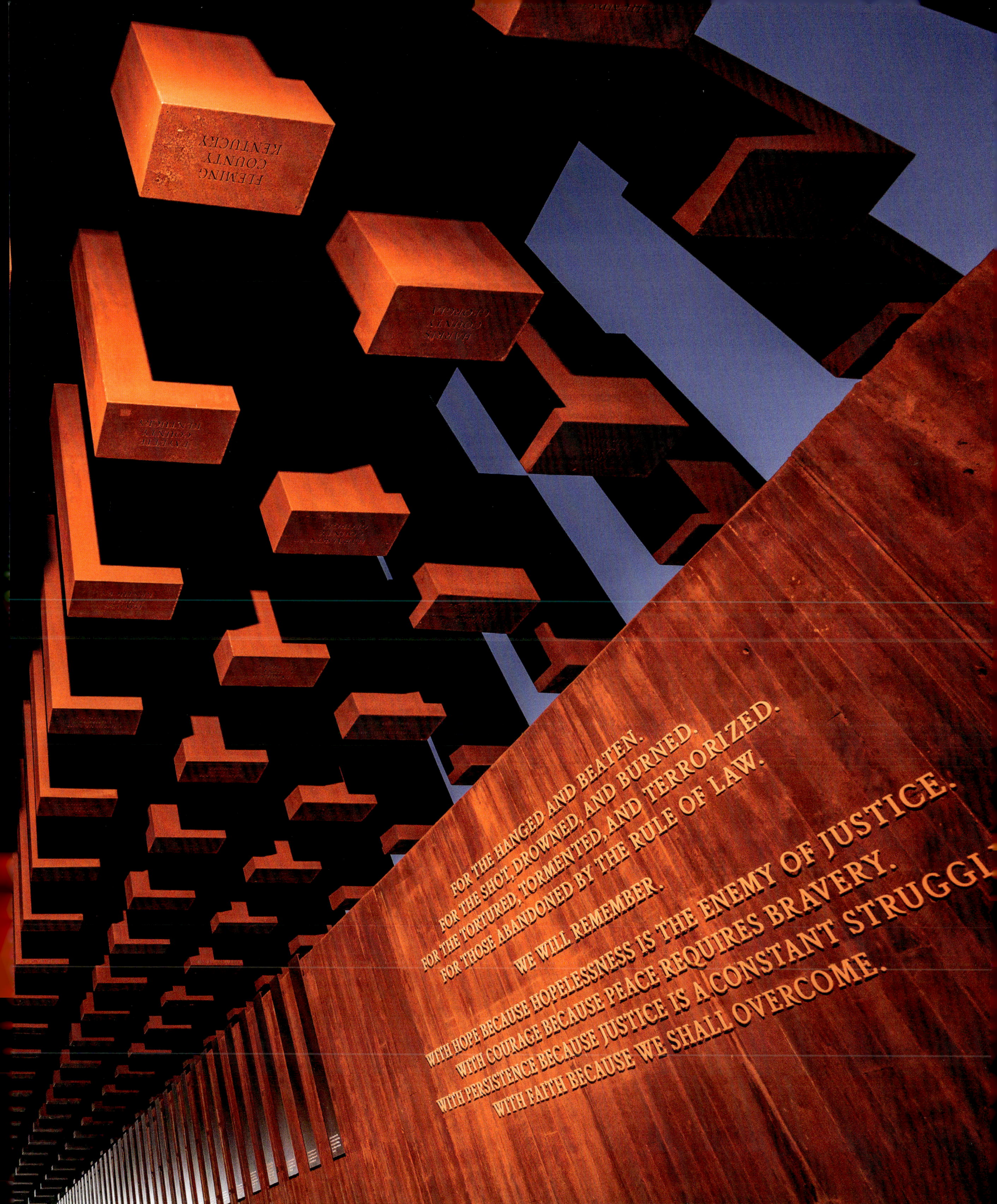
FLEMING
COUNTY
KENTUCKY
HARRIS
COUNTY
GEORGIA
FOR THE HANGED AND BEATEN.
FOR THE SHOT, DROWNED, AND BURNED.
FOR THE TORTURED, TORMENTED, AND TERRORIZED.
FOR THOSE ABANDONED BY THE RULE OF LAW.
WE WILL REMEMBER.
WITH HOPE BECAUSE HOPELESSNESS IS THE ENEMY OF JUSTICE.
WITH COURAGE BECAUSE PEACE REQUIRES BRAVERY.
WITH PERSISTENCE BECAUSE JUSTICE IS A CONSTANT STRUGGL
WITH FAITH BECAUSE WE SHALL OVERCOME.

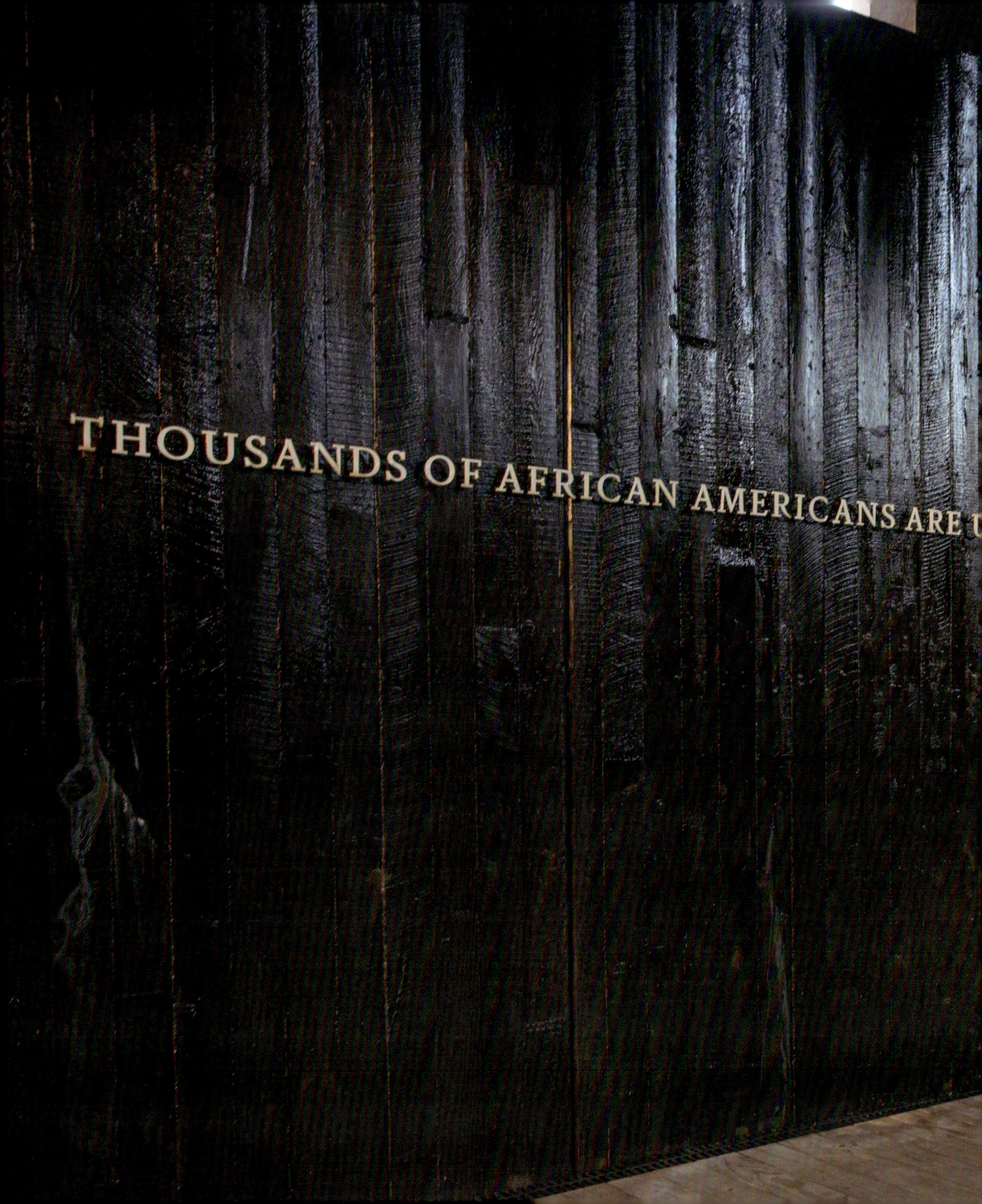

THOUSANDS OF AFRICAN AMERICANS ARE

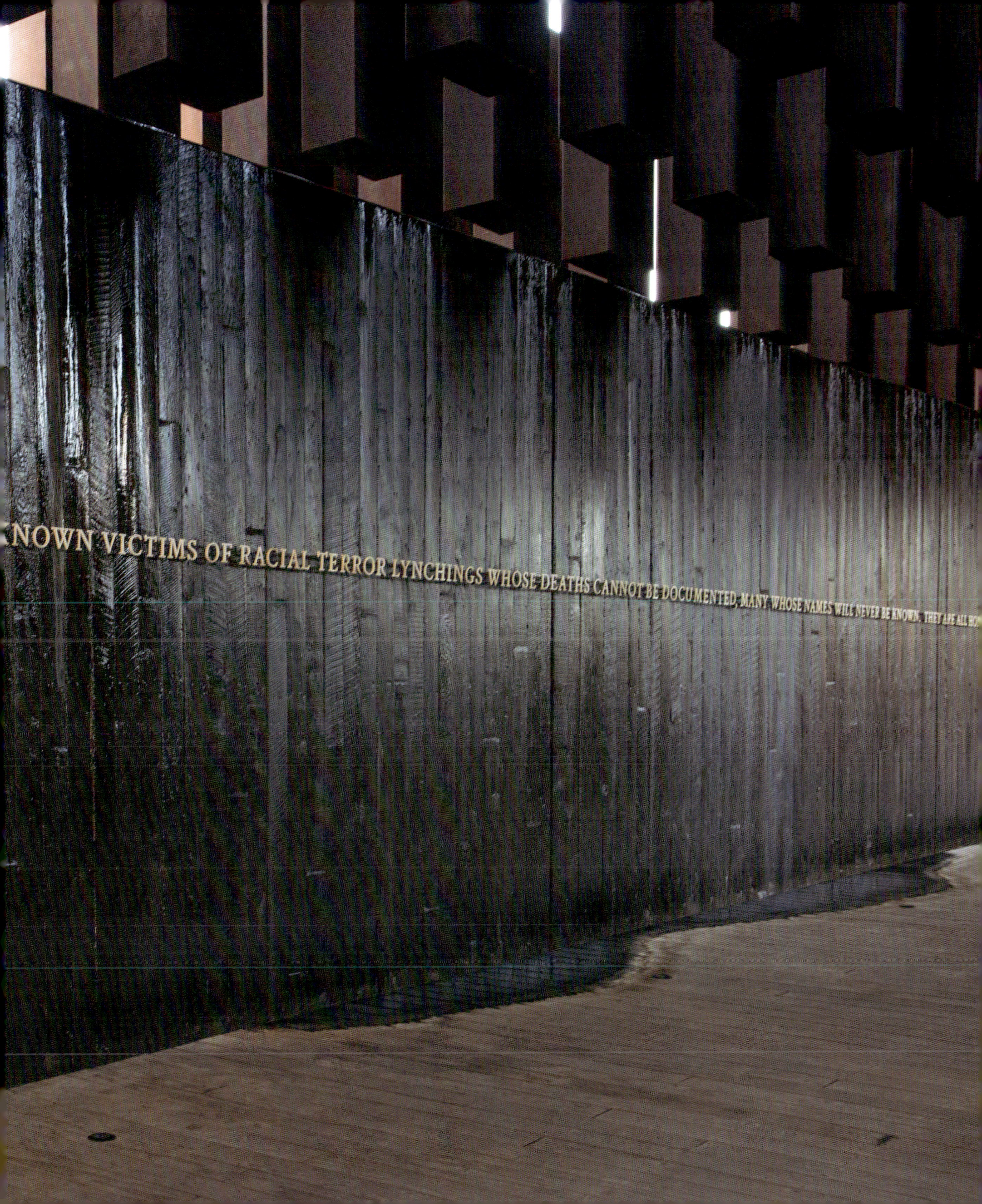
NOWN VICTIMS OF RACIAL TERROR LYNCHINGS WHOSE DEATHS CANNOT BE DOCUMENTED, MANY WHOSE NAMES WILL NEVER BE KNOWN. THEY ARE ALL HO

David Hunter was lynched in Laurens County, South Carolina, in 1898 for leaving the farm where he worked without permission.

Two Black men were lynched, whipped to death while being "interrogated" in the woods, after an overcoat went missing from a hotel in Tifton, Georgia, in 1900.

Calvin Kimblern was lynched by a mob of at least three thousand people in Pueblo, Colorado, in 1900.

Ballie Crutchfield was lynched in Rome, Tennessee, in 1901 by a mob searching for her brother.

Fred Rochelle, aged sixteen, was burned alive in a public spectacle lynching before thousands in Polk County, Florida, in 1901.

Fred Alexander, a military veteran, was lynched and burned alive before thousands of spectators in Leavenworth, Kansas, in 1901.

Nathan Bird was lynched near Luling, Texas, in 1902, for refusing to turn his teenaged son over to a mob; his son, accused of fighting with a white boy, was also lynched.

David Walker, his wife, and their four children were lynched in Hickman, Kentucky, in 1908 after Mr. Walker was accused of using inappropriate language with a white woman.

William Miller was lynched in Brighton, Alabama, in 1908 for organizing local coal miners.

William Donegan was lynched in Springfield, Illinois, in 1908 for having a white wife.

Bird Cooper was lynched in Claiborne Parish, Louisiana, in 1908 after he was acquitted of murder charges.

John Stoner was lynched in Doss, Louisiana, in 1909 for suing the white man who killed his cow.

Laura Nelson and her teenaged son, **L.D.**, were lynched without trial in Okemah, Oklahoma, in 1911 after a white man was found dead.

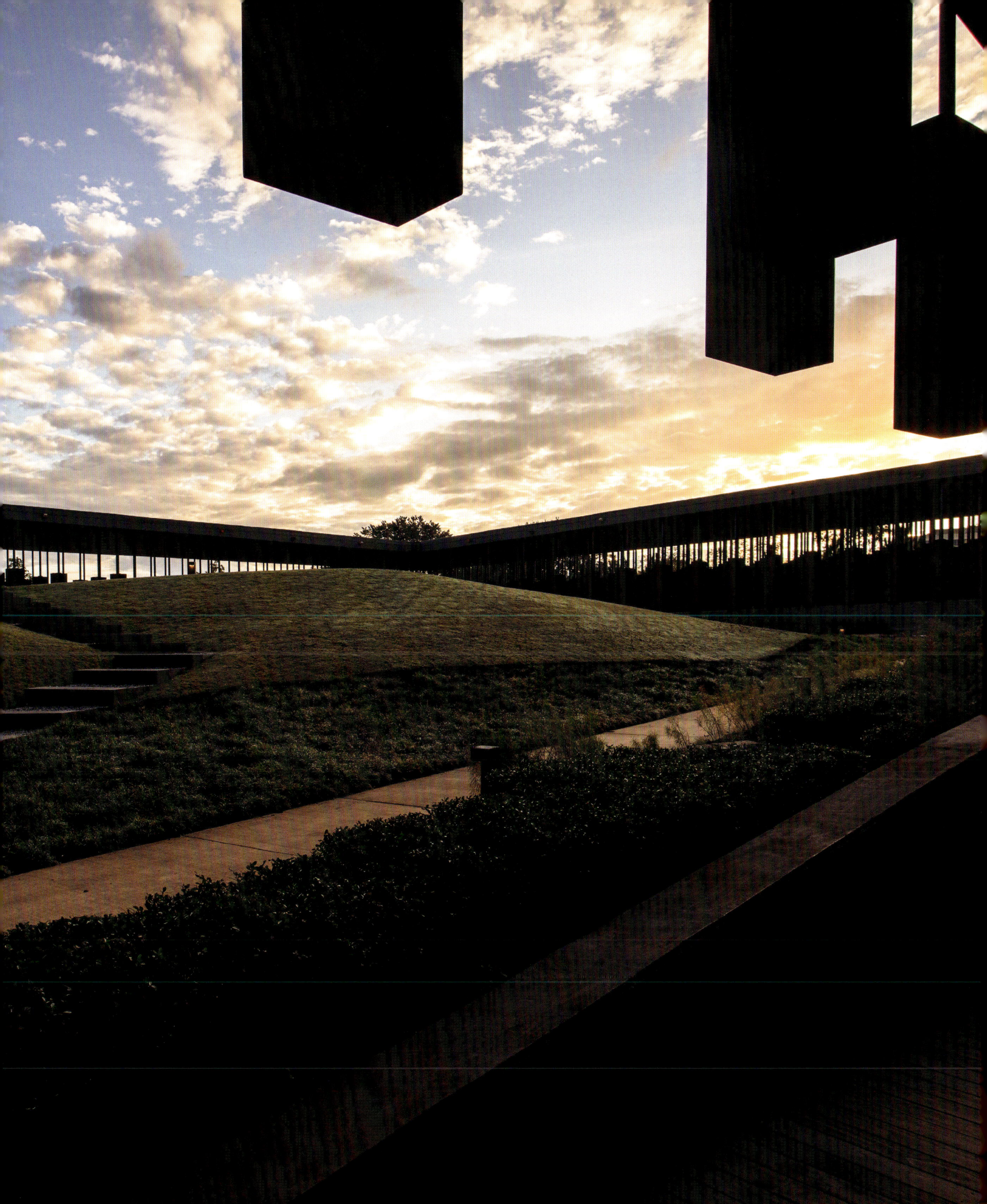

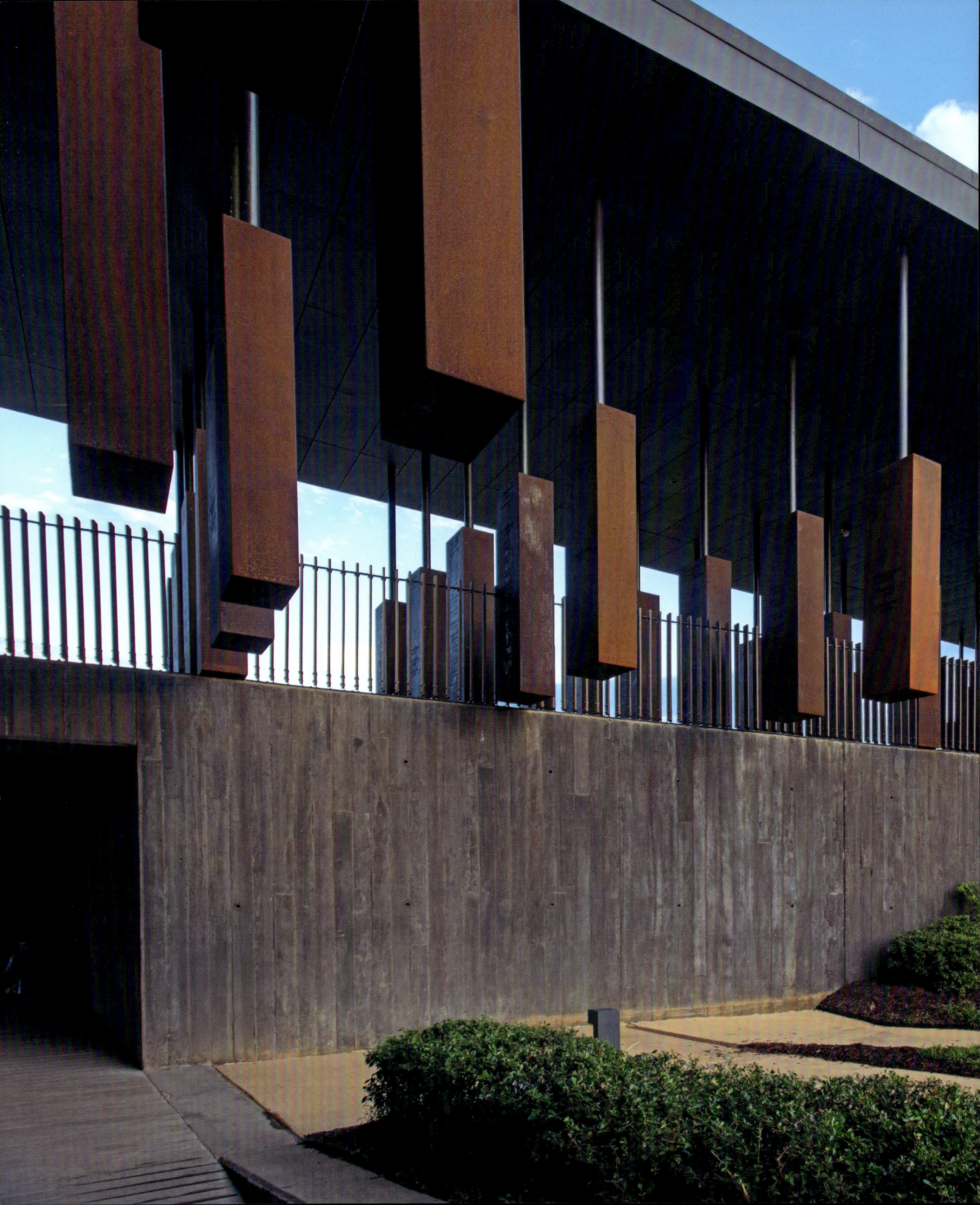

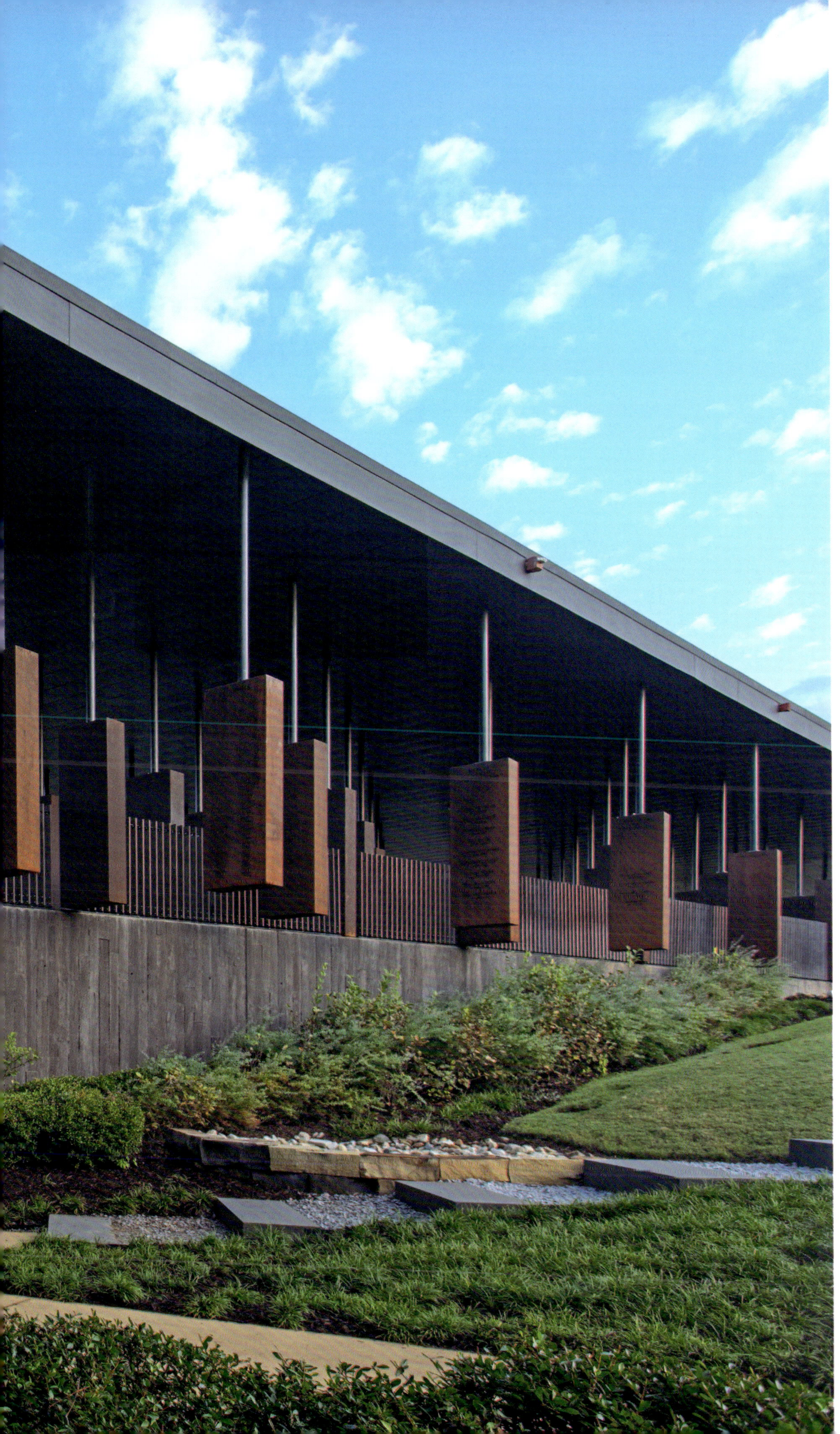

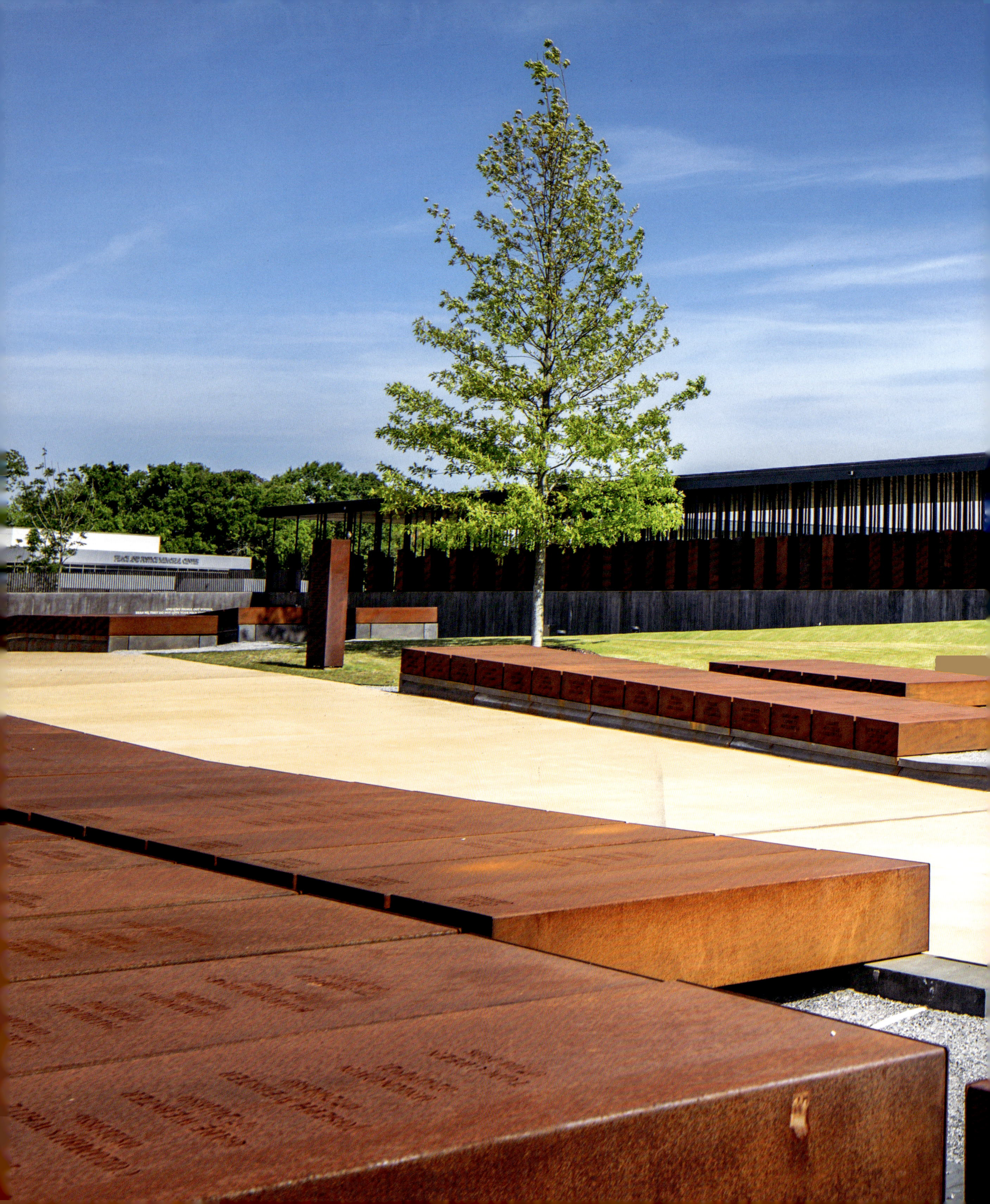

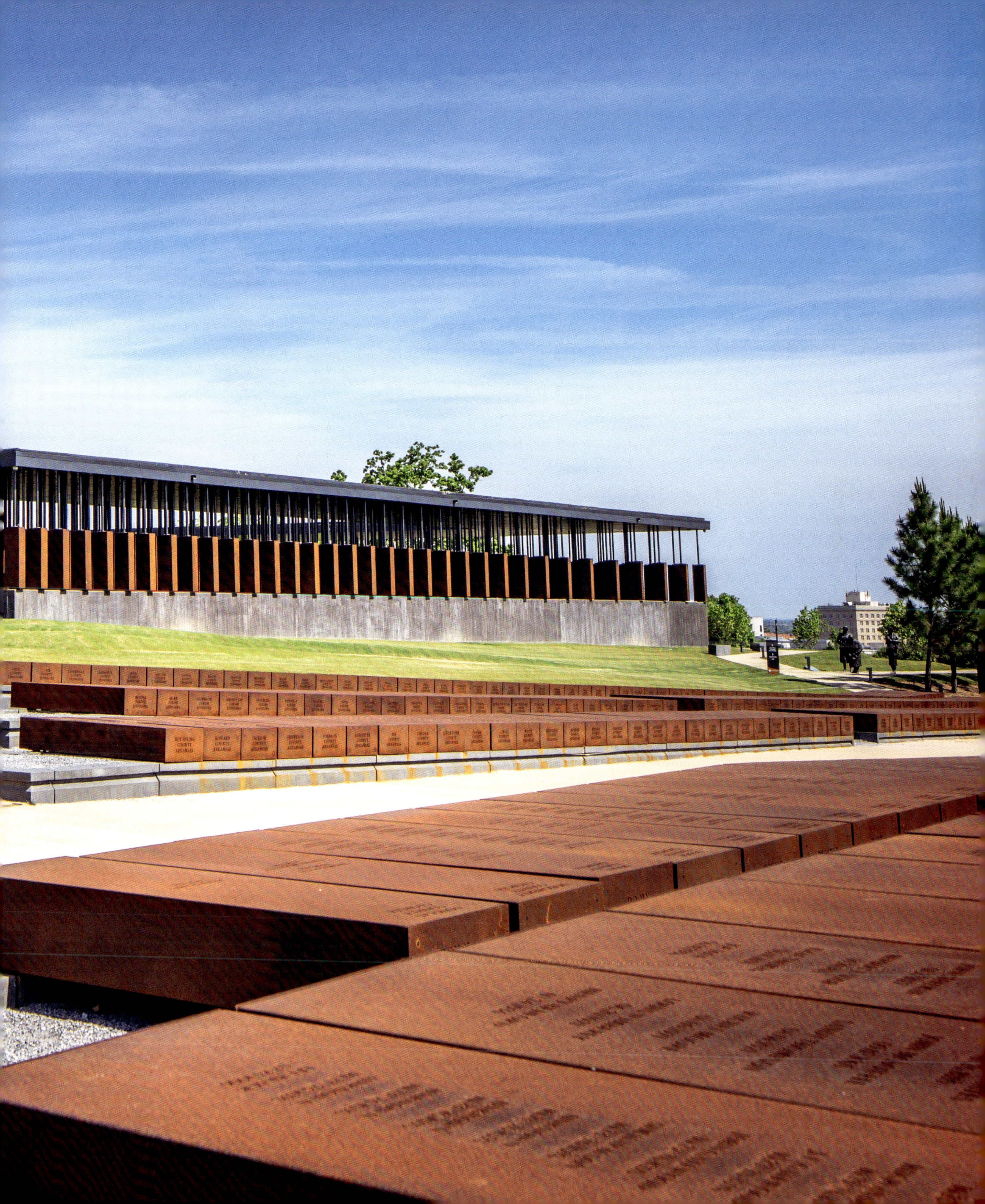
HOT SPRING COUNTY ARKANSAS
HOWARD COUNTY ARKANSAS
JACKSON COUNTY ARKANSAS
JEFFERSON COUNTY ARKANSAS
JOHNSON COUNTY ARKANSAS
LAFAYETTE COUNTY ARKANSAS
LEE COUNTY ARKANSAS
LINCOLN COUNTY ARKANSAS
LITTLE RIVER COUNTY ARKANSAS

The way to right wrongs is to turn the light of truth upon them.

—IDA B. WELLS

Some lynching victims were targeted for their efforts to organize Black communities for political and economic equality. Others were lynched for refusing to address a white man as "sir" or for demanding to be served at the counter in a segregated soda shop. Hundreds were lynched based on accusations of offenses like arson, robbery, nonsexual assault, and vagrancy. In a strictly maintained racial caste system, white lives and white property held heightened value, while the lives of Black people held little or none.

Nearly 25 percent of African American lynching victims were accused of sexual assault and nearly 30 percent were accused of murder. Because African Americans were presumed guilty and dangerous, accusations lodged against them were rarely scrutinized. Nearly all were lynched without an investigation, much less a trial. Efforts to pass federal anti-lynching legislation repeatedly failed because of opposition by Southern elected officials. Only 1 percent of lynchings committed after 1900 led to a criminal conviction.

With no protection from the constant threat of death, nearly six million Black Americans fled the South between 1910 and 1970. Many left behind their homes, families, businesses, and jobs to flee racial terror as traumatized refugees. Lynching profoundly reshaped the geographic, political, social, and economic conditions of African Americans in ways still evident today.

Lynchings in America were not isolated hate crimes committed by rogue vigilantes; they were targeted acts of racial violence perpetrated to uphold an unjust social order. Lynchings were terrorism.

Racial terror lynching left thousands dead; significantly marginalized Black people politically, financially, and socially; and inflicted deep trauma on the entire African American community. White people who witnessed, participated in, and socialized their children in a culture that tolerated gruesome lynchings also were psychologically damaged. State officials' tolerance of lynching created enduring national and institutional wounds that have not yet healed.

Lynchings occurred in communities where African Americans today remain marginalized, disproportionately poor, overrepresented in prisons and jails, and underrepresented in decision-making roles in the criminal justice system.

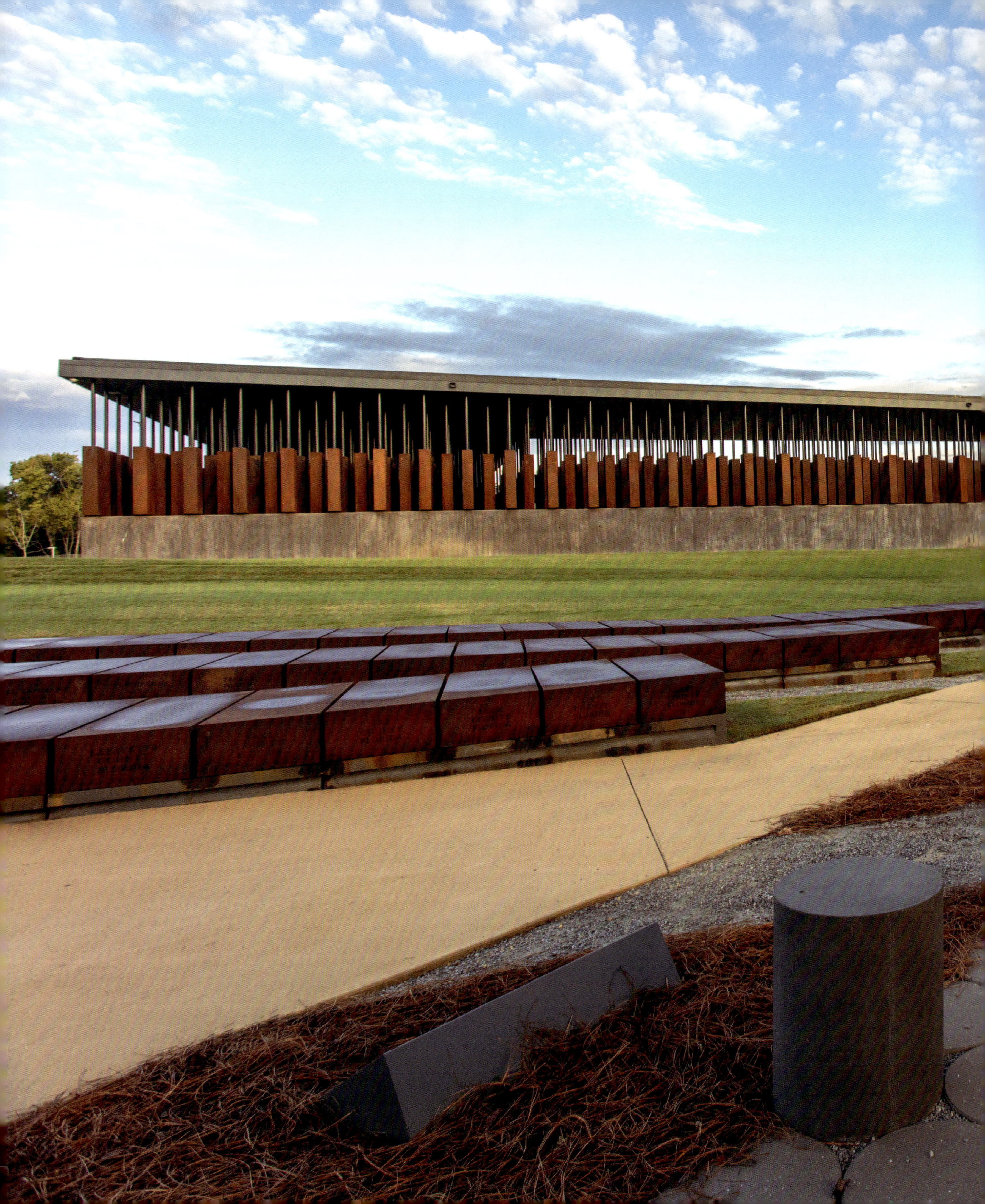

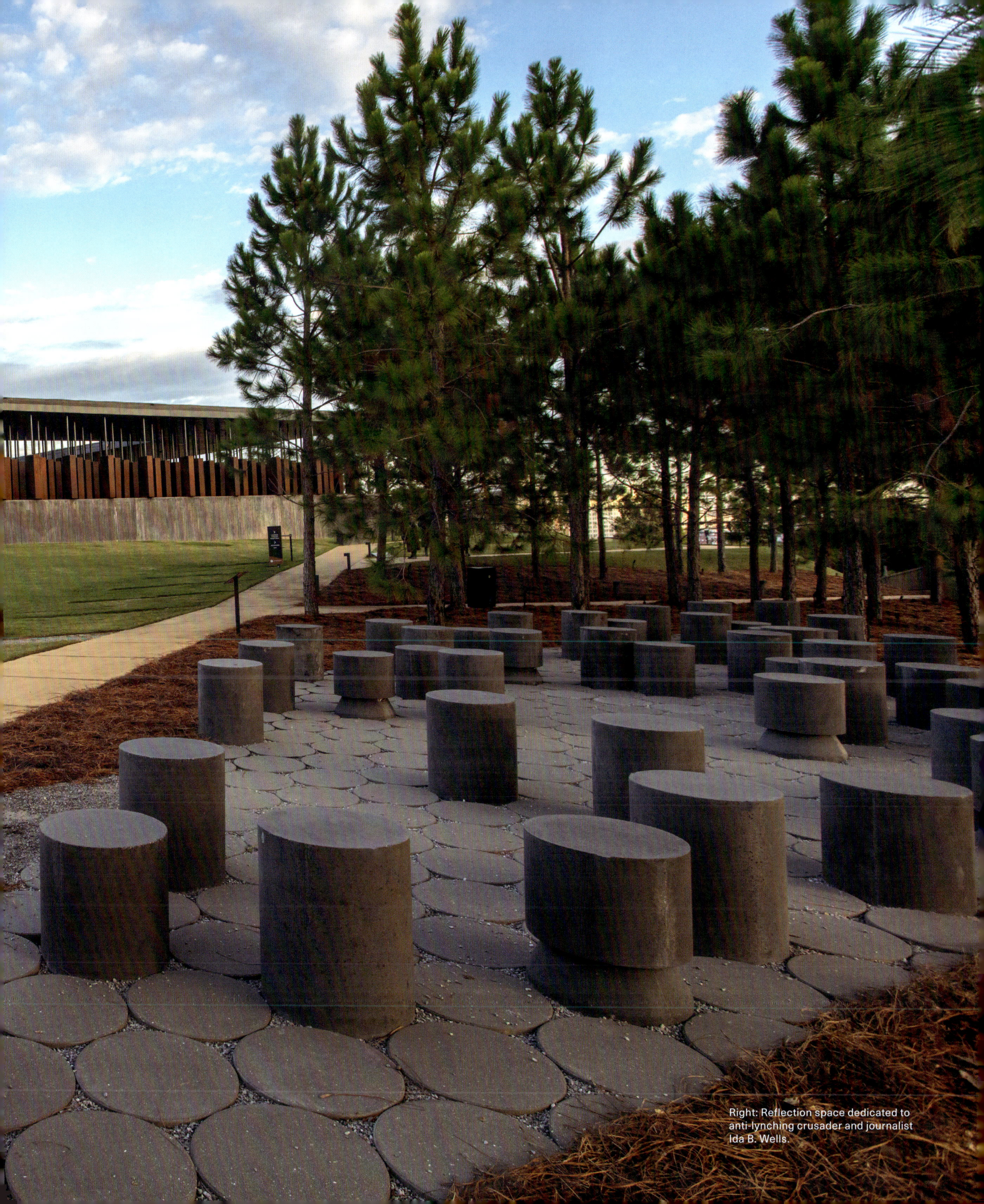

Right: Reflection space dedicated to anti-lynching crusader and journalist Ida B. Wells.

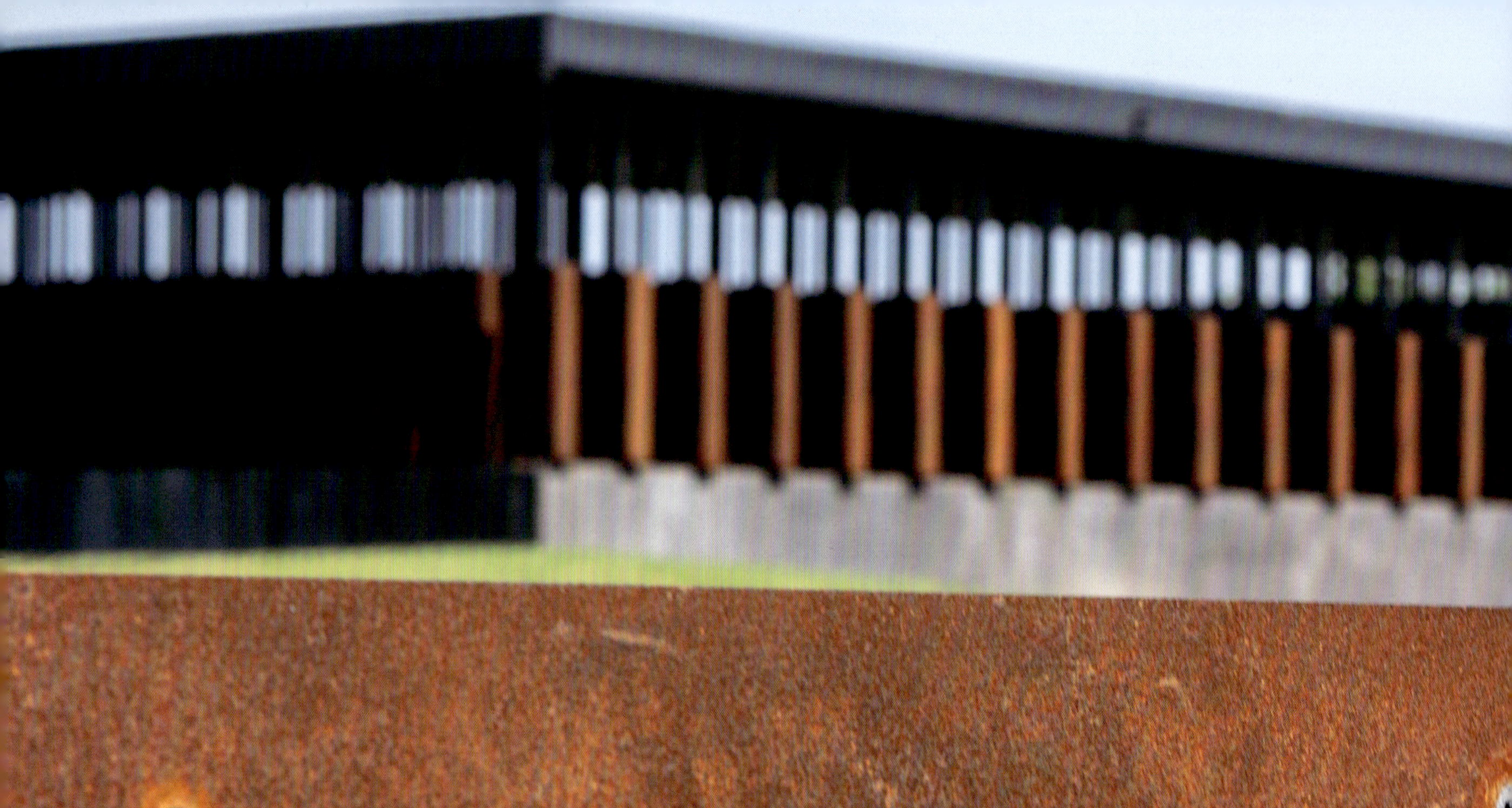
SCOTT
COUNTY
MISSISSIPPI

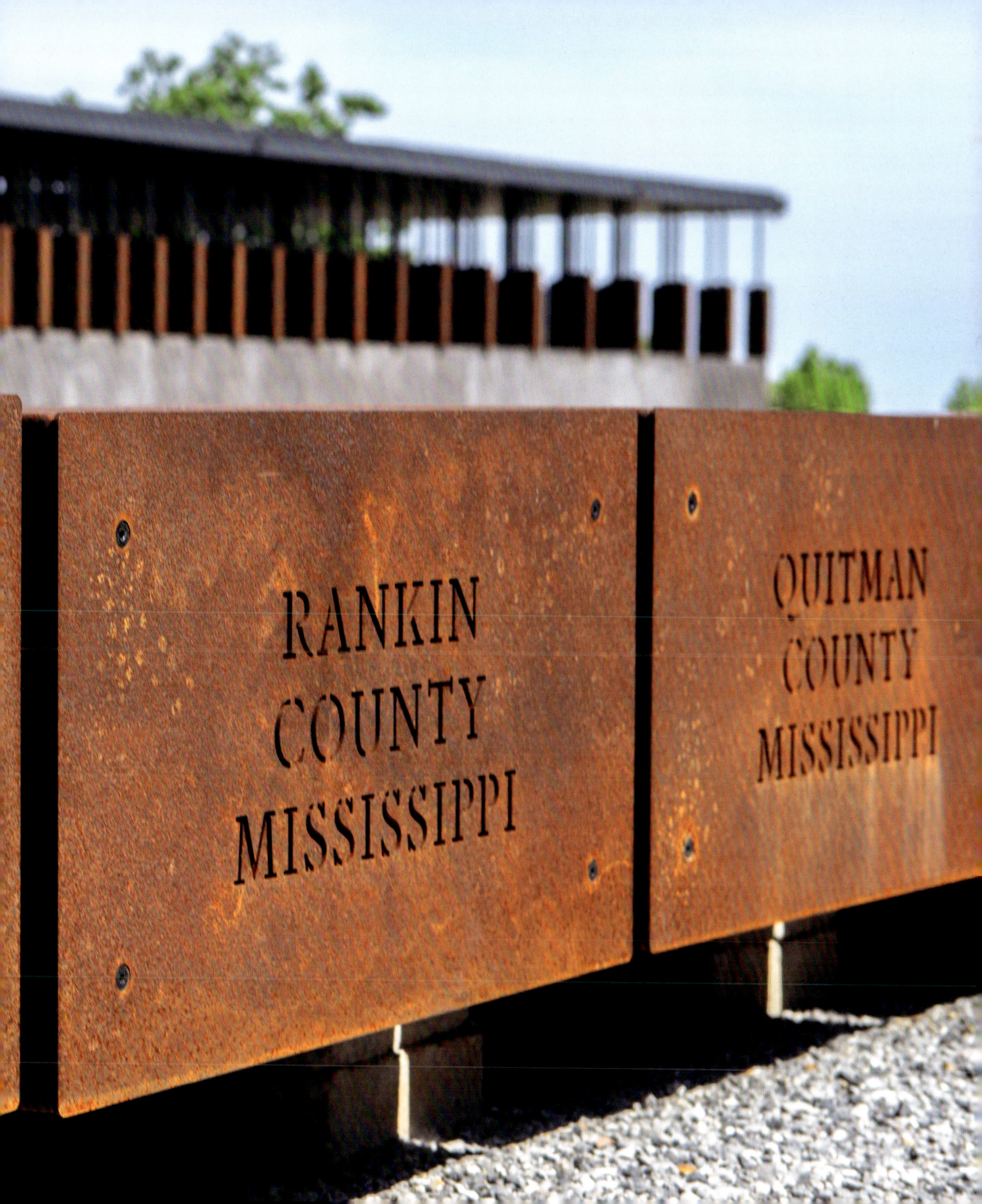
RANKIN
COUNTY
MISSISSIPPI
QUITMAN
COUNTY
MISSISSIPPI

At this memorial, we remember the thousands killed, the generations of Black people terrorized, and the legacy of suffering and injustice that haunts us still. We remember the countless victims whose deaths were not recorded in news archives and cannot be documented, those who are recognized solely in the mournful memories of those who loved them.

We believe that telling the truth about the age of racial terror and reflecting together on this period and its legacy can lead to a more thoughtful and informed commitment to justice today. We hope this memorial will inspire individuals, communities, and this nation to claim our difficult history and commit to a just and peaceful future.

In 1915, Mamie Lang Kirkland was just seven years old when her father and his friend were threatened with lynching and her family was forced to flee their home in Ellisville, Mississippi. The friend returned to Ellisville and was brutally killed by a mob of thousands in a lynching that was advertised on the front page of newspapers as far away as New Orleans.

She married and raised a family of her own, but Mrs. Kirkland never forgot the terror of running from home or the lynching that could have happened to her father. Though she could not recall the lynched man's name, she held strong the duty to remember and made sure her children knew the story. She vowed never to return to Mississippi.

But in 2015, when her son Tarabu showed her an article printed in EJI's report "Lynching in America" that detailed the lynching of John Hartfield in Ellisville in 1919, she instantly recognized the name of her father's friend. "That's him," she said. Tarabu decided to go to Ellisville, and Mrs. Kirkland went with him, returning to her birthplace one hundred years after she fled in terror.

At the opening of the National Memorial for Peace and Justice, Mamie Kirkland exemplified the power of memorializing this history as she vowed, "I will never forget."

Thousands of African Americans are unknown victims of racial terror lynchings whose deaths cannot be documented, many whose names will never be known.

They are all honored here.

Tell my people to go west. There is no justice for them here.

—THOMAS MOSS, LAST WORDS BEFORE HE WAS LYNCHED IN MEMPHIS, TENNESSEE, IN 1892

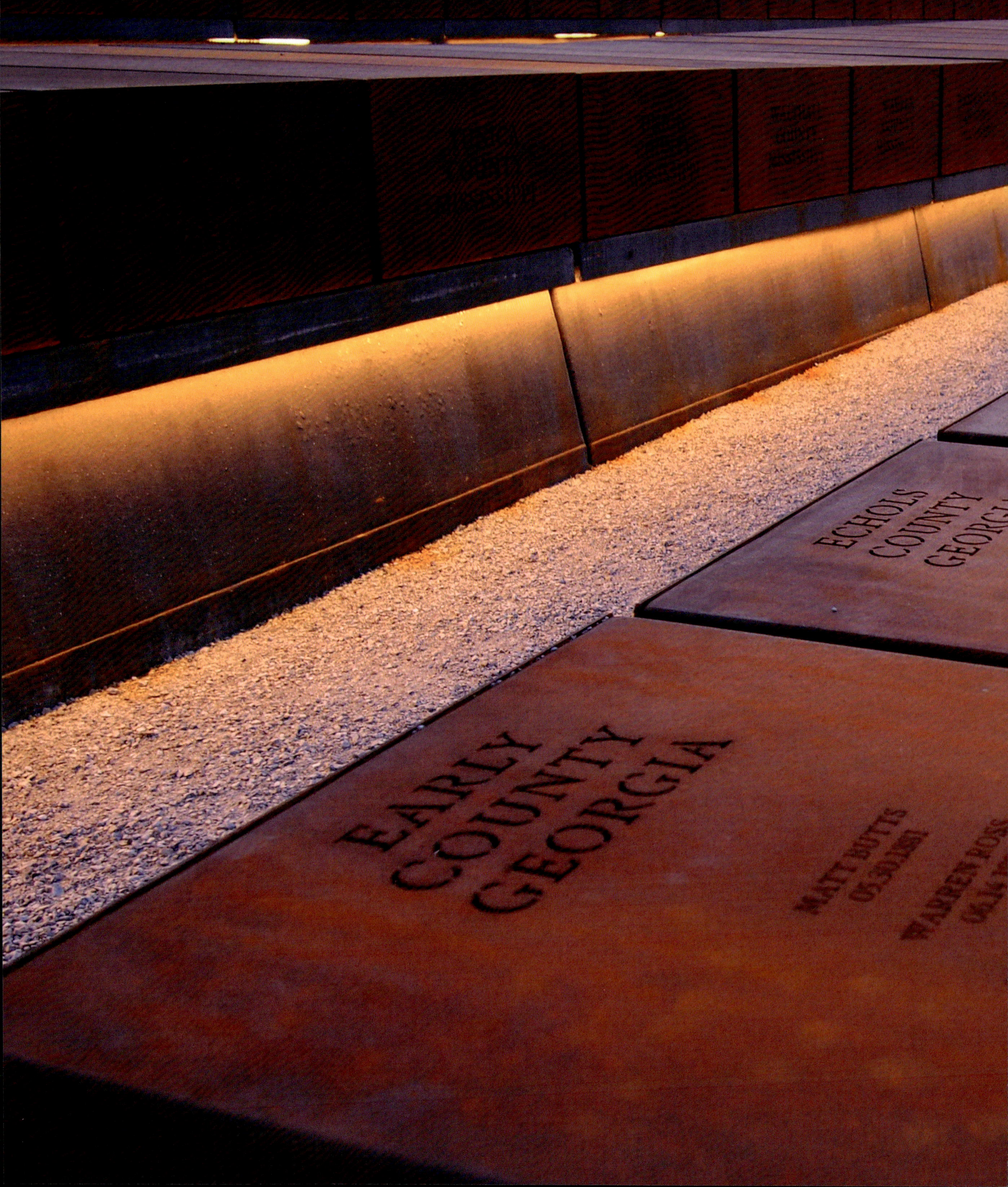
ECHOLS
COUNTY
EARLY
COUNTY
GEORGIA
MATT BUTTS
WARREN ROSS

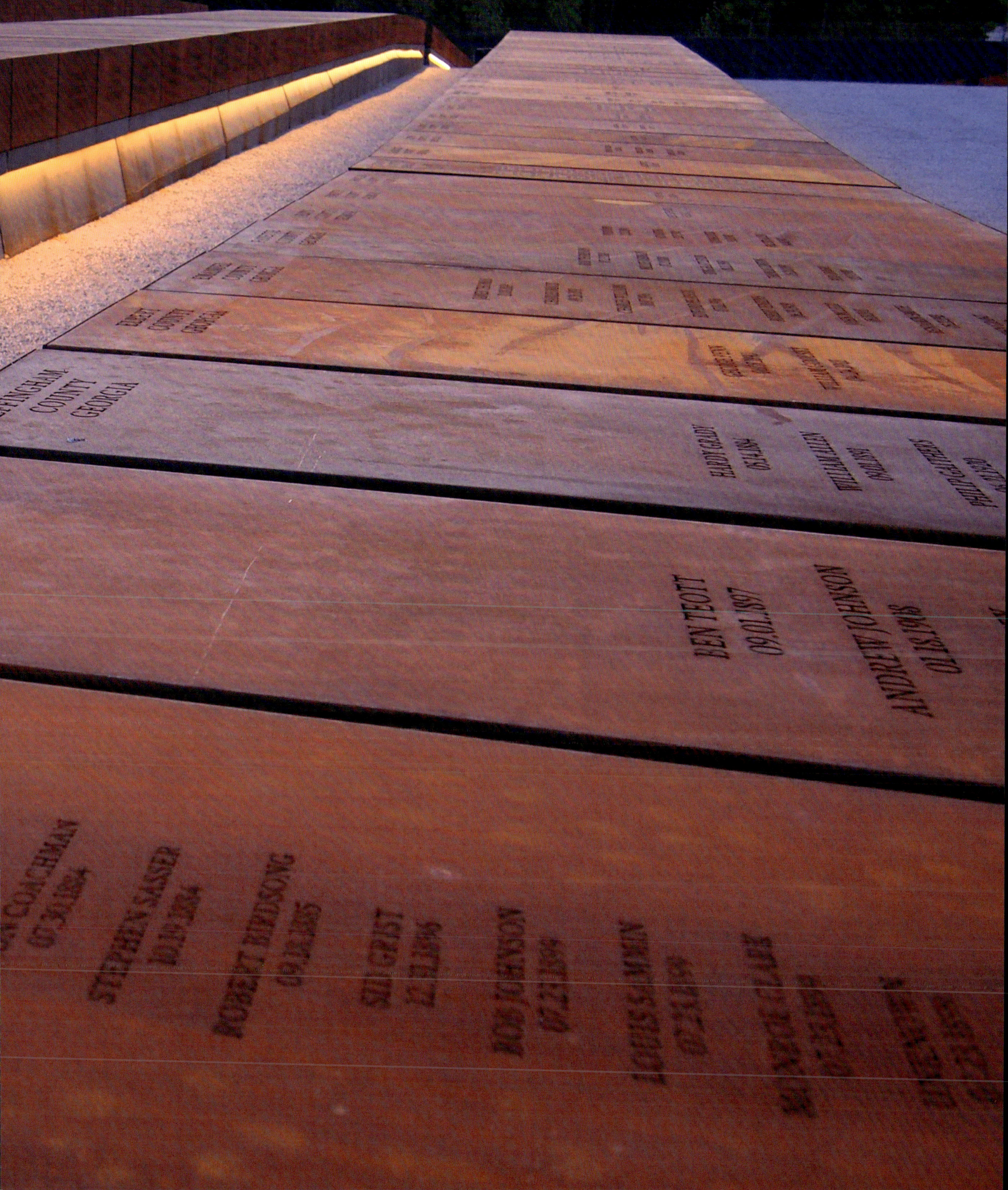
COUNTY
GEORGIA
HARDY GRADY
WILLIAM ALLEN
BEN TEOTT
09.01.1897
ANDREW JOHNSON
STEPHEN SASSER
ROBERT BIRDSONG
BOB JOHNSON

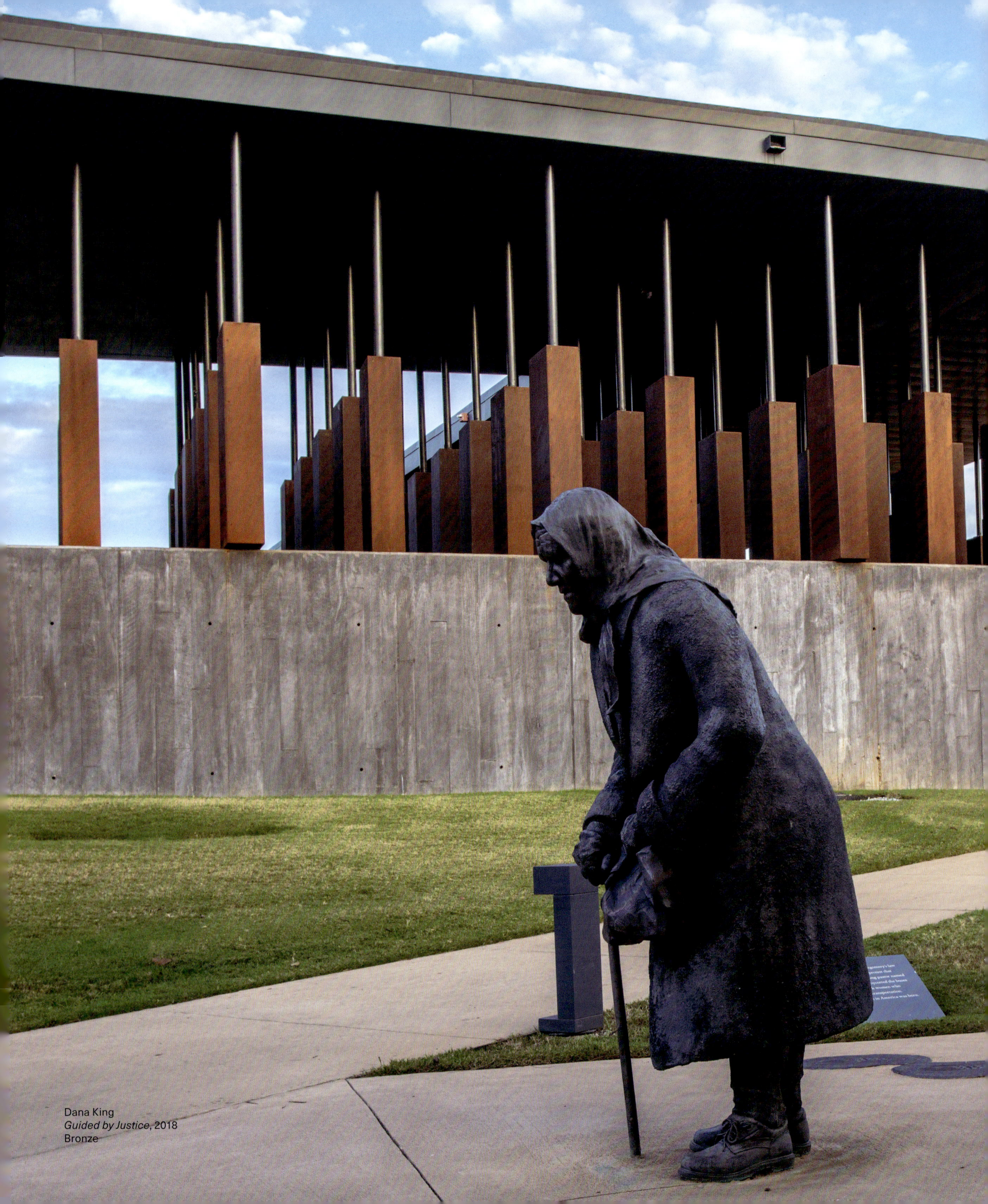

Dana King
Guided by Justice, 2018
Bronze

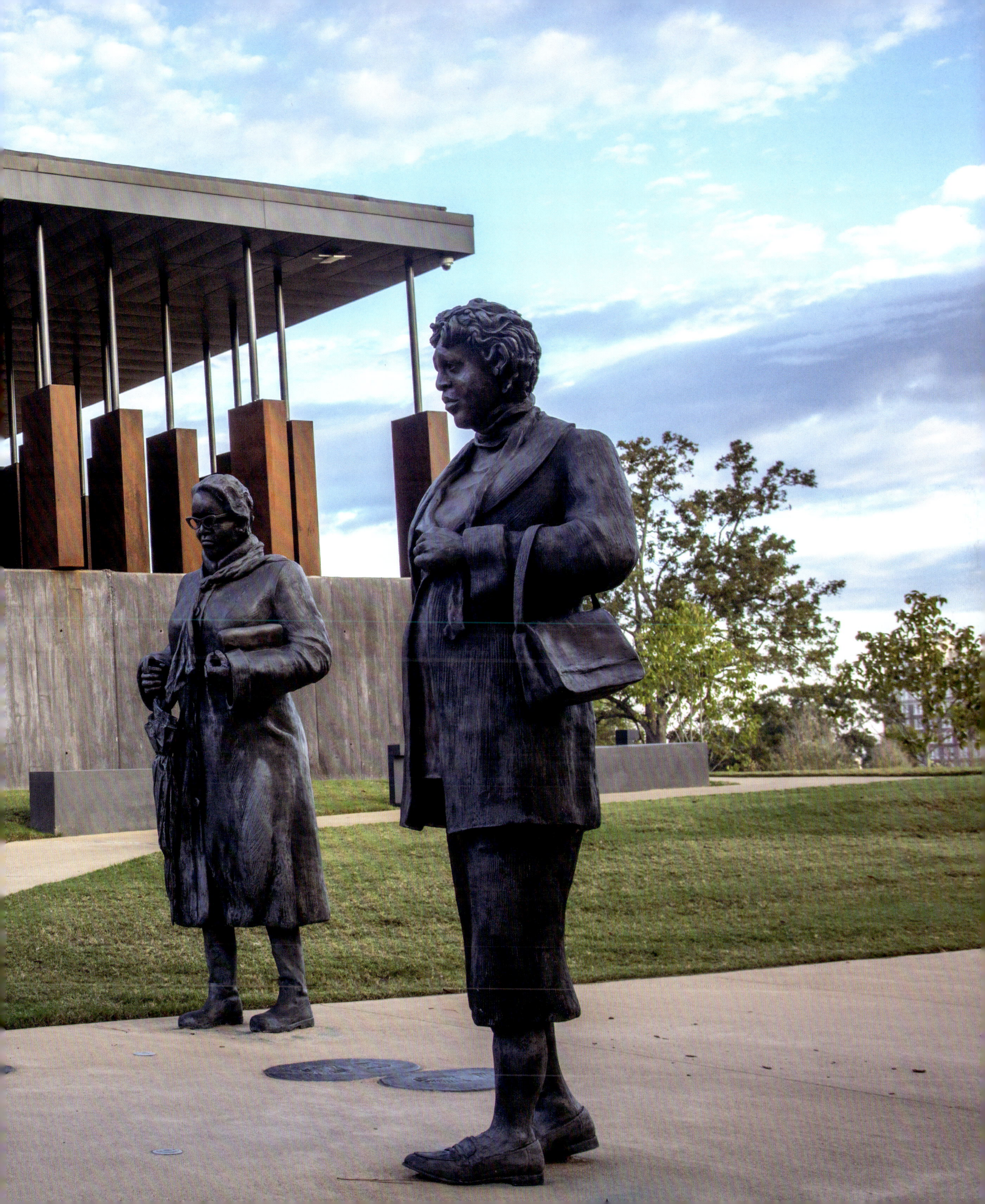

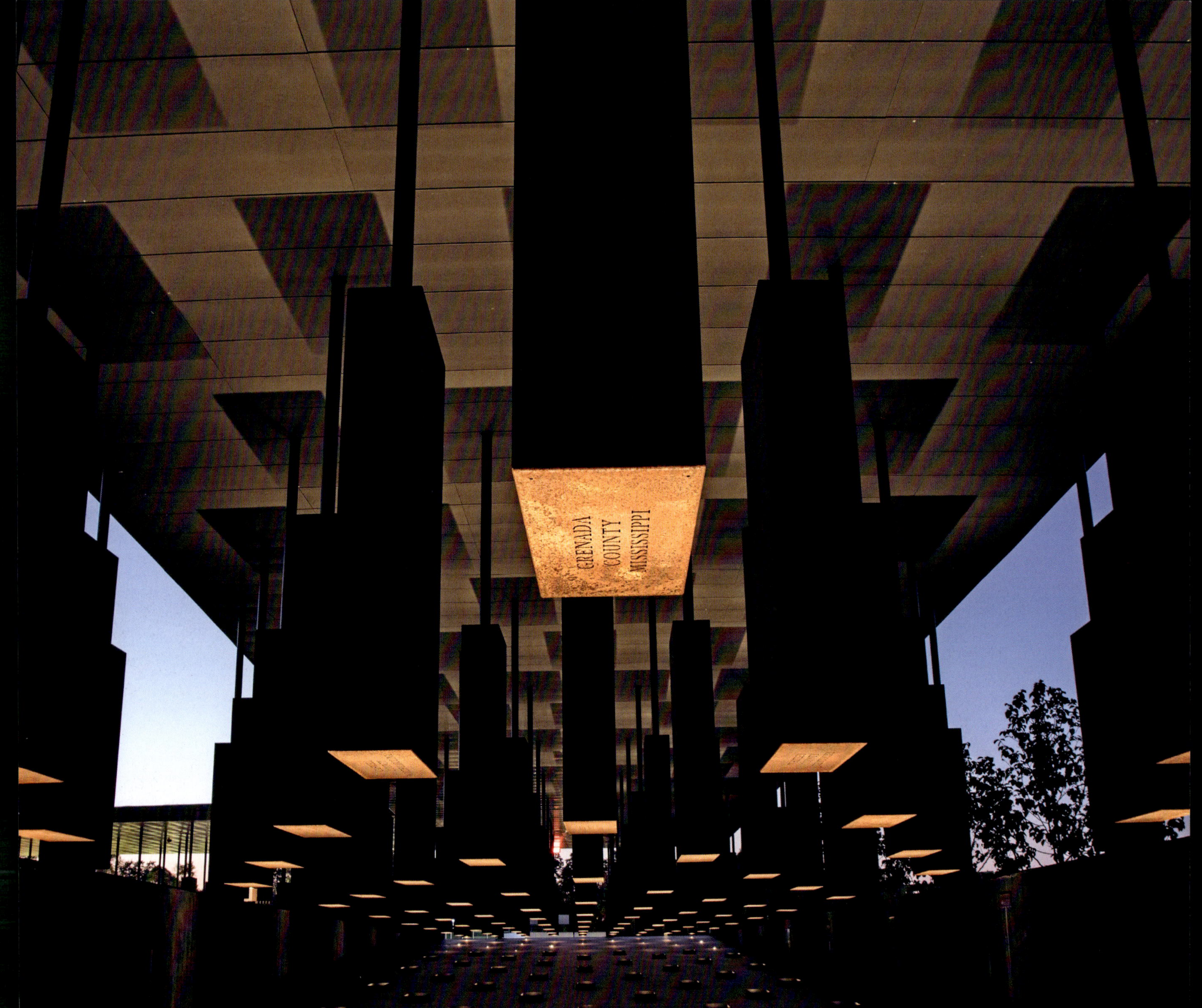
GRENADA
COUNTY
MISSISSIPPI

Zachariah Walker was burned alive by a lynch mob of more than one thousand men, women, and children in Coatesville, Pennsylvania, in 1911.

Thomas Miles Sr., was lynched in Shreveport, Louisiana, in 1912 for allegedly writing a note to a white woman.

Anthony Crawford was lynched in Abbeville, South Carolina, in 1916 for rejecting a white merchant's bid for cottonseed.

Dozens of men, women, and children, were lynched in a massacre in East St. Louis, Illinois, in 1917.

Marcel Ruffin was lynched in Garyville, Louisiana, in 1917, after he was accused of vagrancy.

Ell Persons was lynched by a mob of five thousand people in Memphis, Tennessee, in 1917.

Charles Shipman was lynched in Fort Bend County, Texas, in 1918 for arguing with the white owner of the plantation where he lived and worked.

Mary Turner was lynched, with **her unborn child**, at Folsom Bridge at the Brooks-Lowndes County line in Georgia in 1918 for complaining about the recent lynching of her husband, **Hayes Turner**.

Hundreds of Black men, women, and children were lynched in the Elaine Massacre in Phillips County, Arkansas, in 1919.

Will Brown was lynched in Omaha, Nebraska, in 1919 by a riotous white mob of up to fifteen thousand people.

Elias Clayton, **Isaac McGhie**, and **Elmer Jackson** were lynched by a mob of ten thousand people in Duluth, Minnesota, in 1920.

George Hawkins, **Carrie Diamond**, **Eliza Talbot**, and **Nelson Talbot** were among dozens lynched during the Tulsa Massacre in Tulsa, Oklahoma, in 1921.

Charles Atkins, fifteen, was burned alive in 1922 by a white mob of more than one thousand people in Washington County, Georgia.

Grant Cole was lynched in Montgomery, Alabama, in 1925 after he refused to run an errand for a white woman.

Henry Patterson was lynched in LaBelle, Florida, in 1926 for asking a white woman for a drink of water.

Laura Wood was lynched in Barber, North Carolina, in 1930 after a white merchant said she stole a ham.

Lacy Mitchell was lynched in Thomasville, Georgia, in 1930 for testifying against a white man accused of raping a Black woman.

George Armwood was lynched and burned by a mob of more than one thousand people in Princess Anne, Maryland, in 1933.

Elizabeth Lawrence was lynched in Birmingham, Alabama, in 1933 for reprimanding white children who threw rocks at her.

Henry Bedford, a seventy-four-year-old formerly enslaved man, was lynched in Pelahatchie, Mississippi, in 1934 for "talking disrespectfully" to young white men.

The Reverend T. A. Allen was lynched in Hernando, Mississippi, in 1935 for organizing local sharecroppers.

Otis Price was lynched in Perry, Florida, in 1938 for walking past a window while a white woman was inside bathing.

Jesse Thornton was lynched in Luverne, Alabama, in 1940 for addressing a white police officer without the title "mister."

Elbert Williams was lynched in Brownsville, Tennessee, in 1940 for working to register Black voters as part of the local NAACP.

Ernest Green and **Charlie Lang**, both fourteen years old, were lynched in Shubuta, Mississippi, in 1942 after a white girl said they were threatening.

Malcolm Wright was lynched in Chickasaw County, Mississippi, in 1949 for yielding too little of the roadway to white men as he passed in his wagon.

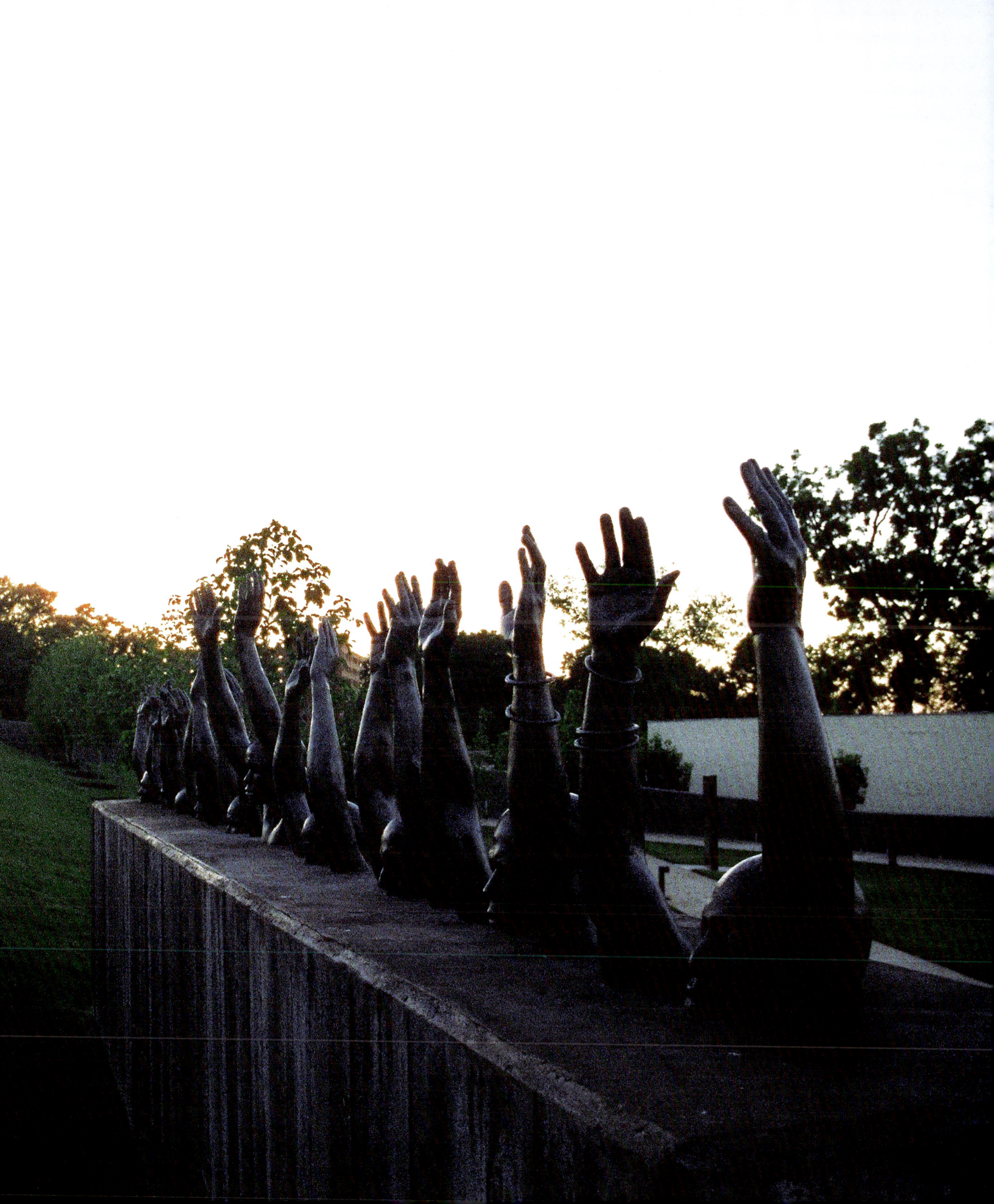

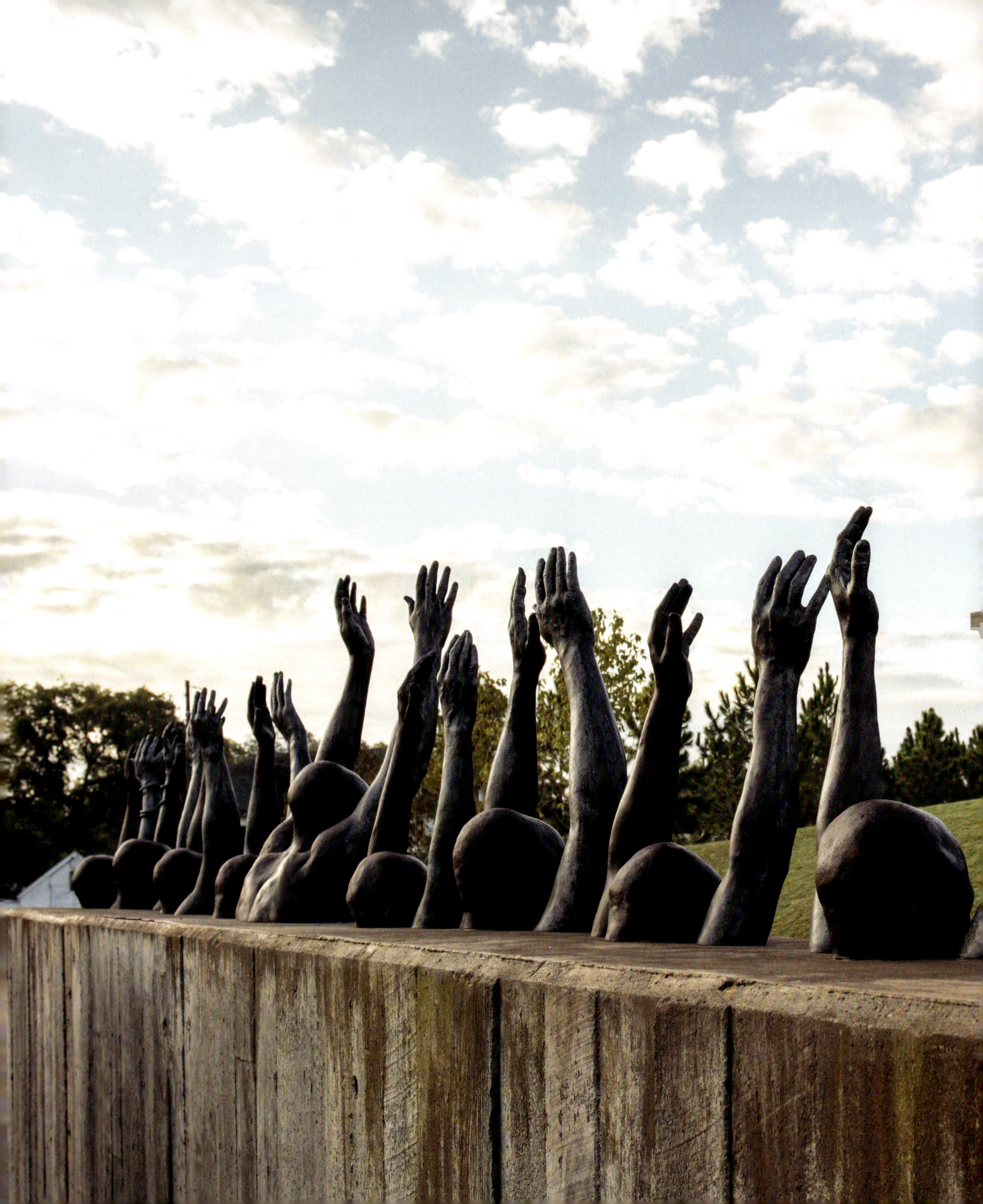

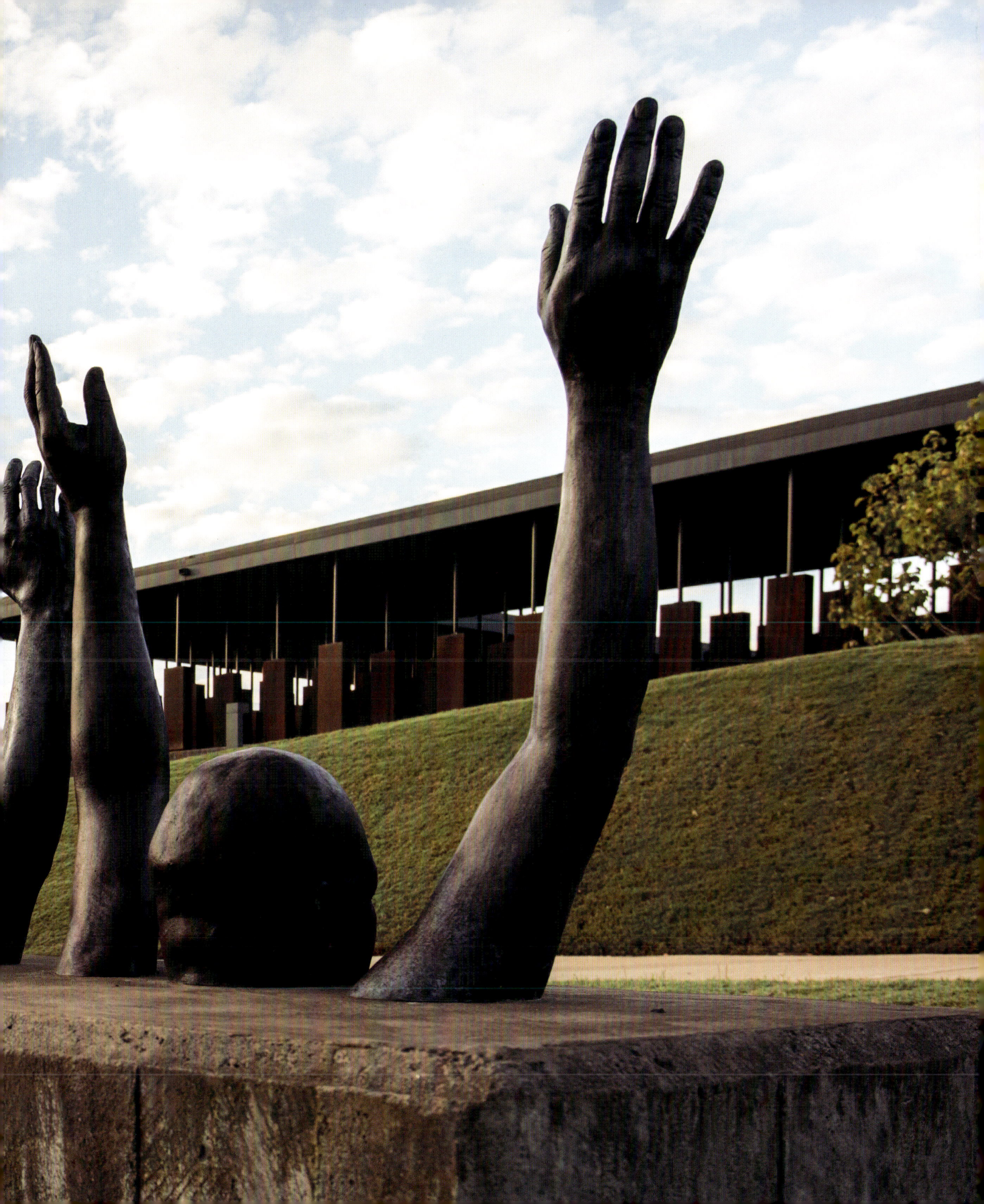

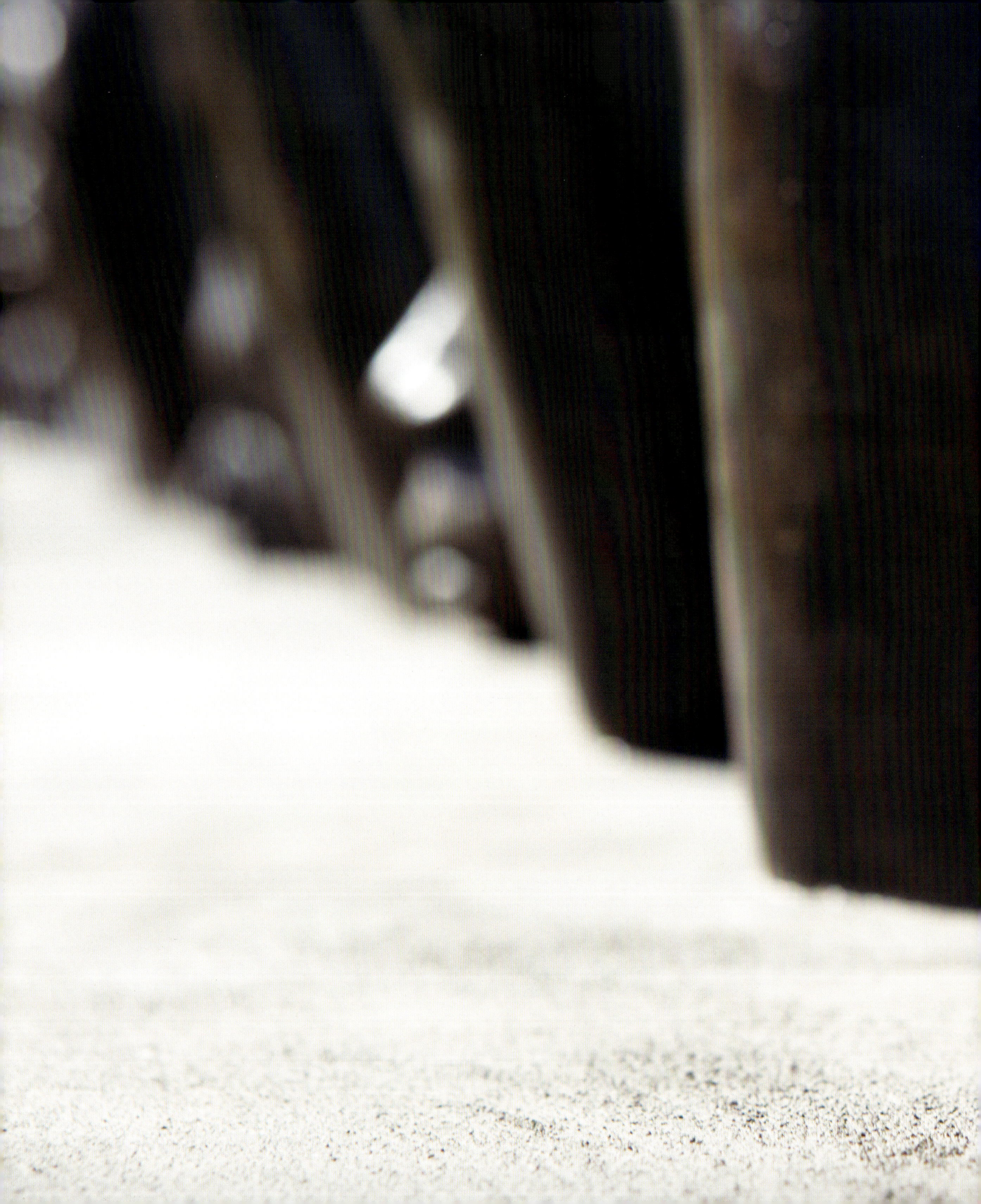

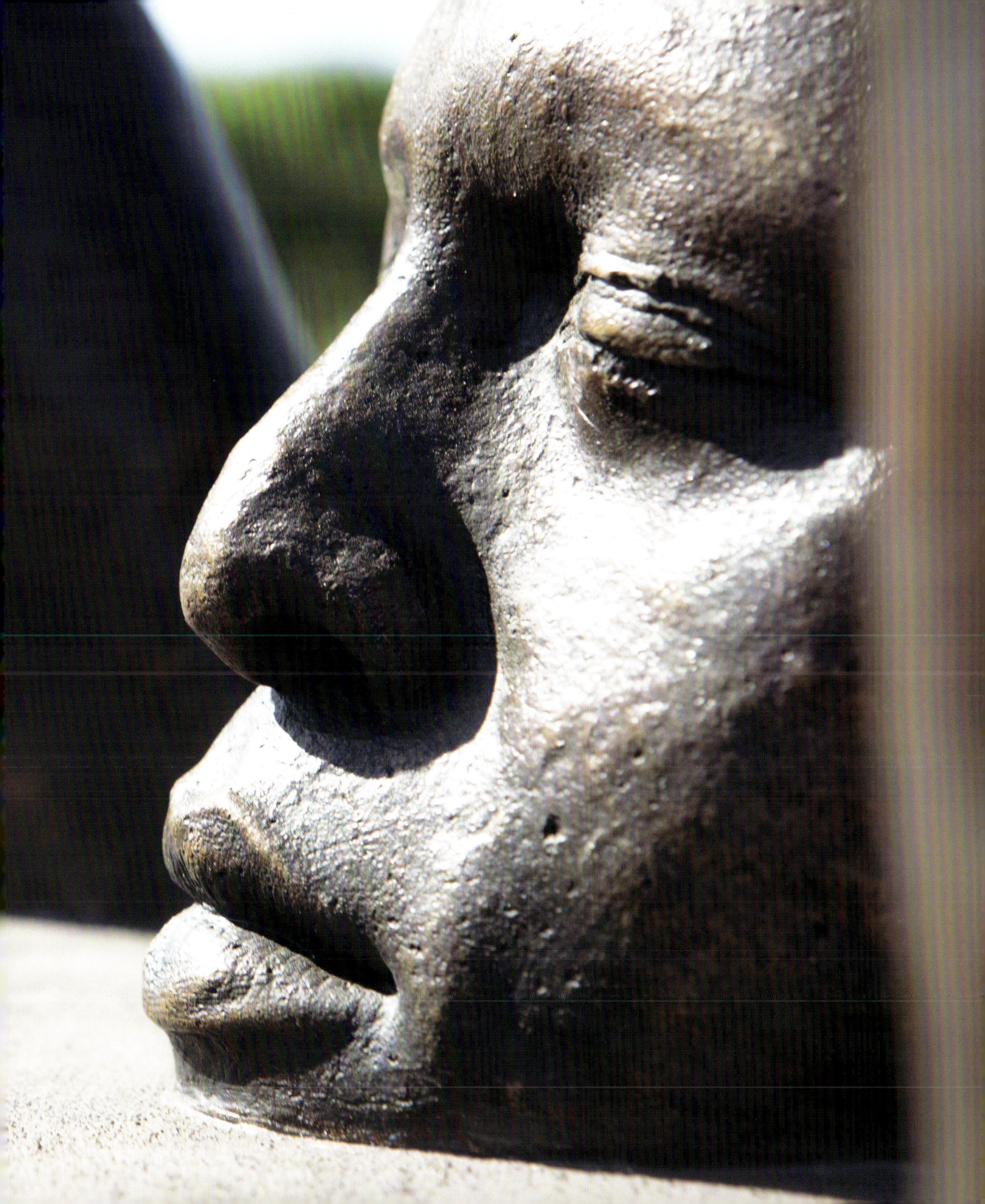

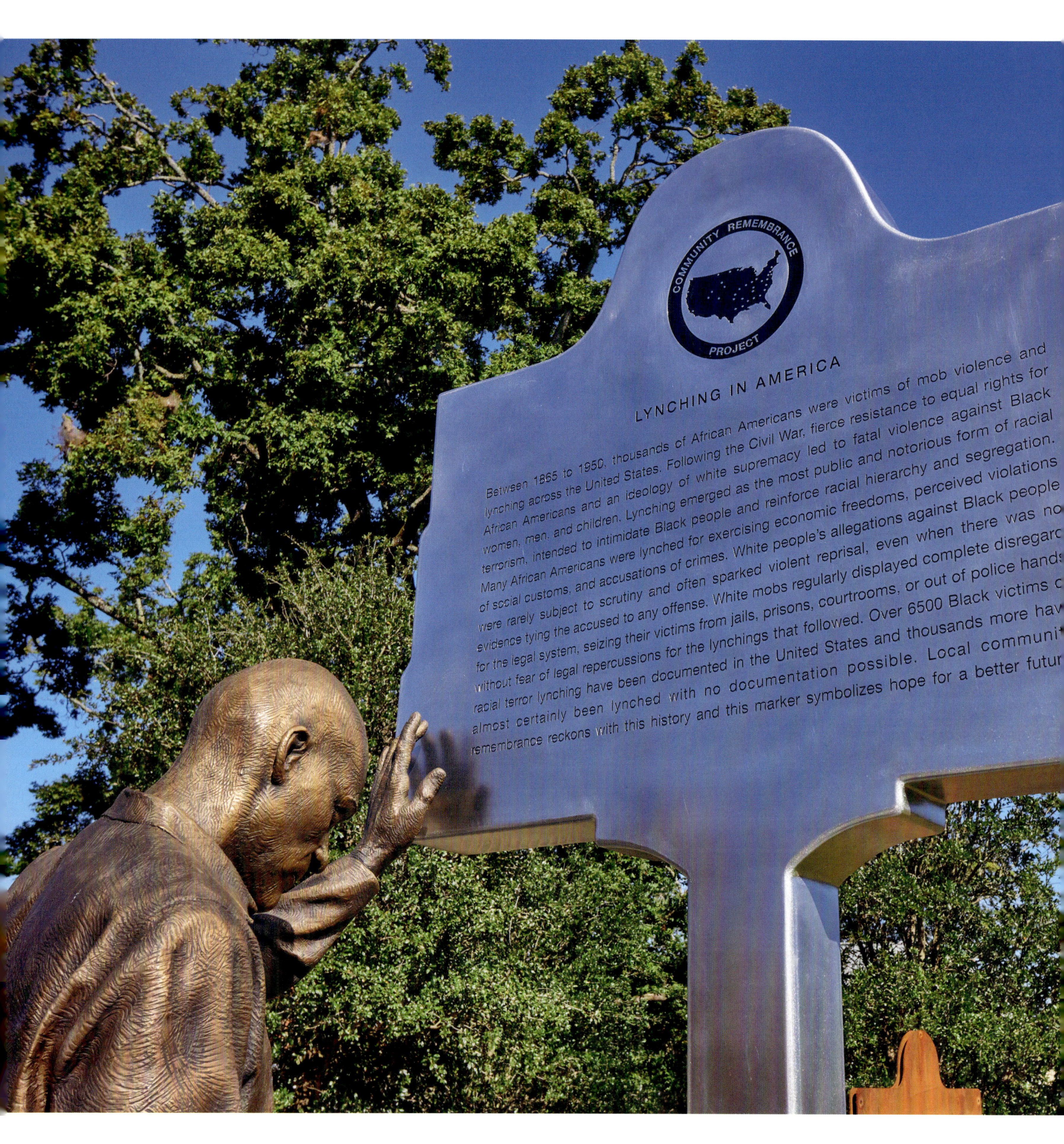
COMMUNITY REMEMBRANCE
PROJECT
LYNCHING IN AMERICA
Between 1865 to 1950, thousands of African Americans were victims of mob violence and
lynching across the United States. Following the Civil War, fierce resistance to equal rights for
African Americans and an ideology of white supremacy led to fatal violence against Black
women, men, and children. Lynching emerged as the most public and notorious form of racial
terrorism, intended to intimidate Black people and reinforce racial hierarchy and segregation.
Many African Americans were lynched for exercising economic freedoms, perceived violations
of social customs, and accusations of crimes. White people's allegations against Black people
were rarely subject to scrutiny and often sparked violent reprisal, even when there was
evidence tying the accused to any offense. White mobs regularly displayed complete
for the legal system, seizing their victims from jails, prisons, courtrooms, or out of police
without fear of legal repercussions for the lynchings that followed. Over 6500 Black victims
racial terror lynching have been documented in the United States and thousands more
almost certainly been lynched with no documentation possible. Local
remembrance reckons with this history and this marker symbolizes hope for a better

Above and pages 168–71:
Branly Cadet
Arise, 2022
Bronze

Community Reckoning

The Memorial expanded in 2022 with the addition of *Arise*, a sculpture by Branly Cadet, and nearly 100 marker monuments that memorialize racial terror lynchings across the U.S. *Arise* features six figures, cast in bronze, who are all modeled on living descendants of a person who was lynched. The marker monuments provide detailed narratives about documented lynchings that amplify and deepen visitors' opportunities to learn about racial terror lynchings in America.

Since 2015, hundreds of community coalitions have partnered with EJI's Community Remembrance Project to install historical markers that memorialize victims of racial terror lynchings in dozens of communities across more than twenty states.

The sculpture celebrates the thousands of citizens engaged in this vital truth and justice work in their own communities.

The Peace and Justice Memorial Garden

Near the entrance to the Memorial, the Peace and Justice Memorial Garden is a serene and beautiful setting for reflection and remembrance. A brick "memory wall" built at the garden's edge bears witness to Montgomery's history of enslavement. Despite the brutality of slavery, enslaved Black people developed highly refined skills as carpenters, blacksmiths, brickmasons, wheelwrights, and engineers.

In the late 1850s, enslaved people made bricks to build the Montgomery Theater, which opened downtown in 1860. The remarkable skill of these enslaved masons is evident in bricks that have endured for more than 150 years. The garden's memory wall is constructed with bricks made by Black people enslaved in Montgomery who endured the humiliation of bondage with strength and skill that remain tangible today.

The Peace and Justice Memorial Center

Located at 414 Caroline Street, across from the entrance to the Memorial, the Peace and Justice Memorial Center opened in 2019 as an extension of the Memorial. Built to enhance the public and community education goals of the Legacy Museum and the Memorial, the center hosts community events with acclaimed artists, writers, and scholars, as well as film screenings and other programs.

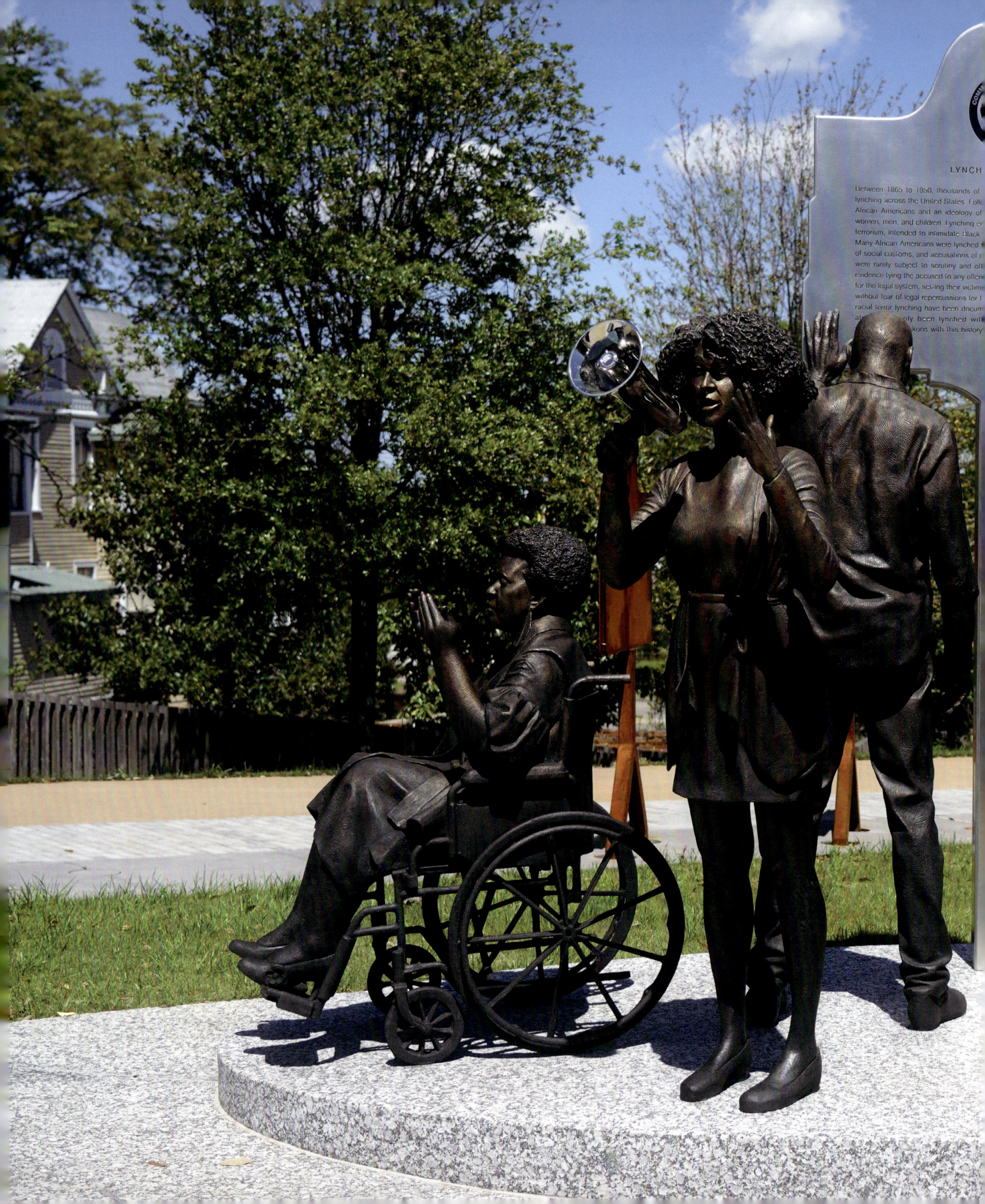

LYNCH
Between 1865 to 1950, thousands of
lynching across the United States.
African Americans and an ideology of
women, men, and children. Lynching
terrorism, intended to intimidate Black
Many African Americans were lynched
of social customs, and accusations of
were rarely subject to scrutiny and
evidence tying the accused to any
for the legal system, seizing their
without fear of legal repercussions for
racial terror lynching have been
been lynched
with this history

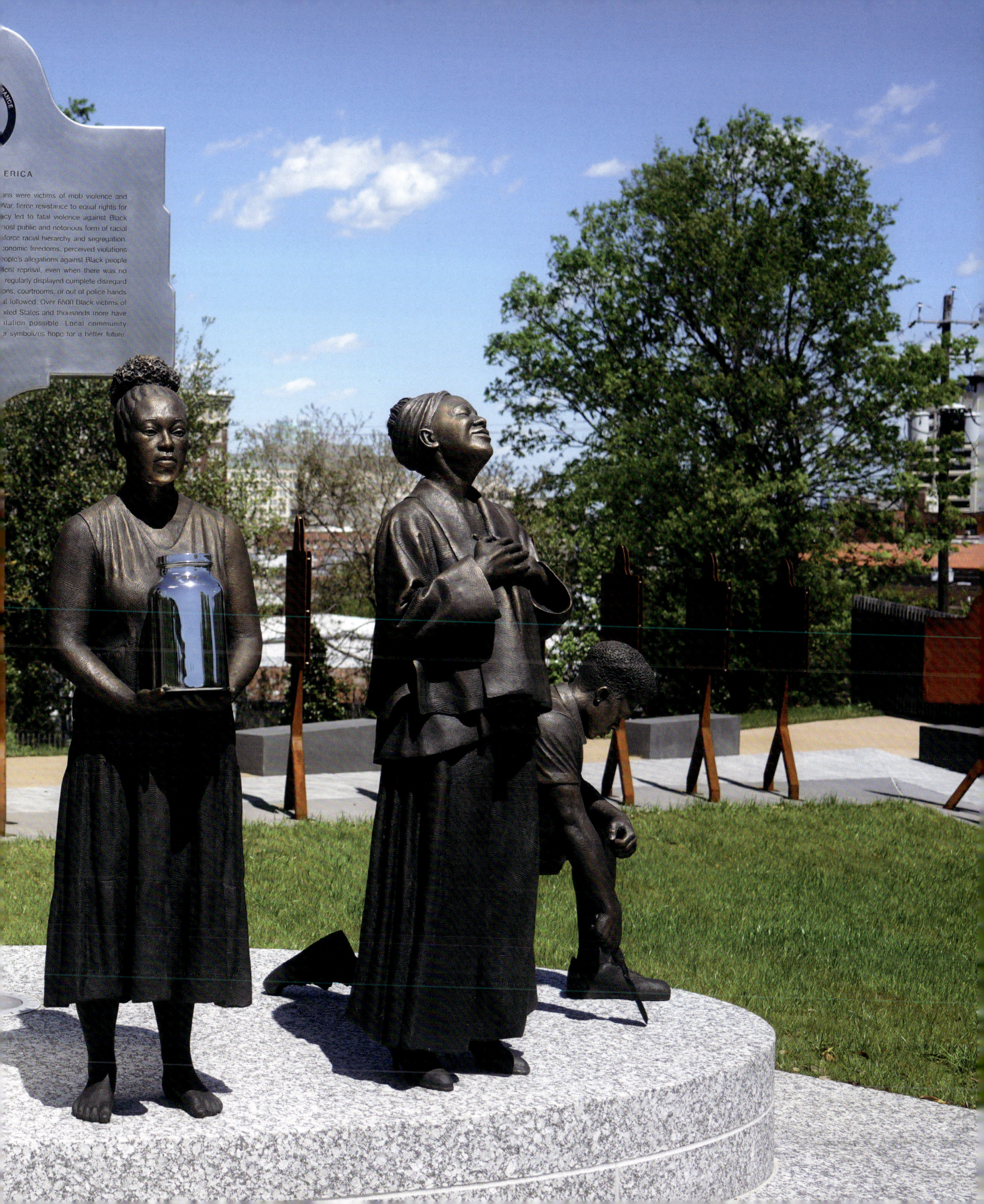
were victims of mob violence and
fierce resistance to equal rights for
led to fatal violence against Black
public and notorious form of racial
racial hierarchy and segregation.
freedoms, perceived violations
allegations against Black people
reprisal, even when there was no
regularly displayed complete disregard
courtrooms, or out of police hands
followed. Over 6500 Black victims of
States and thousands more have
possible. Local community
symbolizes hope for a better future.

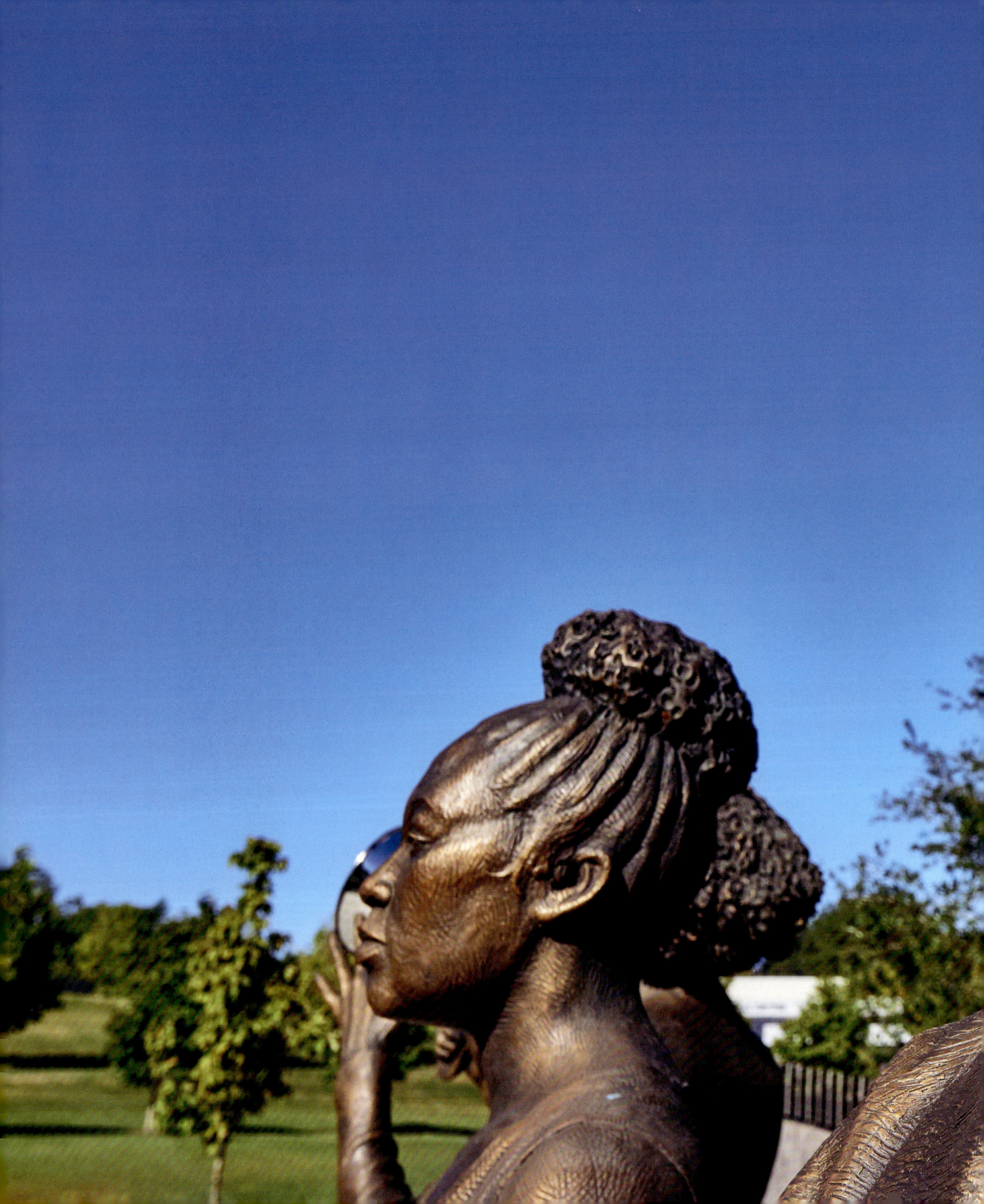

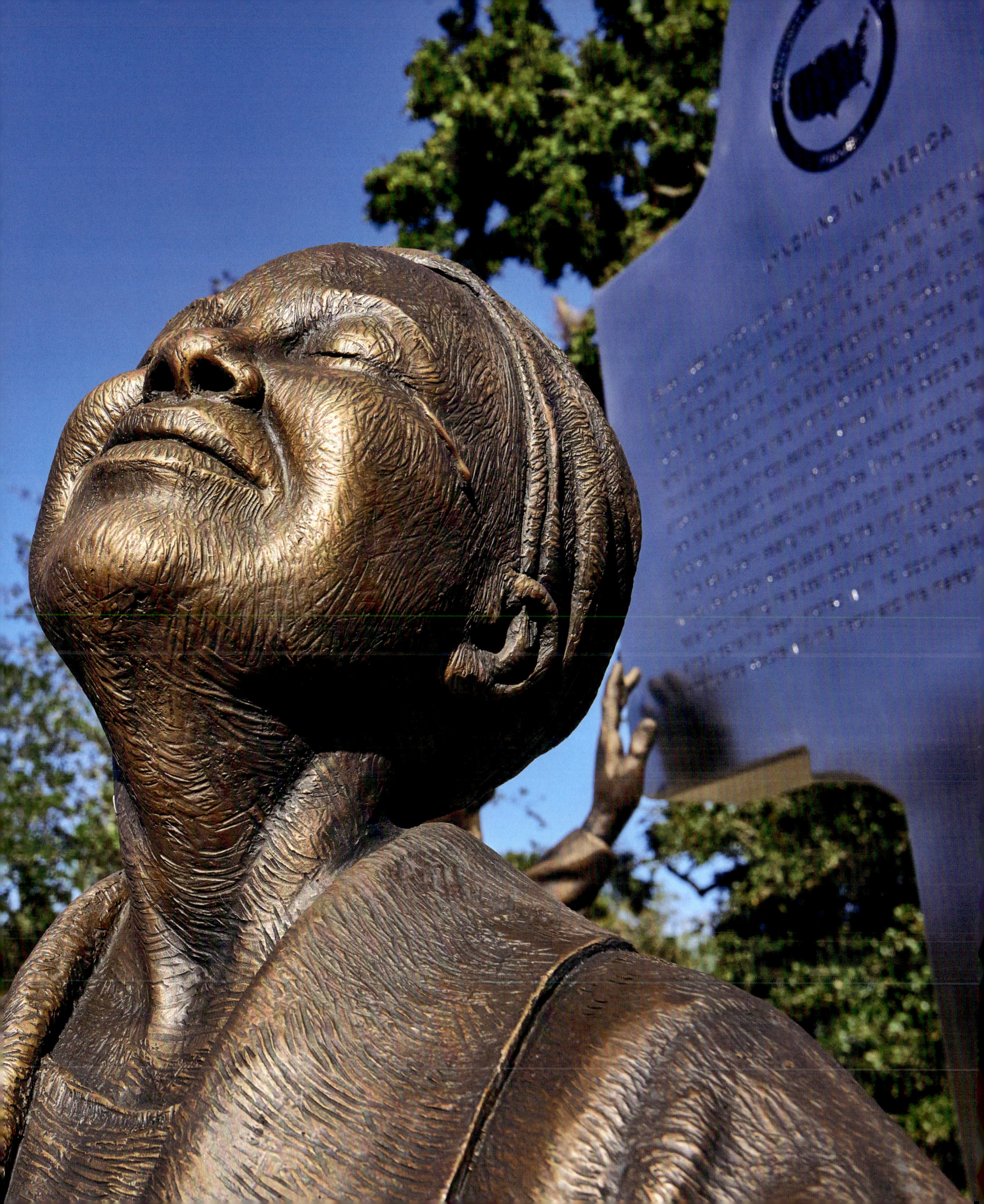
LYNCHING IN AMERICA

It is a space where visitors can continue to learn about America's history of racial inequality, explore the work of EJI, and engage with artists and thought leaders.

The Memorial documents the most active era of racial terror lynchings, from 1877 to 1950. But racially motivated violence and lynchings continued after 1950, often targeting early civil rights leaders and Black people whose success challenged white supremacy.

On April 29, 2019, EJI dedicated a monument at the Peace and Justice Memorial Center that commemorates twenty-four men and women who were lynched or killed in racially motivated attacks during the 1950s, including Emmett Till and voting rights activists Harry and Harriette Moore.

At the dedication ceremony, representatives for each victim laid white roses at the base of the monument as a visual and tangible tribute to their loved ones' lives.

Their deaths sparked protests and activism that fueled more than a decade of social changes. We remember them for their leadership, their humanity, and their role in a long and continuing struggle.

Lynching in Alabama

In Alabama alone, more than 360 lynching victims were shot, hanged, burned, or mutilated, often without even the allegation of a criminal offense, and always without trial or process.

EJI works with communities to commemorate and recognize the traumatic era of racial terror by collecting soil from lynching sites. The Community Soil Collection Project provides a tangible way for community members to confront the legacy of racial terror lynchings and memorialize the African American victims whose lives were lost.

Hundreds of people have visited lynching sites across Alabama to gather soil from them. More than 250 jars of soil are exhibited at the Peace and Justice Memorial Center.

By gathering soil from lynching sites, EJI aims to bear witness to this history and the devastation that racial terrorism wrought upon individuals, families, communities, and our nation as a whole.

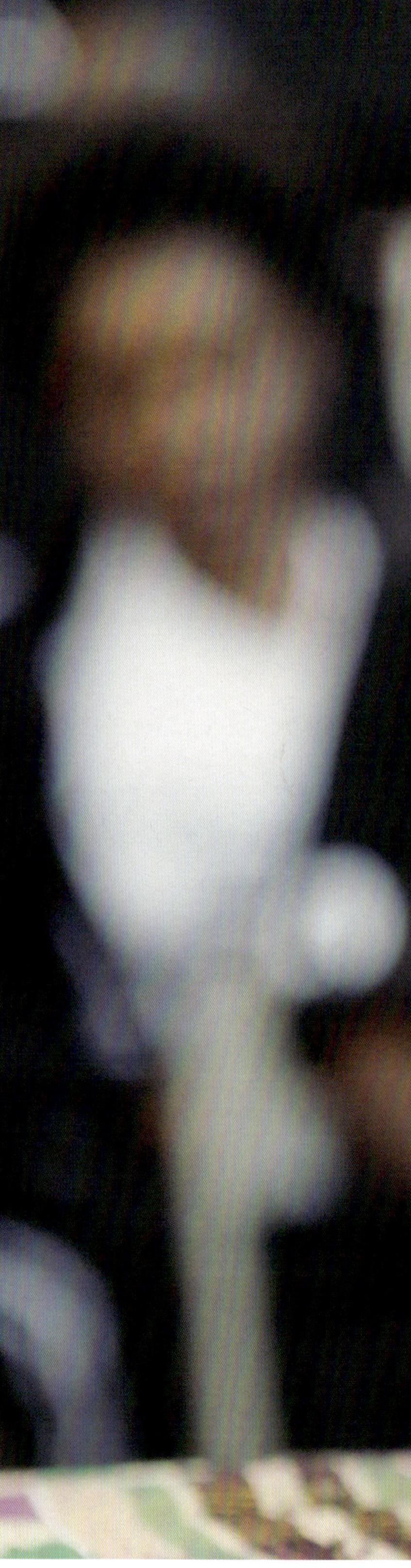

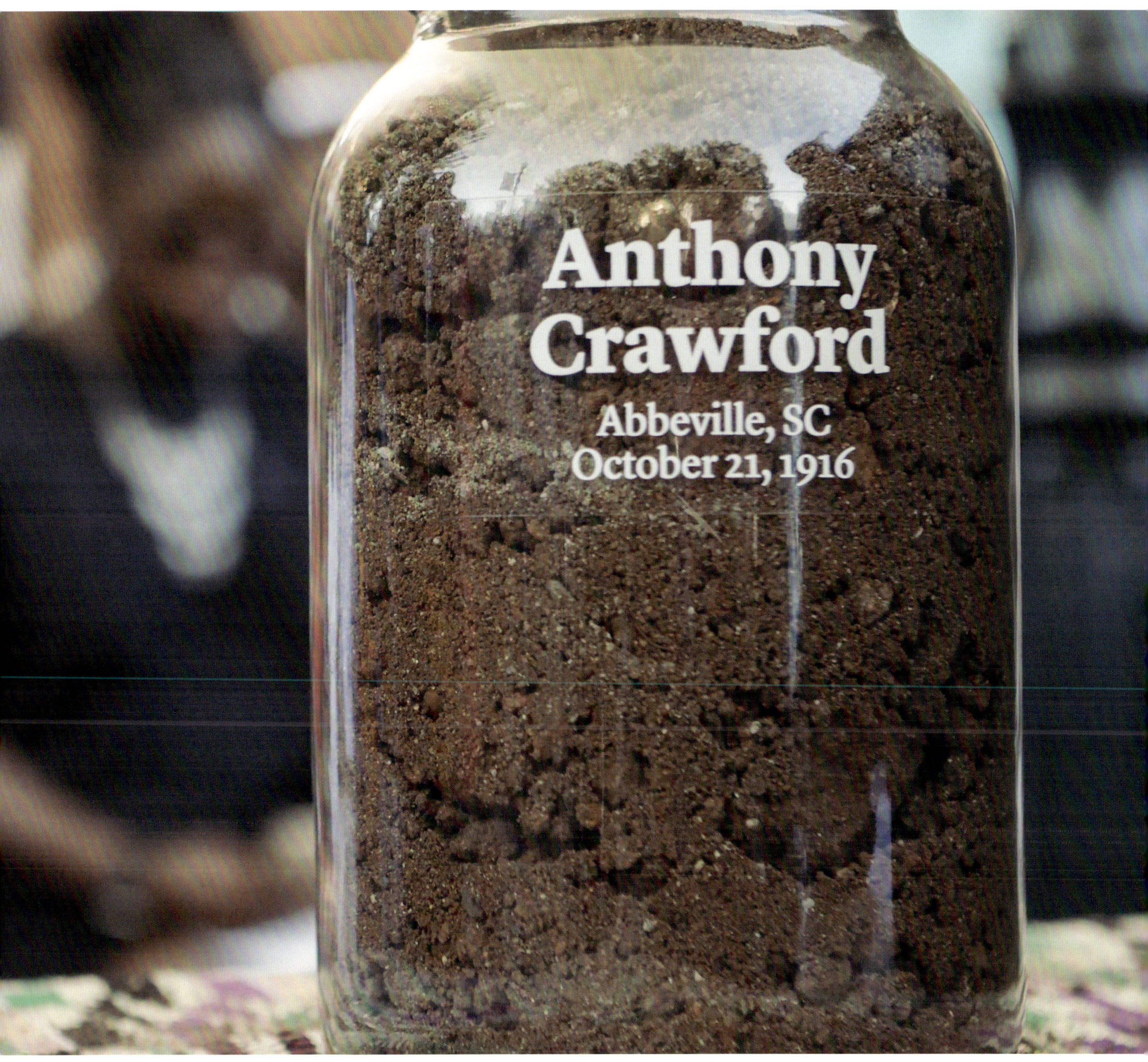
Anthony
Crawford
Abbeville, SC
October 21, 1916

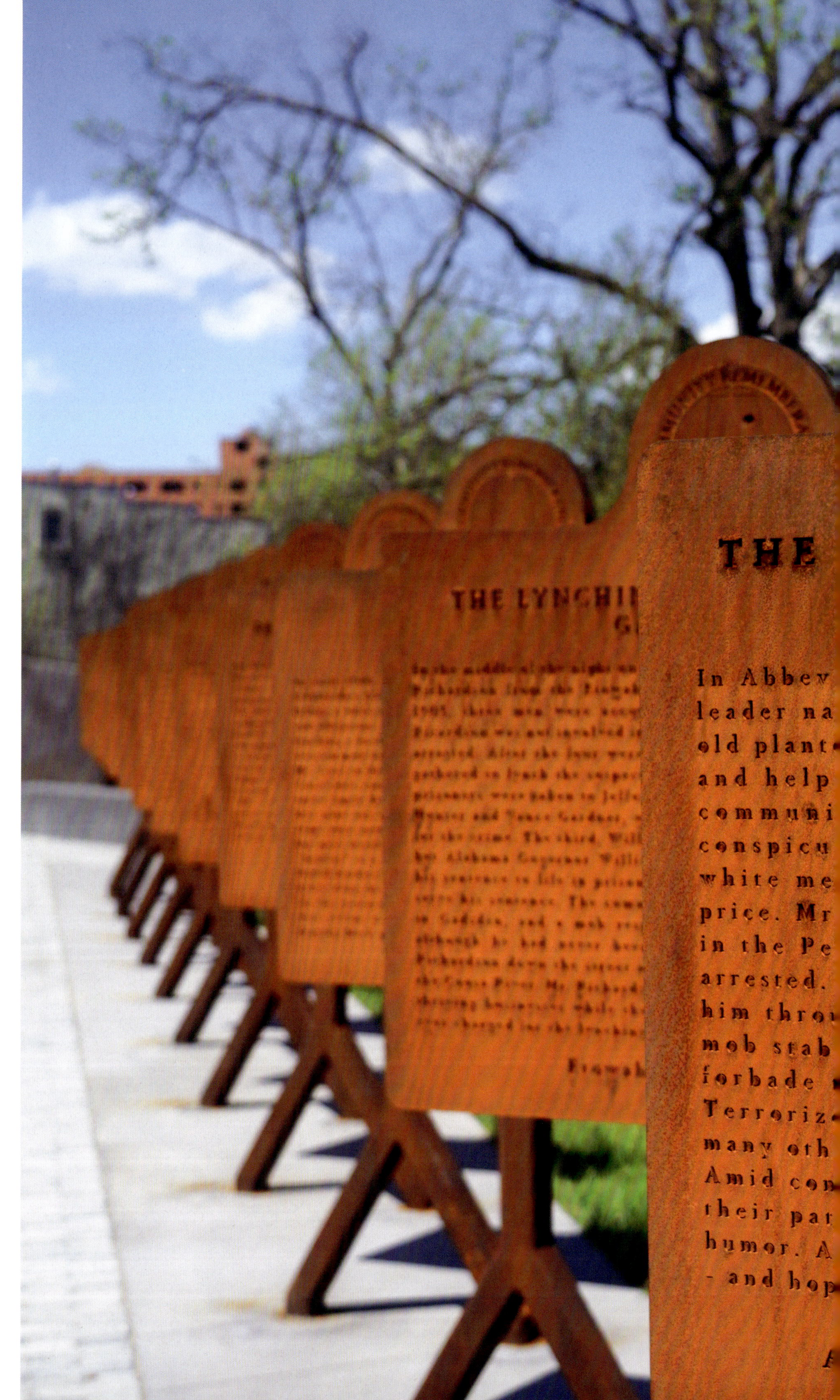
THE
In Abbev
leader na
old plant
and help
communi
conspicu
white me
price. Mr
in the Pe
arrested.
him thro
mob stab
forbade
Terroriz
many oth
Amid con
their pa
humor. A
- and hop

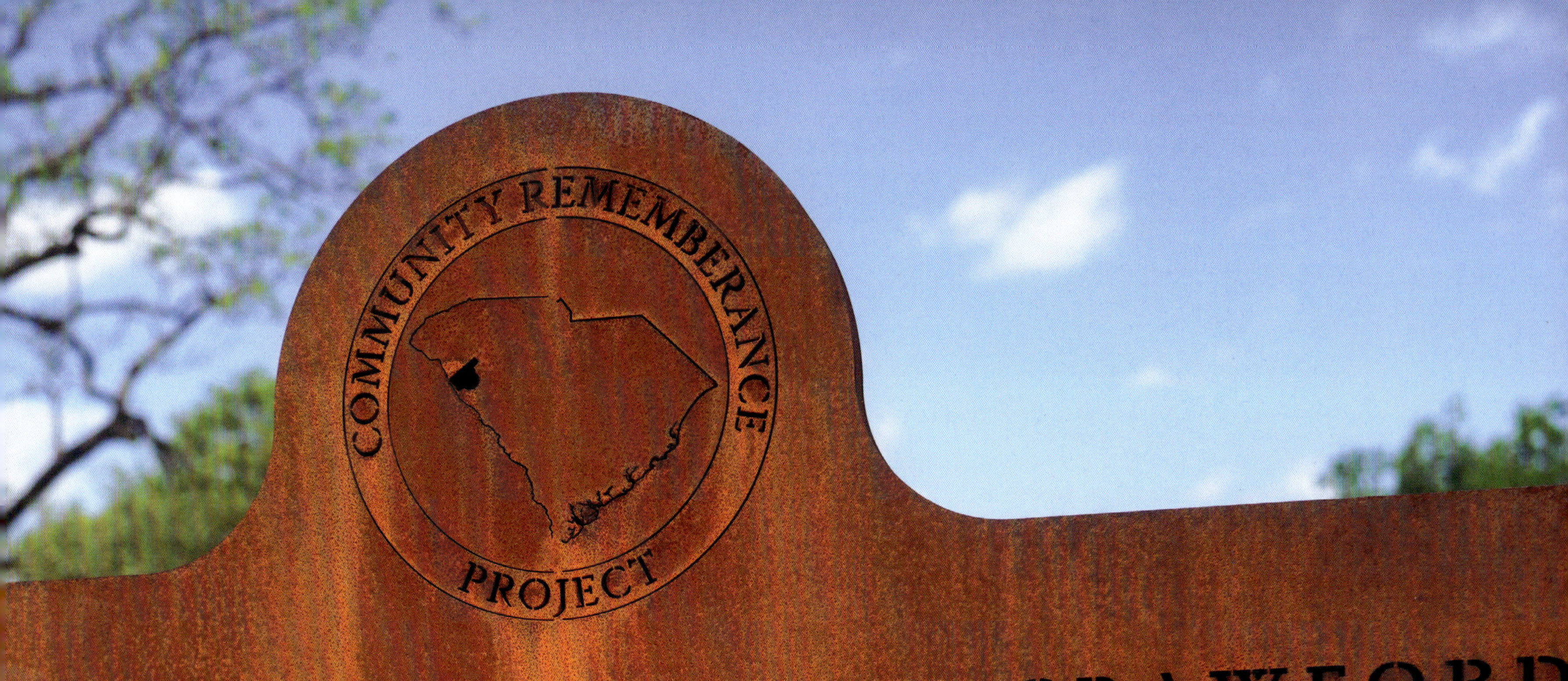
COMMUNITY REMEMBRANCE
PROJECT
NCHING OF ANTHONY CRAWFORD
Abbeville, South Carolina
on Saturday, October 21, 1916, a white mob lynched a Black
Anthony Crawford for arguing with a white man. A 56-year
Grandpa" Crawford owned 427 acres of land, had 13 children,
stablish a school, a church, and farms in the local Black
During the Jim Crow era, successful Black people were
-and arguing with white people was dangerous. That day, a
ant demanded to buy Mr. Crawford's cottonseed for a lower
awford, who used to tell his family he'd rather "throw the seed
Creek," refused to sell. After an argument, Mr. Crawford wa
ew hours later, 300 white men seized him from jail and dragged
town behind a buggy. Finally stopping at the fairgrounds, the
, beat, hanged, and shot Mr. Crawford over 200 times - then
Crawford family to remove his hanging body from the tree.
the well-established, multi-generational Crawford family and
ocal Black people realized that Abbeville was not safe for them.
ed threats, most of the family fled North, leaving behind what
ch had built, and carrying the painful loss of his wisdom and
tury later, this marker symbolizes their continued remembrance
at Abbeville never forget or repeat that horrendous October day
beville County

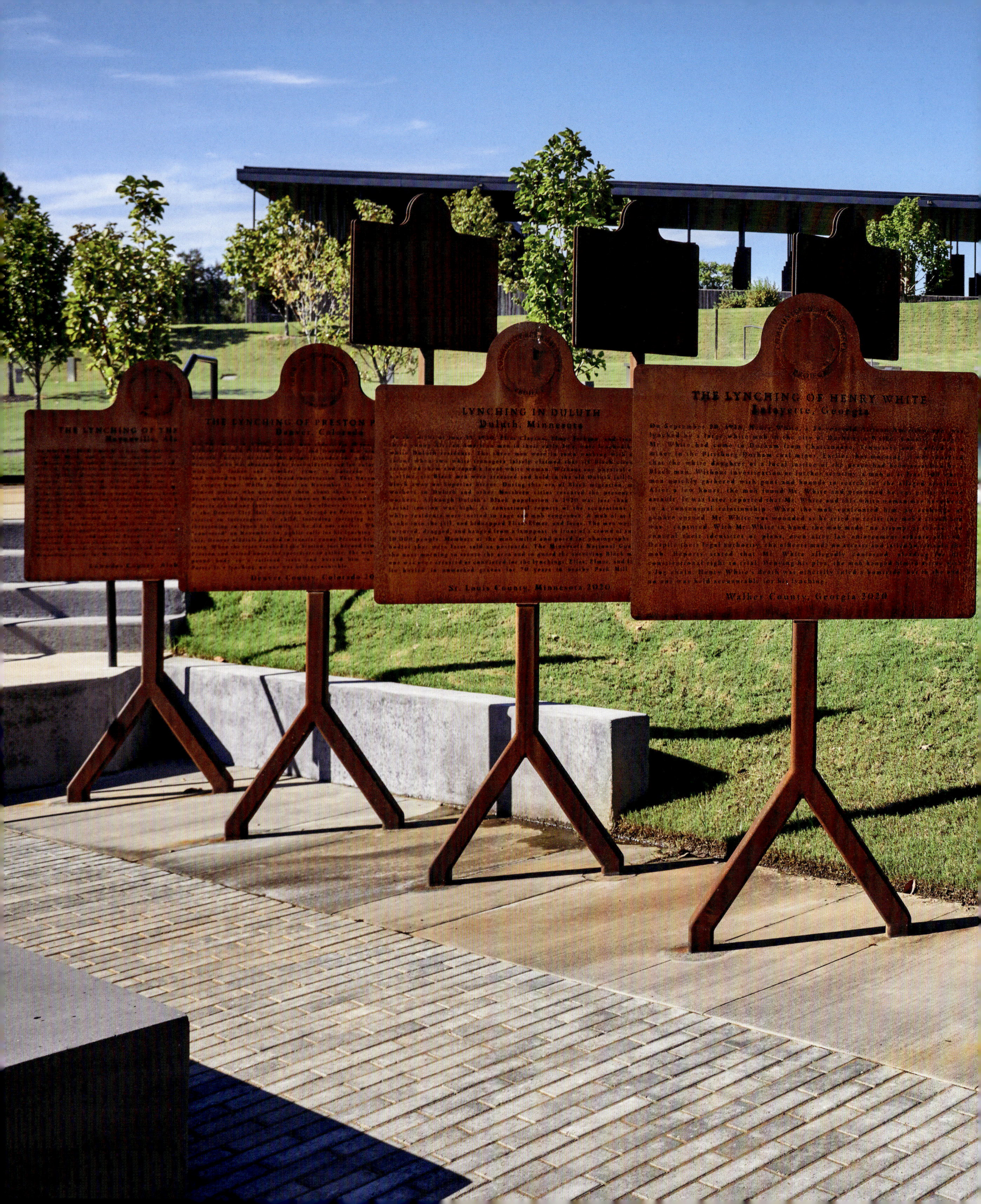

LYNCHING IN DULUTH
Duluth, Minnesota
St. Louis County, Minnesota 2020
THE LYNCHING OF HENRY WHITE
Lafayette, Georgia
Walker County, Georgia 2020

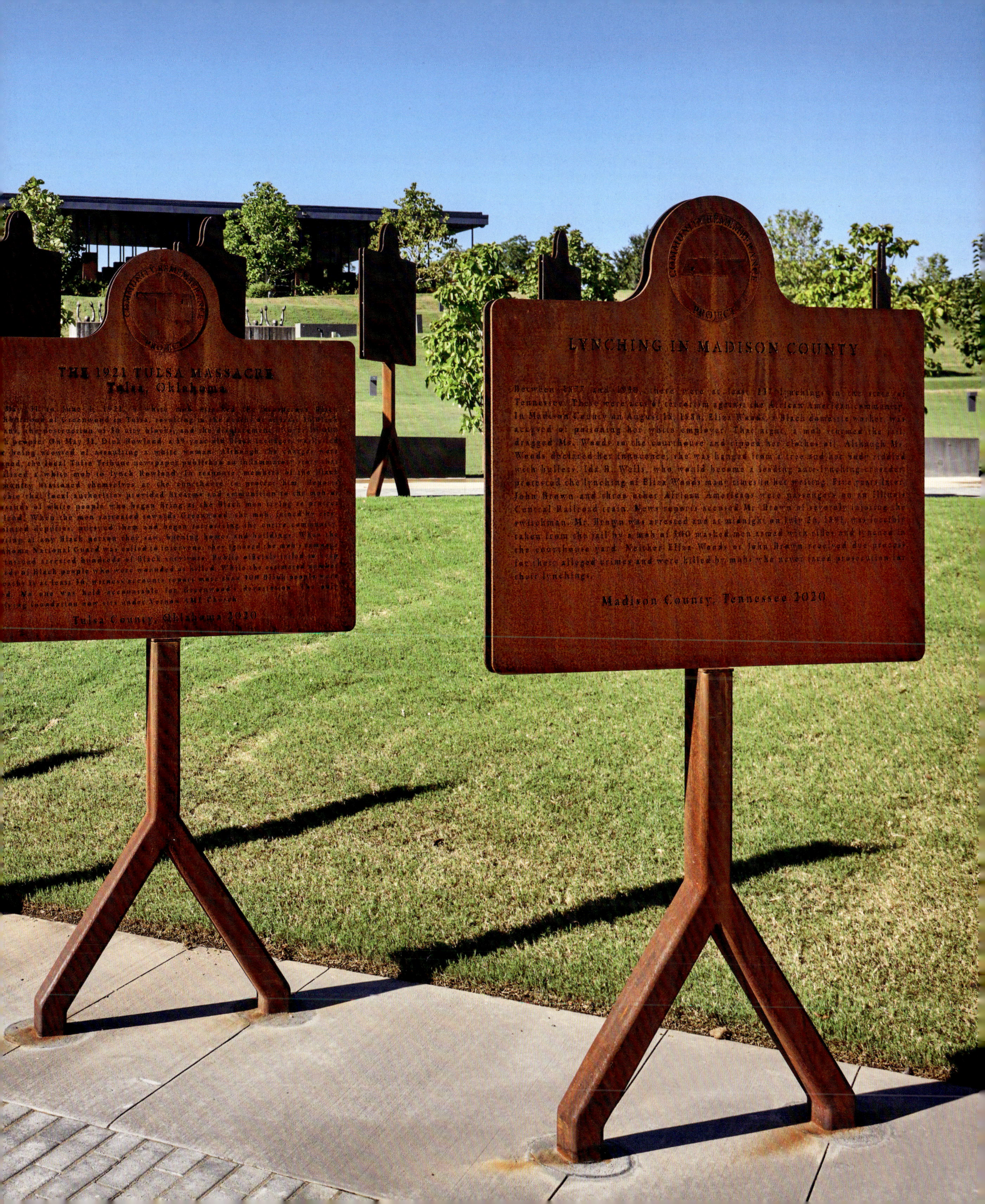
THE 1921 TULSA MASSACRE
Tulsa, Oklahoma
Tulsa County, Oklahoma 2020
LYNCHING IN MADISON COUNTY
Madison County, Tennessee 2020

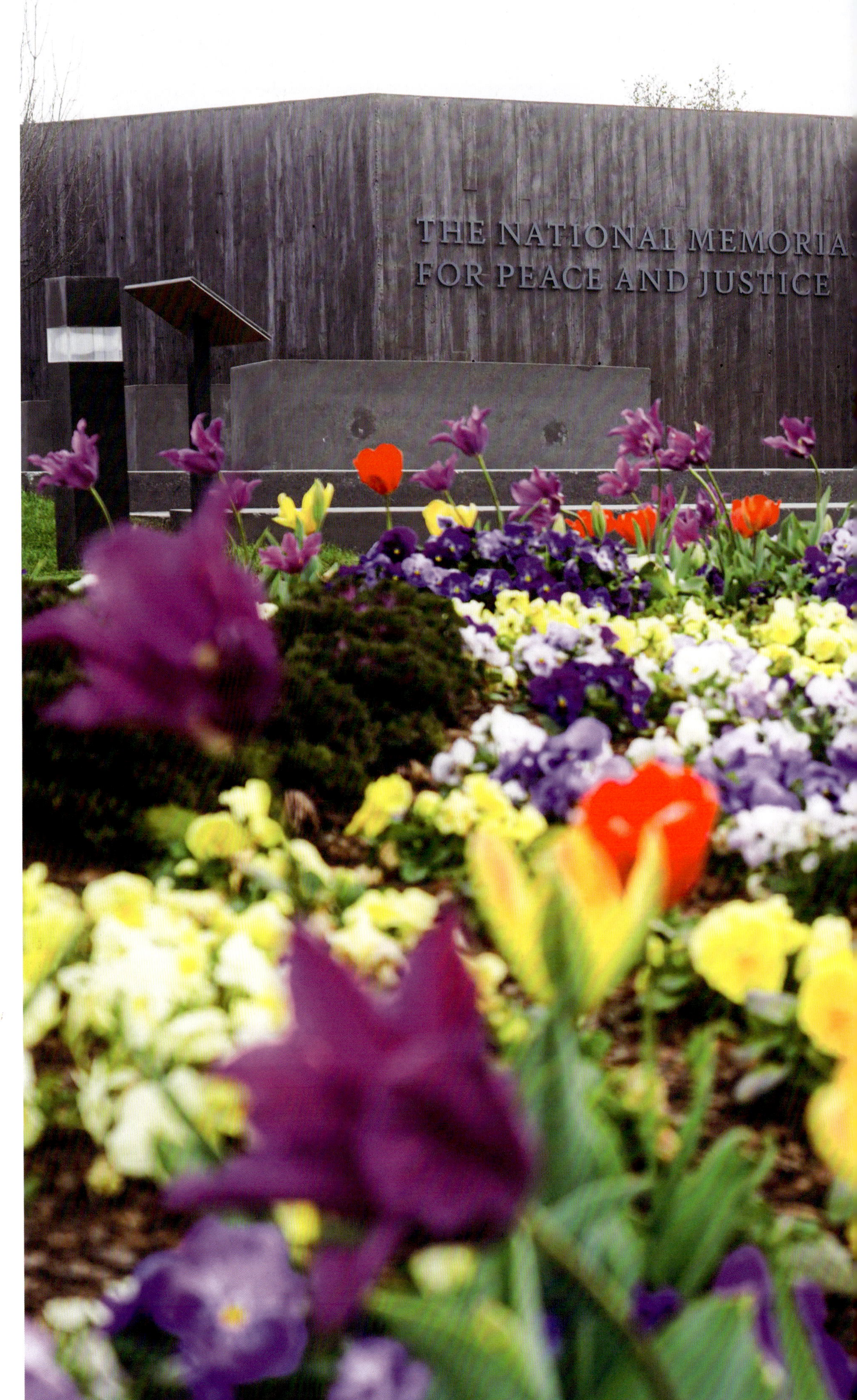
THE NATIONAL MEMORIA
FOR PEACE AND JUSTICE

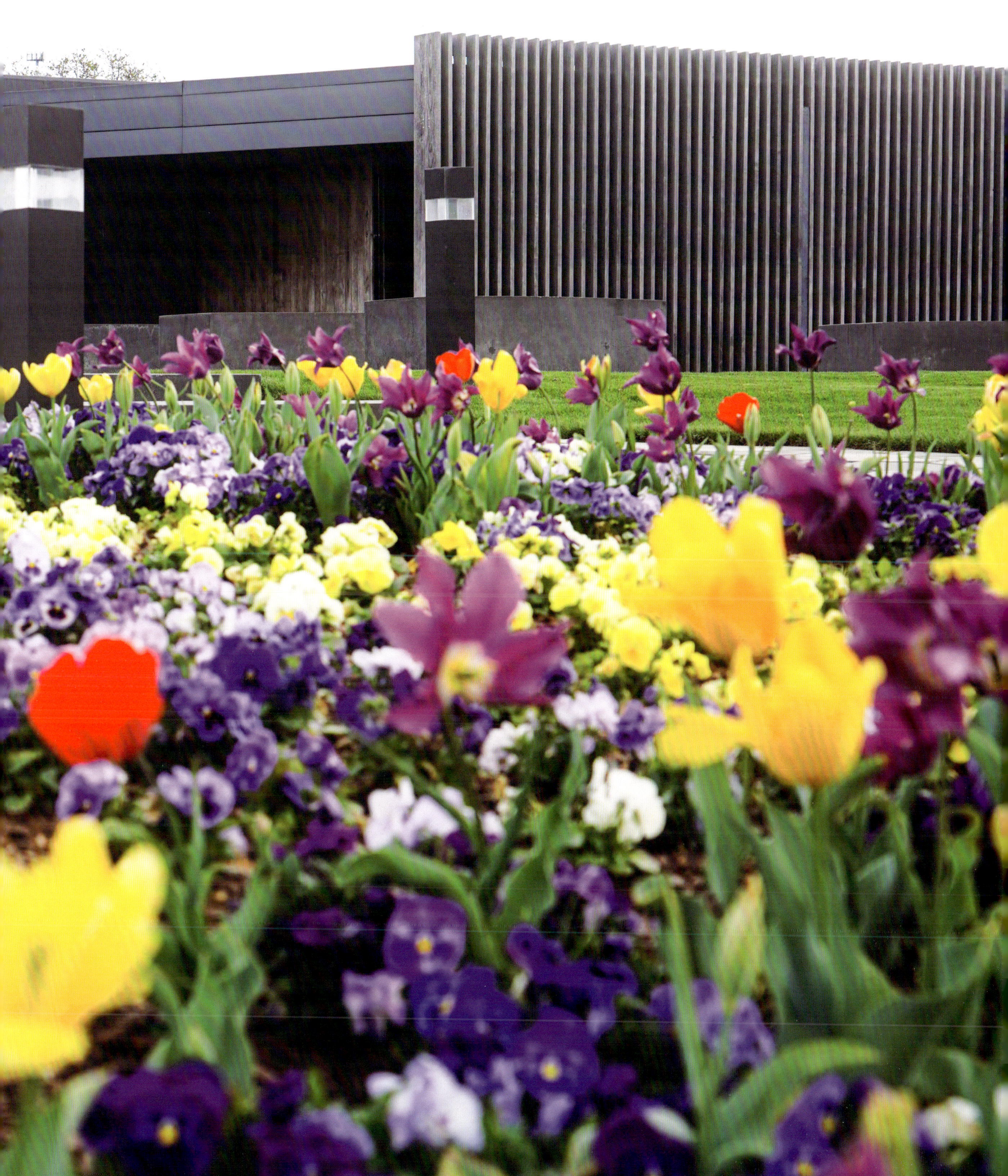

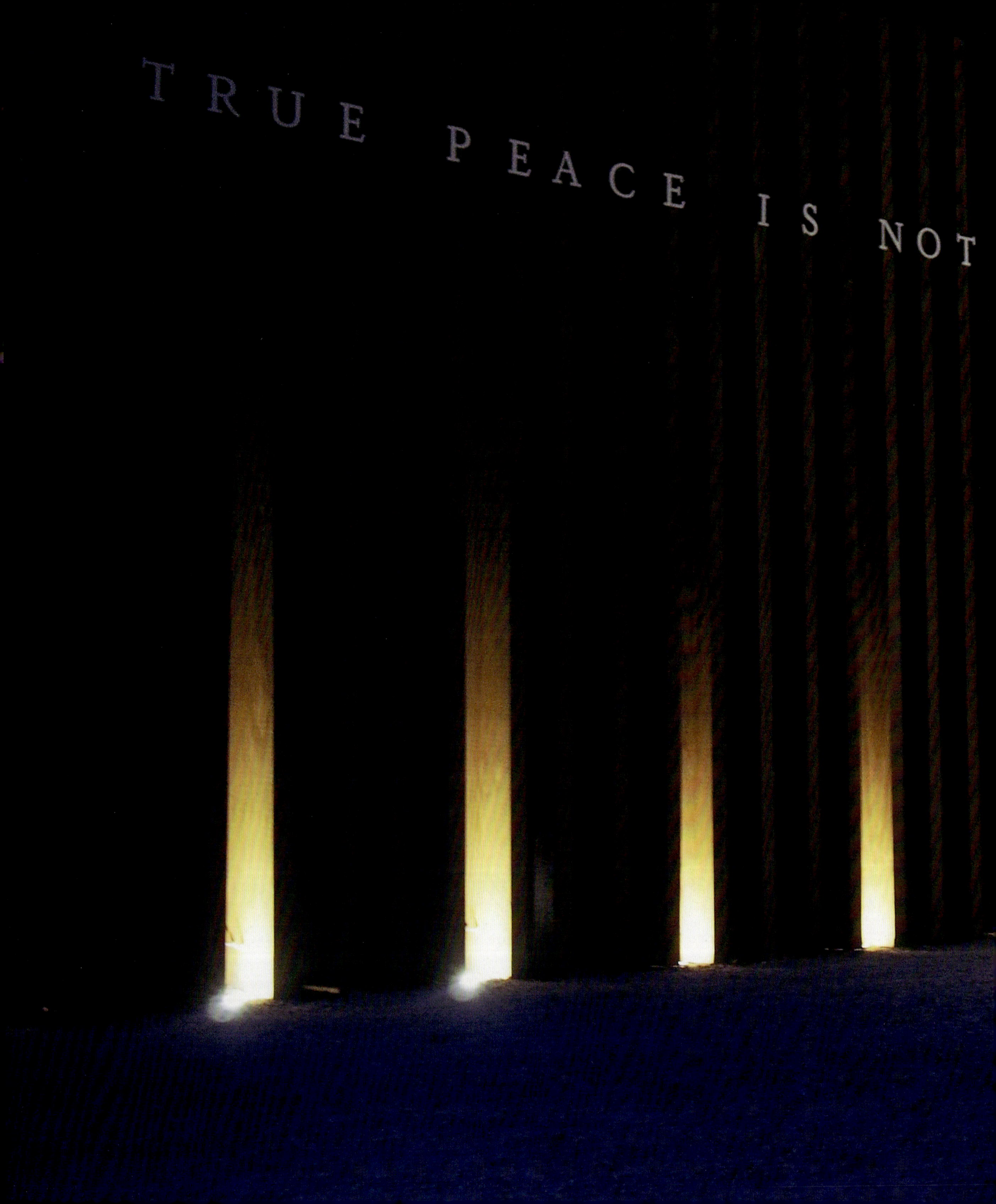

TRUE PEACE IS NOT

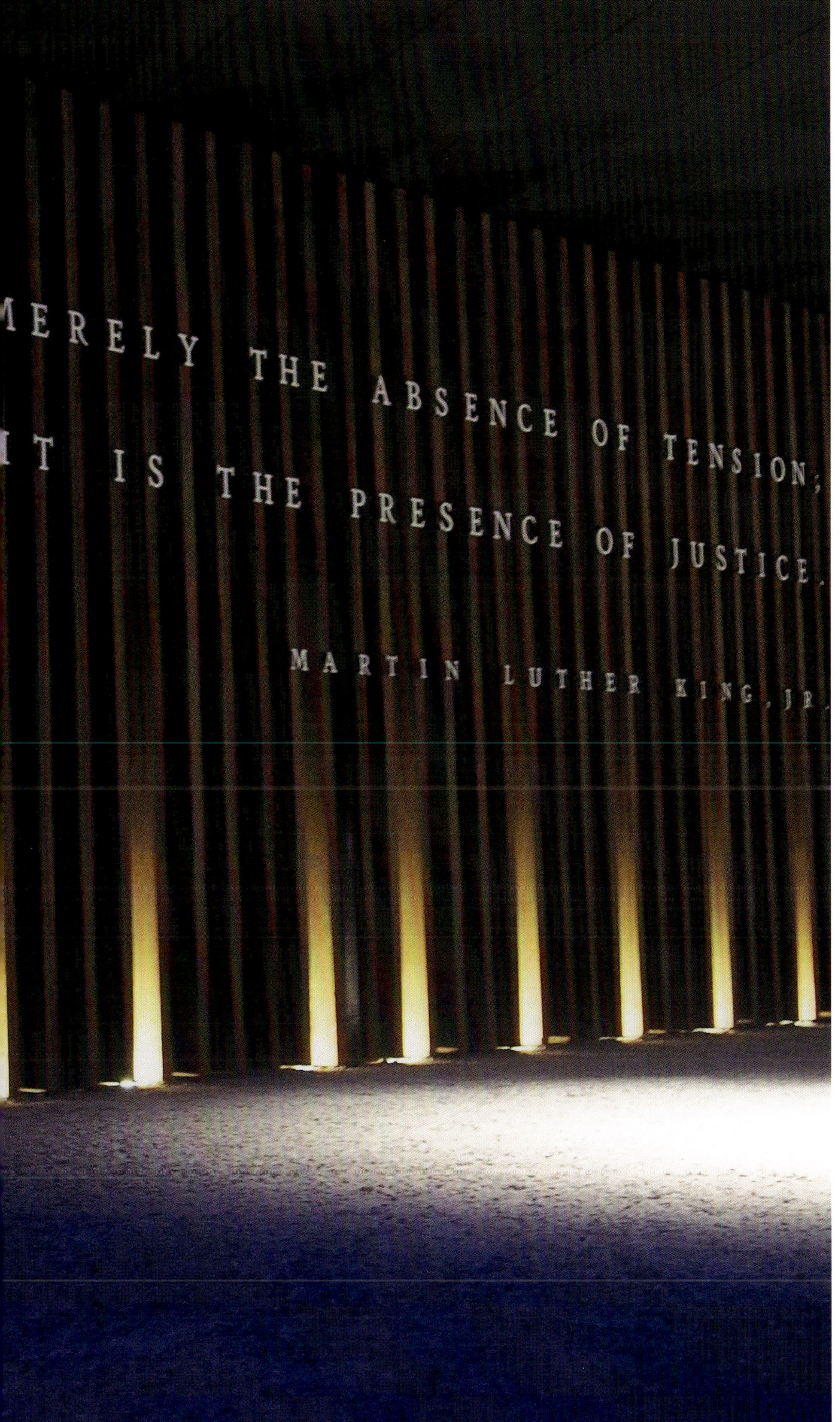
MERELY THE ABSENCE OF TENSION;
IT IS THE PRESENCE OF JUSTICE
MARTIN LUTHER KING, JR.

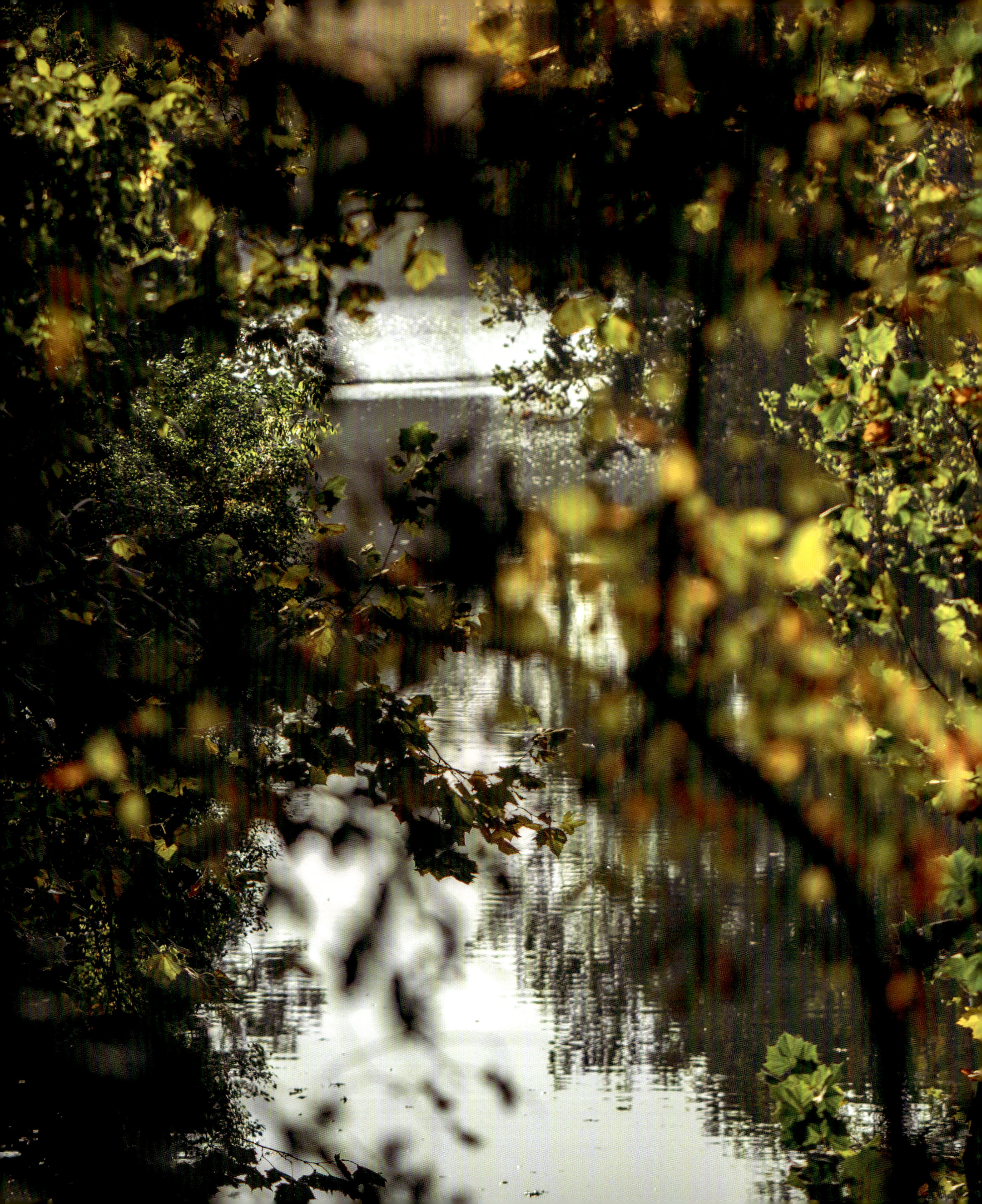

FREEDOM MONUMENT SCULPTURE PARK

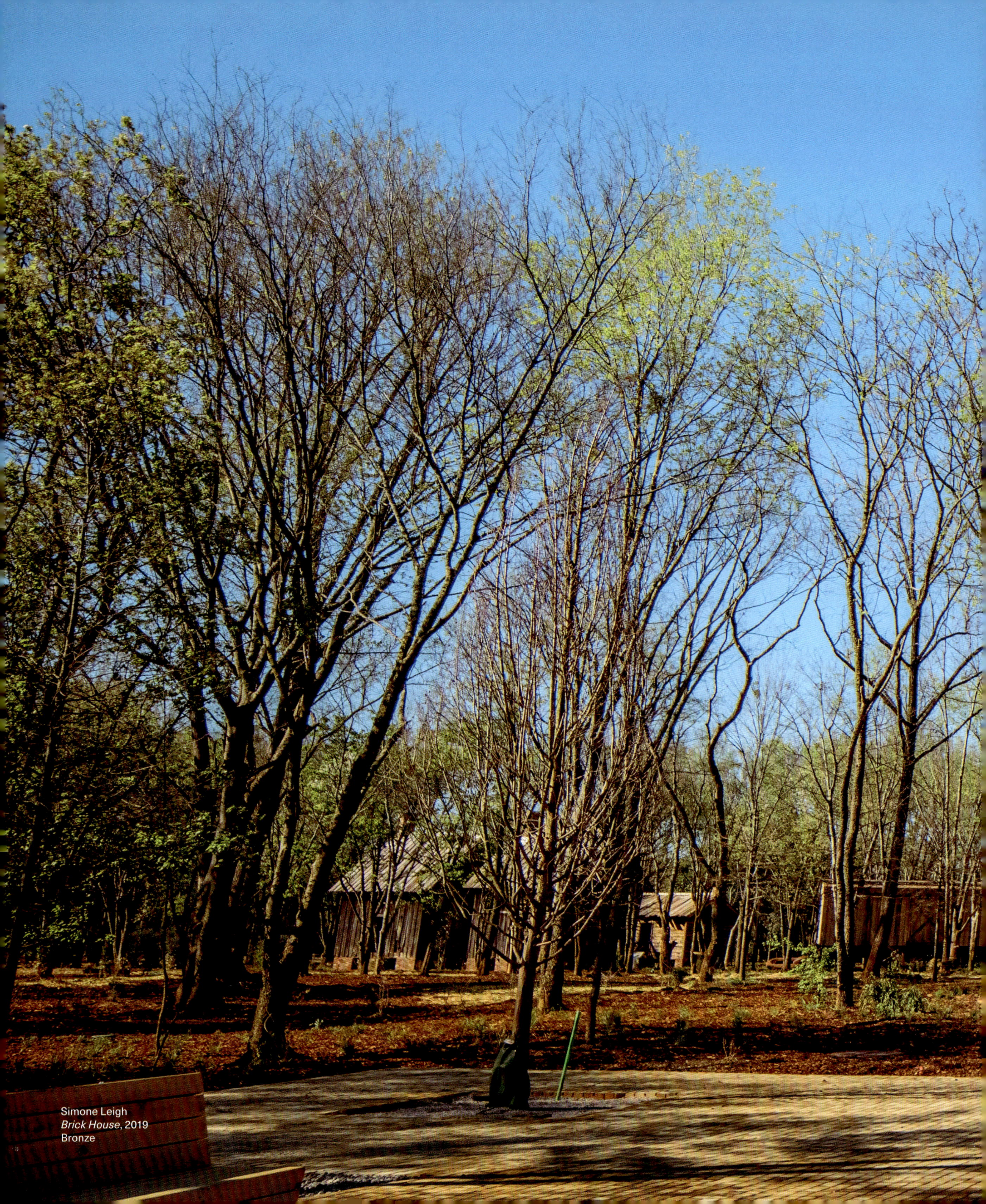

Simone Leigh
Brick House, 2019
Bronze

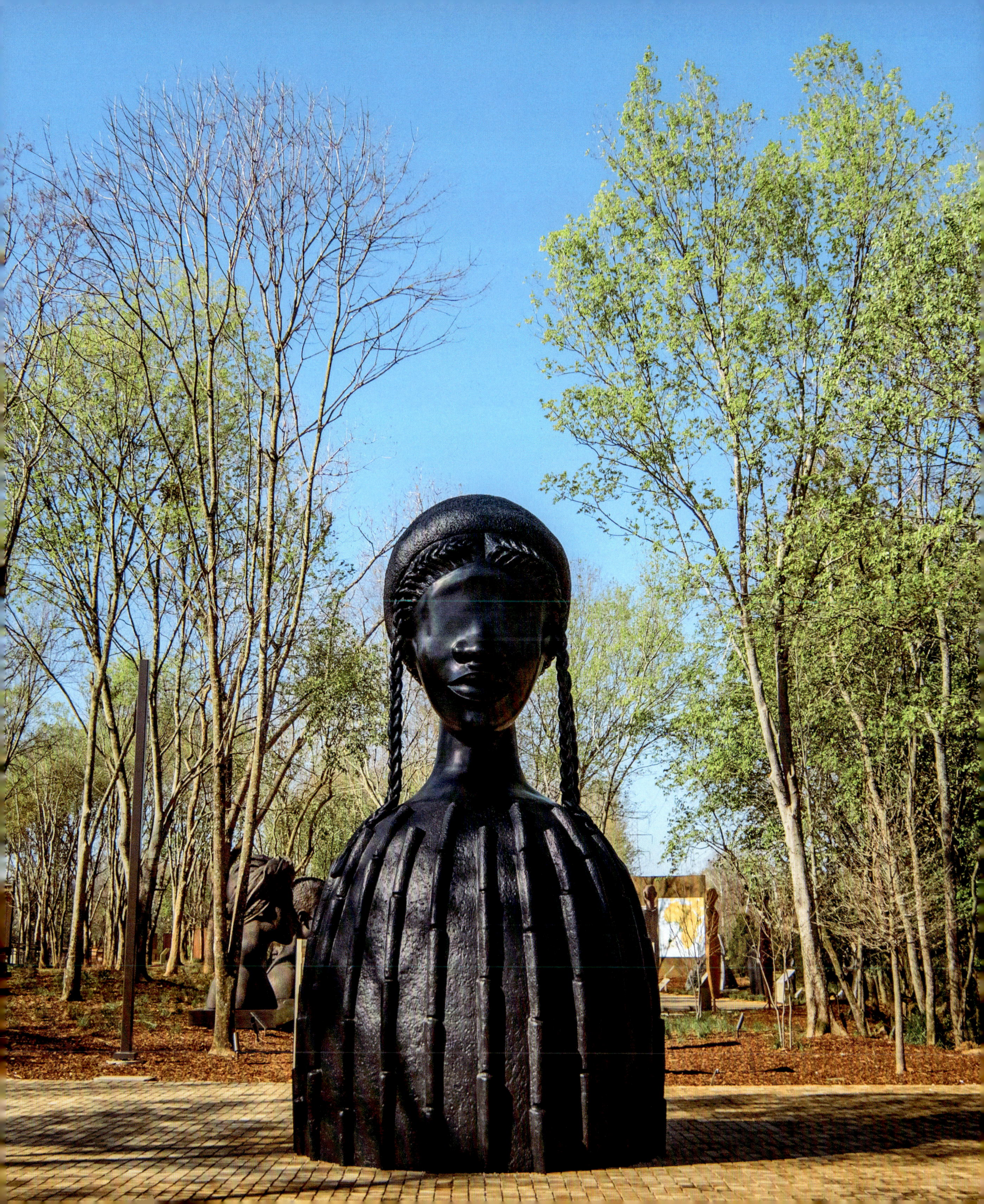

Overlooking the Alabama River, Freedom Monument Sculpture Park honors the lives and memories of the ten million Black people who were enslaved in America and celebrates their courage and resilience.

Freedom Monument Sculpture Park is a seventeen-acre site on the banks of the Alabama River, near railroad tracks on which enslaved people were trafficked during the nineteenth century. Plantations and forced labor camps bordered the Alabama River, creating a region with one of the largest populations of enslaved people in the country. The nearby trafficking and forced labor of enslaved people makes this a historically significant space. At this site, the lives and legacy of enslaved people are explored, remembered, and honored.

We also acknowledge and honor the Indigenous Peoples who occupied these lands for thousands of years before the arrival of Europeans.

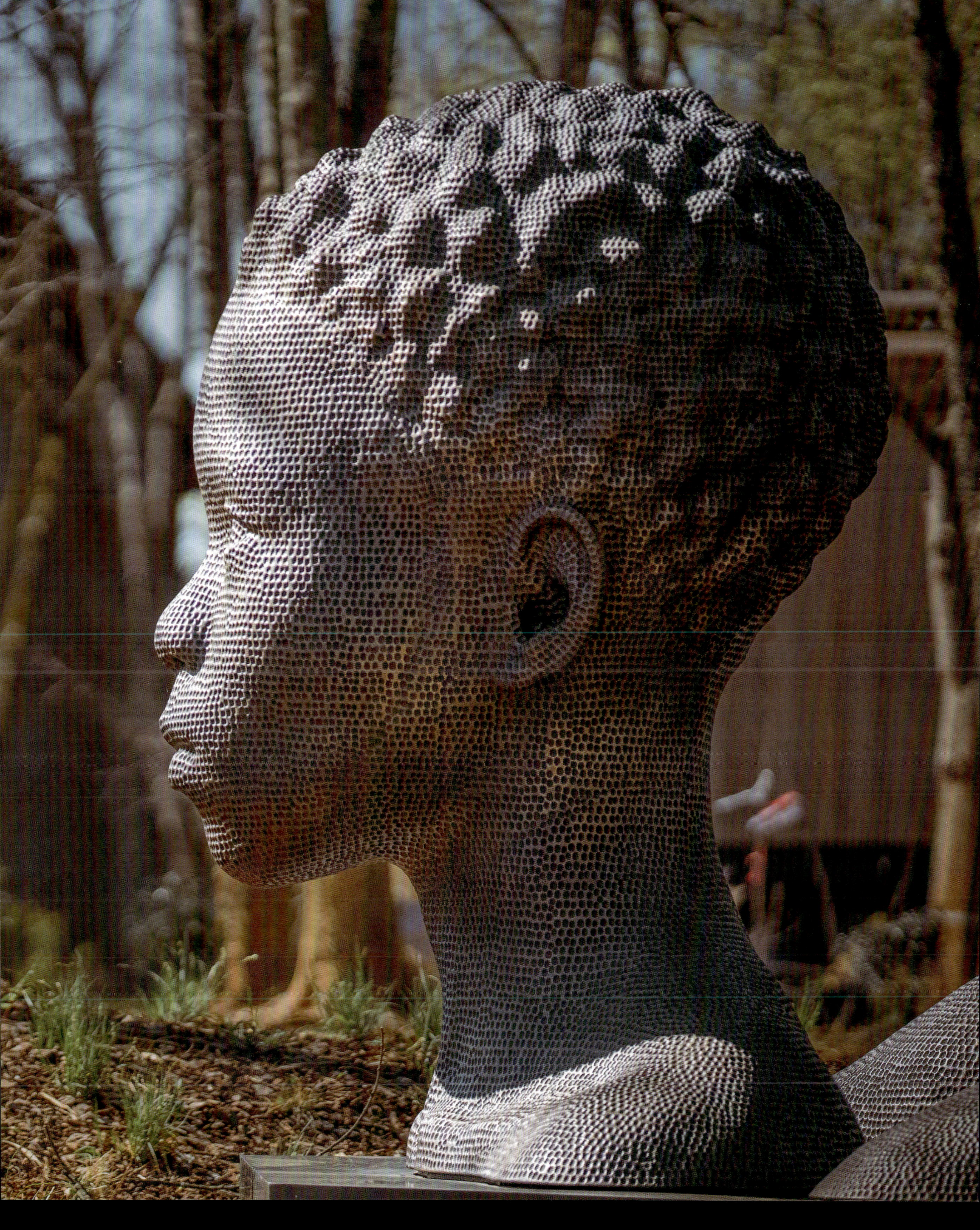

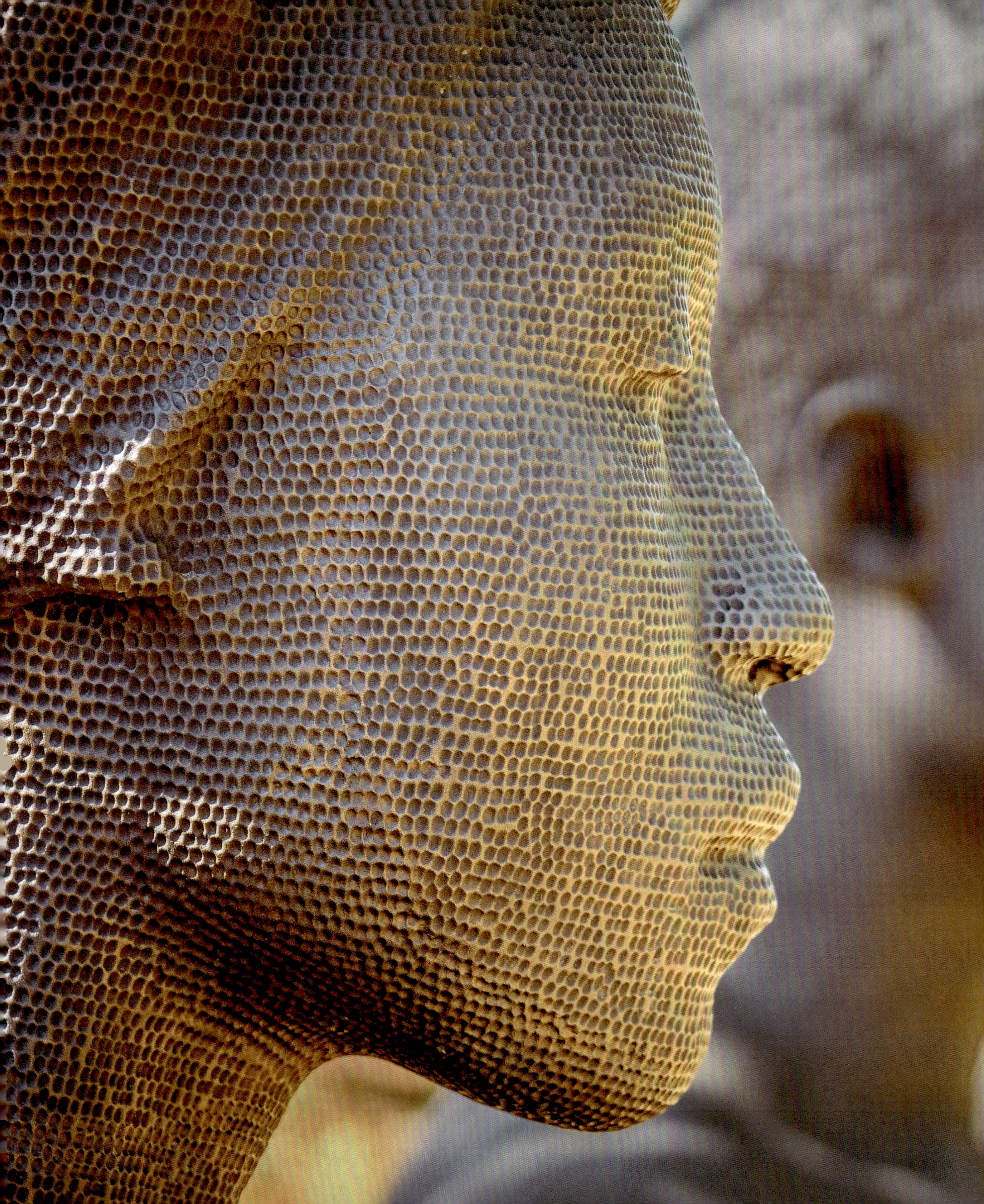

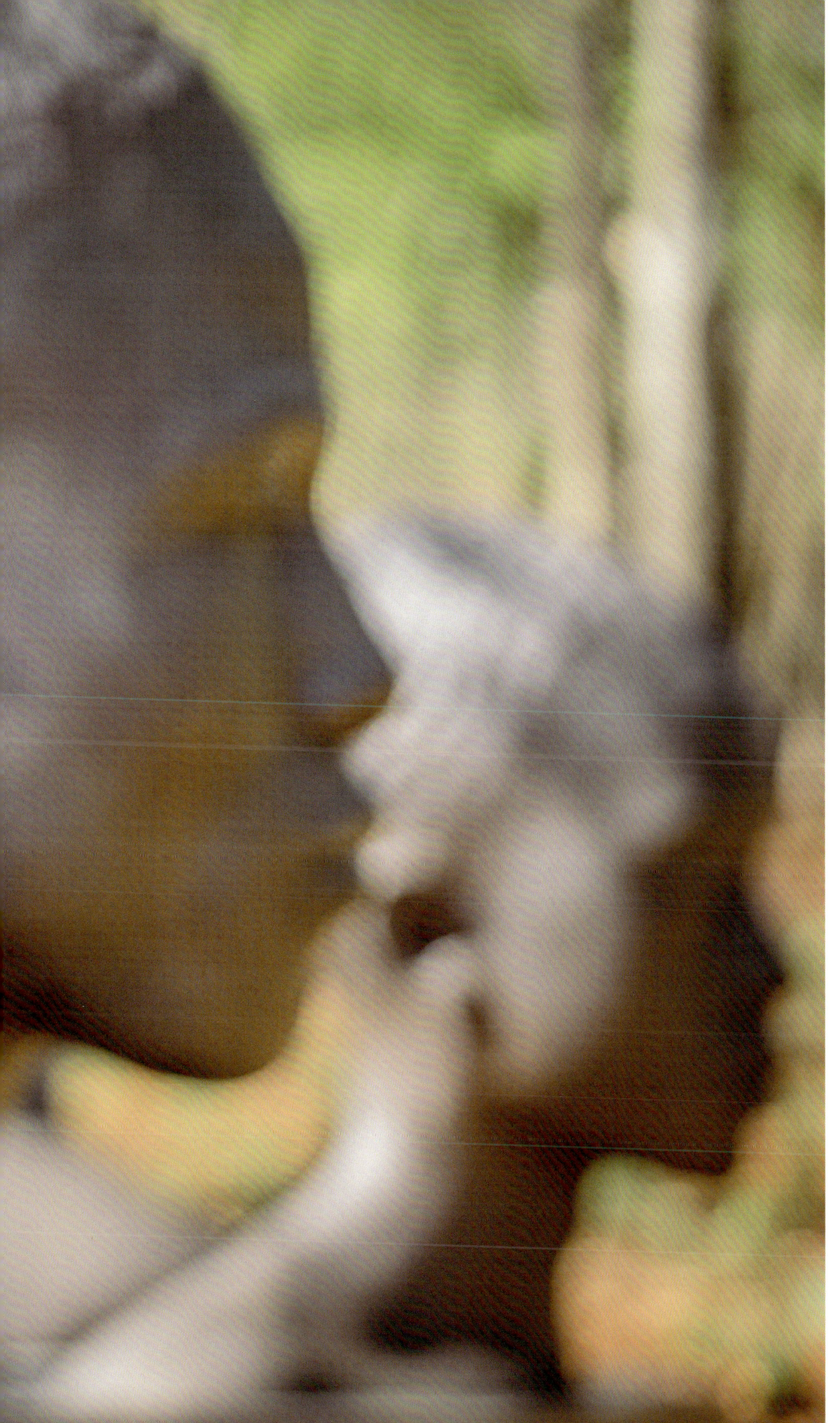

Opposite and page 187:
Rayvenn D'Clark
Black Renaissance, 2023
Bronze

The Power of Place

Nearly two million people from across the country and the world have visited the Legacy Museum and the National Memorial for Peace and Justice in Montgomery, Alabama. This level of interest in learning about our nation's history of racial injustice and its legacy energized and inspired us to begin thinking about how to create a new space focused on the institution of slavery.

Despite the centrality of slavery in our nation's history, little has been done to comprehensively detail the human scale of this tragic institution. The enslavement of ten million Black people had a profound impact on the legal, cultural, social, and economic character of the United States, but there is an absence of authentic and historically significant places in America that explore the lives of enslaved people and the history of slavery and its legacy.

We began searching for a site to address this lack of education. We also felt the need to counter the harmful myth that Africa was underdeveloped before Europeans arrived and to push back on the claim that slavery was beneficial to Black people. Visiting plantations in Charleston and across the South, we were struck by the difficulty of telling an honest story about slavery in spaces where the built architecture is so committed to racial hierarchy. The "big house" dominates everything, centering the lives of enslavers while the lives of enslaved Black people are literally marginalized.

We began to think if we had an outdoor space filled with great art that helps people understand both the brutality of slavery and the humanity of the enslaved, it would help us navigate the tragic history that leads up to this triumphant, extraordinary emancipation that represents so much more than we've acknowledged.

We found a site near the Legacy Museum, overlooking the Alabama River, next to railroad tracks that were originally laid by enslaved people. Given the site's proximity to the river, we wanted to talk about the history of Indigenous Peoples before the arrival of Europeans. We were frustrated that the existing narrative landscape tended to start with the arrival of Europeans, as if there were no Indigenous Peoples here before. We consulted a nearby Maskoke community that lives as their ancestors did in precolonial times.

The park also describes the empires of Africa and their achievements in metallurgy, astronomy, and agriculture, long before Europe. And it recognizes the consequences for the continent of the kidnapping and trafficking of millions of African people. Because there's not much in the visual record of this era that conveys the humanity of enslaved people, we created one of the most significant narrative art collections

Dotun Popoola
Irinkemi Asake, 2021–24
Scrap metals, mild steel, galvanized pipes, automobile parts, stainless steel, gold-coated balls, and wrought iron

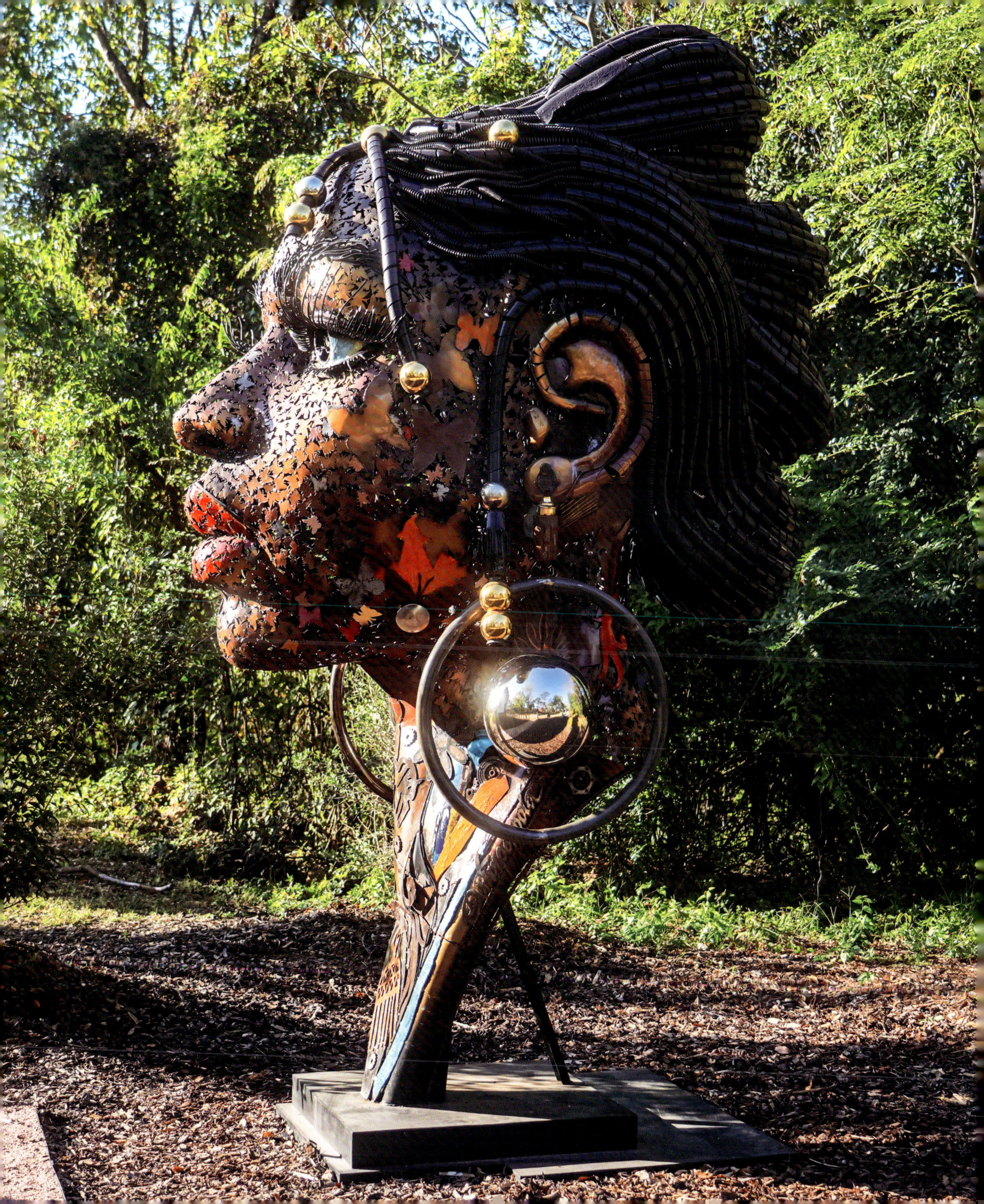

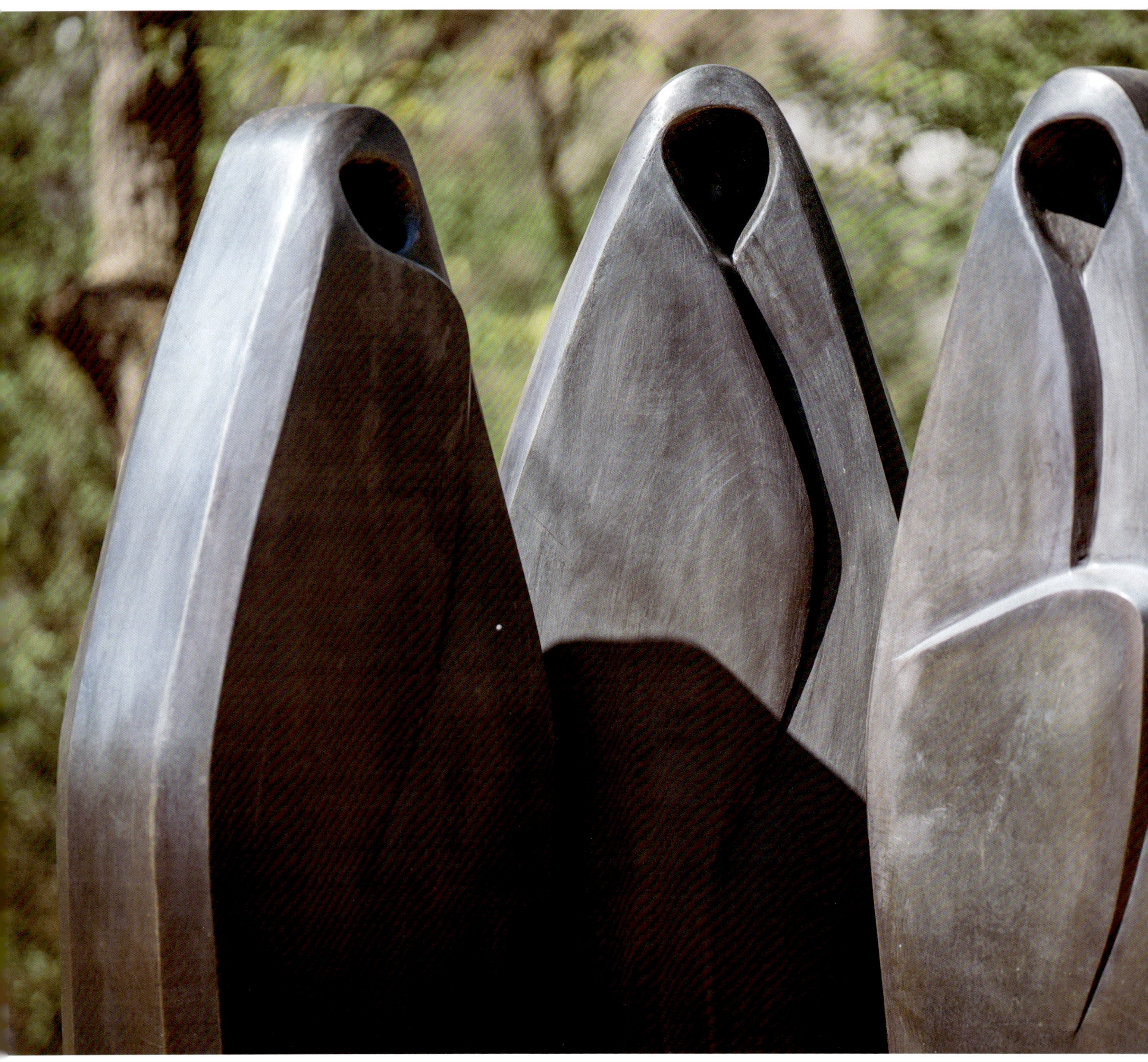

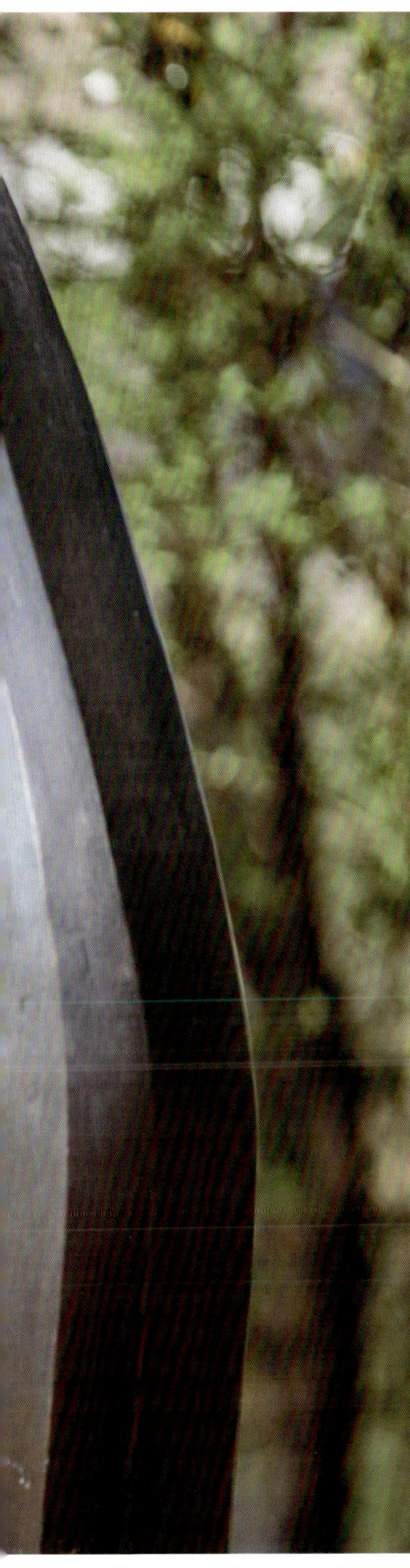

Allan Houser
When Friends Meet, 1987
Bronze

in the world, with more than fifty sculptures by globally renowned artists who depict the humanity and dignity of people in the midst of brutality and violence.

Freedom Monument Sculpture Park is an exploration of the institution of slavery that is centered on the lives of enslaved people. The culmination of the sculpture park is the National Monument to Freedom, standing 43 feet tall and 155 feet wide in the shape of an open book. Inscribed with 122,000 surnames that formerly enslaved people chose and officially recorded in the 1870 census, the monument celebrates this extraordinary exercise of freedom.

No matter where you are in the park, even in the midst of really challenging parts of our history such as the laws of slavery and the holding pen, you can see that monument and know that freedom is coming. Which is not what our enslaved foreparents knew.

We hope visitors to Freedom Monument Sculpture Park will be persuaded that we owe the people who were enslaved in this country more recognition, more acknowledgment, and more honor for their remarkable decision to commit to building community and exercising citizenship in America after Emancipation instead of seeking retribution or revenge. If we can face the ugliest parts of the history of slavery, then we will gain the courage and power to create an era of truth and justice, truth and repair, truth and reconciliation, and truth and restoration.

We also hope the park provides Black Americans with an opportunity to discover that descendants are not just the heirs of enslavement and bondage, pain and suffering, lynching and segregation, and racial violence and discrimination. That legacy is real, but the descendants of the enslaved are also the heirs of people who found a way to persevere, to stand strong, to hold on to their dignity and their faith, to love in the midst of sorrow. This power, beauty, and strength have to be acknowledged.

There is trauma in our history that courses still through our bodies and our consciousness—but there's also triumph and unimaginable fortitude. We need to embrace the legacy of hope and strength, and recognize in ourselves the power and ability to overcome.

Indigenous Peoples in the Americas

Indigenous Peoples have thrived on this continent for thousands of years, cultivating corn, beans, squash, and other crops; strategically hunting large game; and adapting to environmental changes.

At least five million Indigenous People inhabited what is now the U.S. before Europeans arrived.

More than two hundred languages were spoken by Indigenous Peoples in more than five hundred distinct nations and communities that fostered ancestral wisdom traditions, built extensive road and waterway transportation networks, produced hundreds of inventions and innovations, created vast social and political systems, and established cities with as many as forty thousand residents.

In the late 1400s, Europeans brought violence, disease, and exploitation that ultimately resulted in the loss of more than 90 percent of the continent's Indigenous population. Survivors formed modern nations, including the Cherokee, Choctaw, Chickasaw, Seminole, and Maskoke in the Southeast.

False narratives about Indigenous Peoples' subhuman or primitive status were used to justify land seizures, mass murder, and enslavement. By 1715, as many as 50,000 Indigenous People in the South had been sold by British traffickers. The U.S. government launched a brutal campaign to take more than a billion acres of land through violence and forcible removals that, together with disease and starvation, reduced the population of Indigenous People to only 300,000 by 1900.

Today, many Indigenous People face environmental threats, discrimination and exclusion, and a host of other challenges.

Indigenous Peoples in the Alabama River Region

Modern Indigenous nations descended from ancient Mississippian chiefdoms including Moundville, Cahokia, Coosa, and Tascaluza formed in the Alabama River Region between the 1500s and 1700s. Maskoke—called "Creeks" by Europeans—occupied large swaths of what would become Alabama in 1819. The Maskoke Nation encompassed many socially and politically diverse peoples with their own languages, geographic origins, and creation stories.

The Alabama River was home to abundant animal life and vegetation, and its spring flooding rejuvenated soil for Indigenous farmers, who engineered dams to fish. Indigenous Peoples established numerous towns along or near the Alabama River, including Atahachi about three miles below Montgomery, and Uxapita, located where an interstate highway currently crosses the Alabama River in Montgomery.

Montgomery was significant in the forced removal of Indigenous Peoples from the area. In the 1830s, Maskoke who were captured while resisting forced removal were held in the Montgomery County Jail, and in 1836, some 2,300 Maskoke were loaded onto steamboats in Montgomery and forcibly removed.

Later that year, President Andrew Jackson ordered the forced removal of the remaining members of the Maskoke Nation from their ancestral homelands. Hundreds perished while being forced to walk hundreds of miles on the "Trail of Tears."

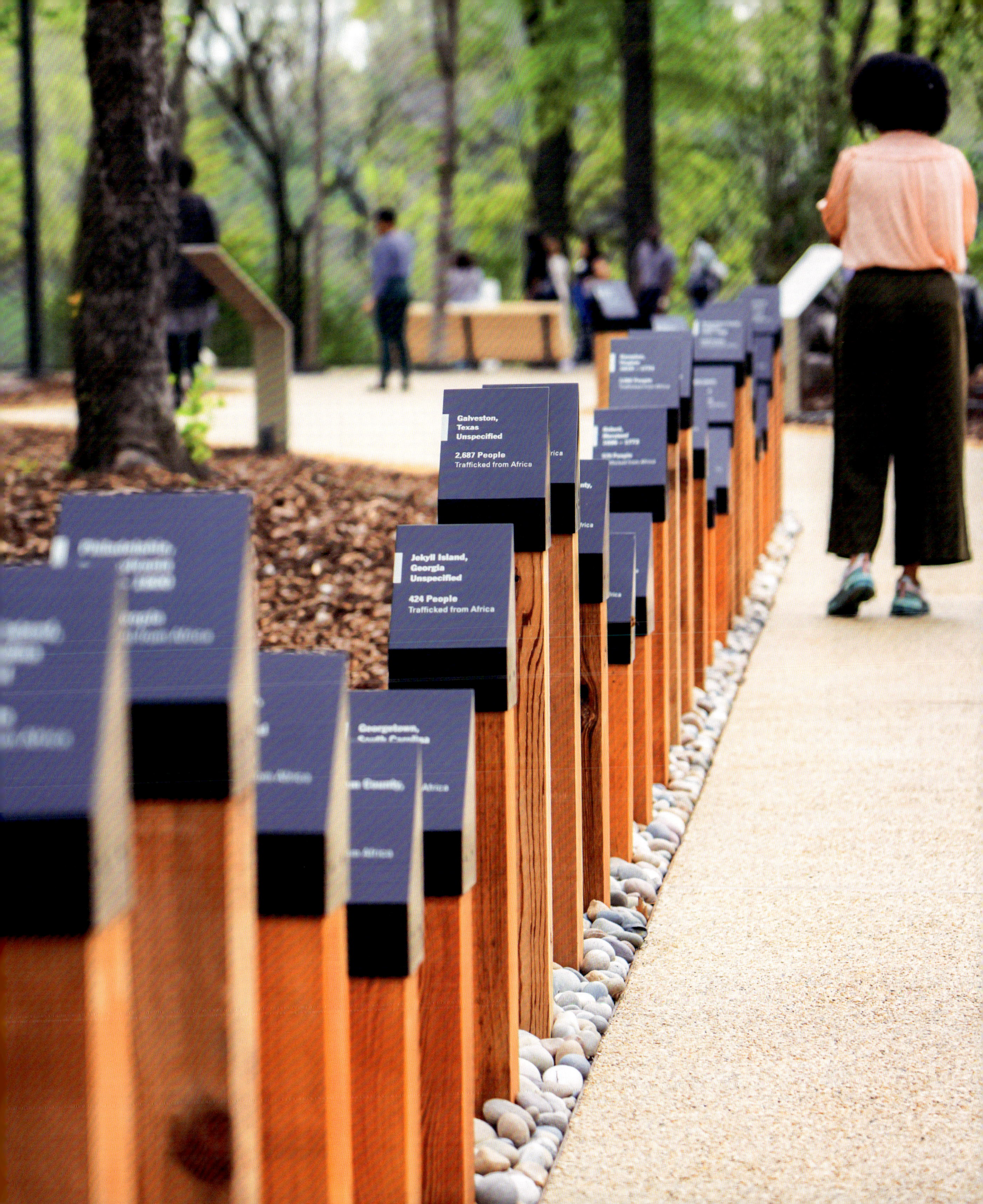
Galveston,
Texas
Unspecified
2,687 People
Trafficked from Africa
Jekyll Island,
Georgia
Unspecified
424 People
Trafficked from Africa

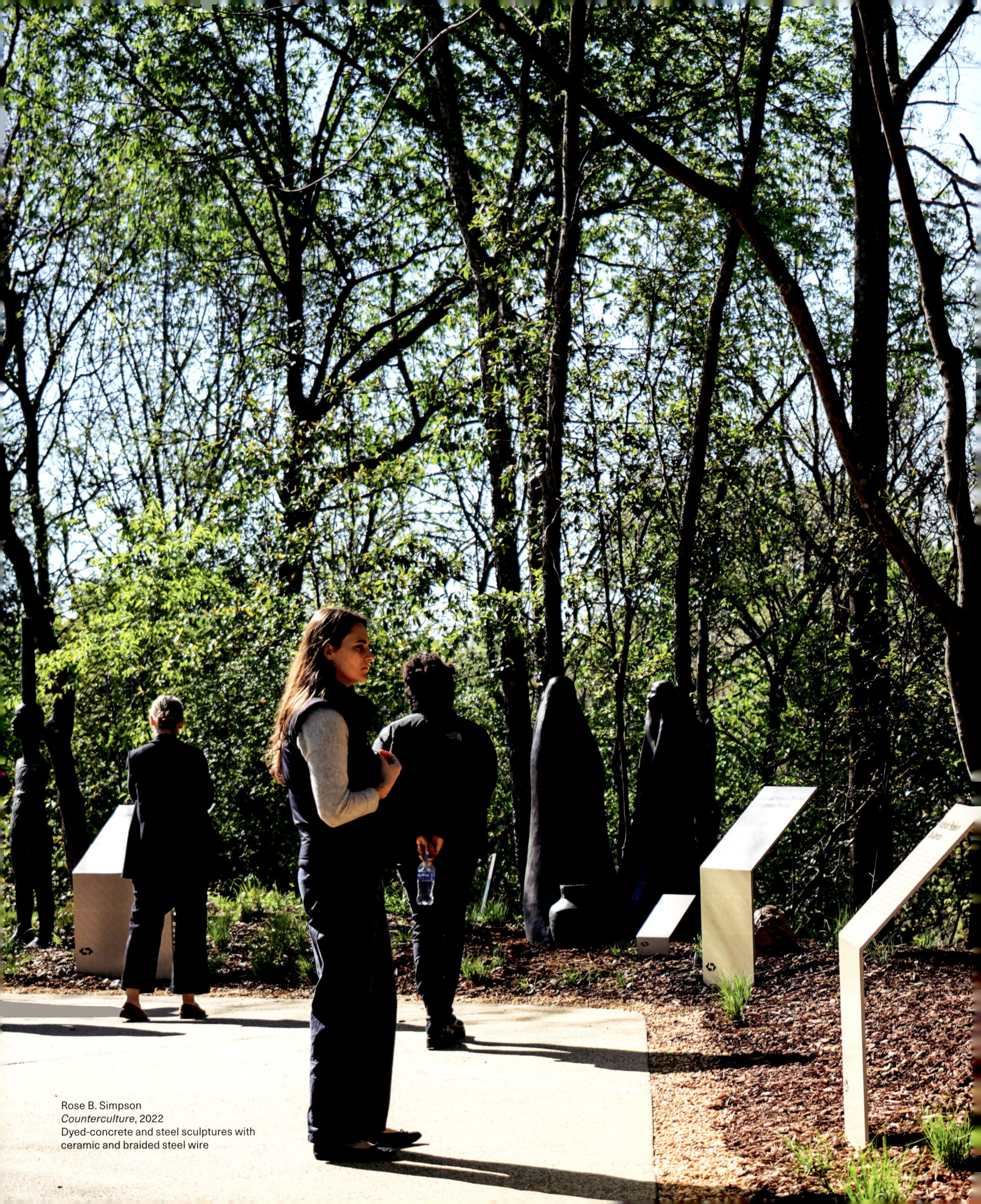

Rose B. Simpson
Counterculture, 2022
Dyed-concrete and steel sculptures with ceramic and braided steel wire

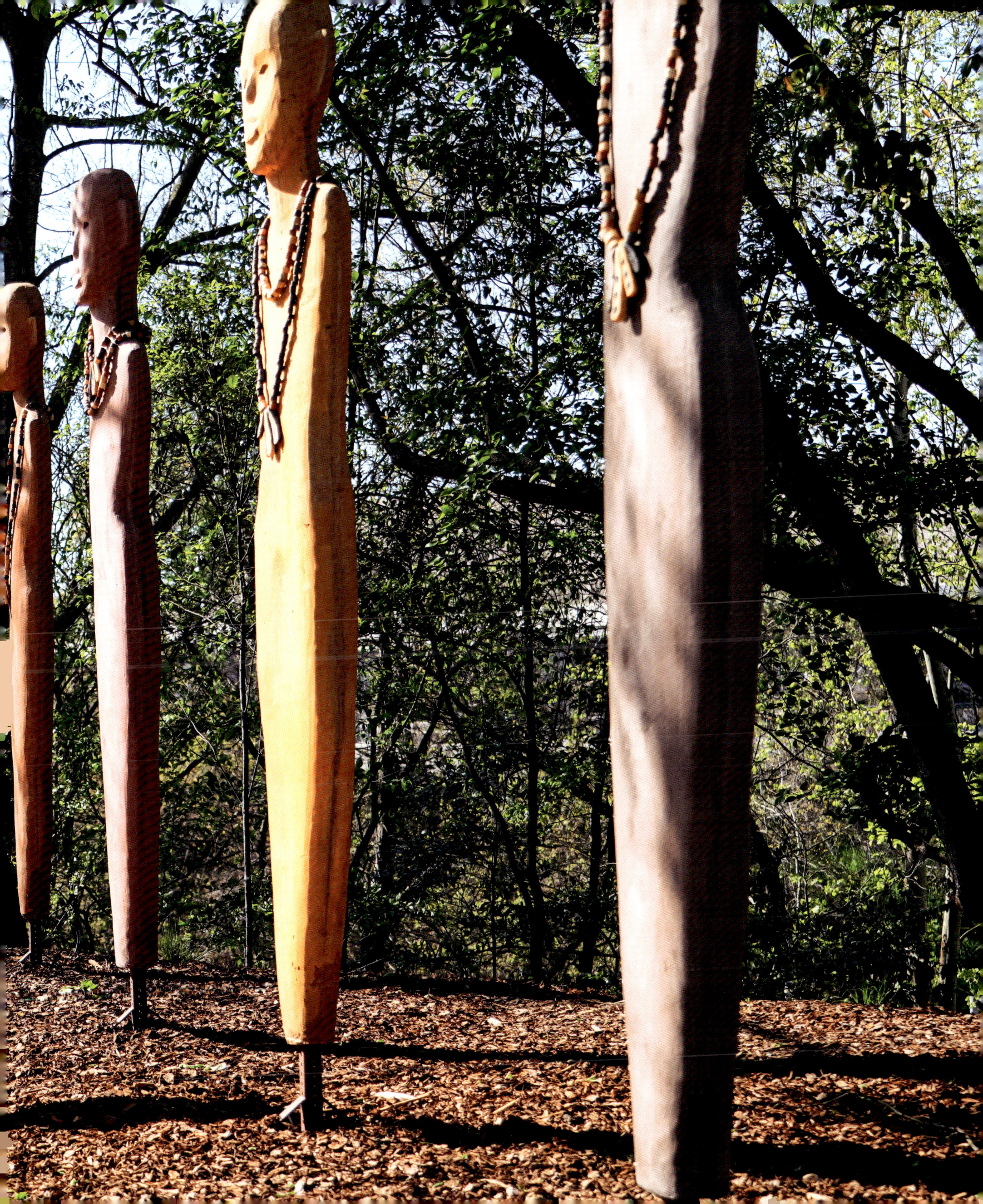

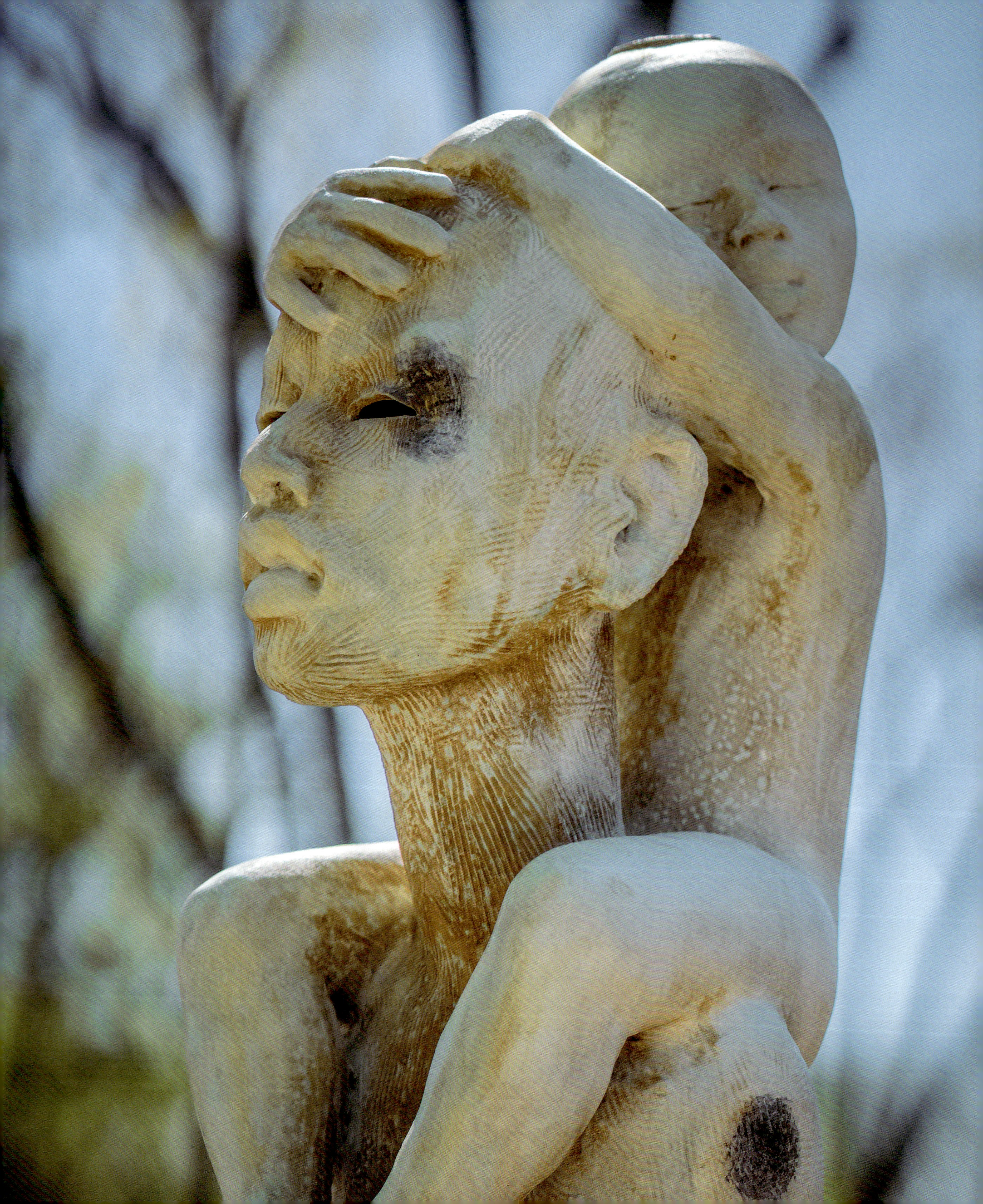

Rose B. Simpson

Rose B. Simpson (b. 1983) was born in Santa Clara Pueblo, New Mexico, to a long line of ceramic artists. An enrolled member of the Santa Clara Pueblo (Kha'po Owingeh), based just south of Española, Simpson lives and works in the place where her ancestors have lived for hundreds of years. Her work reflects on the history and culture of her homeland and honors the power and resilience of her ancestors.

Simpson is a mixed-media artist who works in ceramic, metal, fashion, painting, music, performance, and installation. She is best known for figurative sculptures that she creates using a technique she devised and calls "slap-slab" to shape her clay sculptures by hand. She throws a slab of clay sideways until it is very thin, then tears off pieces and attaches them to each other, so that the seams, pinches, and her fingerprints are visible in the finished sculpture.

Counterculture honors generations of marginalized people, many of whom were forcibly removed from the land they had called home for centuries. The figures are "witnesses of that really difficult history" of colonization. Simpson told *The Berkshire Eagle* in 2022. "[T]hese could be put anywhere on this planet and they'd still be, in a sense, surveying that difficult history."

Each sculpture's eyes are holes that show the sky and land behind them and let the light stream through. "The eyes go through the form, all the way through to the back of the head, to sort of wake them up," she said. "They are watching."

In addition to *Counterculture*, her sculptures *Cairn: bronze* and *Heights I* are included at the Freedom Monument Sculpture Park.

Rose B. Simpson
Cairn: bronze (detail), 2023
Patinated and painted bronze

Agnes Nyanhongo

Agnes Nyanhongo (b. 1960) is a Zimbabwean sculptor renowned for her mastery in stone carving. Born into a family of artists and sculptors, she draws inspiration from the rich cultural heritage of her roots. Nyanhongo's sculptures often reflect themes of womanhood, family, and traditional rituals, characterized by fluid forms and intricate detailing.

She is considered one of Zimbabwe's most important artists. Her works have been exhibited at the National Gallery of Zimbabwe and around the world, earning her recognition and acclaim in contemporary African art. Chapungu Sculpture Park in Harare, where she was a resident artist, calls her the country's most acknowledged sculptress.

Agnes Nyanhongo
Keeping the History, 2023
Springstone

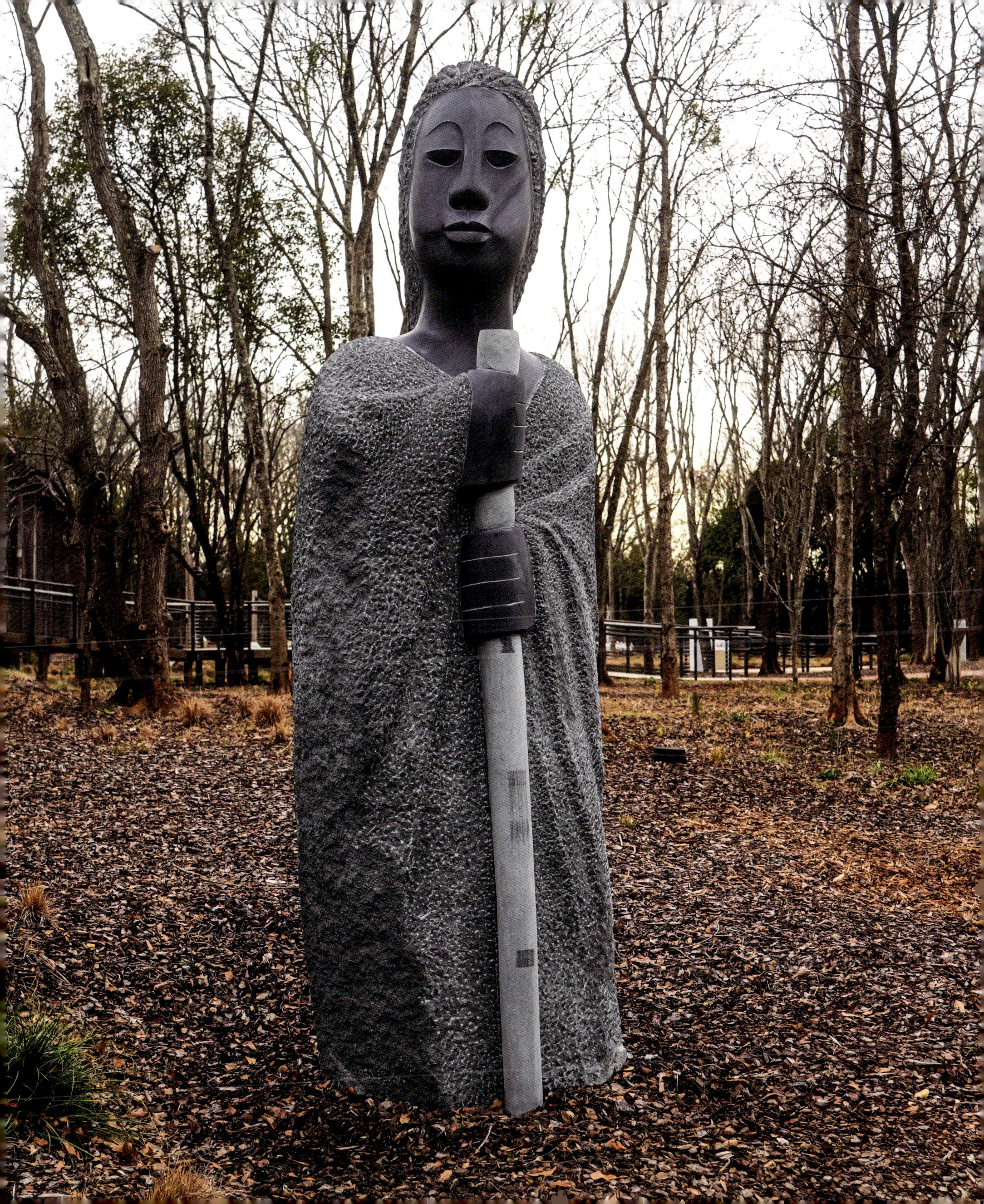

Africa: Cradle of Civilization

Africa is the birthplace of humankind and the site of countless human milestones, including the creation of the first stone tools, first astronomical sites, and first works of art. While many parts of the world remained dormant, cultures and civilizations on the African continent thrived.

Some seven thousand years ago, the great civilizations of Egypt and Kush established vast empires that reigned for more than a thousand years. Around 2000 BCE, the Bantu people spread advanced knowledge of ironworking and agricultural science as they expanded across the continent from West Africa.

In the early centuries of the Common Era, the Kingdom of Aksum, centered in modern-day Ethiopia, organized extensive trade routes between China, India, and Rome and was renowned for its monumental architecture.

On the East African coast, commercial city-states like Mogadishu, Mombasa, Kilwa, and Sofala attracted merchants from across the Indian Ocean buying gold, ivory, and specialized goods such as camel-hair cloth and high-grade iron ore.

In the medieval period, the West African kingdoms of Ghana, Songhai, and Mali were among the world's largest economies and featured highly prestigious centers of learning. Other West African peoples such as the Edo, the Yoruba, and the Asante created eminent works of sculpture in bronze, terra-cotta, and gold.

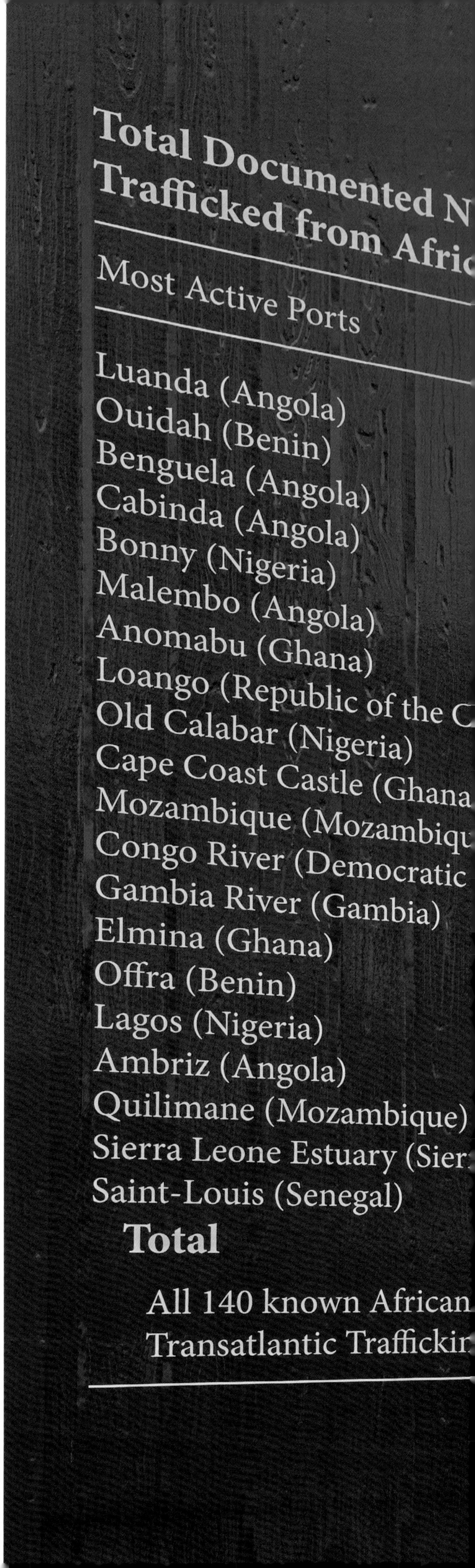

...er of Kidnapped People ...Ports, 1501 –1867

	Number of People Trafficked
	2,826,000
	1,004,000
	764,000
	753,000
	672,000
	549,000
)	466,000
	418,000
	412,000
	318,000
	293,000
...ublic of the Congo)	276,000
	258,000
	255,000
	231,000
	230,000
	206,000
	159,000
...one)	148,000
	145,000
	10,383,000
...s for ...mbined	12,520,000

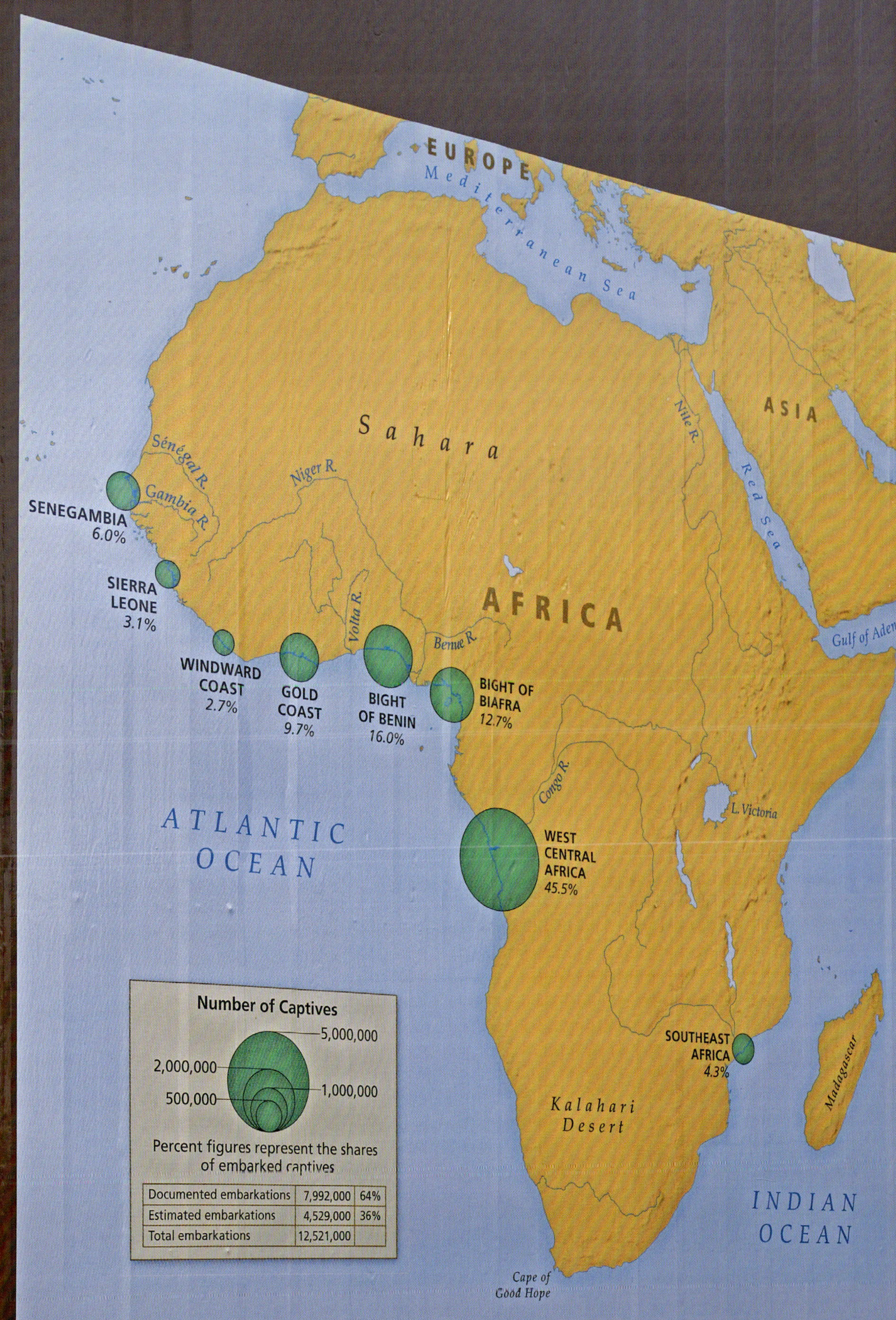

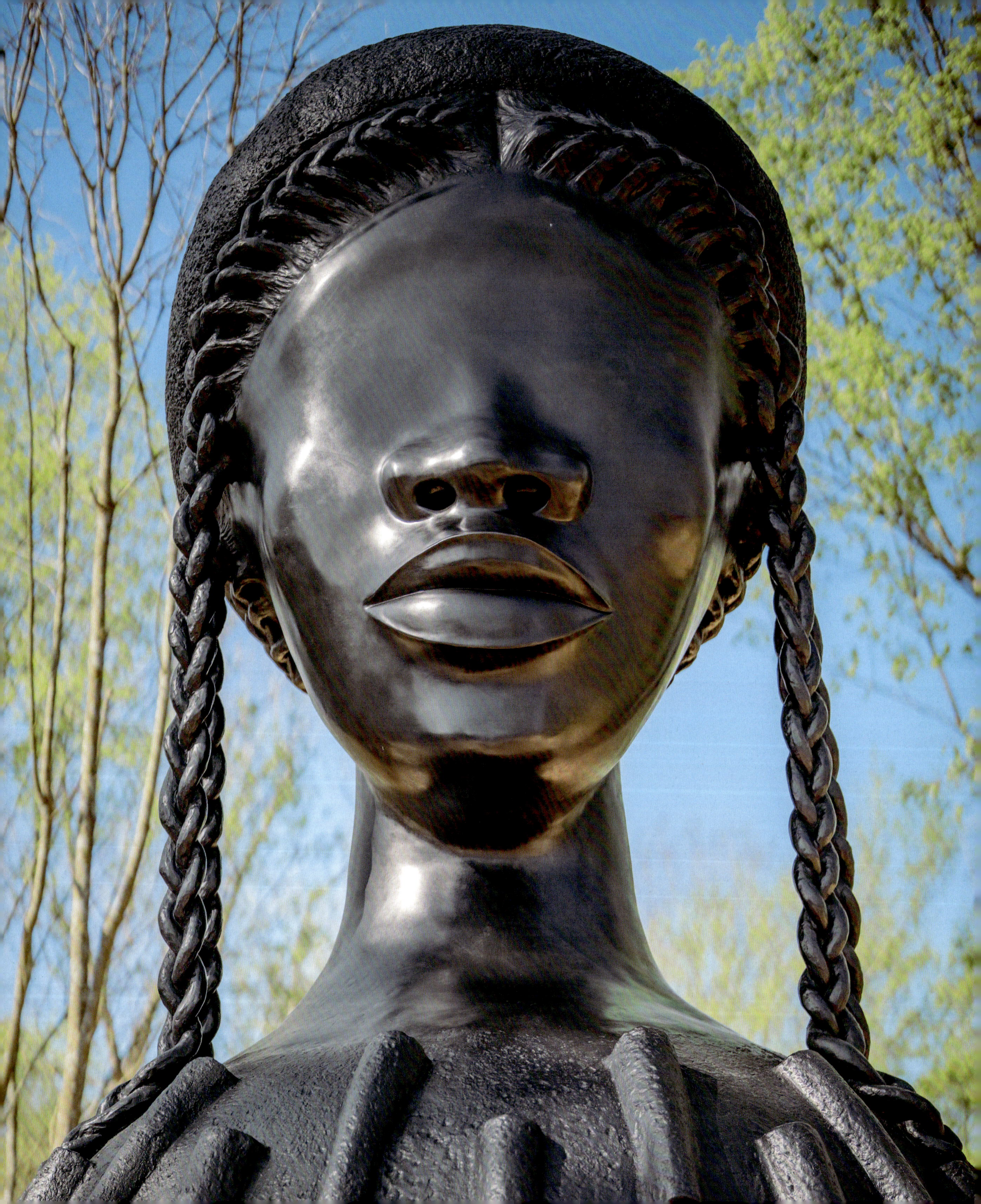

Simone Leigh

Born in Chicago, Simone Leigh (b. 1967) is a sculptor and video installation artist based in Brooklyn. She describes her work practice as "auto-ethnographic," informed by her Black female identity and rooted in African cultural traditions. Recognizing the lack of preservation of Black history, Leigh also evokes narrative and fiction in her work. Her experience as the daughter of Jamaican missionaries led to her dedication to exploring the histories of Black women.

Her work has been exhibited at the Guggenheim Museum in New York, the Tate Gallery in London, the Studio Museum in Harlem, and the Hammer Museum in Los Angeles, among other prominent institutions worldwide. A major retrospective of her work started a national tour in 2023 that included the Institute of Contemporary Art/Boston, the Hirshhorn Museum and Sculpture Garden in Washington, D.C., and the Los Angeles County Museum of Art in a joint presentation with the California African American Museum.

Early in her career, she was told that her ceramic sculptures would never be shown in contemporary arts spaces. Her work was excluded and ignored for many years, but she used that time to develop her craft, even if no one would see or appreciate her work or the messages she hoped to convey.

Leigh was one of the first artists to be commissioned for the High Line Plinth in New York City, where her commission, *Brick House*, was unveiled in April 2019. *Brick House* celebrates the strength and beauty of Black women in a public space, where the worth and humanity of Black women has often been diminished. Leigh has been widely recognized for her sculptures of Black women and commentary on their labor. In 2022, Leigh became the first Black woman to represent the U.S. at the Venice Biennale, where she won the Golden Lion for the year's best artist.

Leigh's works explore themes of traditional African cultures, Black feminism, postcolonial theory, and racial politics. She often centers the history of Black emancipation and connects it to Black liberation organizations. In addition to *Brick House*, her sculptures *109 (Face Jug Series)*, *Jug*, and *Anonymous* are also included at the art gallery in the Legacy Museum.

Brick House (detail)

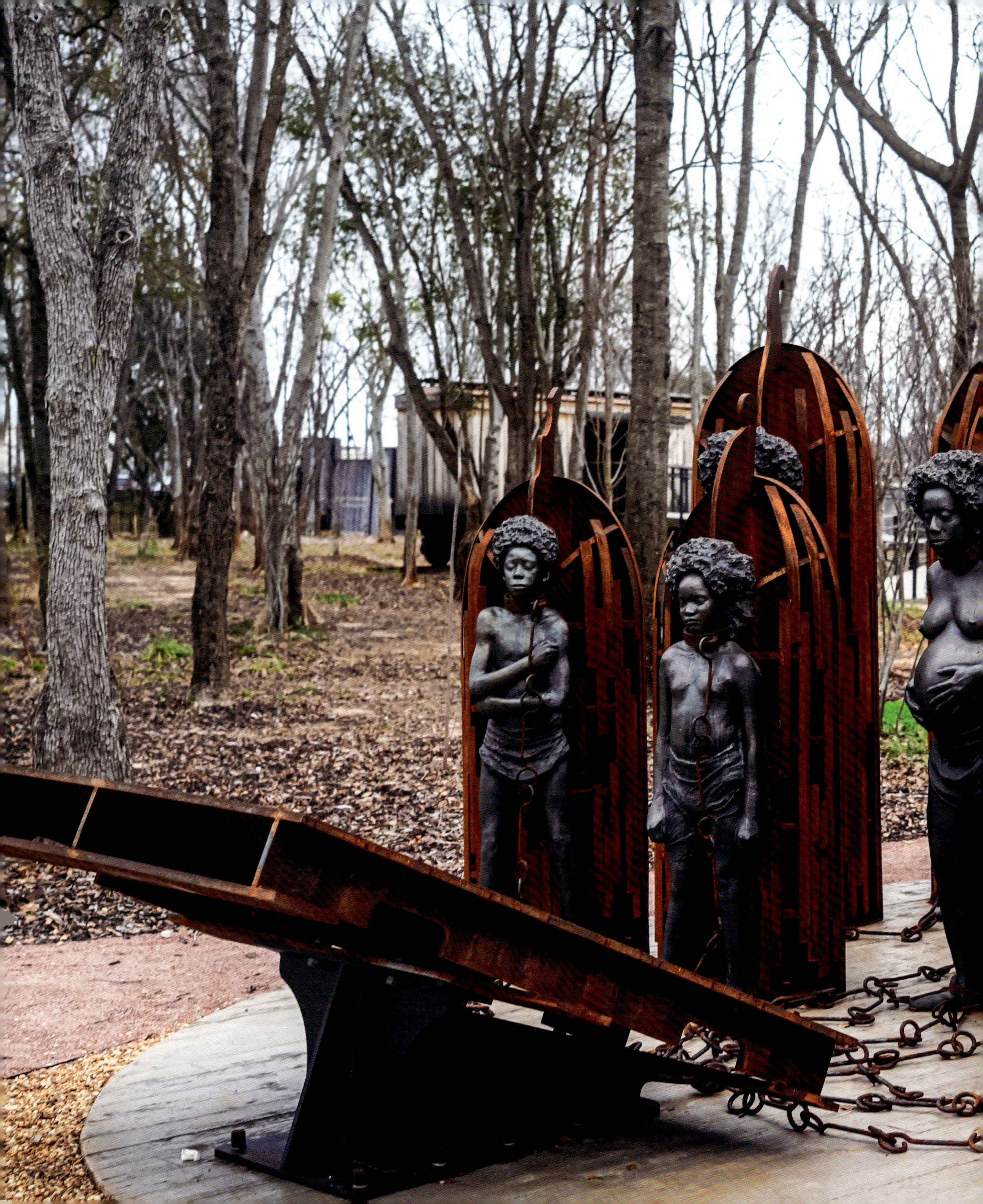

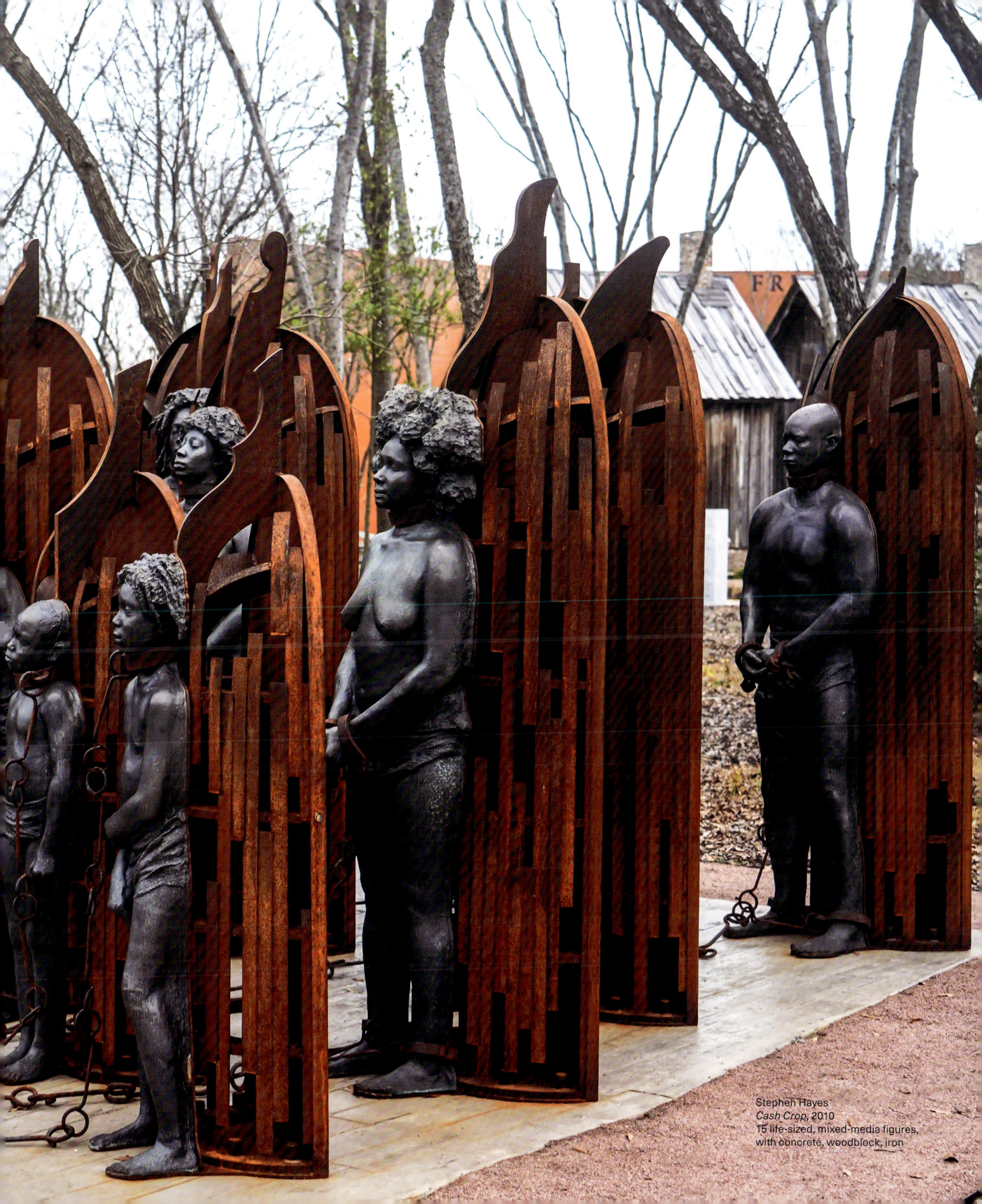

Stephen Hayes
Cash Crop, 2010
15 life-sized, mixed-media figures, with concrete, woodblock, iron

The Transatlantic Trade of Enslaved People

The enslavement of human beings occupies a painful and tragic space in world history. Denying a person freedom, autonomy, and life through enslavement represents the worst kind of human rights abuse.

An expanded new era of transatlantic enslavement arose in the fifteenth century, when ships from Europe and the Americas began trafficking millions of kidnapped Africans to North, Central, and South America. Ships from Portugal and its colony Brazil were responsible for trafficking nearly six million abducted people from Africa. And ships originating in Great Britain were responsible for trafficking more than a quarter of all people taken from Africa from 1501 to 1867. From 1726 to 1800, British ships were the leading traffickers of kidnapped Africans, responsible for taking more than two million people from the African continent in that short time span.

From 1626 to 1867, ships from North America were responsible for trafficking hundreds of thousands of Black people abducted in Africa. In the two years before the U.S. ended the Transatlantic Trade of Enslaved People in 1808, a quarter of all trafficked Africans were carried in ships that flew the U.S. flag. Rhode Island's ports combined to organize voyages responsible for trafficking at least 110,000 kidnapped Africans, making it one of the fifteen largest originating ports in the world.

During the horrendous journey across the Atlantic, women, men, and children were packed into filthy cargo holds without enough food, air, or space. Almost two million Africans died during the Middle Passage.

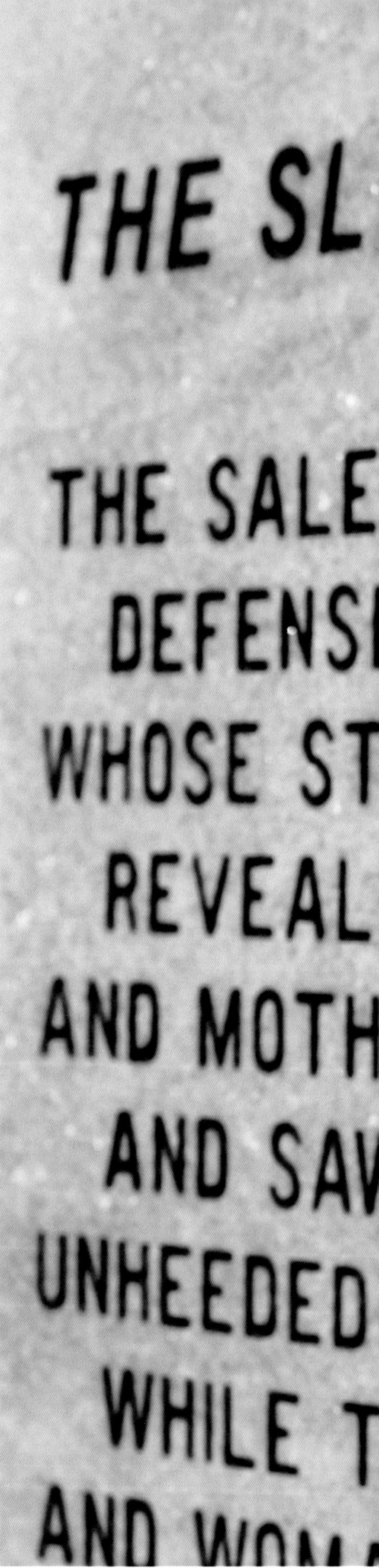

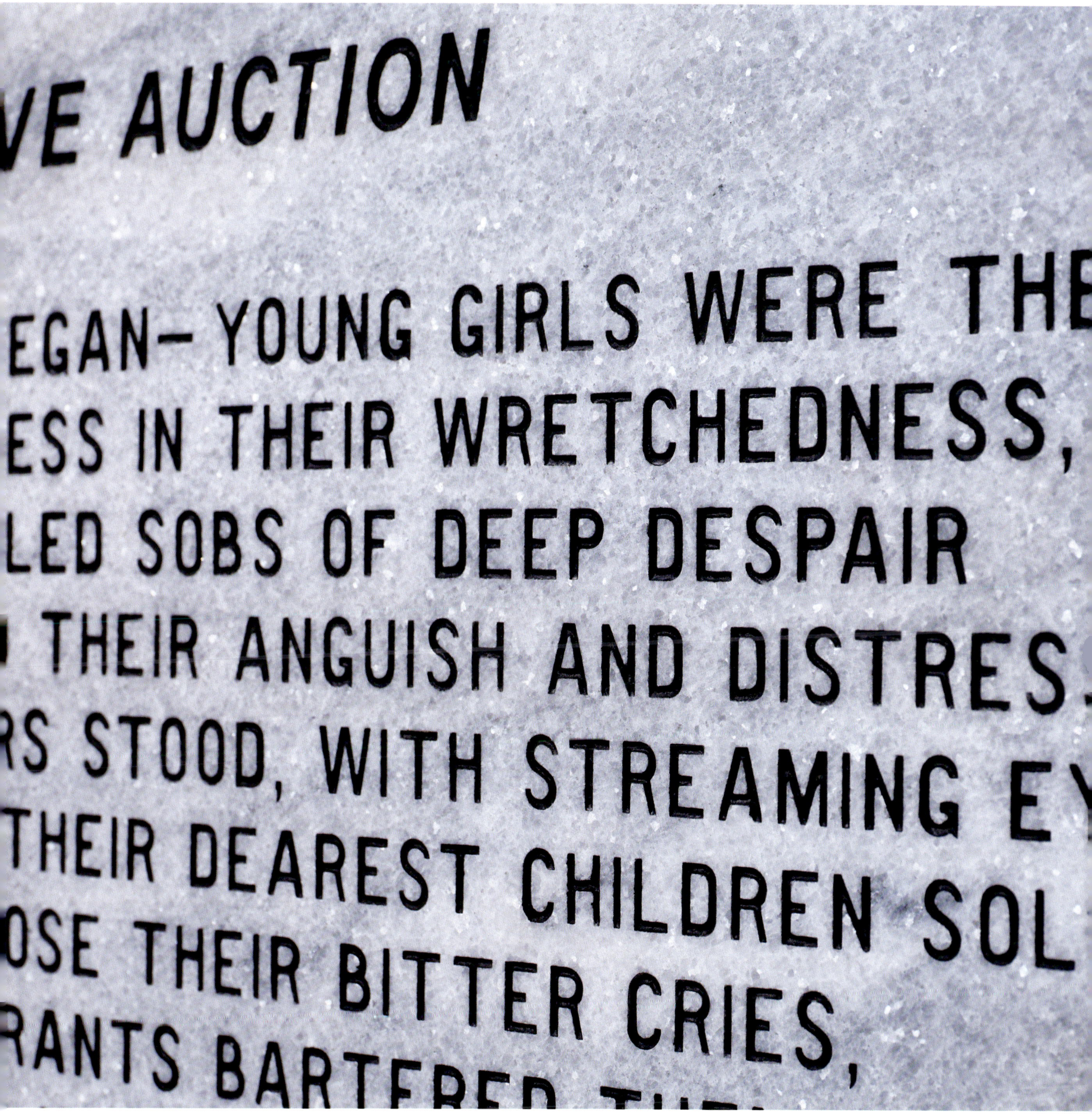

VE AUCTION

EGAN– YOUNG GIRLS WERE THE
ESS IN THEIR WRETCHEDNESS,
LED SOBS OF DEEP DESPAIR
THEIR ANGUISH AND DISTRES
RS STOOD, WITH STREAMING EY
THEIR DEAREST CHILDREN SOL
OSE THEIR BITTER CRIES,
RANTS BARTERED

Kwame Akoto-Bamfo

Kwame Akoto-Bamfo (b. 1983) is a Ghanaian sculptor and installation artist whose work is dedicated to preserving African heritage. He has a Master of Fine Arts degree from Kwame Nkrumah University of Science and Technology in Kumasi and leads Osramba Studio, which is committed to empowering and educating multimedia artists, architects, designers, and craftsmen in Accra.

He founded the Ancestor Project, which he describes as "a conscious effort by the creators (artists and volunteers) and participants (everybody else) to promote African heritage values through the use of art, music, and performance." In 2015, he won the Kuenyehia Art Prize, Ghana's top award for contemporary art.

His best known work is *Nkyinkyim Installation*, which depicts the trauma of enslavement and racial violence and the diverse culture, history, and heritage of African people. This ever-growing collection of humanistic sculptures spans both sides of the Atlantic, with hundreds of sculpted heads installed in Ghana and connected works at our Legacy Sites in Montgomery.

"Each sculpture has a story," Akoto-Bamfo has said. "Traditionally in African art, the head represents everything—your soul, your being. It has your eyes. So in the faces you can see their identity. These were living beings; you can relate to them. It's that that I'm trying to capture."

Akoto-Bamfo conveys the resilience of enslaved people in connected sculptures at Freedom Monument Sculpture Park. *We Am Very Cold* portrays survivors of the Middle Passage who reappear and affirm their love and strength in *Mama, I hurt my hand*. "We should become conscious that this is a continuum," he told *Harper's Bazaar*. "We like to forget or cut things off, but it is a continuum; and you and I, we all play a part of this narrative."

The sculpture park documents brutal violence against Black people during and since enslavement and ultimately celebrates those who resisted hopelessness and persevered. "I can vent in the works, show the harshness, be explosive," Akoto-Bamfo said, because violence does not get the last word at the park. Instead, "there is closure or a way forward for people who visit," which inspires him to see his work with EJI as "a canvas of peace."

Opposite and pages 212–
Kwame Akoto-Bamfo
We Am Very Cold, 2023
Bronze

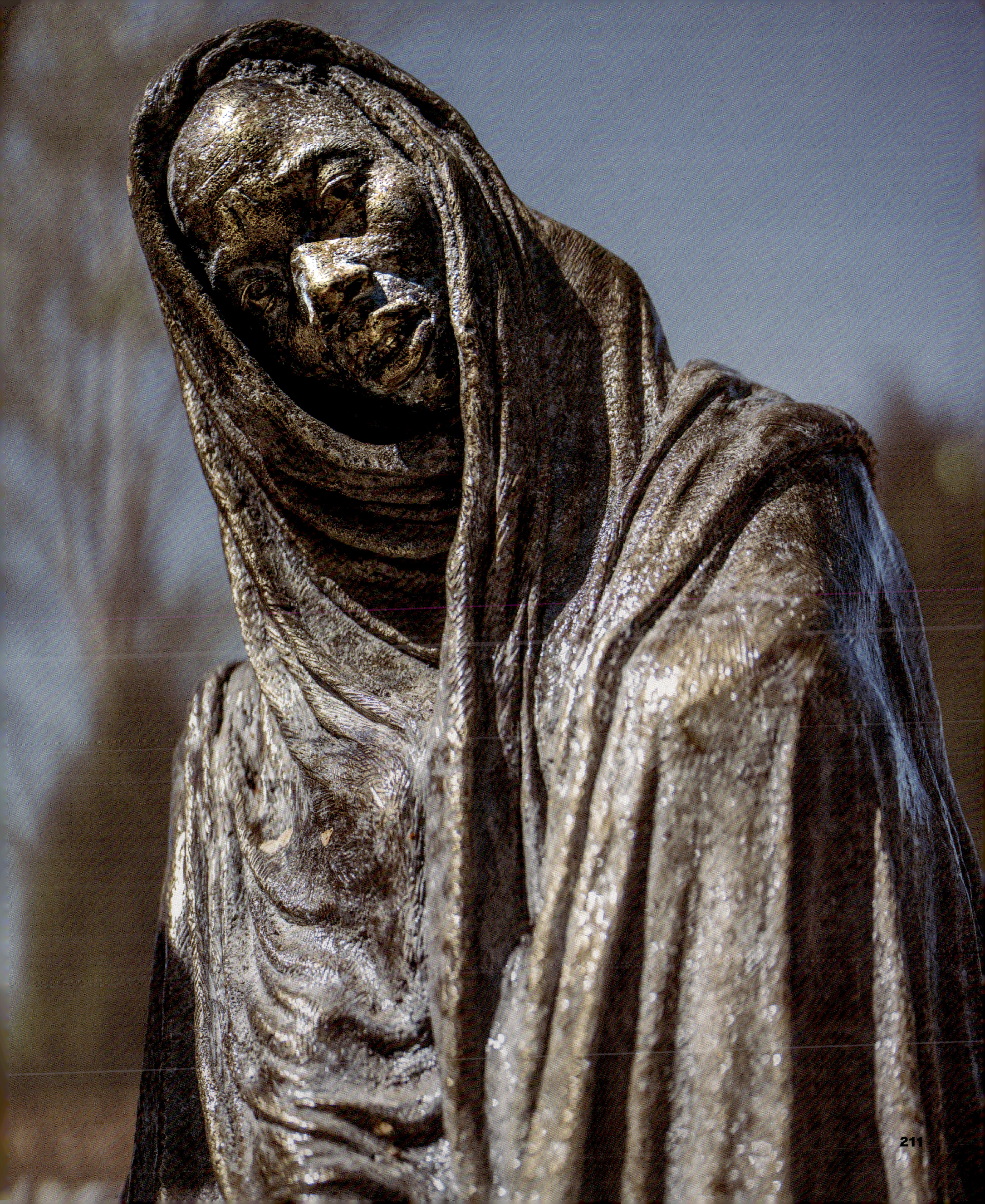

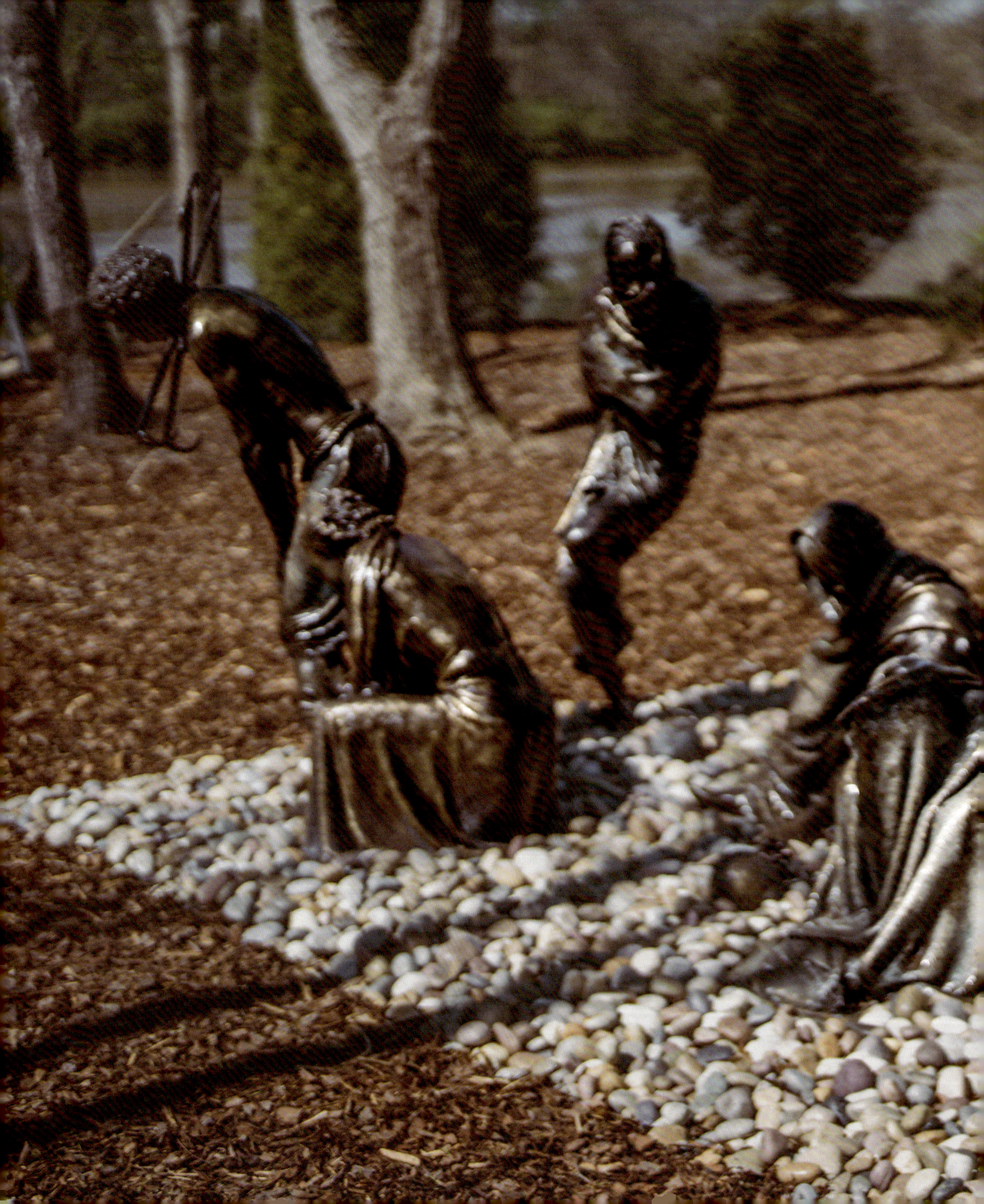

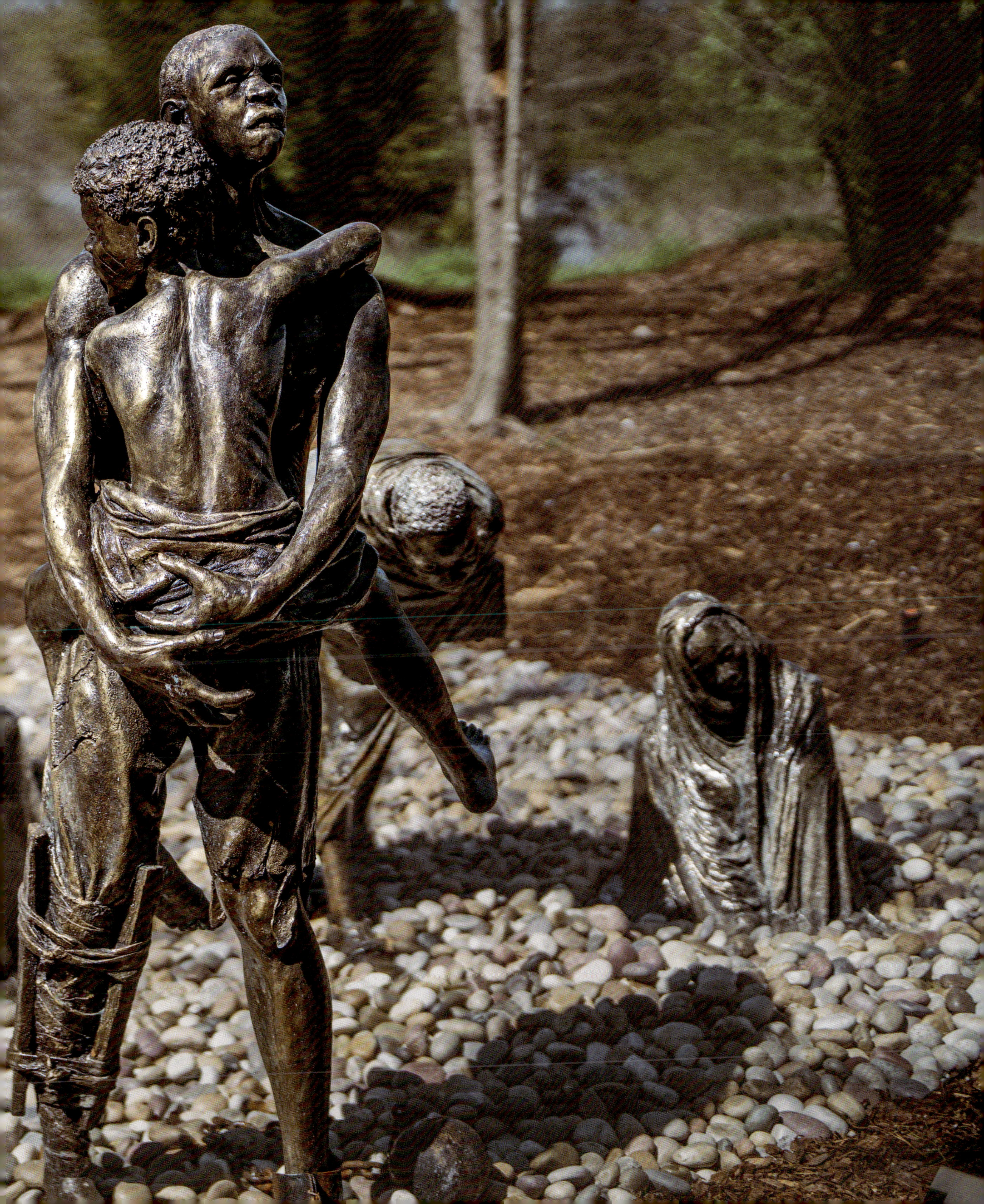

As all were chained together night and day, it was impossible to sleep, being annoyed by the bustle and crowd of the passengers on board; by the terrible thought that we were destined to be sold in markets as sheep or oxen; and annoyed by the galling chains that cramped our wearied limbs.

— HENRY BIBB, *NARRATIVE OF THE LIFE AND ADVENTURES OF HENRY BIBB, AN AMERICAN SLAVE* (1815–1854)

Trafficking by River

Tens of thousands of enslaved people were trafficked by boat on the Alabama River in the nineteenth century. Steamboats greatly reduced the amount of time it took to traffic enslaved people. By the 1840s, steamboats carrying more than two hundred enslaved people at a time could complete a 250-mile journey in less than a day.

Some ships were specifically built to traffic enslaved people, and traffickers used steamships to communicate with enslavers up and down the river to arrange sales and secure financial backing.

Many enslaved people lived in terror of being separated from their loved ones and trafficked by steamship to the especially brutal plantations in the Deep South. The constant threat of being "sold down the river" was an enormous burden.

Enslaved people endured horrific conditions aboard riverboats, where they were crowded together and confined with little protection from the elements. They were kept away from the edges of the boat to prevent escape. Some who were able to make it to the edge of the ship drowned themselves in the river.

Enslaved people were brought to Montgomery from Mobile and New Orleans via the Alabama River. Once they arrived at a port, enslavers would parade enslaved people through the streets to be sold in "slave markets," after which they were loaded on another ship or marched to a plantation or other forced labor site.

Thousands of enslaved people were forced to work on steamships, performing the most difficult and dangerous jobs. Every year, hundreds of trafficked and laboring enslaved people died or suffered serious injuries on steamboats from disease, privation, boiler explosions, and other hazards.

White passengers traveled in close proximity to people who were being trafficked in inhumane conditions, but most were largely indifferent to the suffering of enslaved people. One enslaved person forced to work on a riverboat recalled, "A drove of slaves on a southern steamboat, bound for the cotton or sugar regions, is an occurrence so common, that no one, not even the passengers, appear to notice it, though they clank their chains at every step."

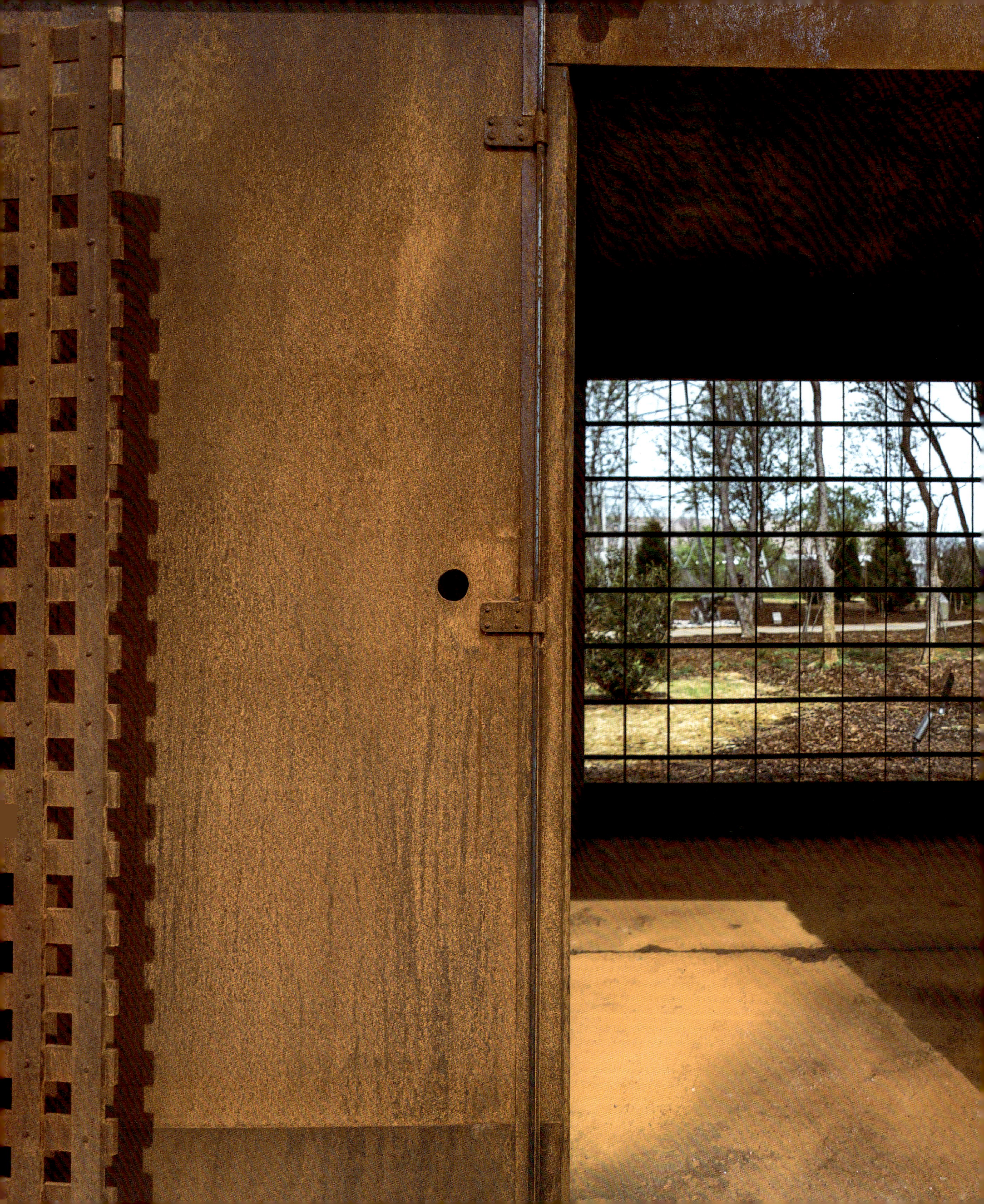

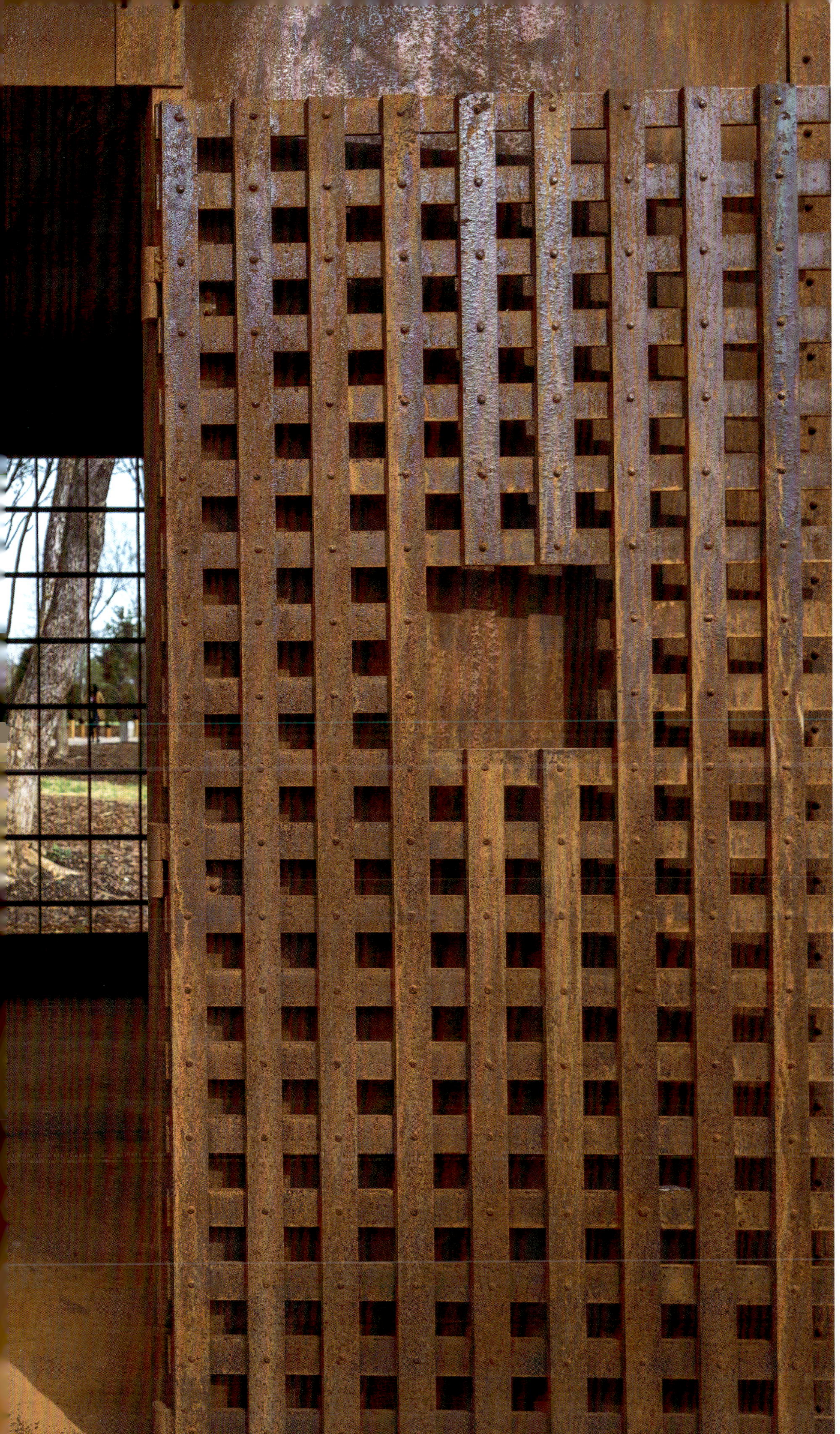

Holding pens like this one were used to imprison enslaved people waiting in agony to be sold at auctions alongside livestock and farming implements.

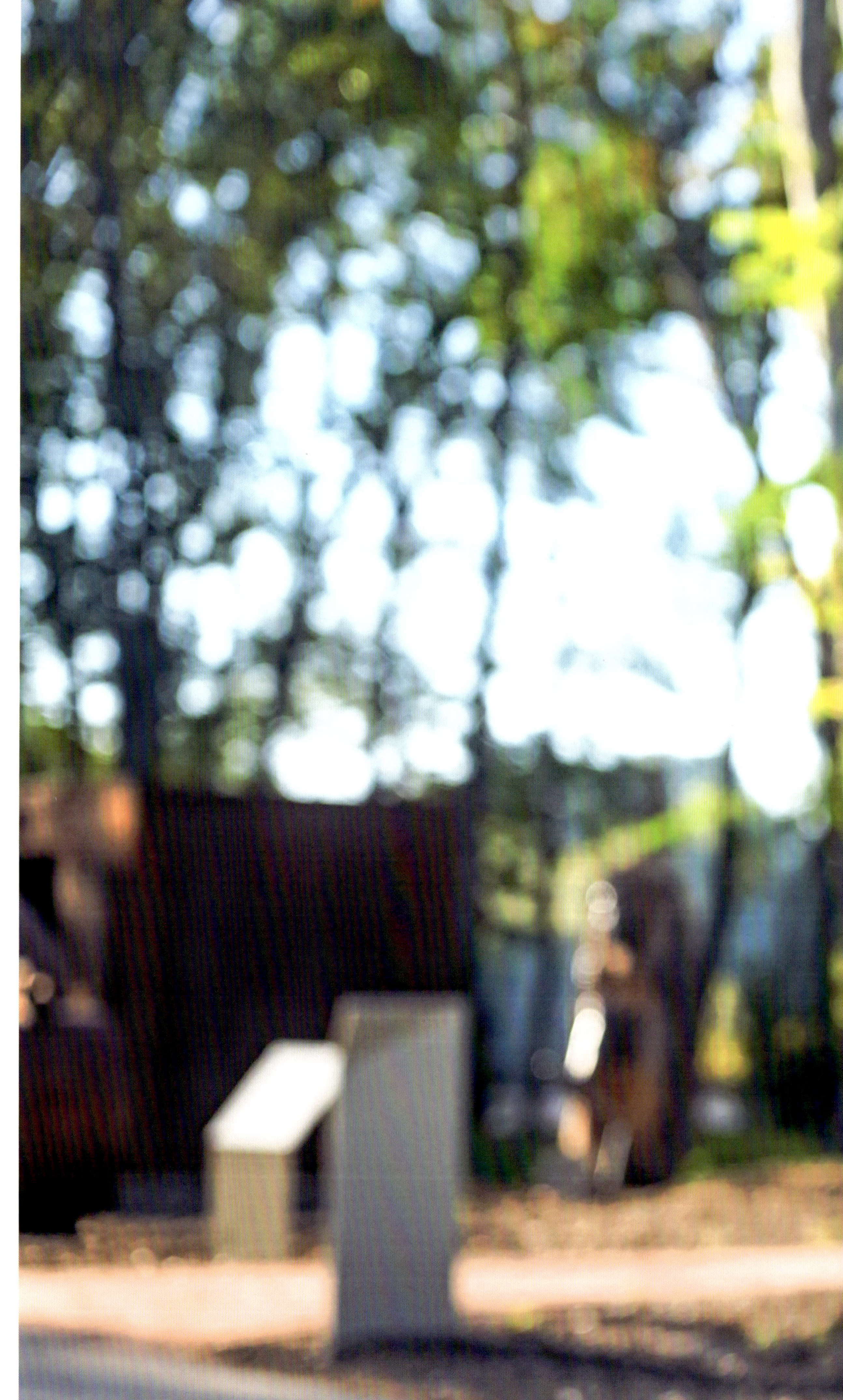

Vinnie Bagwell
Waiting for Auction (detail), 2024
Bronze

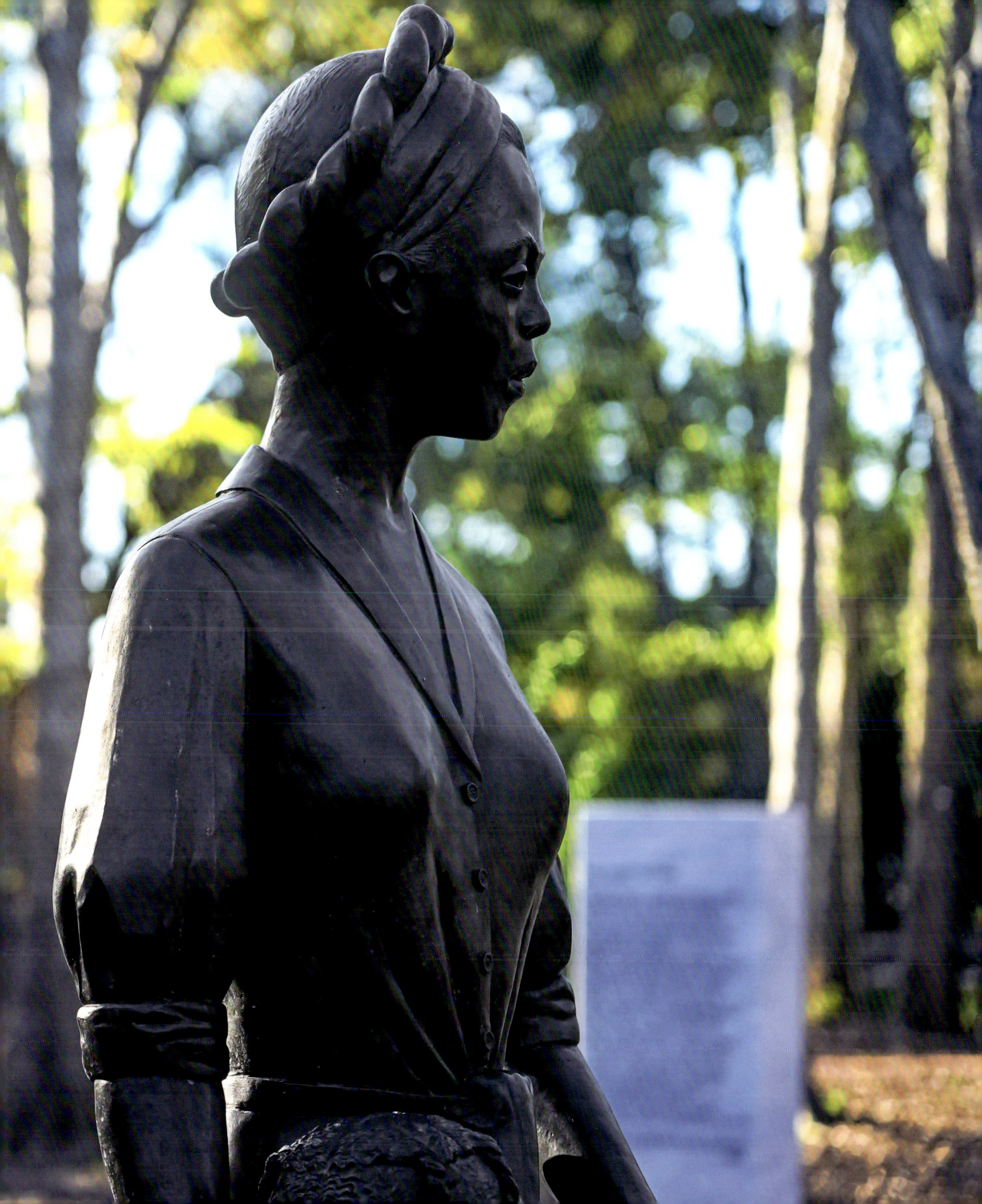

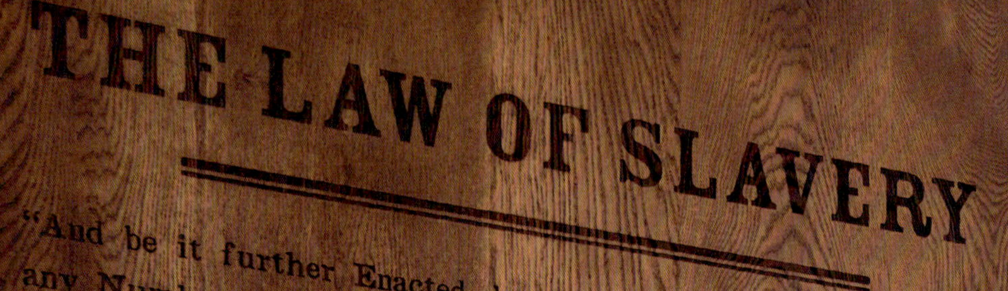

"And be it further Enacted, by the Authority aforesaid, That if any Number of Negroes or other Slaves, that is to say, Three or more, shall at any Time hereafter, consult, advise or conspire to rebel, or make insurrection, or shall plot or conspire the Murder of any Person or Persons whatsoever, every such consulting, plotting, or conspiring, shall be adjudged and deemed Felony; And the Slave or Slaves convicted thereof, in Manner hereafter directed, shall suffer Death."

North Carolina, 1741

"Be it further enacted, That . . . every slave which shall be found out of any town in this province, if such slave lives or is usually employed there, or out of the plantation to which such slave belongs, or in which such slave is usually employed, if such slave lives in the country, without a ticket as aforesaid, or without a white person in his or her company, shall be punished with whipping on the bare back, not exceeding twenty lashes."

Georgia, 1770

And be it further enacted, That if any slave, who shall be out of the house or plantation where such slave doth live, or is usually employed, or without some white person in company of such slave, shall refuse to submit to the examination of any white person, it shall be lawful for any such white person to pursue, apprehend and moderately correct such slave, and if such slave assault and strike such white person, such slave may be lawfully killed."

Georgia, 1770

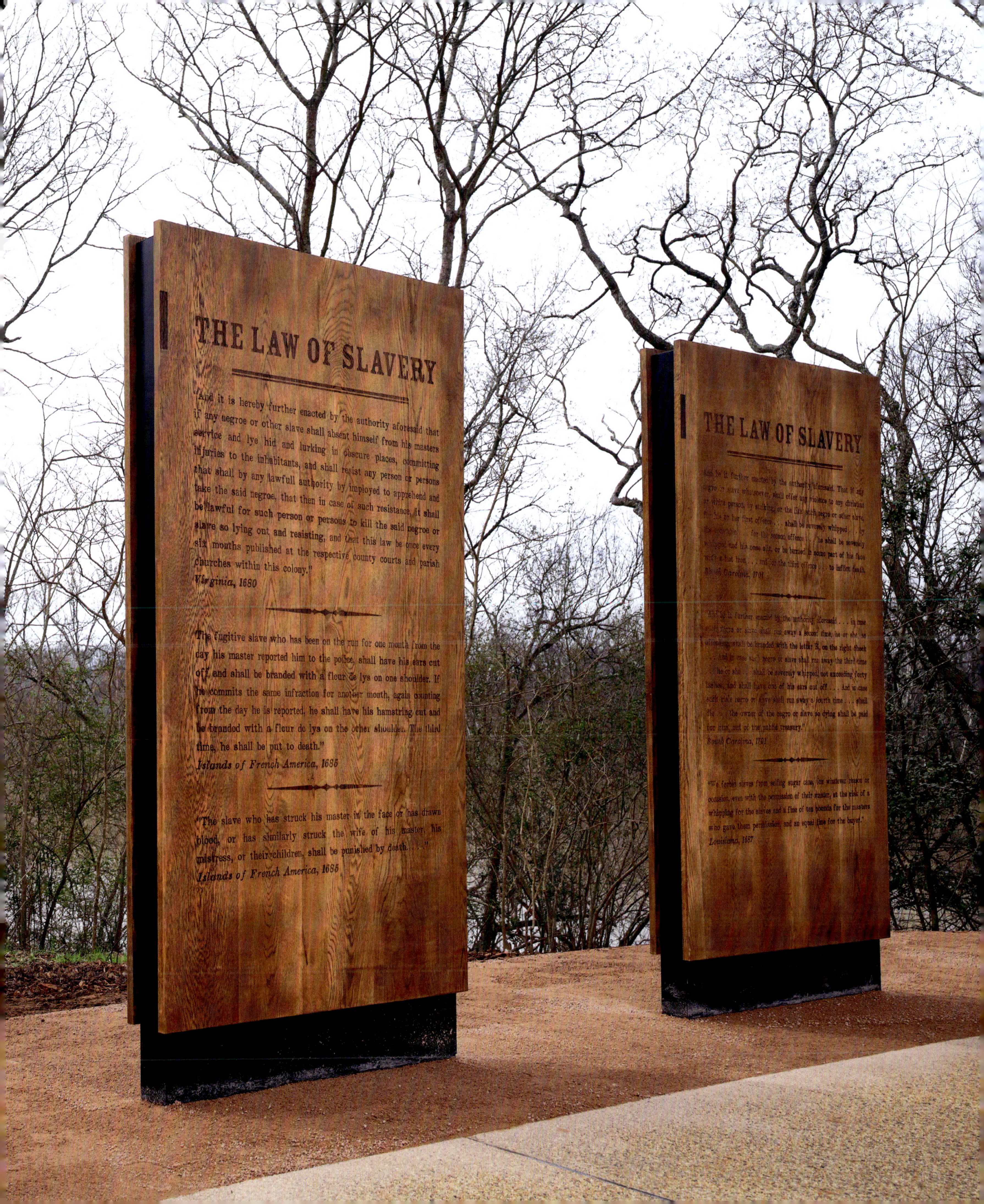
THE LAW OF SLAVERY
"And it is hereby further enacted by the authority aforesaid that if any negroe or other slave shall absent himself from his masters service and lye hid and lurking in obscure places, committing injuries to the inhabitants, and shall resist any person or persons that shall by any lawfull authority by imployed to apprehend and take the said negroe, that then in case of such resistance, it shall be lawfull for such person or persons to kill the said negroe or slave so lying out and resisting; and that this law be once every six months published at the respective county courts and parish churches within this colony."
Virginia, 1680
"The fugitive slave who has been on the run for one month from the day his master reported him to the police, shall have his ears cut off and shall be branded with a fleur de lys on one shoulder. If he commits the same infraction for another month, again counting from the day he is reported, he shall have his hamstring cut and be branded with a fleur de lys on the other shoulder. The third time, he shall be put to death."
Islands of French America, 1685
"The slave who has struck his master in the face or has drawn blood, or has similarly struck the wife of his master, his mistress, or their children, shall be punished by death . . ."
Islands of French America, 1685
THE LAW OF SLAVERY
South Carolina, 1701
"We forbid slaves from selling sugar cane, for whatever reason or occasion, even with the permission of their master, at the risk of a whipping for the slaves and a fine of ten pounds for the masters who gave them permission, and an equal fine for the buyer."
Louisiana, 1687

Rail Trafficking of Enslaved People

The railroad was a source of terror for the thousands of enslaved people who were trafficked by rail. Enslaved people were chained together and forced in groups of twenty or more into twenty-four- to thirty-foot cars. The departure of a train was often a moment of final separation for loved ones. A formerly enslaved person described the "weeping and wailing . . . as far as human voice could be heard" as a train filled with enslaved people left the station.

A traveler in the South reported, "I have not been on or seen a railroad train, departing southward, that did not convey a considerable number" of enslaved people.

Under the guise of upholding fugitive slave laws, "slave traders" kidnapped tens of thousands of free Black people from the North and took many of them to the South by train in efforts to outpace those trying to rescue them.

At Freedom Monument Sculpture Park, visitors can step inside a railcar like those used to traffic enslaved people as they hear trains pass by on a railway originally built by enslaved people more than 160 years ago.

The Law of Slavery

American colonies and states passed laws to create a racial caste system in the U.S. Brutal and violent punishments were imposed to maintain racial domination and preserve the institution of slavery and the enslavement of millions of Black people.

These laws were used to justify and codify the permanent, hereditary, and unending enslavement of Black people for generations.

The laws that regulated slavery reveal the horrors faced by enslaved people and the strategies states used to preserve racial hierarchy. It is impossible to understand the character of slavery in America without knowing about these laws and their legacy.

A whipping post was used to inflict brutal punishment on Black people in Georgetown, Delaware, well into the twentieth century. It was not removed from the town square until 2020 and is now installed at Freedom Monument Sculpture Park.

The Slave Auction

The sale began—young girls were there,
  Defenseless in their wretchedness,
Whose stifled sobs of deep despair
  Revealed their anguish and distress.

And mothers stood, with streaming eyes,
  And saw their dearest children sold;
Unheeded rose their bitter cries,
  While tyrants bartered them for gold.

And woman, with her love and truth—
  For these in sable forms may dwell—
Gazed on the husband of her youth,
  With anguish none may paint or tell.

And men, whose sole crime was their hue,
  The impress of their Maker's hand,
And frail and shrinking children too,
  Were gathered in that mournful band.

Ye who have laid your loved to rest,
  And wept above their lifeless clay,
Know not the anguish of that breast,
  Whose loved are rudely torn away.

Ye may not know how desolate
  Are bosoms rudely forced to part,
And how a dull and heavy weight
  Will press the life-drops from the heart.

—FRANCES ELLEN WATKINS HARPER

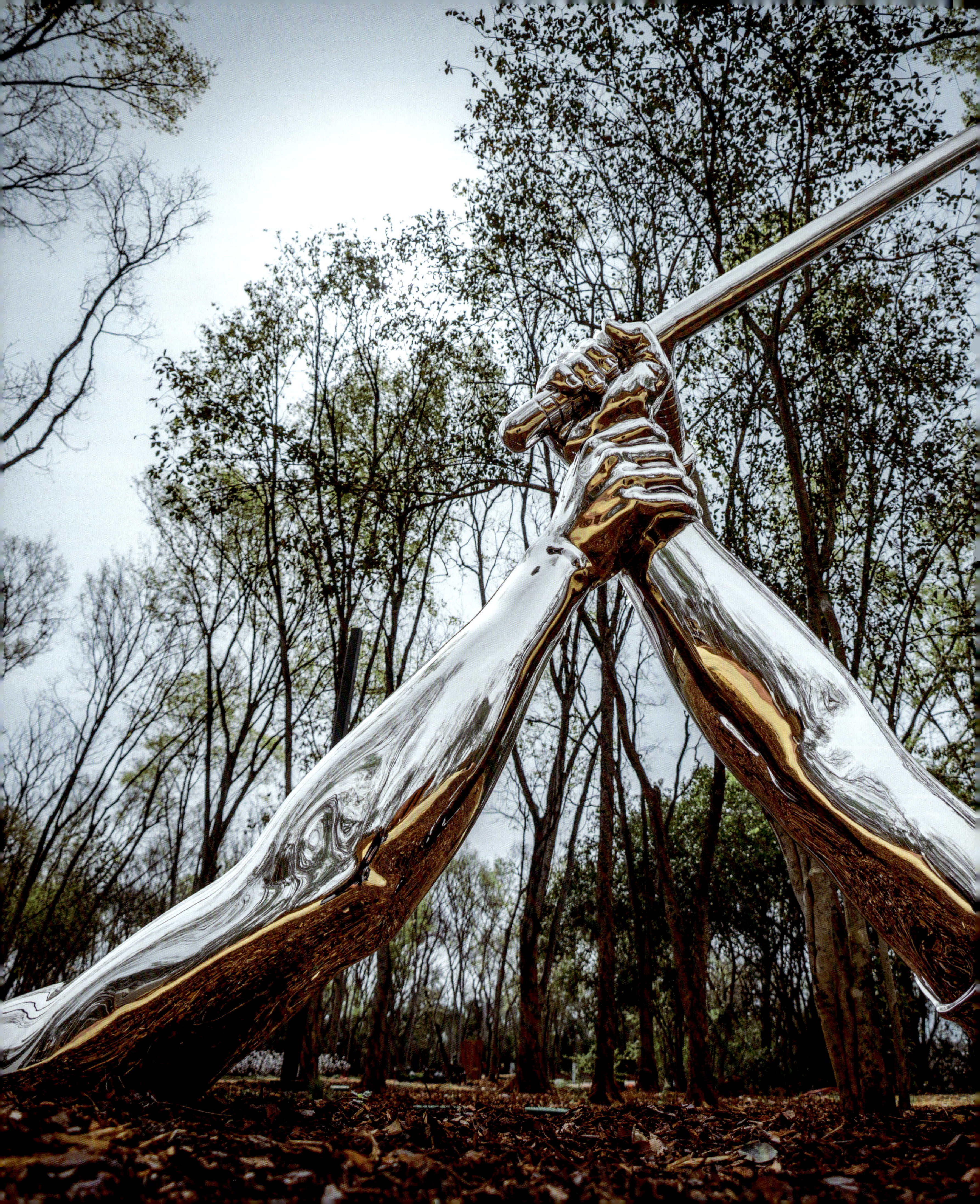

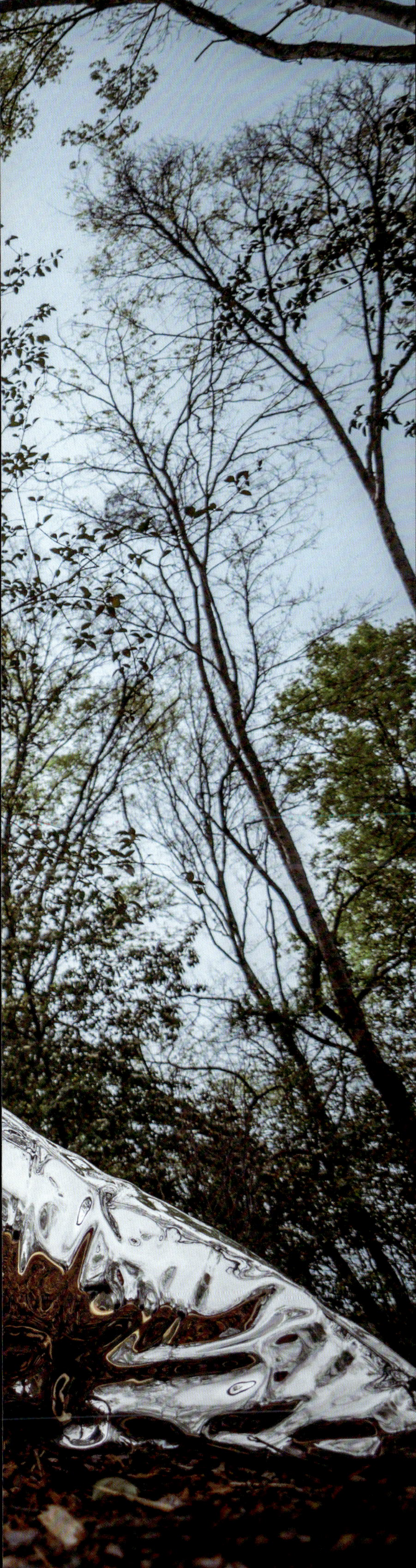

Hank Willis Thomas

Hank Willis Thomas (b. 1976) is a Brooklyn-based mixed-media artist and sculptor. He uses photography, sculpture, and installations to address themes of identity, culture, commodification, media, and perspectives.

Thomas earned a bachelor of fine arts from New York University and a master of fine arts from California College of the Arts. He has received honorary doctorates from the Maryland Institute of Art and the Institute for Doctoral Studies in Visual Arts.

Thomas's work explores the exploitative and stereotypical images of Black people in media and popular culture. He uses imagery from popular media, such as advertisements, to address the ways in which pervasive stereotypes have shaped American culture since enslavement.

He draws connections between the past and present by situating imagery in historical context and highlighting the ways in which the commodification of Black bodies has roots in the era of enslavement and has continued to the present day.

At Freedom Monument Sculpture Park, *Strike* evokes violence and resistance. "I'm also thinking about peace and resolution," Thomas said. "In this case, the gesture of just stopping the brutality begins the opportunity for us to find peace." His art is also featured in the Legacy Museum, where his work *A Luta Continua* is included, and at the National Memorial for Peace and Justice, with *Raise Up*.

Hank Willis Tho
Strike, 2018
Stainless steel

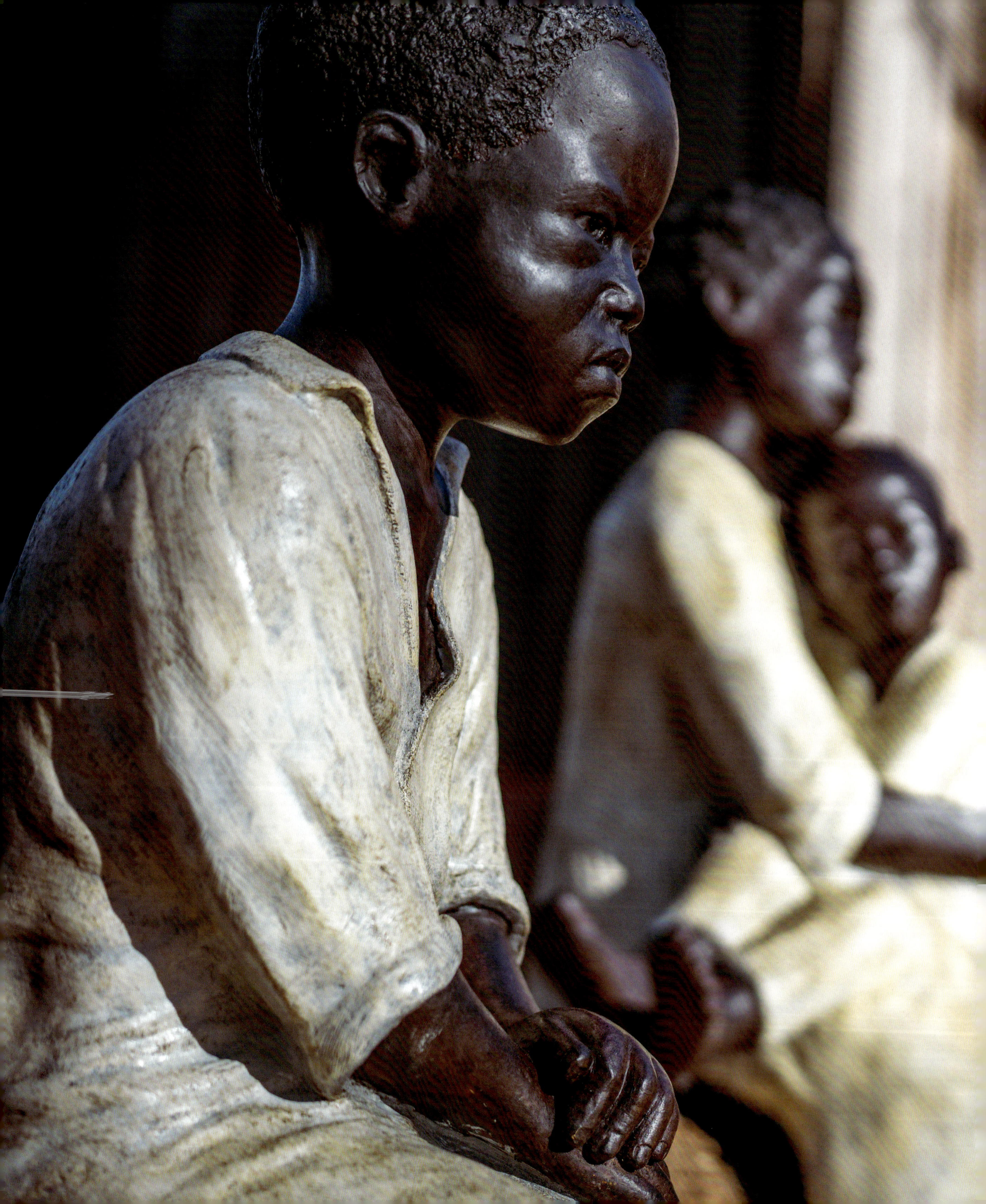

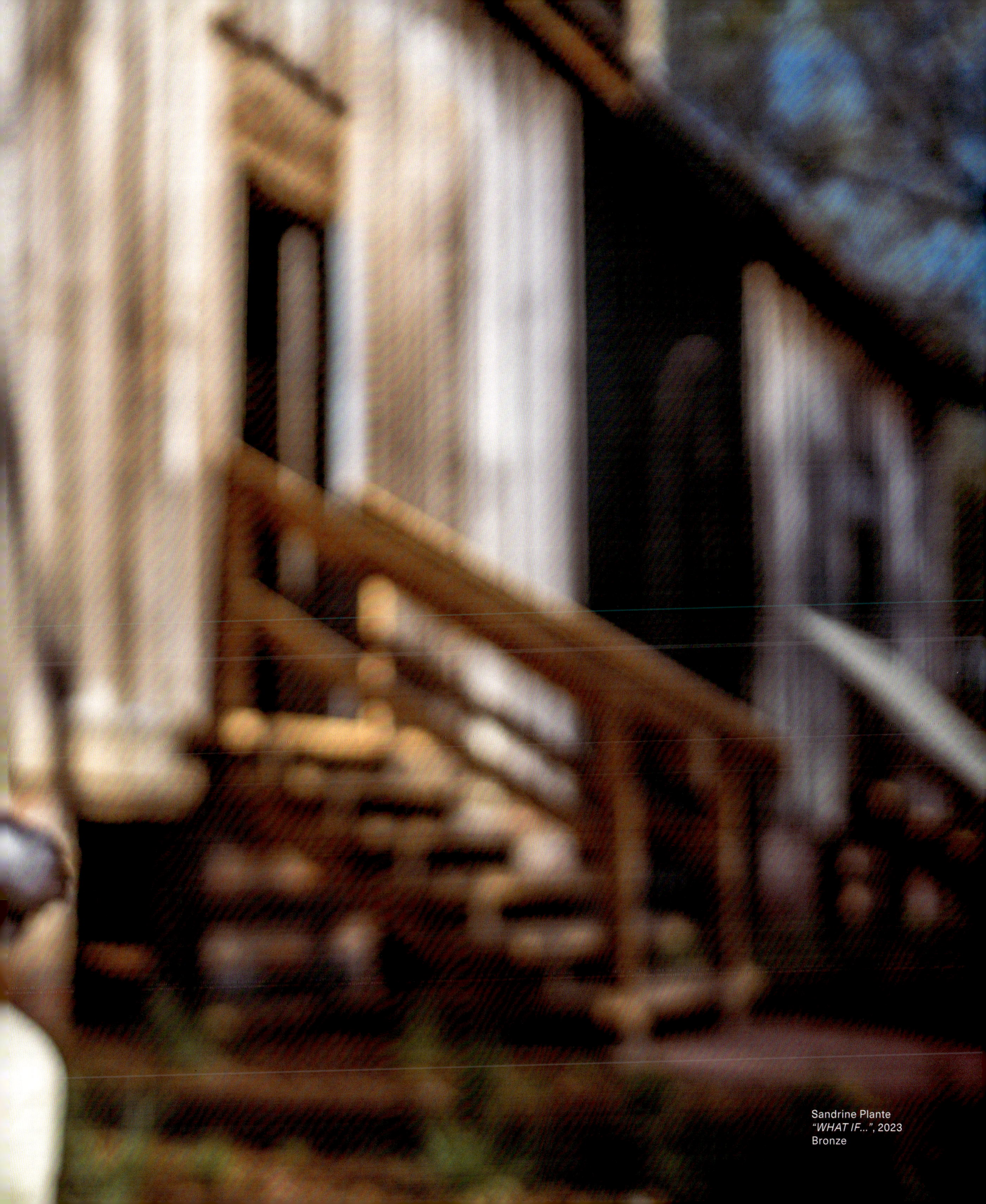

Sandrine Plante
"WHAT IF...", 2023
Bronze

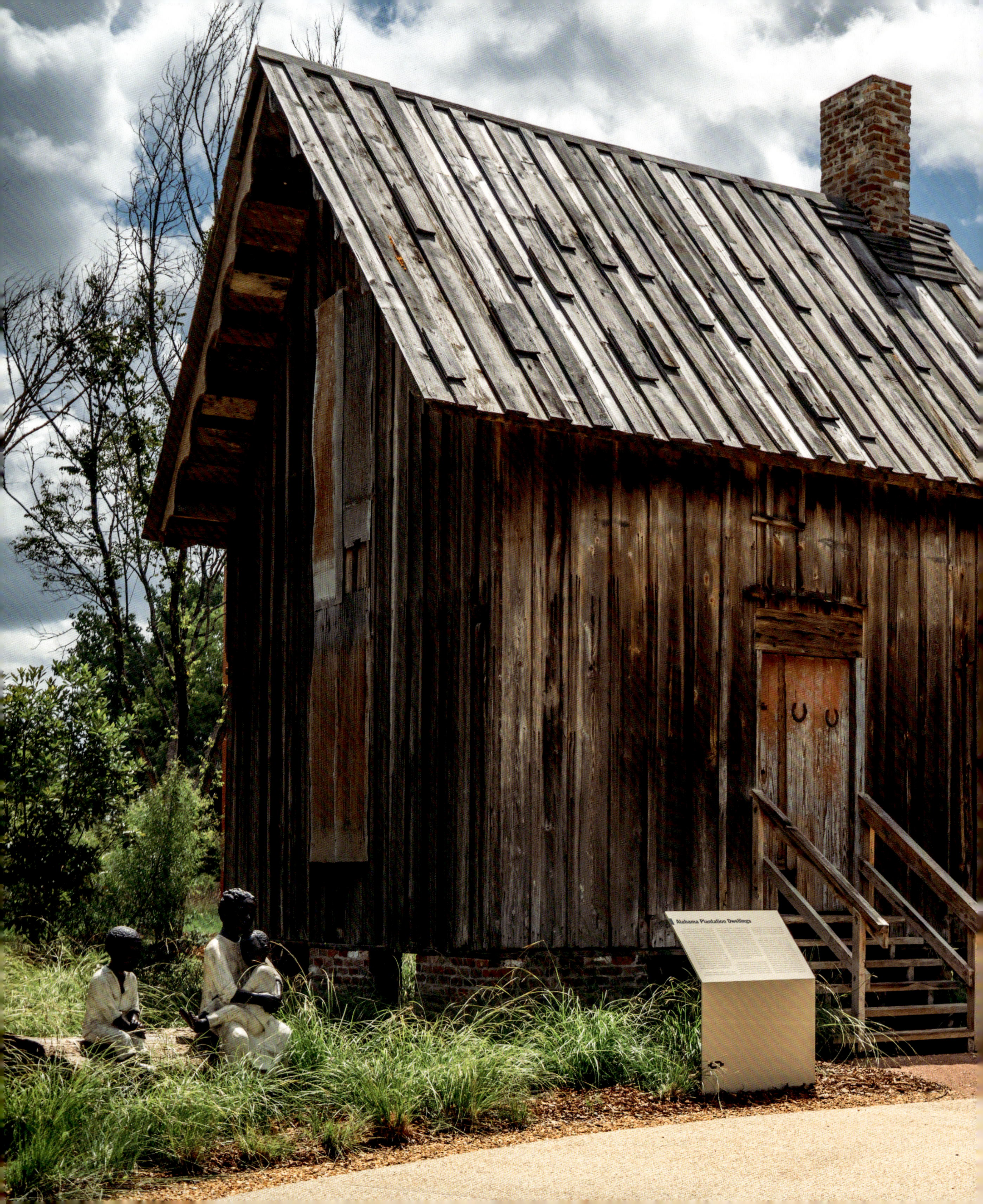
Alabama Plantation Dwellings

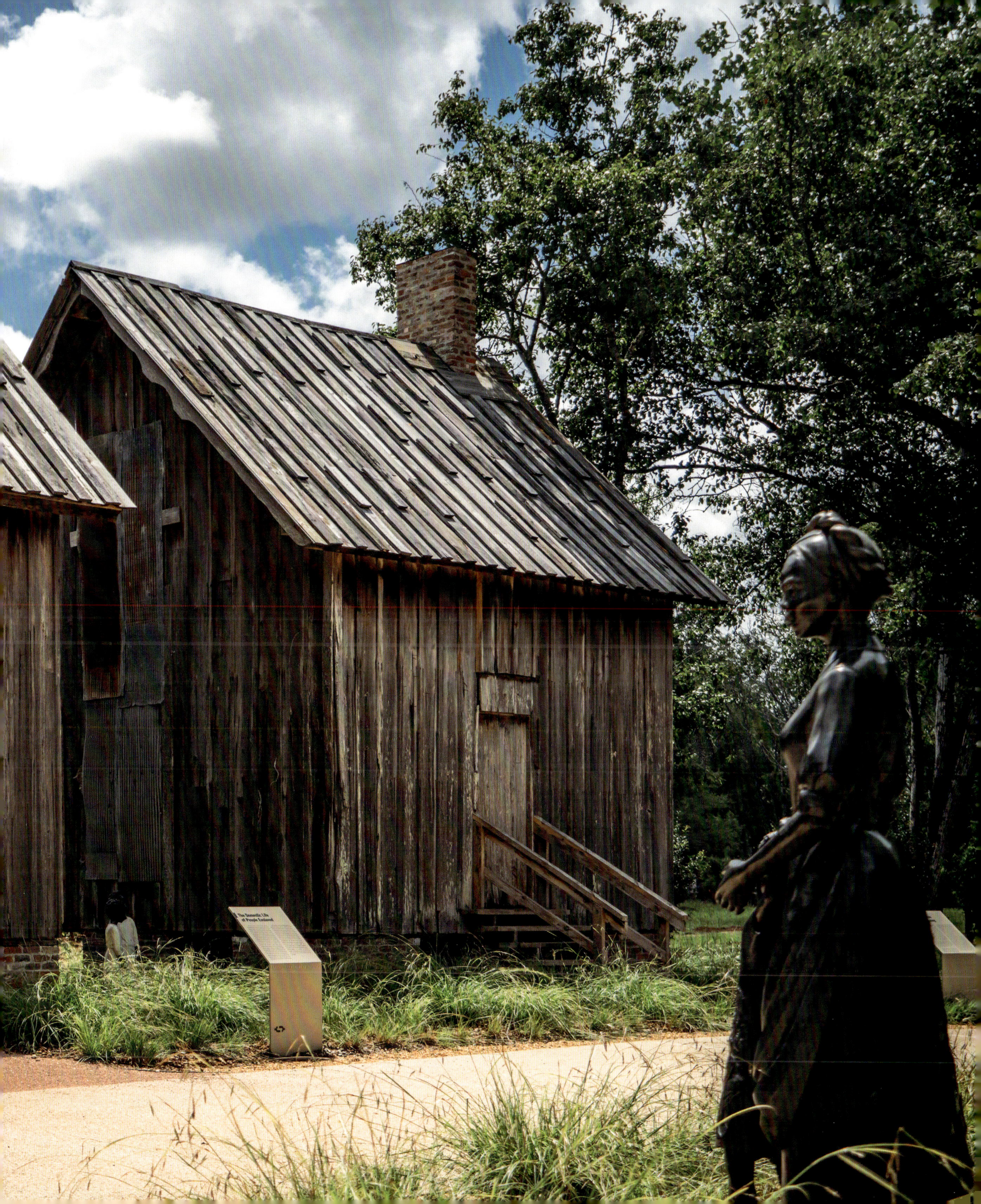

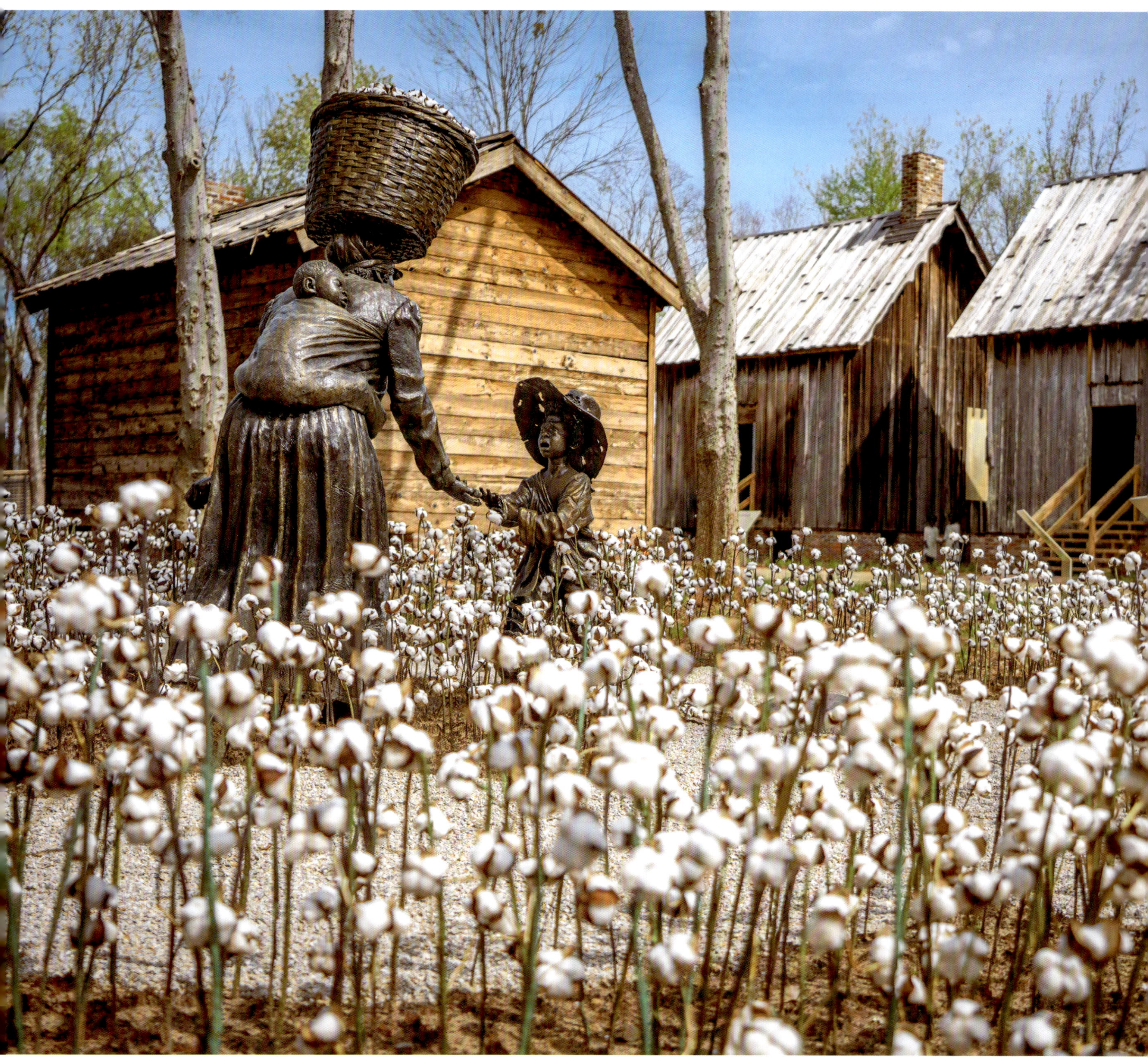

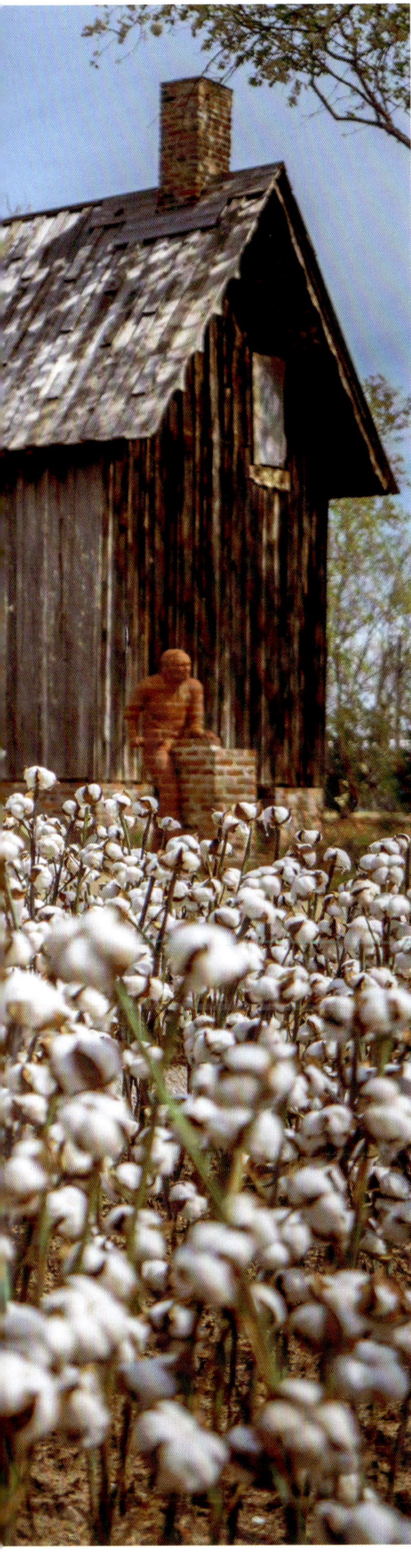

Kwame Akoto-Bamfo
Mama I hurt my hand, 2023
Bronze

Alabama Plantation Dwellings

The two 170-year-old dwellings that now appear at Freedom Monument Sculpture Park were once inhabited by people enslaved at Faunsdale Plantation, eighty miles west of Montgomery in Marengo County. Part of Alabama's Black Belt, Marengo County had one of the highest concentrations of large plantations in the state. A formerly enslaved woman born in Marengo County in the 1850s recalled that dwellings there stretched "as far as your eyes could see."

These two structures were located roughly a third of a mile from the main house at Faunsdale and were built exactly sixty feet apart with a well in the middle—part of a carefully laid out plan for living quarters at the plantation. These structures likely stood in a long row of similar dwellings leading up to the main house. The interiors are sparse, with no sheathing or insulation.

After the end of the Civil War, many formerly enslaved people continued to live in the same structures they had lived in when they were enslaved.

One horror of enslavement was the inability to leave the plantation, but sharecroppers faced the inverse fear—the prospect of being evicted with no other place to live. At Faunsdale, 106 formerly enslaved persons remained living on the plantation as sharecroppers immediately after Emancipation, pursuant to newly drafted and exploitative labor contracts.

> ***"It's a tough place to live, but we didn't have any choice. It was just where you lived."***
> —Junior Meggett, who lived in an enslaved family's dwelling until the mid-twentieth century on Point of Pines Plantation, Edisto Island, South Carolina

In the records kept at Faunsdale, accounts of the challenges formerly enslaved people continued to suffer after Emancipation can be found. Former enslavers documented how they sometimes kicked sharecroppers off the land for minor infractions and accepted their return only after they "begged back."

In Alabama as a whole, tens of thousands of these dwellings had been built by the time of Emancipation, but only a few remain standing today.

The Cotton Economy

The U.S. became the world's leading producer of cotton by forcing enslaved people to cut down forests and create large plantations in the American South. In just thirty years, U.S. cotton production soared from 1.5 million pounds in 1790 to more than 167 million pounds in 1820.

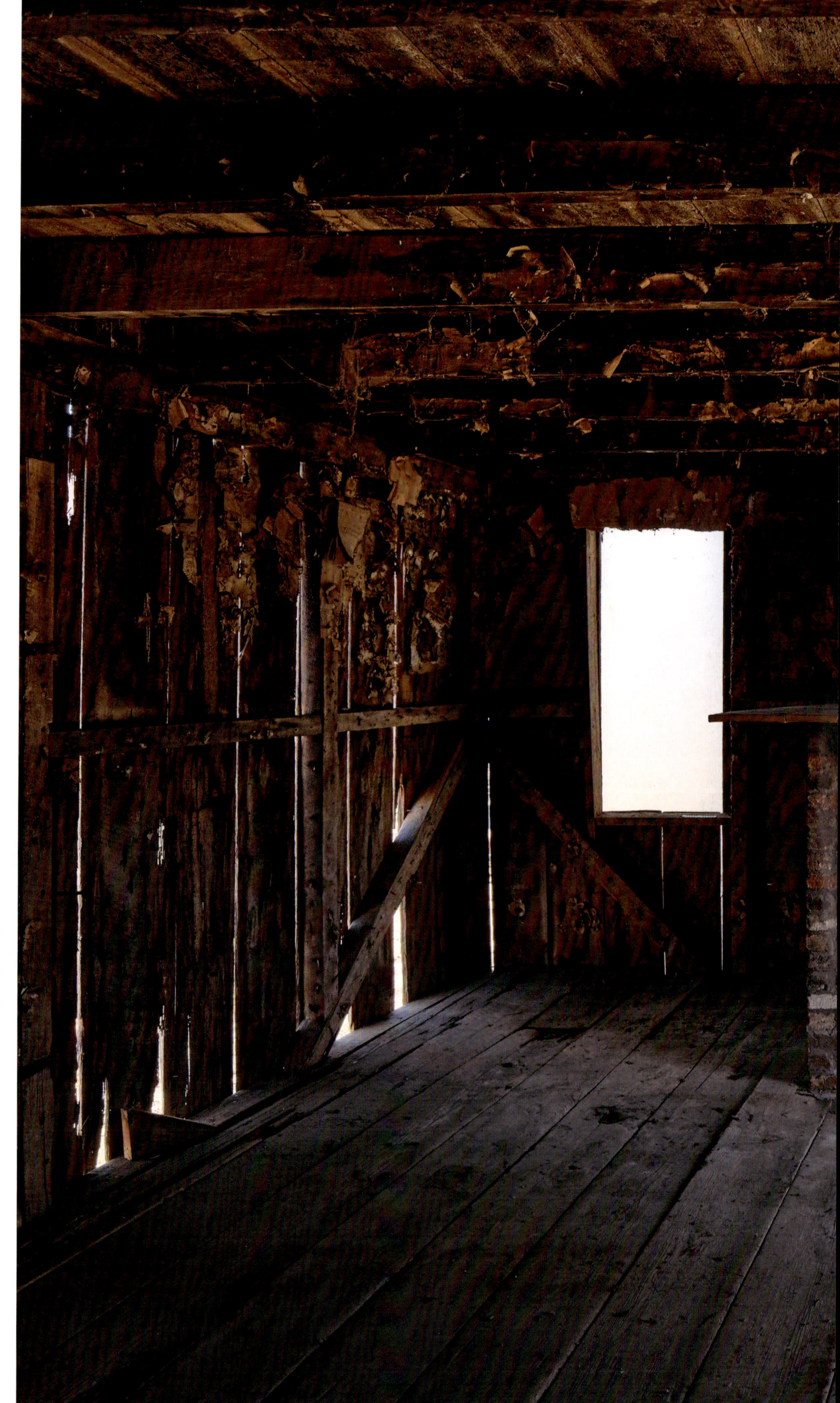

Inside of a 170-year-old dwelling that was once inhabited by enslaved people.

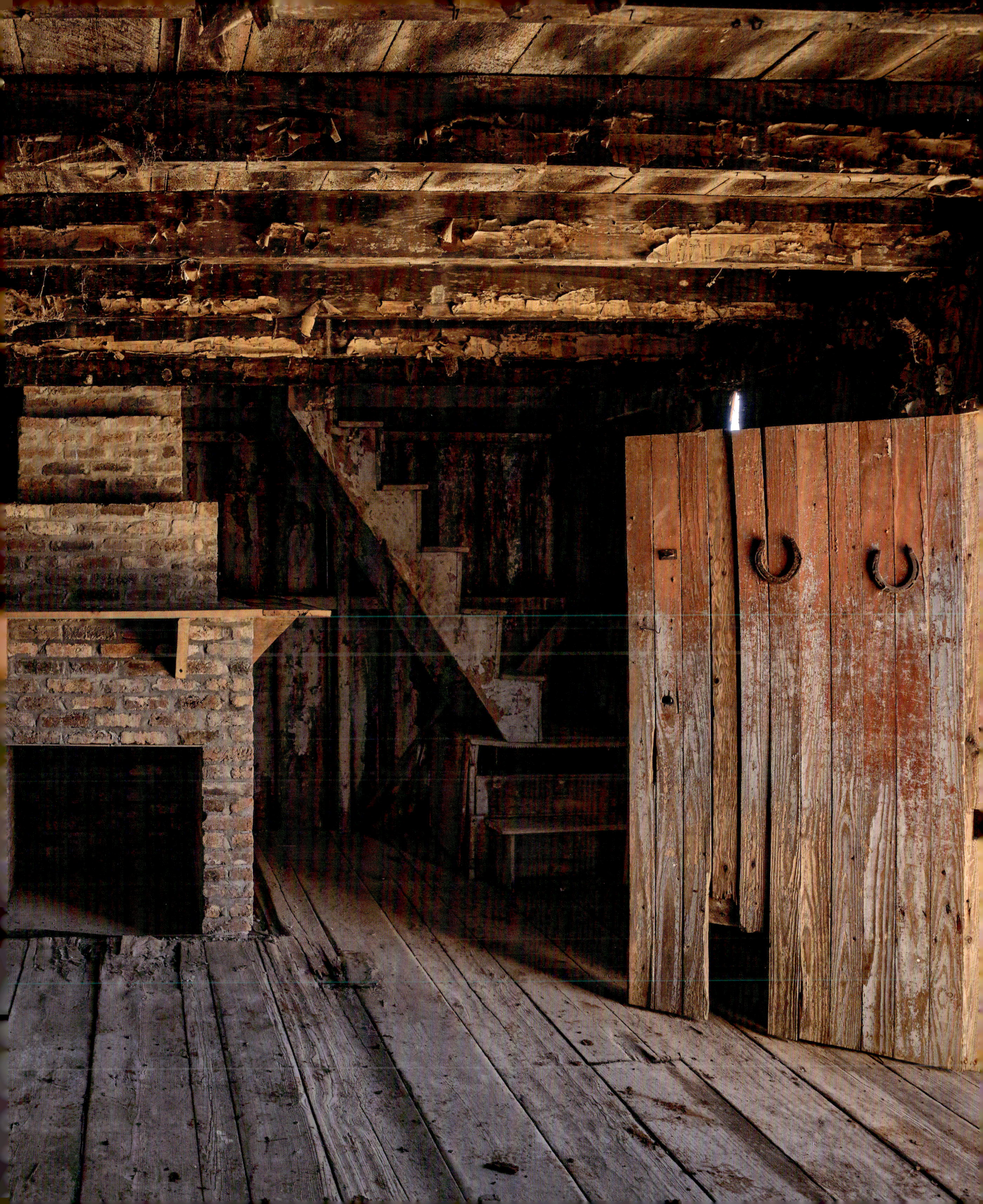

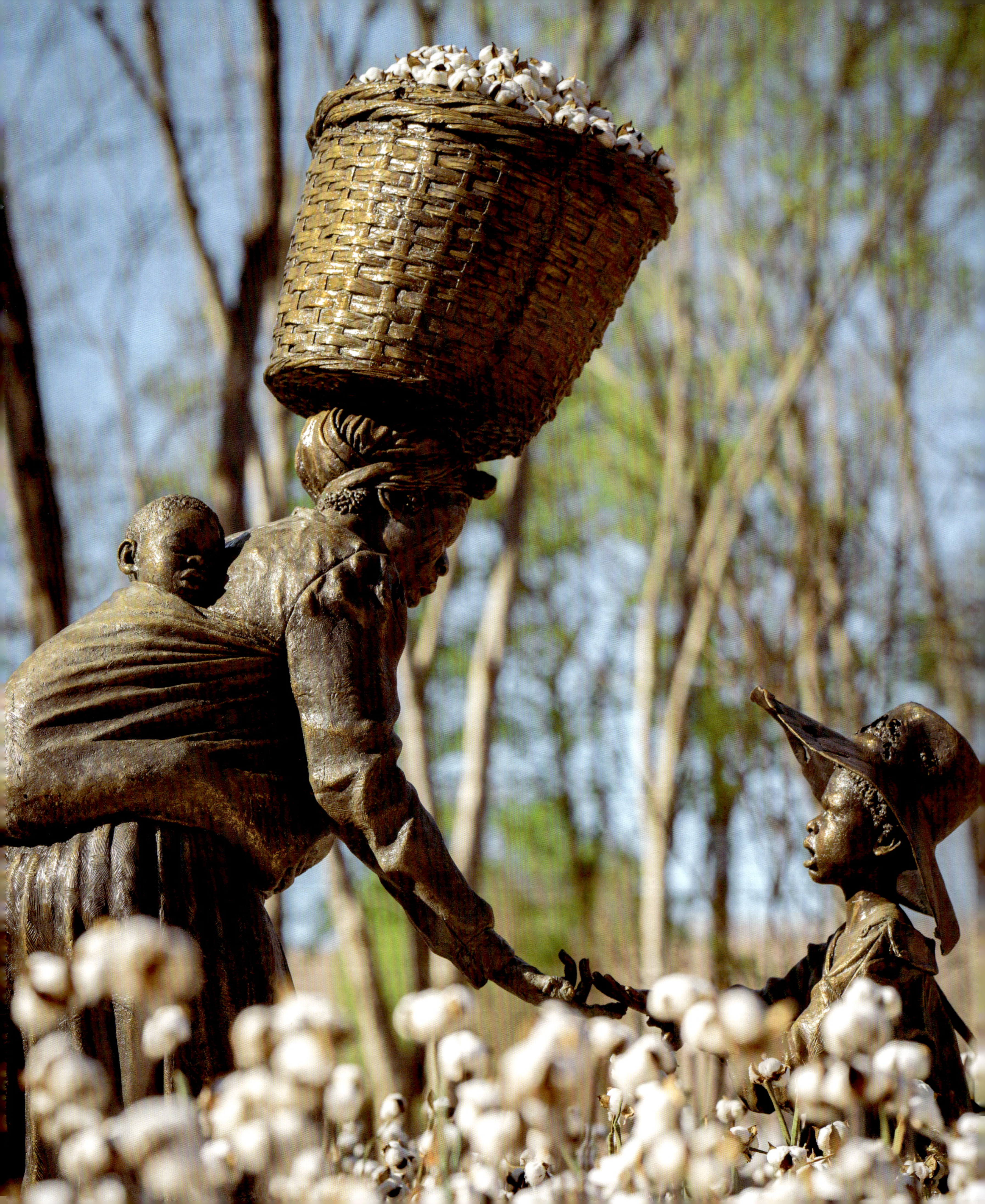

Increased demand for cotton led to the large-scale trafficking of enslaved people from the Upper South to the Lower South. By 1850, an estimated 1.8 million of the 3.2 million enslaved people in the U.S. were forced to produce cotton.

The desire for cotton land brought white planters to Alabama in droves. The enslaved population of the state grew from 47,449 in 1820 to 435,080 in 1860. By 1849, Alabama produced more cotton than any other state and had more than 15,000 cotton plantations.

By 1836, nearly half of the U.S. economy was connected to cotton produced by enslaved people—including hundreds of textile mills in the North.

Three-quarters of the cotton grown in the South was exported, primarily to England, where banks and merchants invested heavily in the American economy sustained by the labor of enslaved people.

Picking cotton was physically demanding and often debilitating, governed by a ruthless "pushing" system in which overseers used surveillance and physical torture to continually increase the amount of cotton picked by enslaved people.

"Let alone the large quantity that each slave must pick every day," one formerly enslaved person wrote. "The bole of the plant when split by ripeness, pricks the fingers, even when you are very careful, and lacerates the flesh round the nails so as to cause a great soreness: besides which, the constant stooping is terribly irksome and painful."

Resistance

Most enslaved people rebelled against enslavement. Some enslaved people disrupted forced labor through work slowdowns, performing haphazard labor, feigning illness, or sabotaging tools, property, or crops. Many fled from forced labor camps and helped others escape.

The most radical form of resistance was survival and refusing to give away the capacity to love. Many enslaved people risked their lives to stay connected with loved ones on nearby plantations or to attend clandestine gatherings to preserve community.

Despite the threat of harsh punishment, thousands of enslaved people acquired literacy and used their knowledge to spread religious and political teachings. Historians and politicians sympathetic to the Antebellum South have attempted to depict enslaved people as generally content with their condition and have sought to conceal laws, practices, and conditions that reveal the horrors of enslavement.

Only recently have historians acknowledged the false narratives created throughout the twentieth century to justify enslavement.

Kwame Akoto-Bamfo
Mama I hurt my hand (detail)

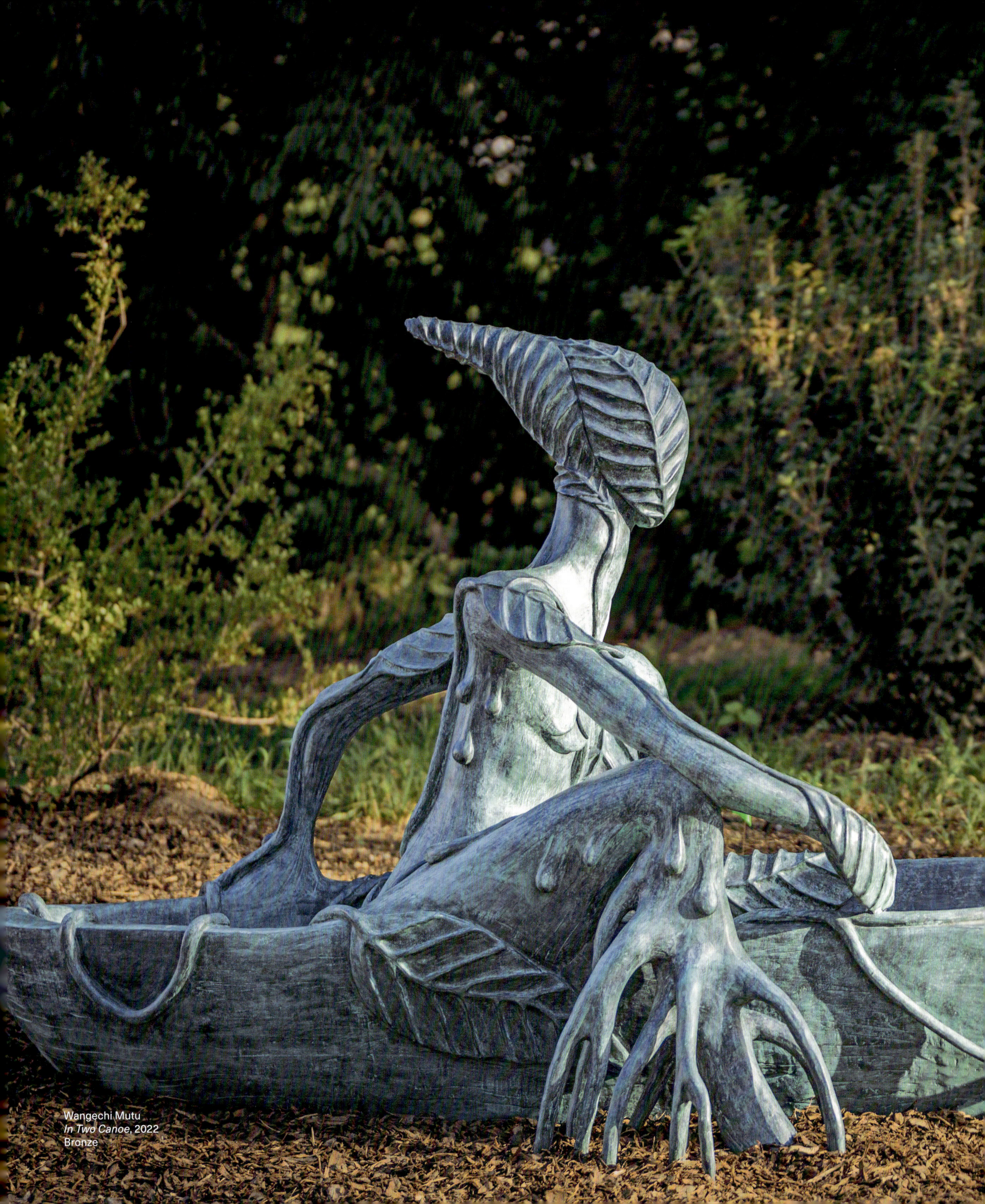

Wangechi Mutu
In Two Canoe, 2022
Bronze

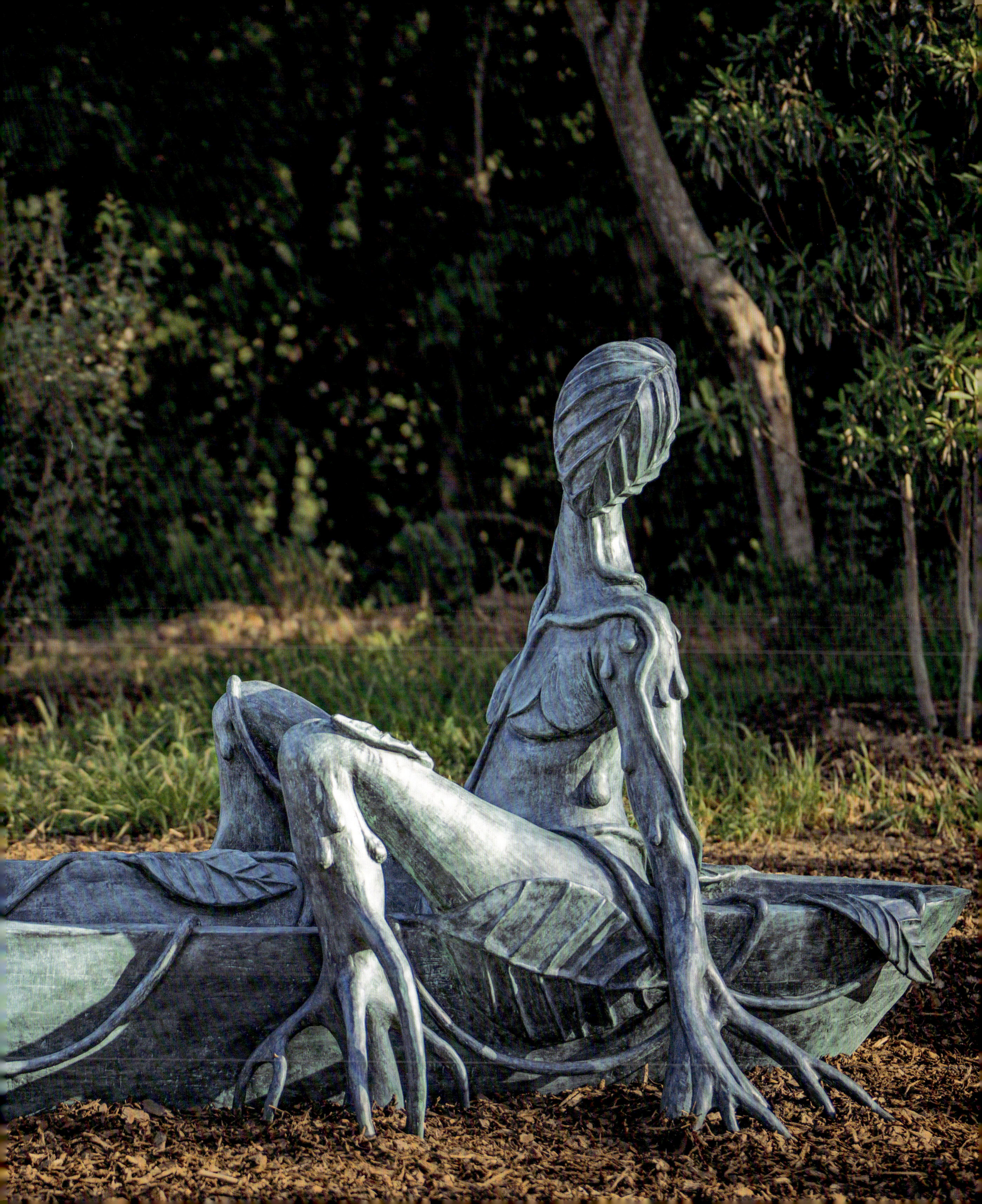

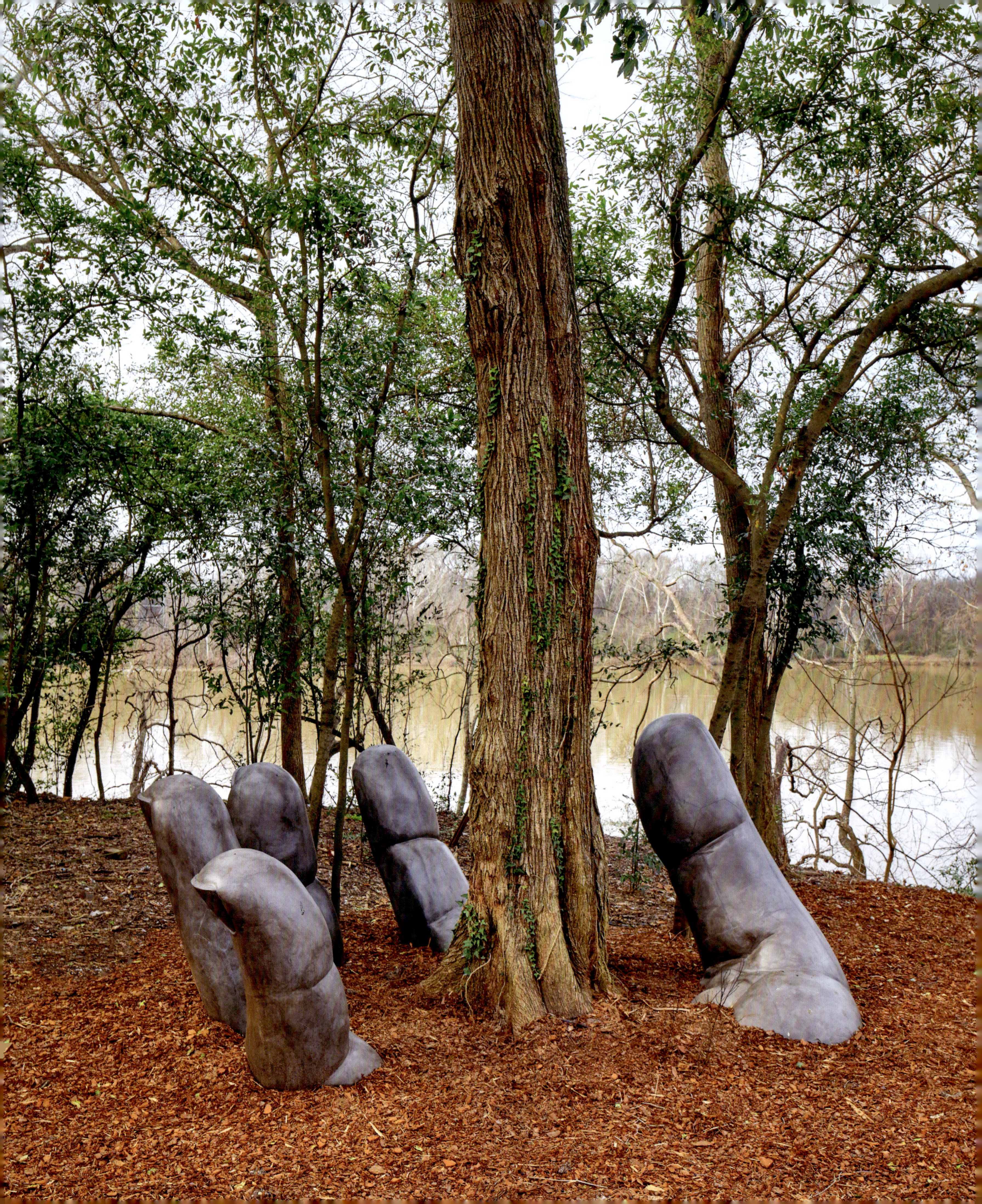

Fugitives, Maroons, and Rebels

Historians estimate that tens of thousands of enslaved people attempted escape. Enslaved people ran away for many reasons, including to avoid violence or being sold. Most often, enslaved people escaped to reunite with loved ones, and many stayed in the vicinity of their former plantations or found refuge in Southern cities rather than going North.

Most who ran away did so alone, but they were aided by others who risked punishment to supply them with food or provide guidance. A large percentage of those who ran away were children.

Some fugitives became "maroons" who formed secret autonomous communities, usually in the woods, mountains, or swamps. They sustained themselves by growing their own food and raiding nearby plantations and towns. At least fifty maroon communities across the South have been documented.

Rebellions also played an important role in enslaved people's resistance. Over 250 rebellions have been documented in the period before the Civil War. Historians credit a widespread rebellion by tens of thousands of enslaved people near the end of the Civil War as a catalyst for the Union's victory over the Confederacy.

Love in the Midst of Agony

Enslaved people formed strong, enduring familial connections with one another despite the hardship, suffering, and constant threat of separation caused by enslavement. Though the extreme physical and emotional stress of life in a forced labor camp made creating a family challenging and often heartbreaking. Nearly half of all enslaved people were separated from close family members at an enslaver's or auctioneer's whim.

Yet it is clear that powerful relationships between parents, children, siblings, and partners were an overwhelming source of strength, perseverance, and hope. Enslaved people took enormous risks to preserve familial bonds and often risked their lives to maintain these connections. Most never gave up hope of finding their loved ones.

Following Emancipation, thousands of formerly enslaved people spent their entire savings to place ads seeking loved ones who had been taken from them.

Eva Oertli and Beat Huber
The Caring Hand, 2014
Concrete

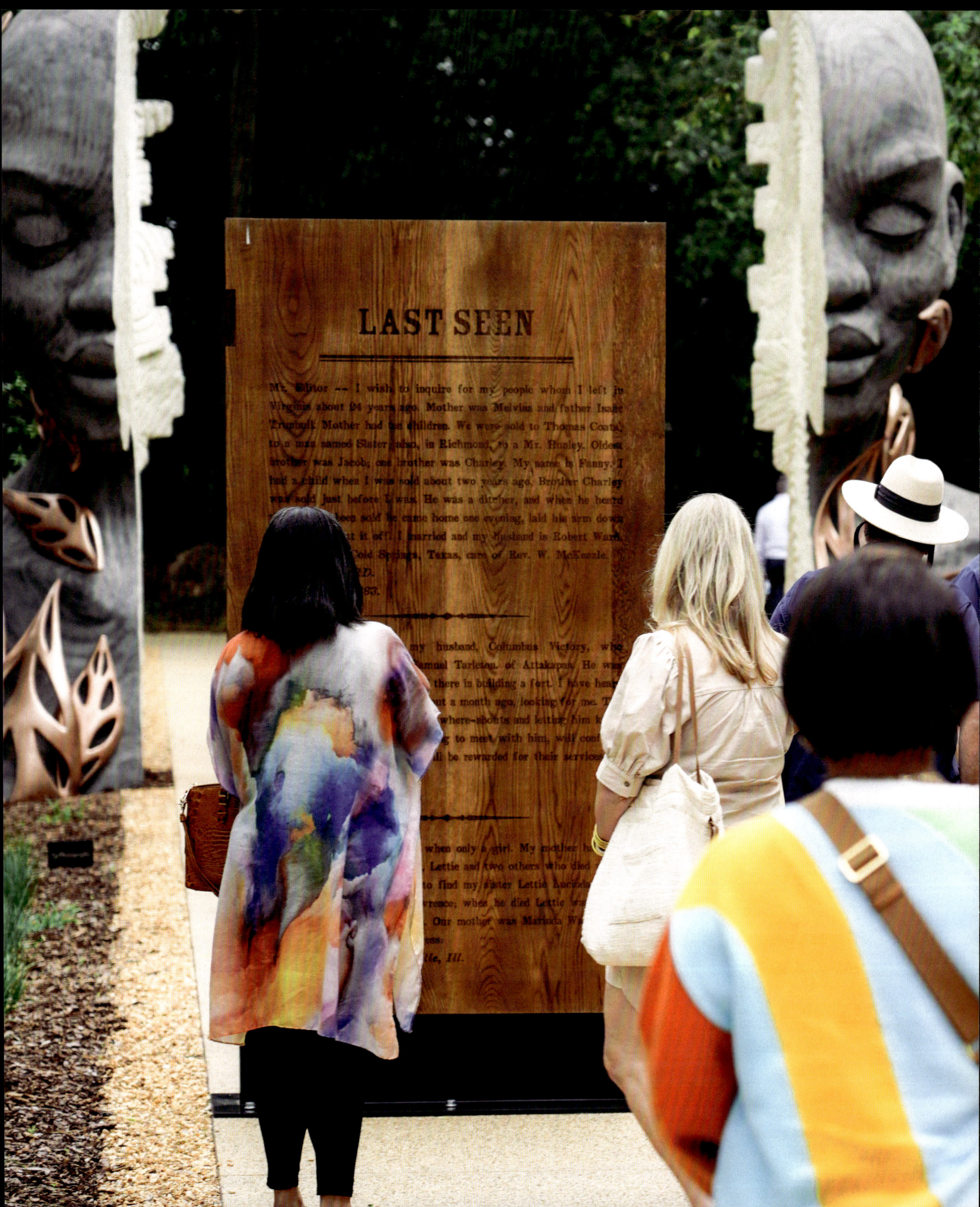
LAST SEEN
Mr. Editor -- I wish to inquire for my people whom I left in
Virginia about 24 years ago. Mother was Melvina and father Isaac
Trumbull. Mother had ten children. We were sold to Thomas Coats,
to a man named Slater, also, in Richmond, to a Mr. Hunley. Oldest
brother was Jacob; one brother was Charley. My name is Fanny. I
had a child when I was sold about two years ago. Brother Charley
was sold just before I was. He was a ditcher, and when he heard
Cold Springs, Texas, care of Rev. W. McKenzie.

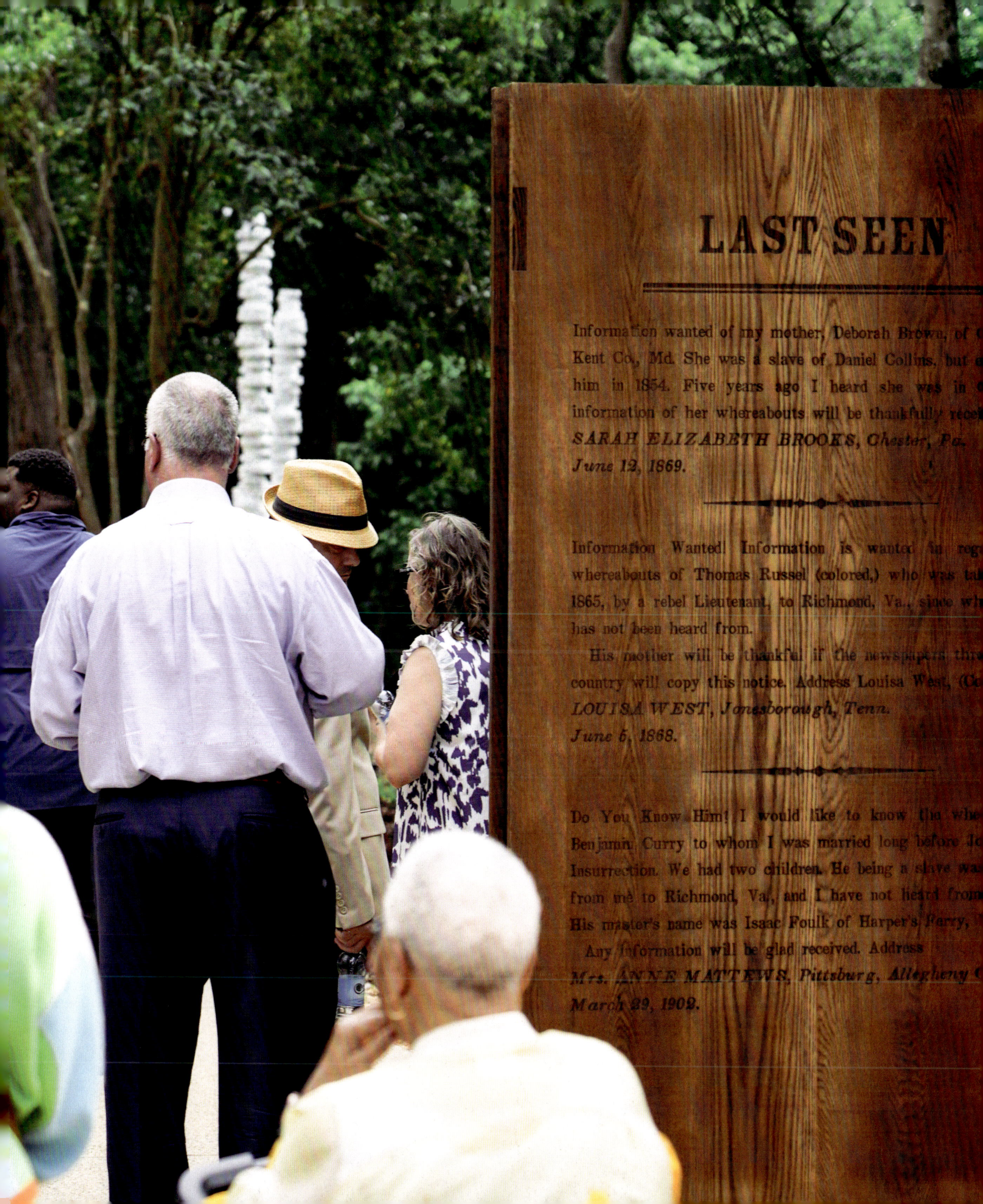

LAST SEEN
Information wanted of my mother, Deborah Brown, of
Kent Co, Md. She was a slave of Daniel Collins, but
him in 1854. Five years ago I heard she was in
information of her whereabouts will be thankfully
SARAH ELIZABETH BROOKS, Chester, Pa.
June 12, 1869.
Information Wanted! Information is wanted in
whereabouts of Thomas Russel (colored,) who was
1865, by a rebel Lieutenant, to Richmond, Va., since
has not been heard from.
His mother will be thankful if the newspapers
country will copy this notice. Address Louisa West,
LOUISA WEST, Jonesborough, Tenn.
June 6, 1868.
Do You Know Him! I would like to know the
Benjamin Curry to whom I was married long before
Insurrection. We had two children. He being a slave
from me to Richmond, Va., and I have not heard
His master's name was Isaac Foulk of Harper's Ferry,
Any information will be glad received. Address
Mrs. ANNE MATTEWS, Pittsburg, Allegheny
March 29, 1902.

A Prayer

O Lord, the hard-won miles
Have worn my stumbling feet:
Oh, soothe me with thy smiles,
And make my life complete.

The thorns were thick and keen
Where'er I trembling trod;
The way was long between
My wounded feet and God.

Where healing waters flow
Do thou my footsteps lead.
My heart is aching so;
Thy gracious balm I need.

— PAUL LAURENCE DUNBAR

Death and Slavery

Death was a constant presence in the lives of enslaved people. Disease, violence, horrific forced labor conditions, trauma, and lack of access to medical care contributed to a much higher mortality rate in the enslaved population than the white population. The discrepancy in mortality was especially large for newborns. Enslaved people who were pregnant were overworked and deprived of health care. Nearly half of enslaved Black babies died within their first year of life. New research suggests that nearly six million Black people died while enslaved in the United States.

State governments placed many restrictions on burial practices for enslaved people. Laws often banned musical instruments, limited funeral attendance, and prevented enslaved Black people from performing the same burial practices as white people. Enslavers sent patrols to watch and even interrupt mourners.

Some enslaved people were forbidden from burying their loved ones altogether. The bodies of the enslaved were sometimes sold to surgeons for dissection under the guise of scientific investigation or utilized by social scientists attempting to contrive theories of racial difference.

Before funerals, the dead were washed, wrapped in cloth, and, in some cases, placed in a simple casket. Funerals included prayer, dance, song, stories, and other rituals. Family and friends put items such as shrouds, jewelry, and coins in the graves, and decorated the outside of burial sites with shells, glass bottles, and crockery.

Because laws prohibited enslaved people from reading and writing, most headstones had no inscriptions.

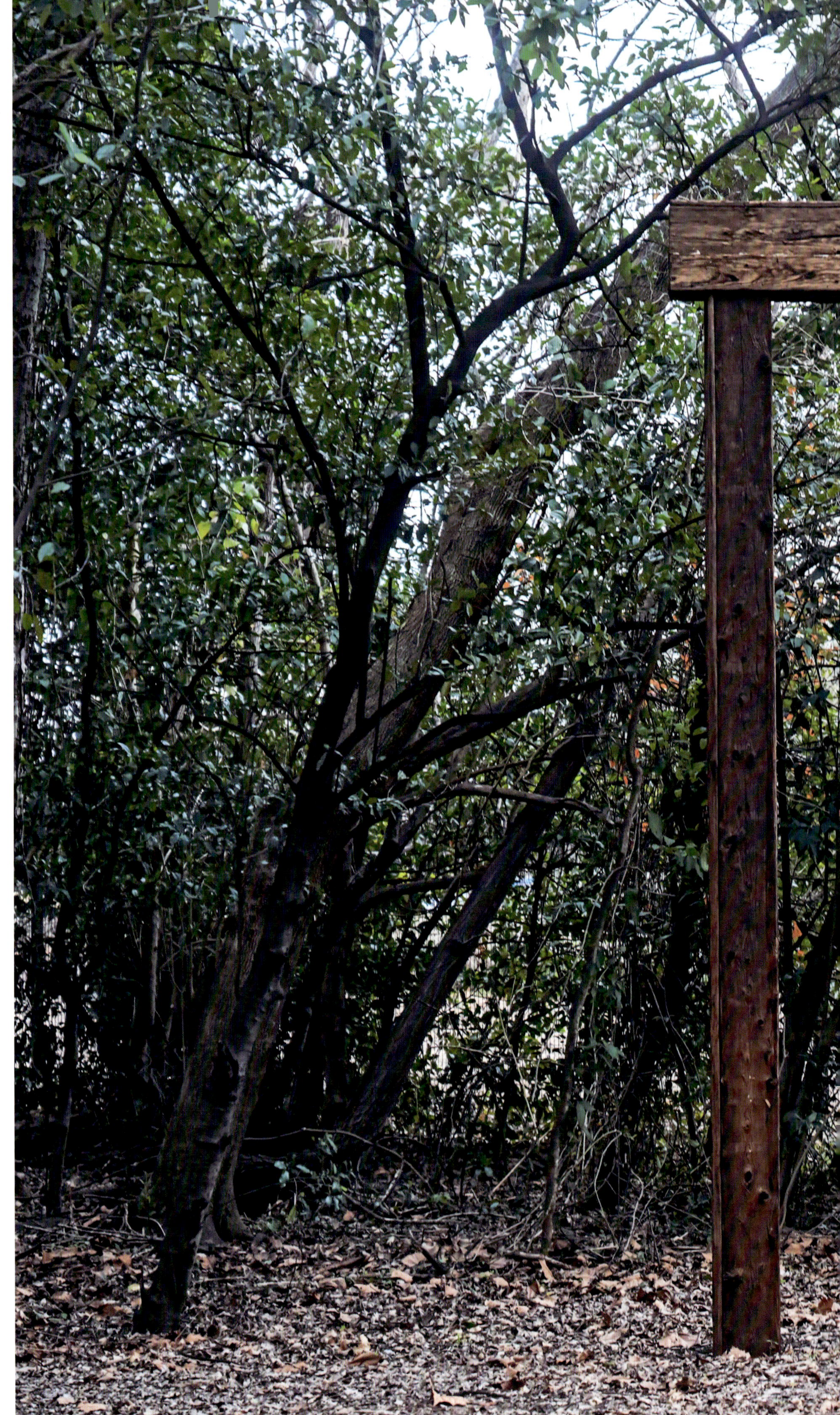

Alison Saar
Travelin' Light, 1999
Cast bronze

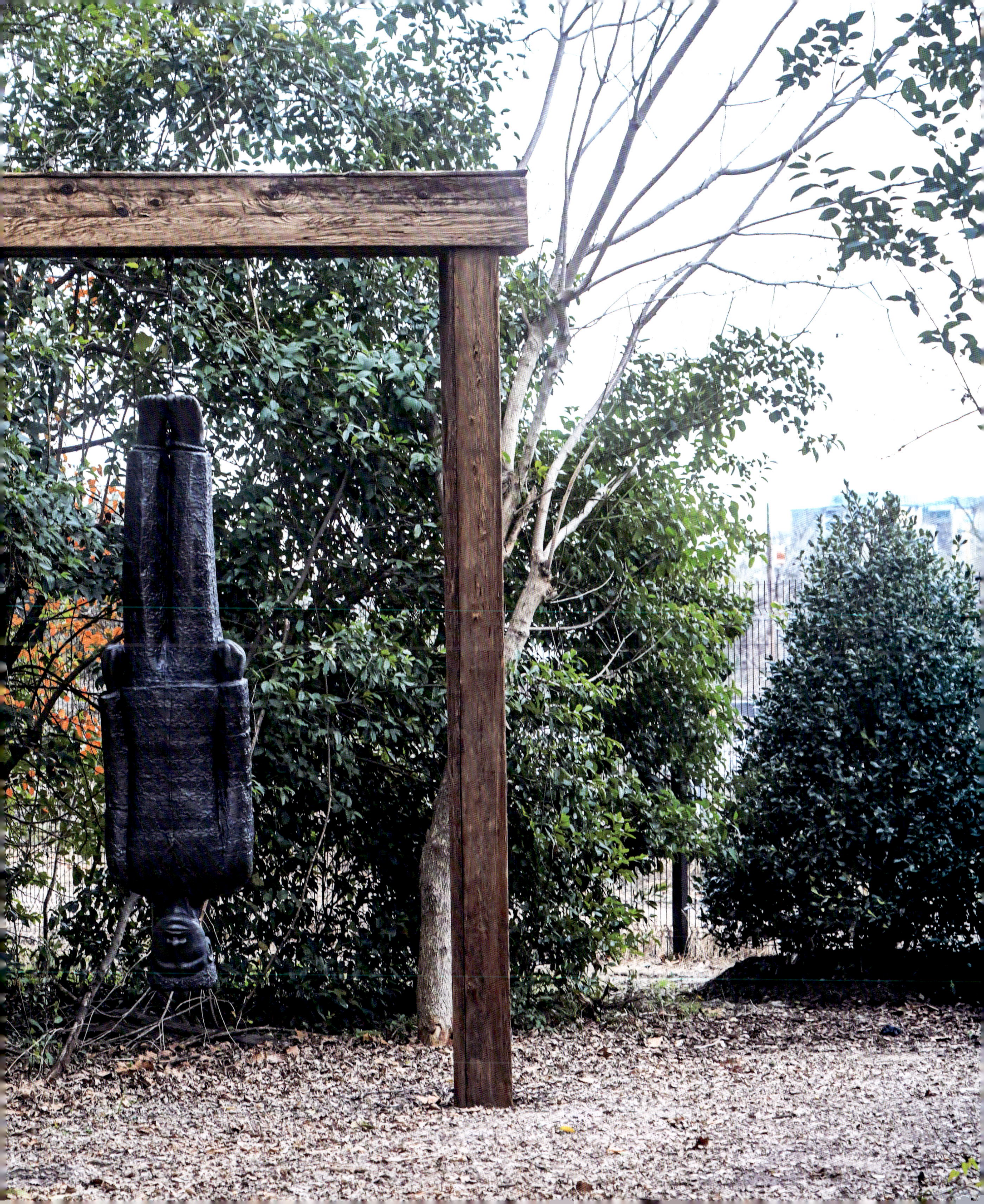

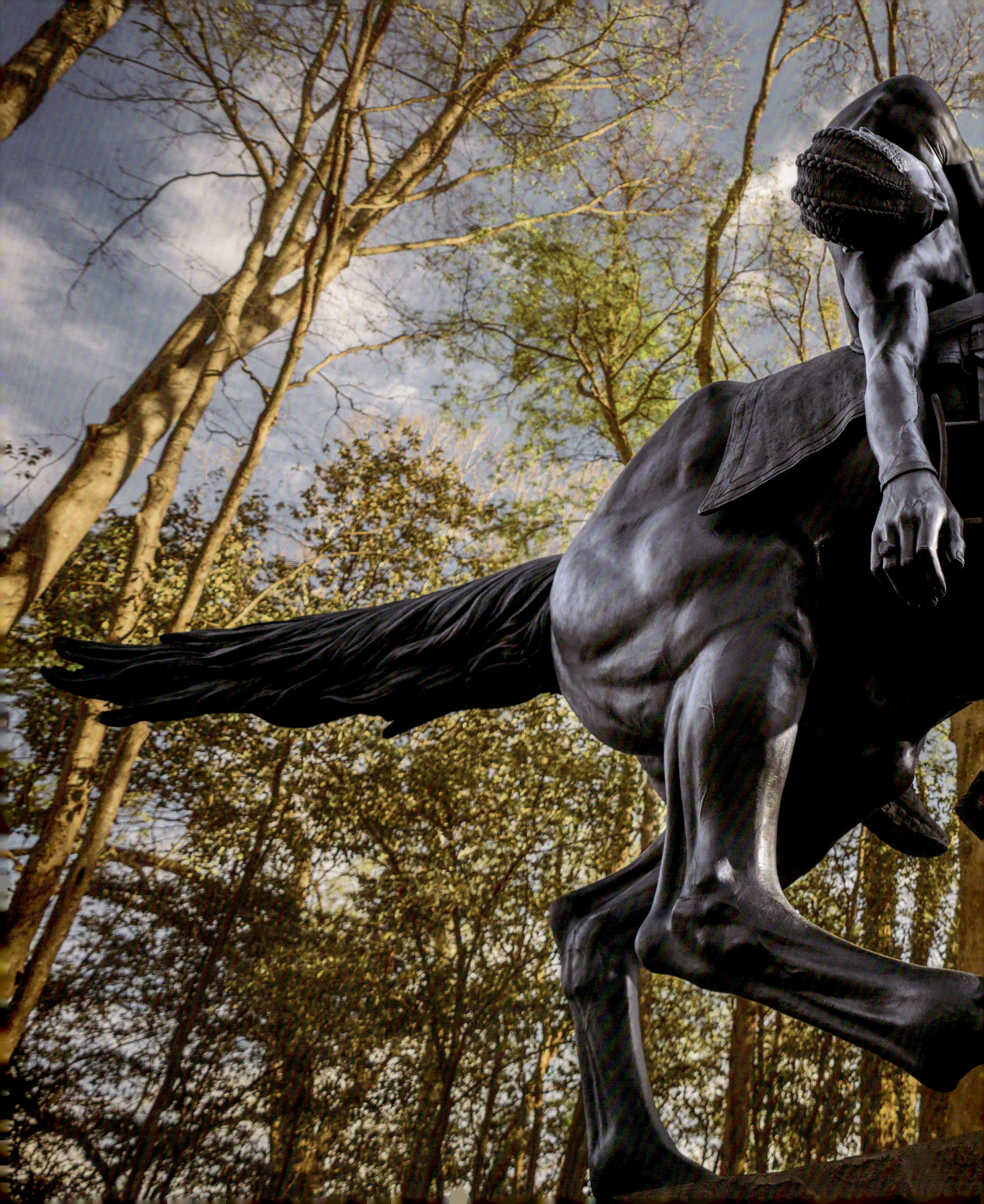

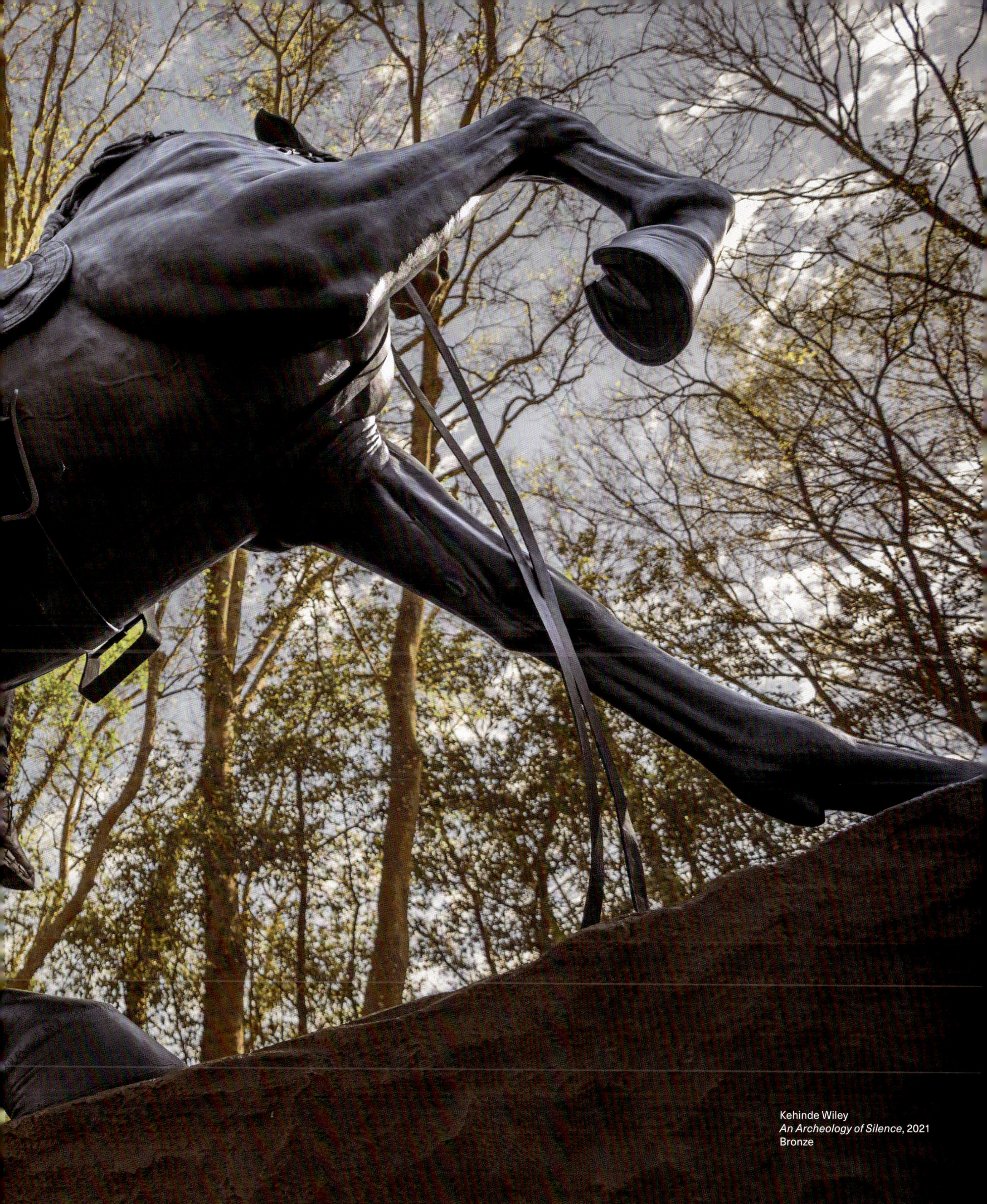

Kehinde Wiley
An Archeology of Silence, 2021
Bronze

Names for Enslaved People

For more than three centuries, enslaved Black people were denied the autonomy to choose their own names. Many enslavers dictated what enslaved people were called, and the U.S. census instructed enslavers to officially record them only with a number.

In 1870, the first census after Emancipation afforded formerly enslaved Black Americans the opportunity to exercise their freedom by officially recording their chosen surnames. To retain bonds with their loved ones, including family members who had been sold away, some formerly enslaved people used surnames associated with their former enslavers.

Safety and assimilation were also important considerations. After Aleck Woodward was told by a military official "that there was no better name than Woodward," his family "took [that] name. It's been a kind of a [protection] to us at times, and none of our immediate family has ever dragged it in a jail or a chain-gang."

Many who joined the Union Army changed their names to avoid identification and retaliation by their former enslavers. Others adopted the surname of a famous person like George Washington, Booker T. Washington, or O.O. Howard, head of the Freedmen's Bureau.

Because enslaved Black people were legally prohibited from learning to read and write, surname spellings were often inconsistent or not carefully recorded. Some shifted from one generation to the next.

More than 120,000 unique surnames were recorded in the 1870 census by four million newly freed Black people. To honor this historic act of freedom, these chosen surnames are inscribed at the National Monument to Freedom, the largest and most comprehensive monument to the descendants of enslaved Black people in the world.

We are thrilled to honor the courageous survivors of enslavement by recognizing the families they created and their millions of descendants, many of whom still bear the names chosen by their formerly enslaved foreparents.

Despite the horror of enslavement, enslaved Black people expressed their dignity, their love, and their never-ending yearning to be free by creating families, communities, and strategies for emancipation.

Because slave life had "busted her legs, back, head, eyes, hands, kidneys, womb and tongue," she had nothing left to make a living with but her heart—which she put to work at once.

—TONI MORRISON, *BELOVED*

Reconstruction and the Continuing Struggle

At the start of the Reconstruction era—the twelve-year period after the Civil War—Black Americans had great hope that Emancipation would mean real freedom and opportunity. Formerly enslaved people embraced education, hard work, faith, and citizenship with extraordinary enthusiasm and devotion.

By 1868, more than 80 percent of Black men who were eligible to vote had registered, schools for Black children became a priority, and courageous Black leaders overcame enormous obstacles to win elections to public office.

But the hope of Reconstruction quickly became a nightmare of unparalleled violence and oppression. Between 1865 and 1877, thousands of Black women, men, and children were attacked, sexually assaulted, terrorized, and killed by white mobs and individuals who were shielded from prosecution. A reign of terror effectively nullified constitutional amendments promising Black people equal protection and the right to vote.

When the federal government retreated from its commitment to protect Black citizens, the Reconstruction era gave way to an era of racial terror lynching, followed by segregation and inequality that persists today.

Black Americans kept fighting for equal rights and working to advance the cultural, social, and economic conditions of formerly enslaved people. The struggle for equality, freedom, and justice has continued across generations since Emancipation. Leaders, advocates, elected officials, activists, writers, celebrities, teachers, artists, journalists, ministers, and ordinary citizens of all racial backgrounds are working to address the harm created by the enslavement of Black people in America.

Freedom Monument Sculpture Park stands in tribute to those who acknowledge the legacy of slavery, the racial inequality it created, and the ongoing struggle for freedom and justice for all.

Daniel Popper
Hallow, 2024
Glass fiber reinforced concrete steel

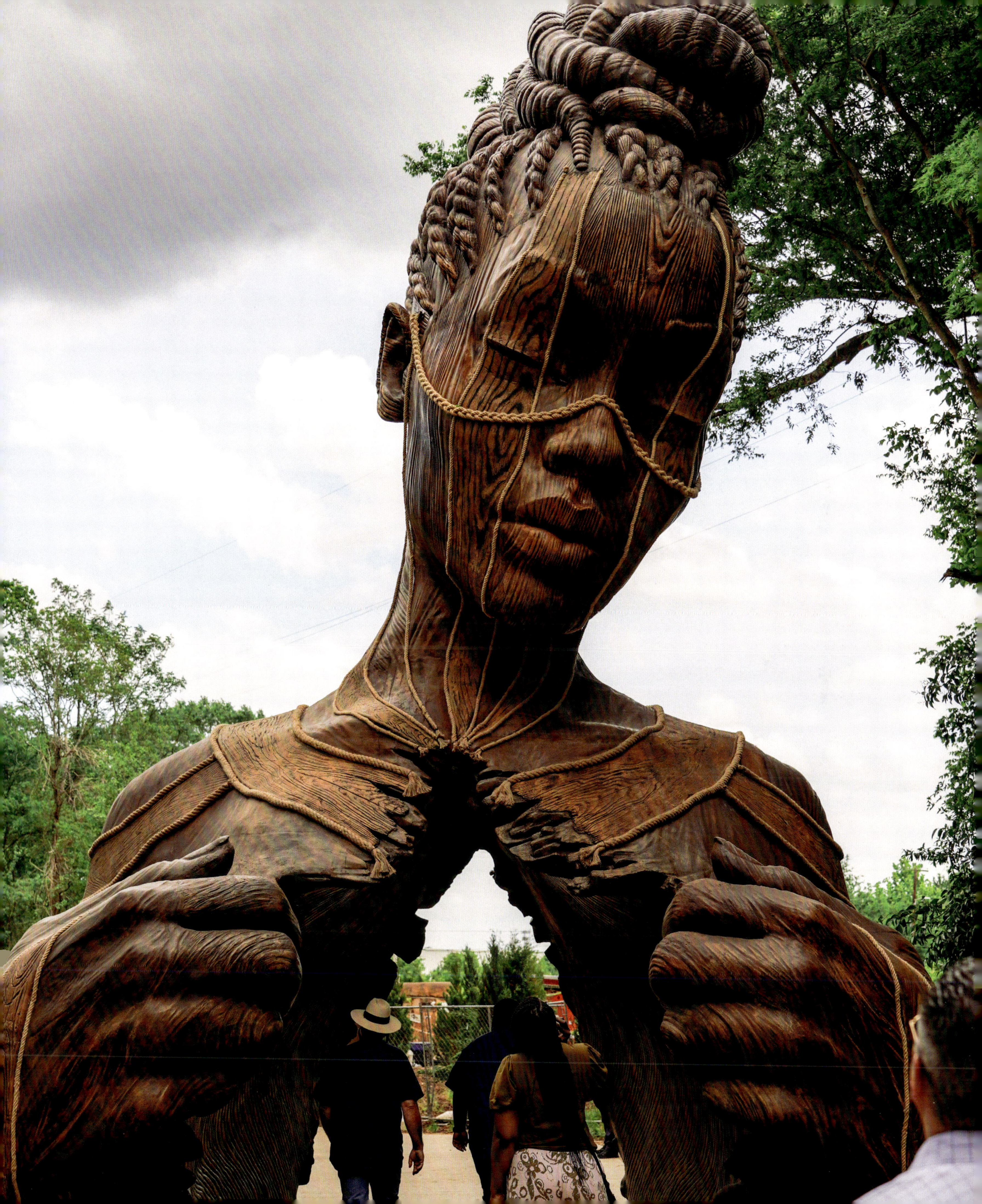

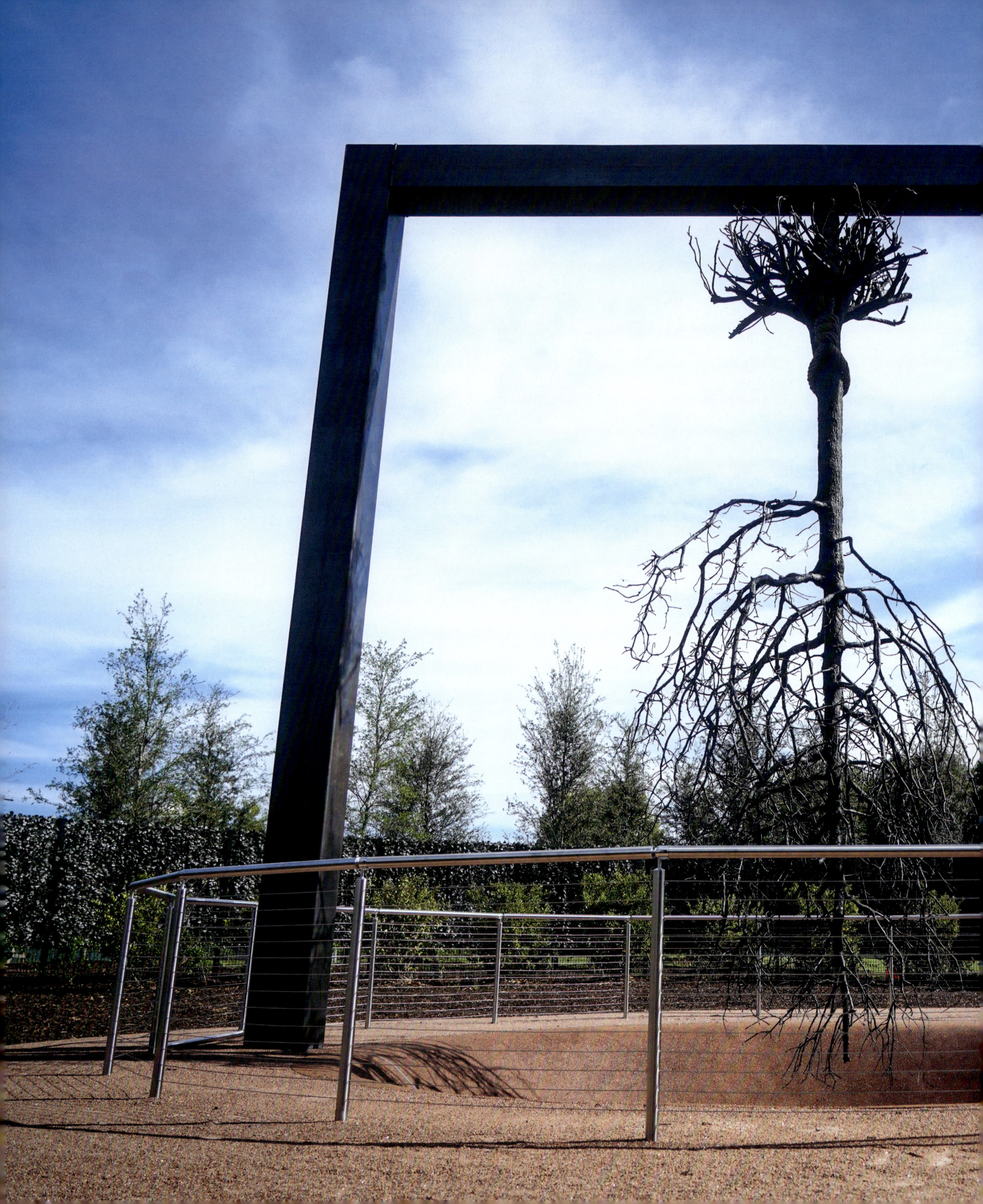

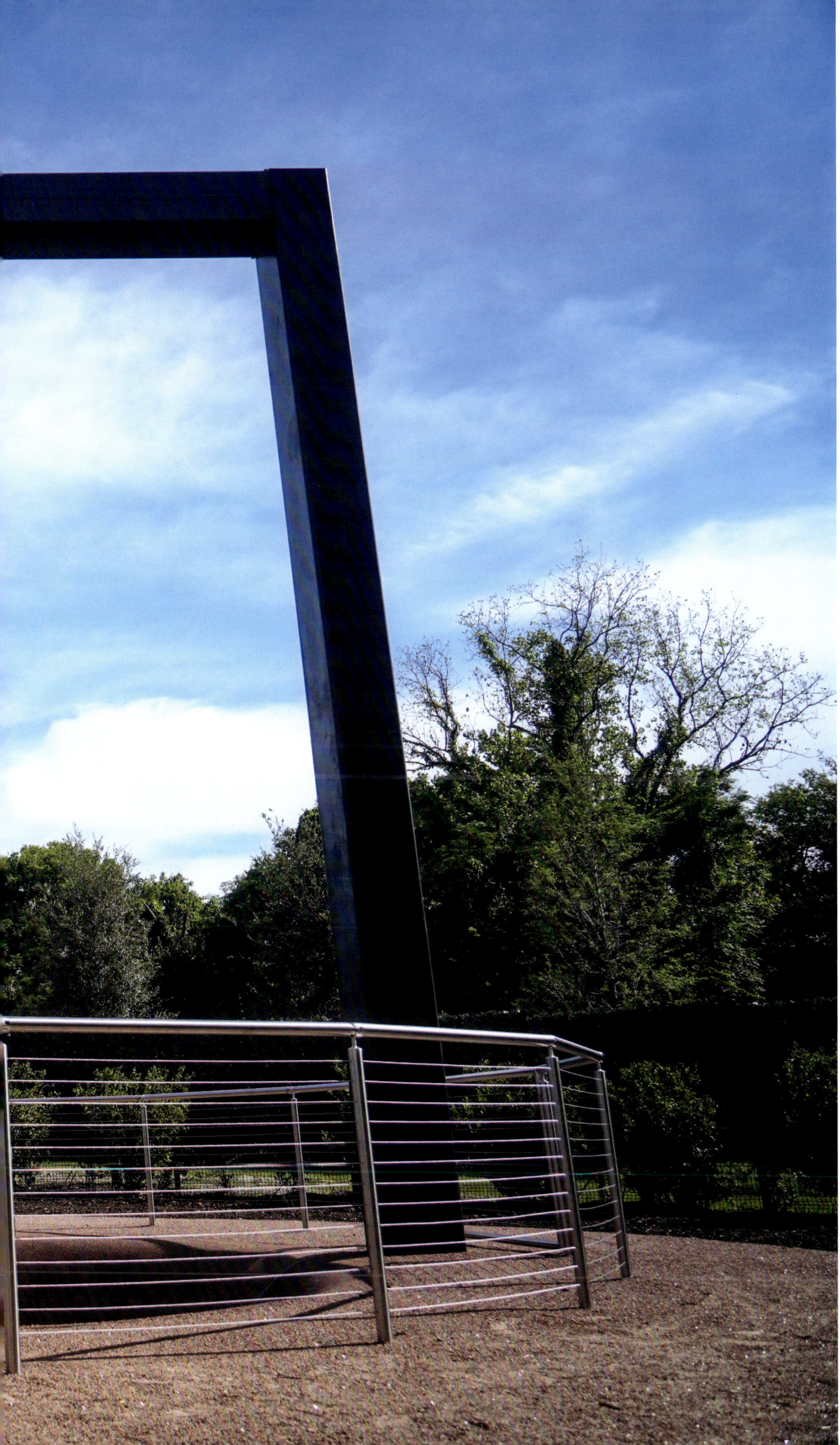

Charles Gaines
Hanging Tree, 2025
Stainless steel, bronze, mechanics

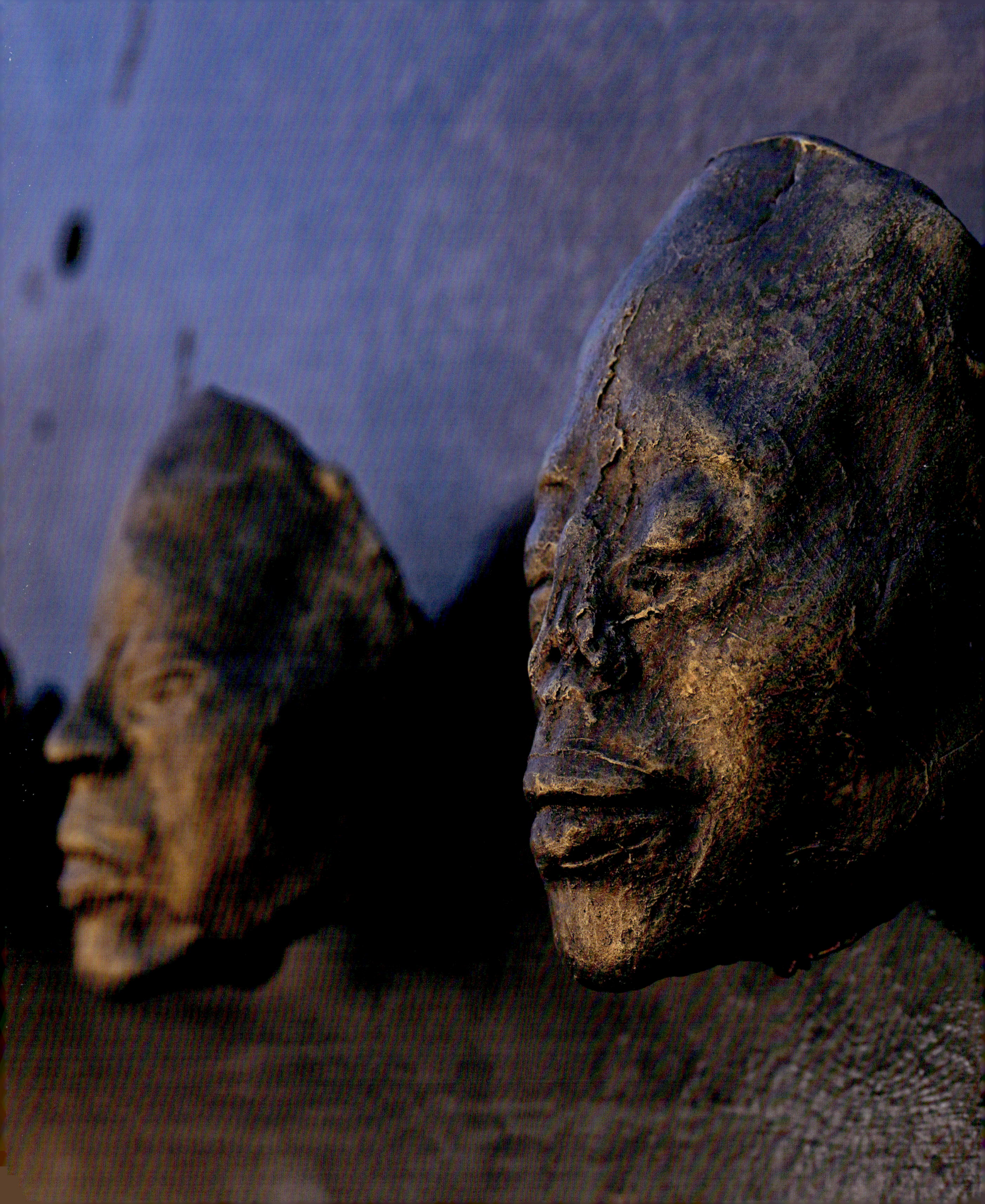

Opposite and following spread:
Nikesha Breeze
108 Death Masks, 2018
Ceramic cast in bronze

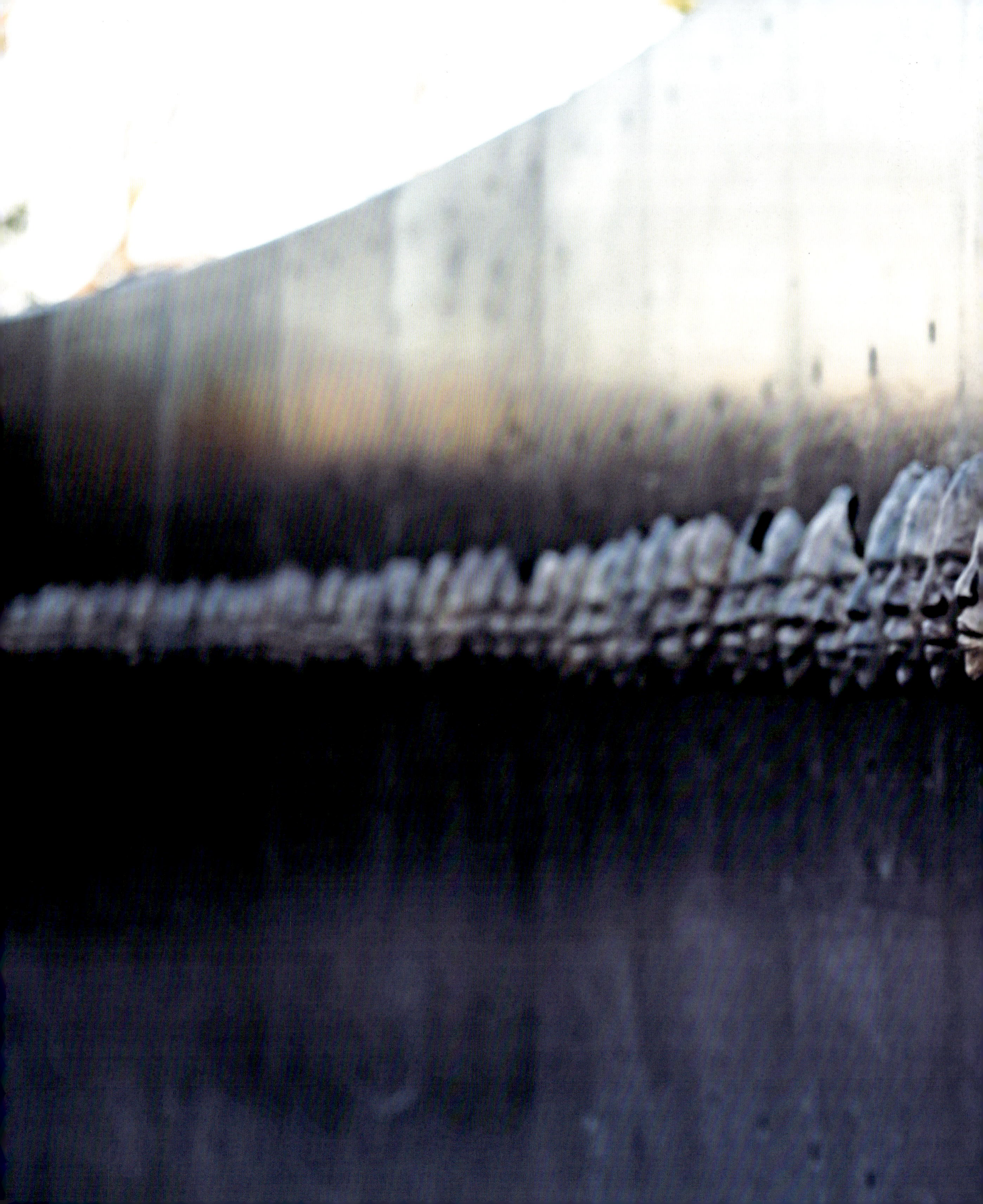

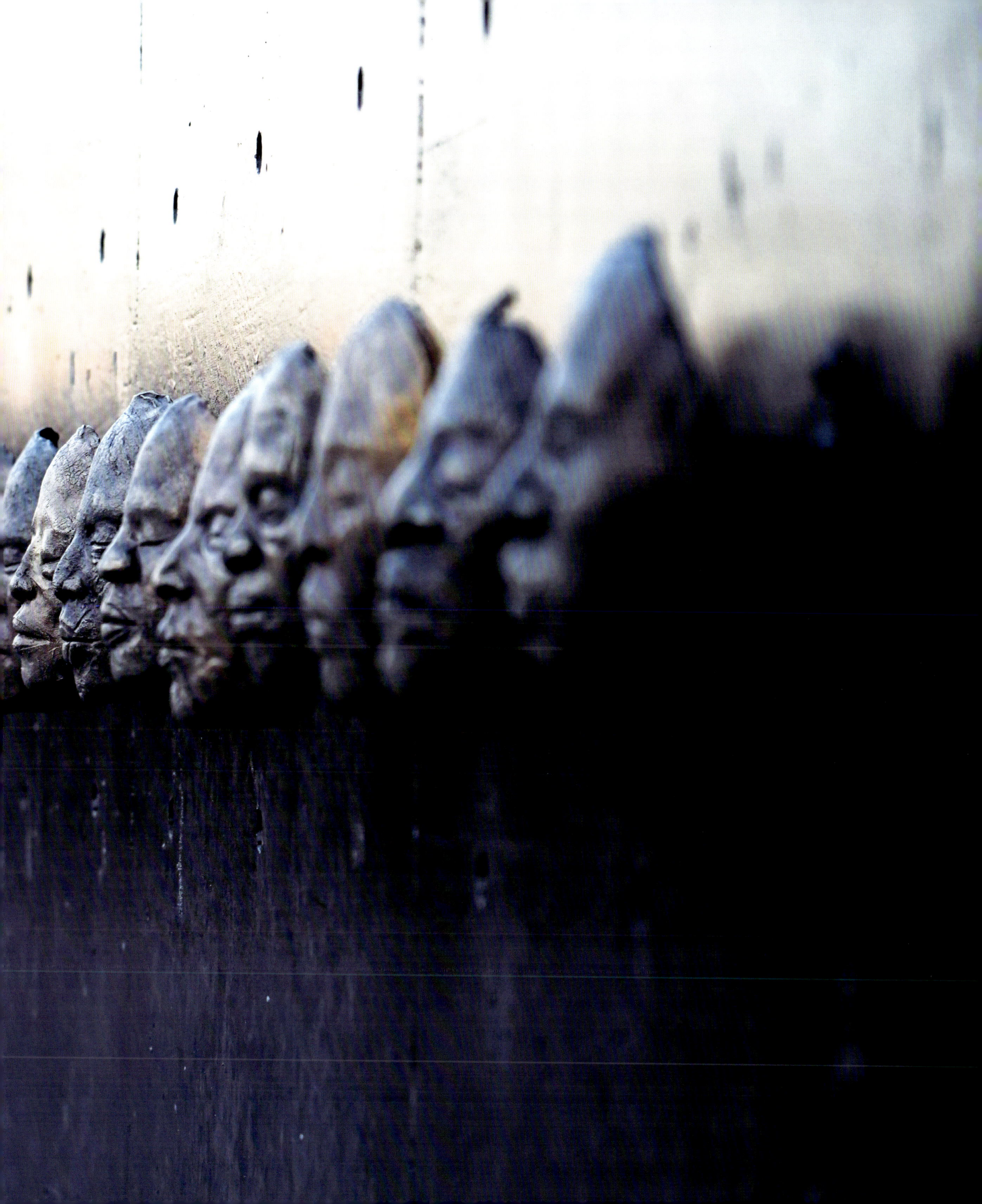

Detail of the National Monument to Freedom.

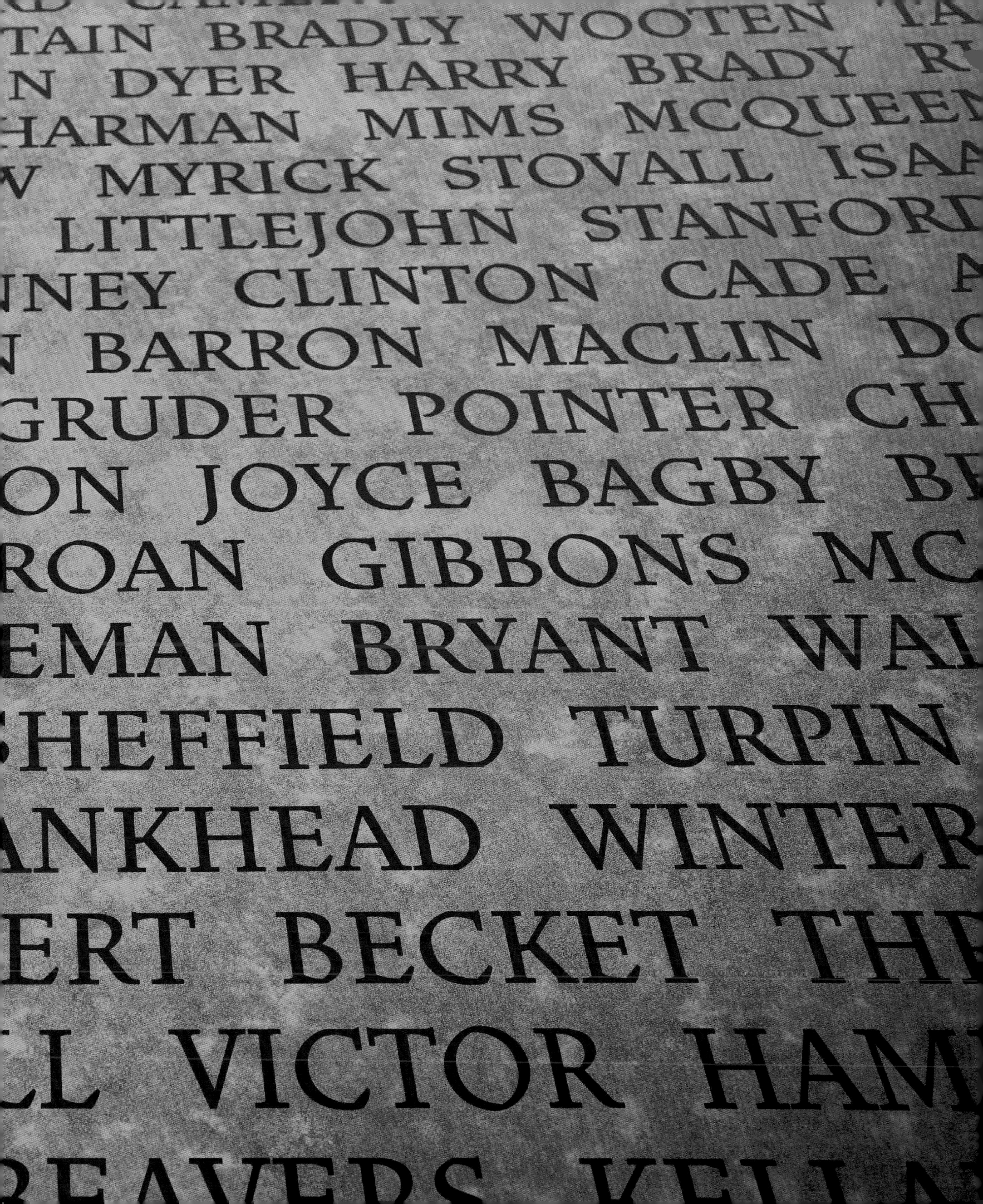

TAIN BRADLY WOOTEN TA
N DYER HARRY BRADY R
HARMAN MIMS MCQUEEN
V MYRICK STOVALL ISAA
LITTLEJOHN STANFORD
NNEY CLINTON CADE A
N BARRON MACLIN DO
GRUDER POINTER CH
ON JOYCE BAGBY BE
ROAN GIBBONS MC
EMAN BRYANT WAL
SHEFFIELD TURPIN
ANKHEAD WINTER
ERT BECKET THE
LL VICTOR HAM
REAVERS KELLIN

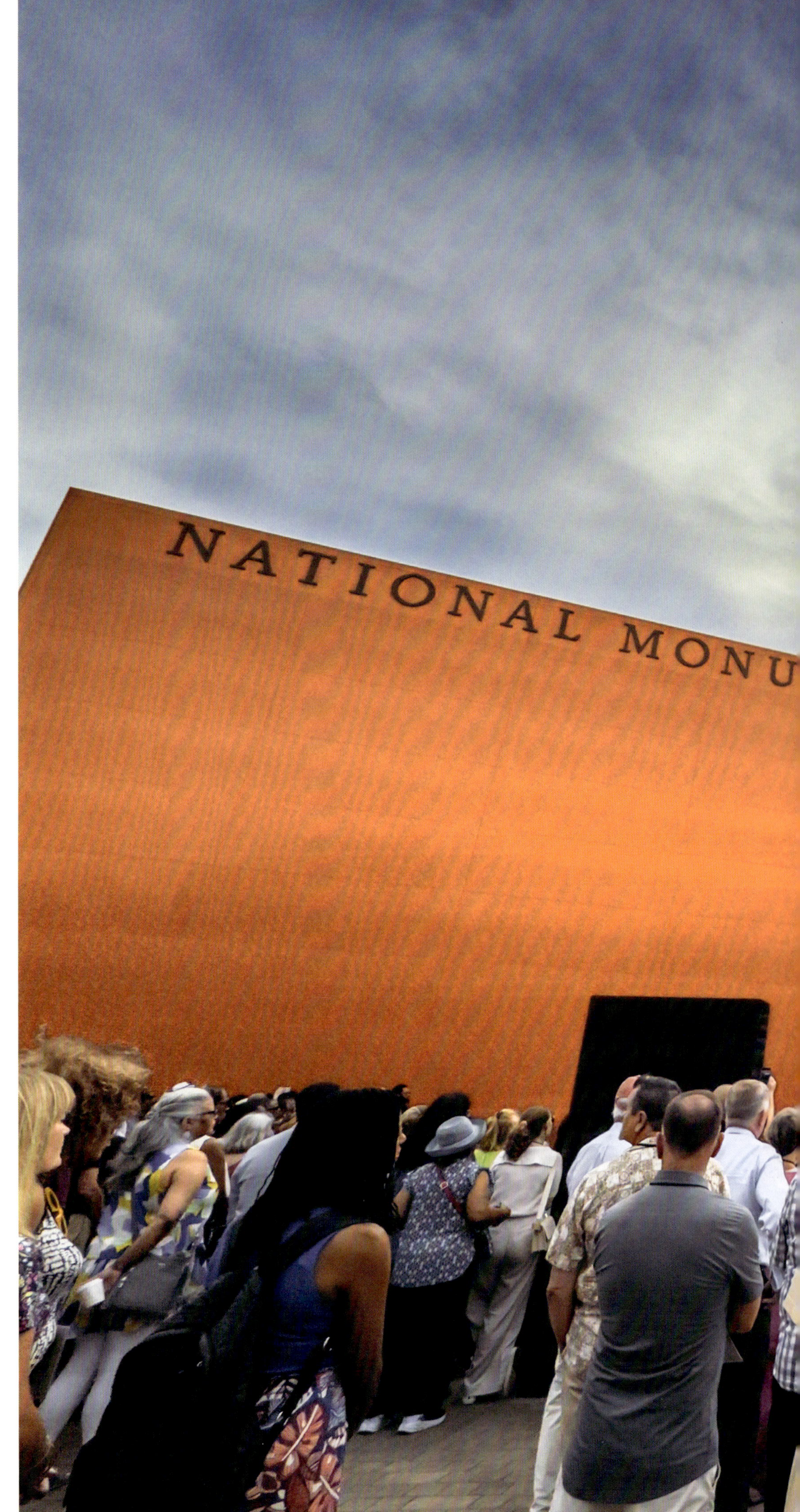

The National Monument to Freedom features more than 120,000 unique surnames recorded in the 1870 census after Emancipation. They represent the names of more than 10 million enslaved people in America and their descendants.

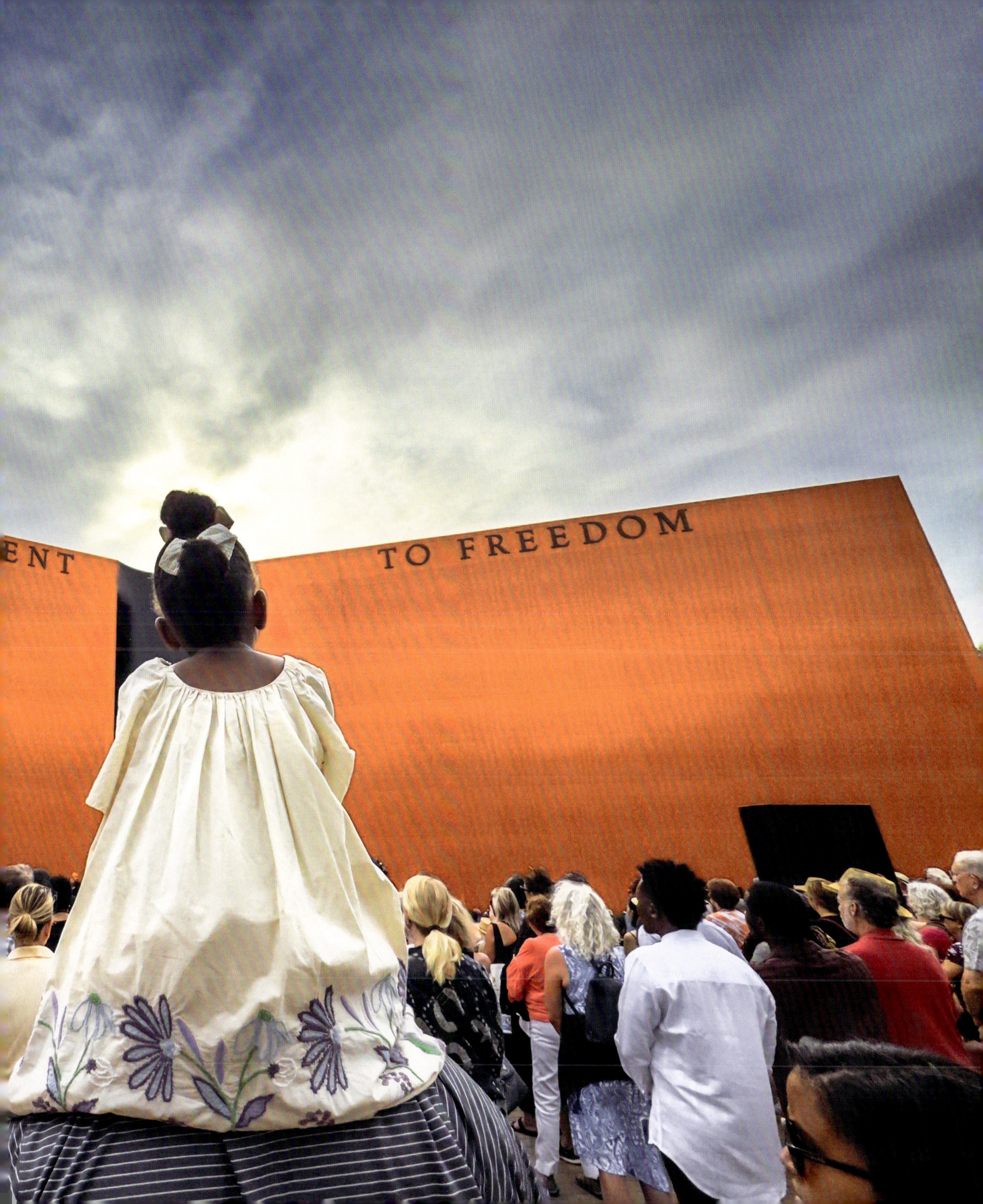
ENT
TO FREEDOM

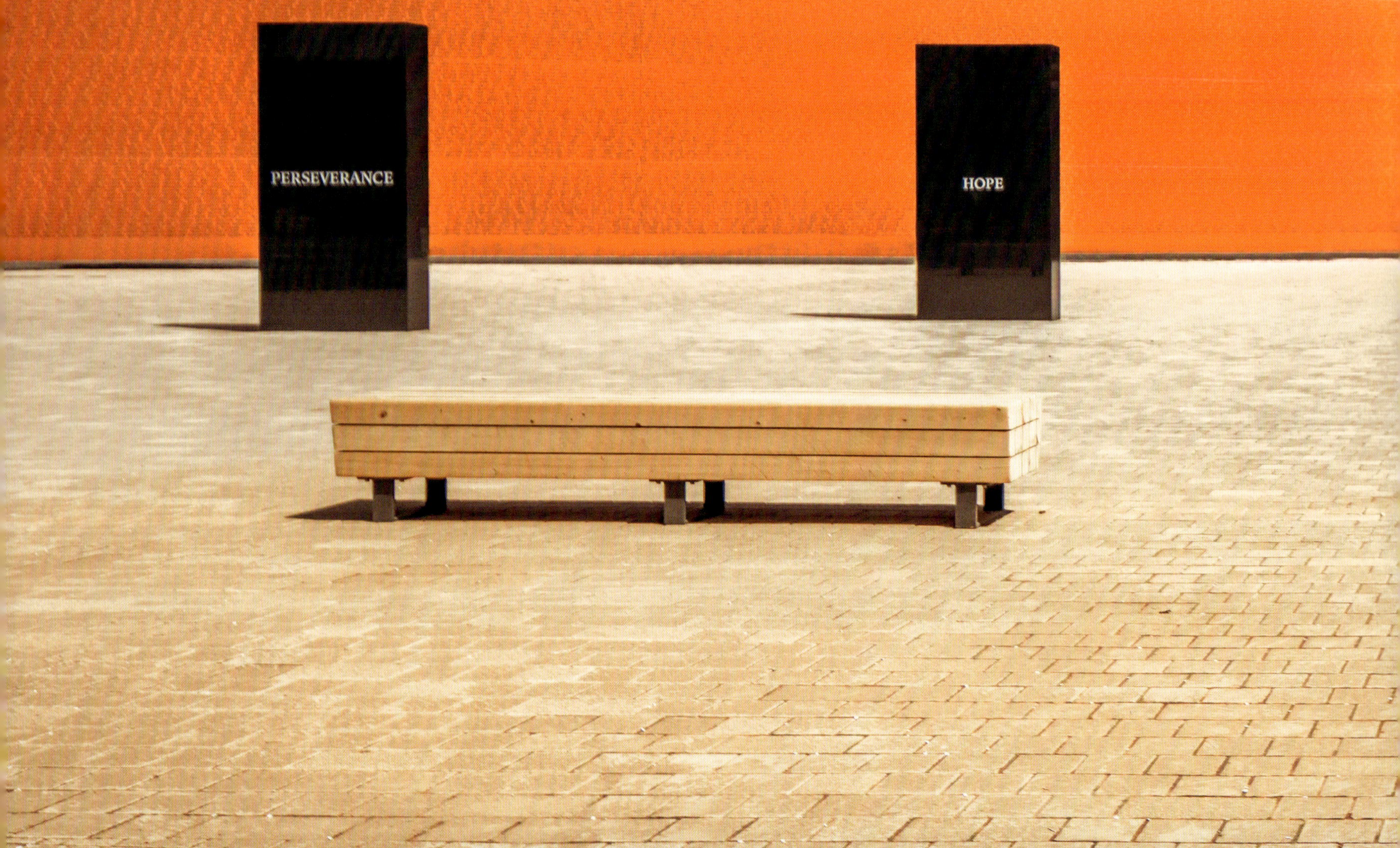
NATIONAL MONUMENT
PERSEVERANCE
HOPE

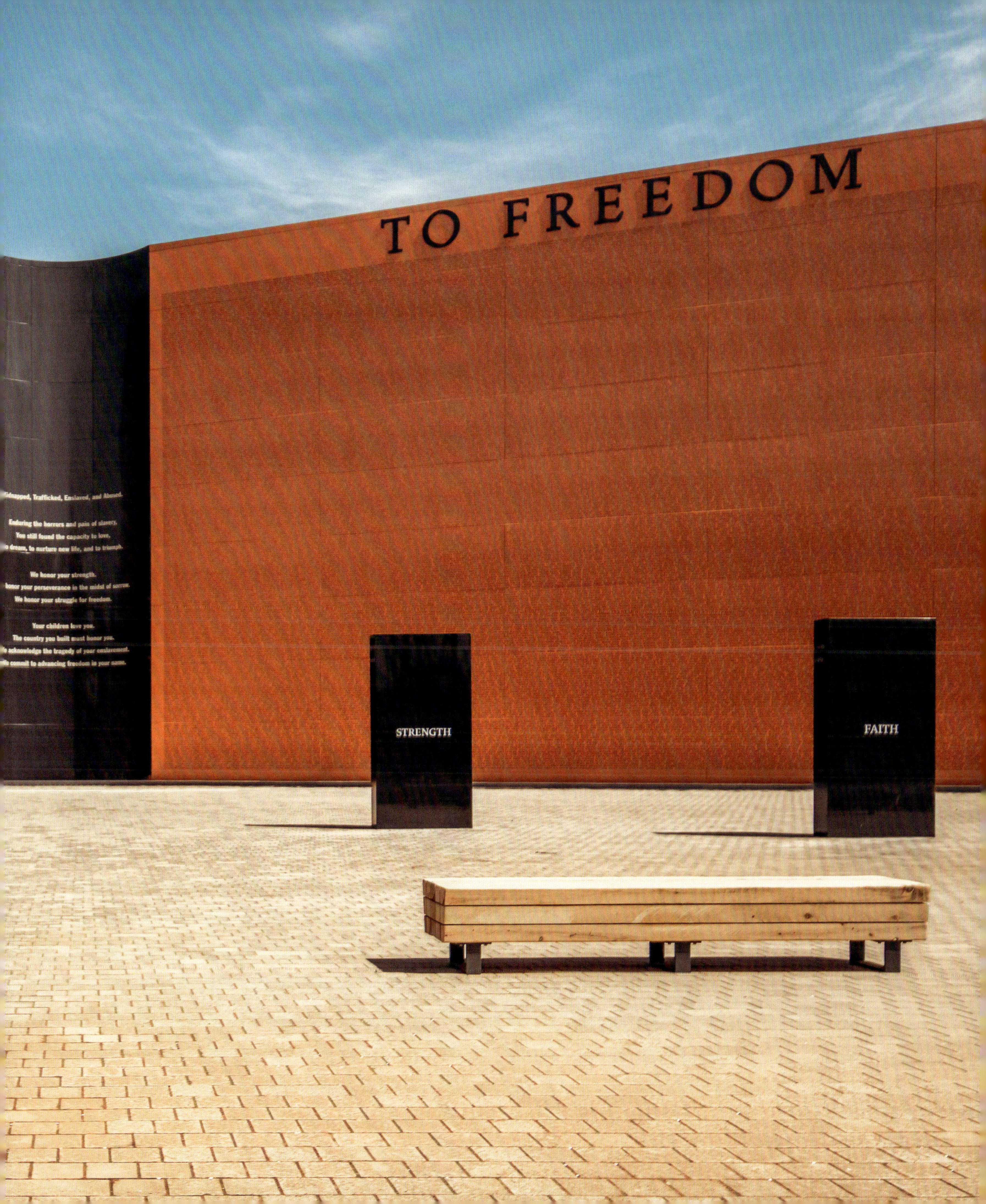
TO FREEDOM
Trafficked, Enslaved, and Abused.
Enduring the horrors and pain of slavery,
You still found the capacity to love,
dream, to nurture new life, and to triumph.
We honor your strength.
honor your perseverance in the midst of sorrow.
We honor your struggle for freedom.
Your children love you.
The country you built must honor you.
acknowledge the tragedy of your enslavement.
commit to advancing freedom in your name.
STRENGTH
FAITH

Kidnapped, Trafficked, Enslaved, and Abused

Enduring the horrors and pain of slavery,
You still found the capacity to love,
to dream, to nurture new life, and to triumph.

We honor your strength.
We honor your perseverance in the midst of sorrow.
We honor your struggle for freedom.

Your children love you.
The country you built must honor you.
We acknowledge the tragedy of your enslavement.
We commit to advancing freedom in your name.

—Inscription on the National Monument to Freedom

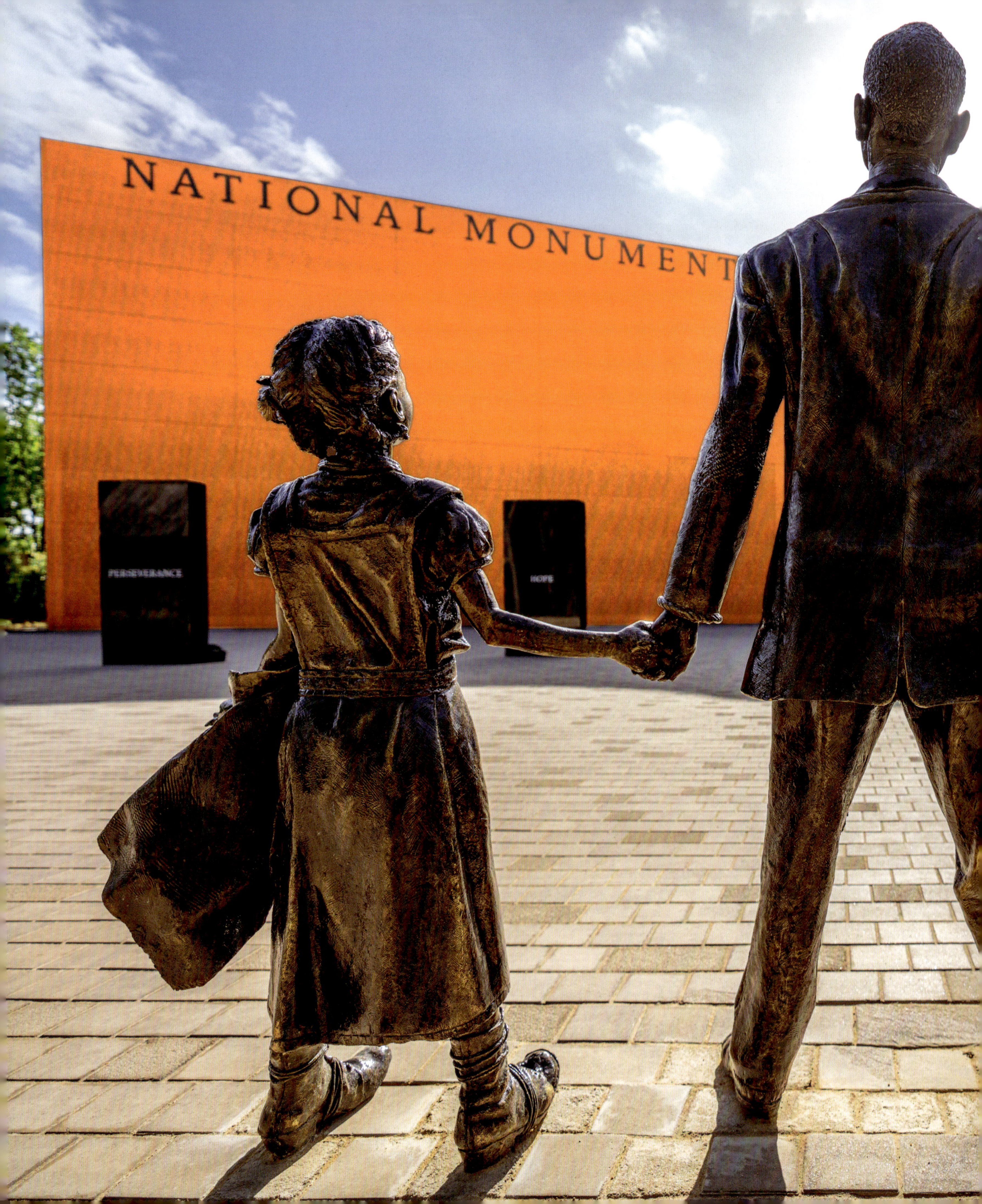
NATIONAL MONUMENT
PERSEVERANCE
HOPE

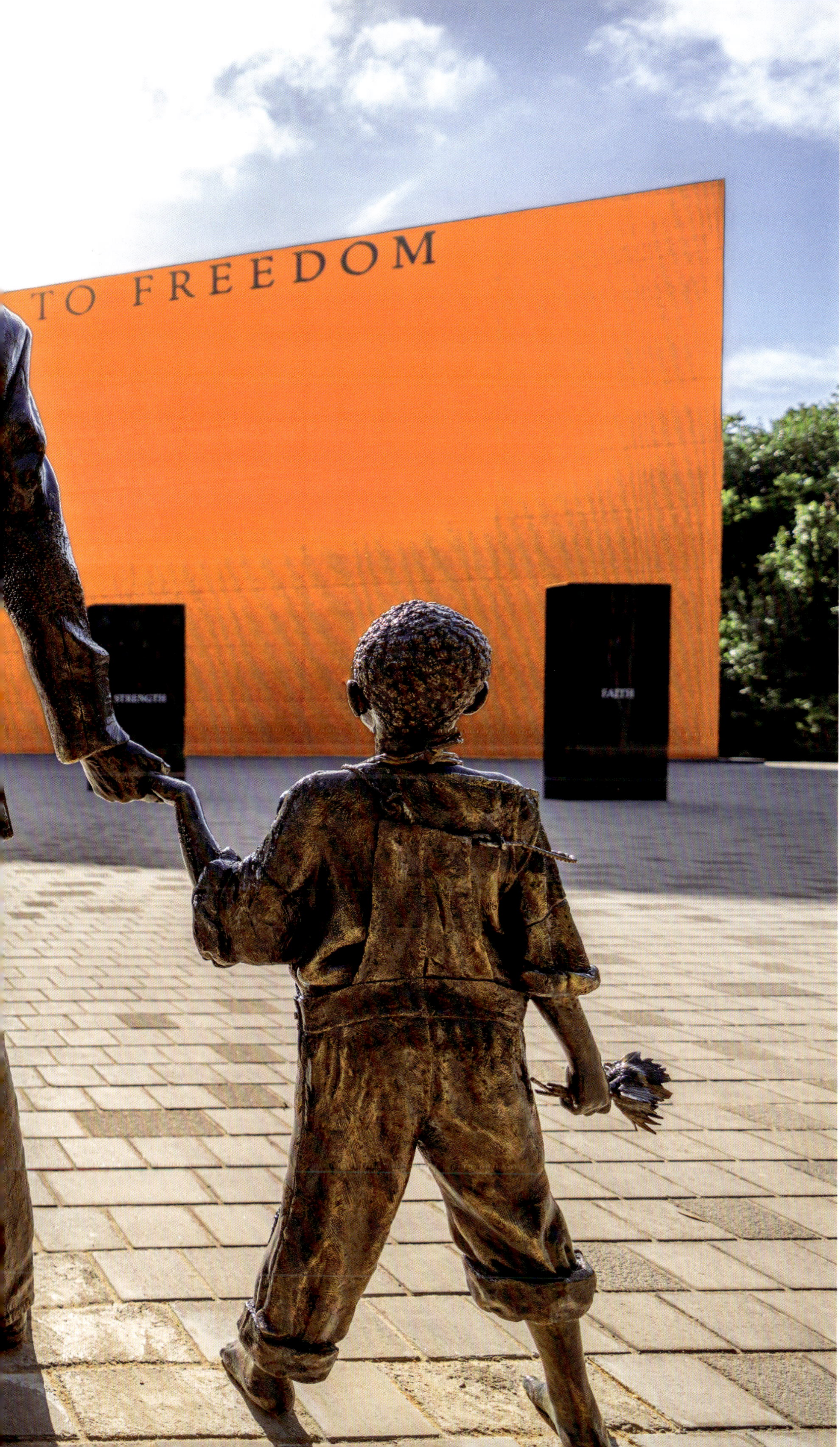

Kwame Akoto-Bamfo
Prayer for the dying, 2023
Bronze

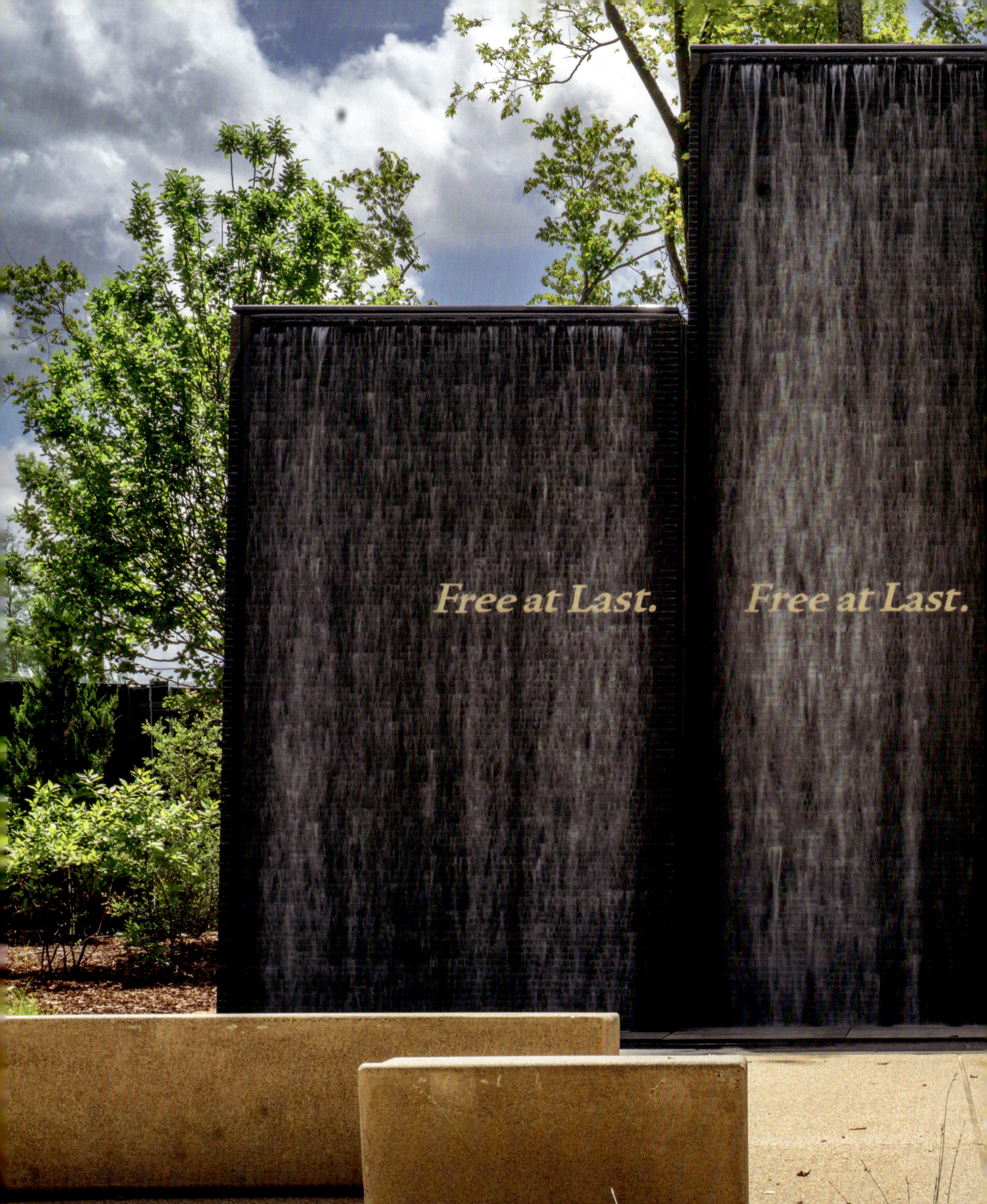
Free at Last.
Free at Last.

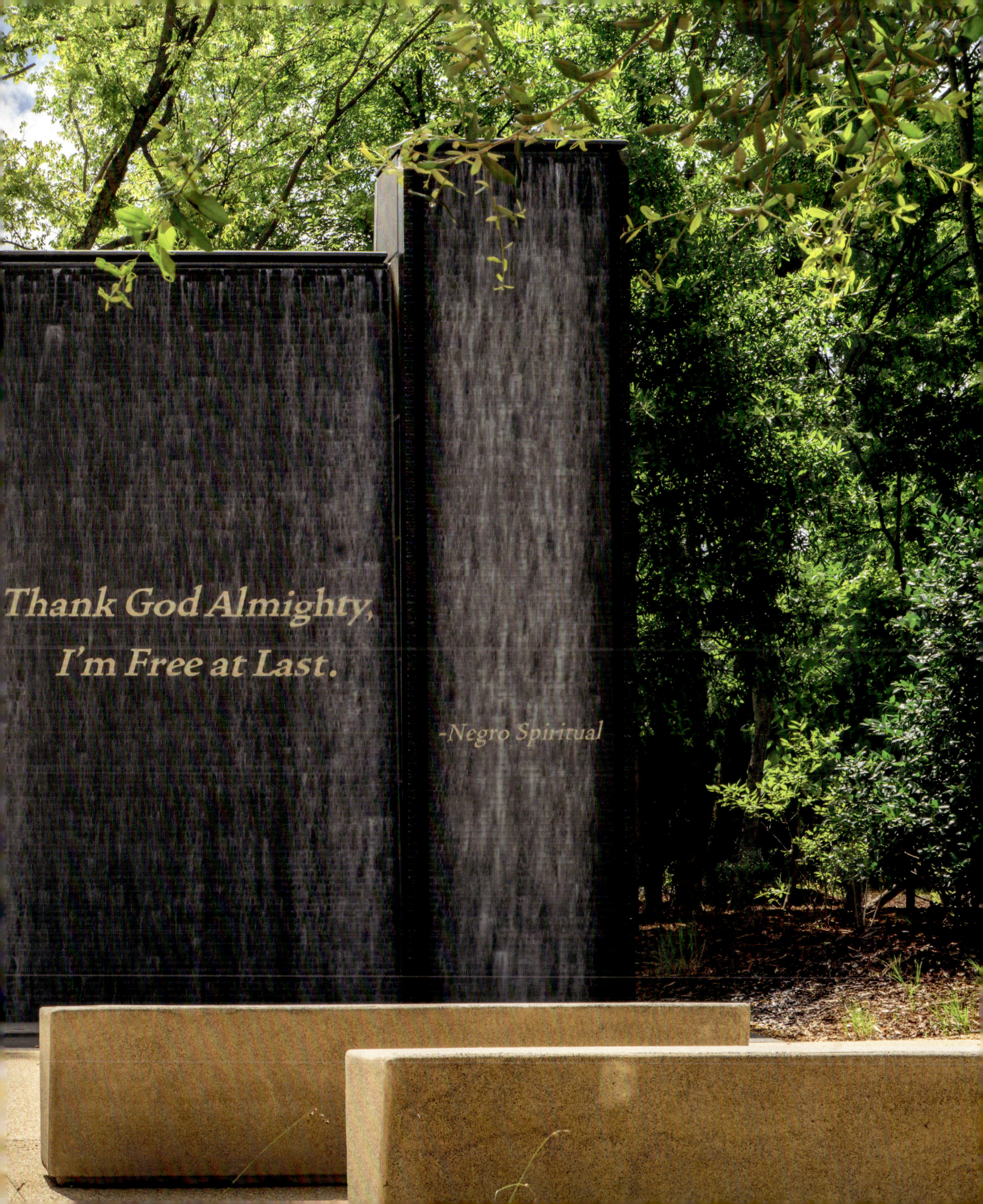

Thank God Almighty,
I'm Free at Last.
-Negro Spiritual

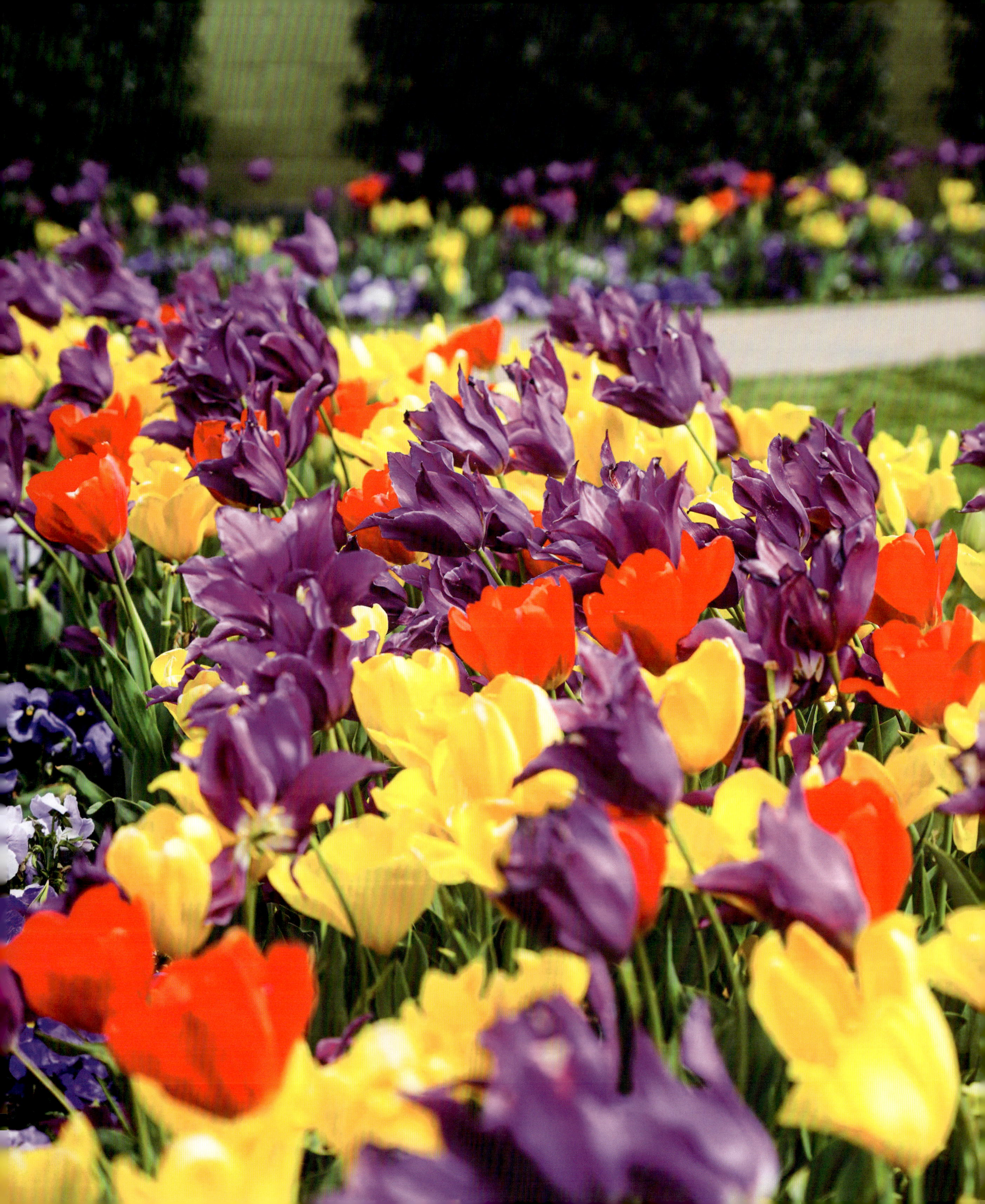

Selected Bibliography

Slavery in America

Ash, Stephen V. *A Massacre in Memphis: The Race Riot That Shook the Nation One Year after the Civil War.* New York: Hill and Wang, 2013.

Baptist, Edward E. *The Half Has Never Been Told: Slavery and the Making of American Capitalism.* New York: Basic Books, 2016.

Benton, Jeffrey C. *Through Others' Eyes: Published Accounts of Antebellum Montgomery, Alabama.* Montgomery: NewSouth Books, 2014.

Berlin, Ira, Marc Favreau, and Steven F. Miller, eds. *Remembering Slavery: African Americans Talk about Their Personal Experiences of Slavery and Emancipation.* New York: The New Press, 2011.

Berry, Daina Ramey. *The Price for Their Pound of Flesh.* Boston: Beacon Press, 2017

Blassingame, John. *The Slave Community: Plantation Life in the Antebellum South.* New York: Oxford University Press, 1979.

Blight, David. *Race and Reunion: The Civil War in American Memory.* Cambridge, MA: Belknap Press, 2001.

Deyle, Steven. *Carry Me Back: The Domestic Slave Trade in America.* New York: Oxford University Press, 2005.

Douglass, Frederick. *Narrative of the Life of Frederick Douglass, An American Slave, Written by Himself.* New York: W. W. Norton & Co., 2016.

Equal Justice Initiative. "Slavery in America: The Montgomery Slave Trade." Montgomery: EJI, 2013.

Foner, Eric. *Gateway to Freedom: The Hidden History of the Underground Railroad.* New York: W. W. Norton & Co., 2015.

Foner, Eric. *Reconstruction: America's Unfinished Revolution, 1863–1877.* New York: HarperCollins, 2002.

Hunter, Tera W. *To Joy My Freedom: Southern Black Women's Lives and Labors after the Civil War.* Cambridge, MA: Harvard University Press, 1997.

Jacobs, Harriet. *Incidents in the Life of a Slave Girl, Written by Herself.* Wokingham, UK: Dodo Press, 2006.

Johnson, Walter. *River of Dark Dreams: Slavery and Empire in the Cotton Kingdom.* Cambridge, MA: Belknap Press, 2013.

Johnson, Walter. *Soul By Soul: Life Inside the Antebellum Slave Market*. Cambridge, MA: Harvard University Press, 1999.

Kendi, Ibram X. *Stamped from the Beginning: The Definitive History of Racist Ideas in America*. New York: Nation Books, 2016.

Lane, Charles. *The Day Freedom Died: The Colfax Massacre, the Supreme Court, and the Betrayal of Reconstruction*. New York: Holt Paperbacks, 2008.

Litwack, Leon F. *Been in the Storm So Long: The Aftermath of Slavery*. New York: Vintage Books, 1979.

Manning, Chandra. *Troubled Refuge: Struggling for Freedom in the Civil War*. New York: Vintage Books, 2016.

McInnis, Maurie D. *Slaves Waiting for Sale: Abolitionist Art and the American Slave Trade*. Chicago: University of Chicago Press, 2011.

Quarles, Benjamin. *Black Abolitionists*. New York: Oxford University Press, 1969.

Rodriguez, Junius P., ed. *Encyclopedia of Slave Resistance and Rebellion, Vols. 1–2*. Westport, CT: Greenwood Press, 2007.

Sublette, Ned and Constance. *The American Slave Coast: A History of the Slave-Breeding Industry*. Chicago: Lawrence Hill Books, 2016.

Tadman, Michael. *Speculators and Slaves: Masters, Traders, and Slaves in the Old South*. Madison: University of Wisconsin Press, 1996.

Racial Terror

Allen, James. *Without Sanctuary: Lynching Photography in America*. Santa Fe, NM: Twin Palms, 2000.

Bailey, Amy Kate, and Stewart E. Tolnay. *Lynched: The Victims of Southern Mob Violence*. Chapel Hill: University of North Carolina Press, 2015.

Berg, Manfred. *Popular Justice: A History of Lynching in America*. Lanham, MD: Government Institutes, 2011.

Blackmon, Douglas. *Slavery by Another Name: The Re-enslavement of Black Americans from the Civil War to World War II*. New York: Anchor Books, 2008.

Brundage, W. Fitzhugh. *Under Sentence of Death: Lynching in the South*. Chapel Hill: University of North Carolina Press, 1997.

Chafe, William H. Raymond Gavins, Robert Korstad et al., eds. *Remembering Jim Crow: African Americans Tell about Life in the Segregated South*. New York: The New Press, 2001.

Cohen, William. *At Freedom's Edge: Black Mobility and the Southern White Quest for Racial Control*. Baton Rouge: Louisiana State University Press, 1991.

Dray, Philip. *At the Hands of Persons Unknown: The Lynching of Black America*. New York: Random House, 2002.

Du Bois, W.E.B. *The Souls of Black Folk*. New Haven, CT: Yale University Press, 2015.

Equal Justice Initiative. "Lynching in America: Confronting the Legacy of Racial Terror." Montgomery: EJI, 2017.

Equal Justice Initiative. "Lynching in America: Targeting Black Veterans." Montgomery: EJI, 2016.

Giddings, Paula. *Ida: A Sword Among Lions.* New York: HarperCollins, 2008.

Ginzburg, Ralph. *100 Years of Lynchings.* Baltimore, MD: Black Classic Press, 1988.

Gonzales-Day, Ken. *Lynching in the West, 1850–1953.* Durham, NC: Duke University Press, 2006.

Gordon, Linda. *The Second Coming of the KKK: The Ku Klux Klan of the 1920s and the American Political Tradition.* New York: Liveright, 2017.

Hoffer, William James. *Plessy v. Ferguson: Race and Inequality in Jim Crow America.* Lawrence: University Press of Kansas, 2012.

Ifill, Sherrilyn. *On the Courthouse Lawn: Confronting the Legacy of Lynching in the Twenty-First Century.* Boston: Beacon Press, 2007.

Jaspin, Elliot. *Buried in the Bitter Waters: The Hidden History of Racial Cleansing in America.* New York: Basic Books, 2008.

King, Gilbert. *Devil in the Grove: Thurgood Marshall, the Groveland Boys, and the Dawn of a New America.* New York: HarperCollins, 2013.

Kousser, J. Morgan. *The Shaping of Southern Politics, Suffrage Restriction and the Establishment of the One-Party South, 1880–1910.* New Haven, CT: Yale University Press, 1974.

Minow, Martha. *Between Vengeance and Forgiveness: Facing History after Genocide and Mass Violence.* Boston: Beacon Press, 1998.

Murray, Pauli, ed. *States' Laws on Race and Color.* Athens: University of Georgia Press, 1997.

Ogletree, Charles J., Jr., and Austin Sarat, eds. *From Lynch Mobs to the Killing State: Race and the Death Penalty in America.* New York: New York University Press, 2006.

Oshinsky, David M. *Worse Than Slavery: Parchman Farm and the Ordeal of Jim Crow Justice.* New York: Simon & Schuster, 1996.

Pfeifer, Michael J. *Lynching Beyond Dixie: American Mob Violence Outside the South.* Chicago: University of Illinois Press, 2013.

Tolnay, Stewart E., and E.M. Beck. *A Festival of Violence: An Analysis of Southern Lynchings, 1882–1930.* Chicago: University of Illinois Press, 1995.

Vandiver, Margaret. *Lethal Punishment.* New Brunswick, NJ: Rutgers University Press, 2006.

Waldrep, Christopher. *African Americans Confront Lynching.* Lanham, MD: Rowman & Littlefield, 2009.

Waldrep, Christopher. *Lynching in America: A History in Documents.* New York: New York University Press, 2006.

Ward, Jason Morgan. *Hanging Bridge: Racial Violence and America's Civil Rights Century.* New York: Oxford University Press, 2016.

Wells-Barnett, Ida B. *Crusade for Justice: The Autobiography of Ida B. Wells.* Chicago: University of Chicago Press, 1970.

Wells-Barnett, Ida B. *On Lynchings.* Mineola, NY: Dover, 2014.

Whitaker, Robert. *On the Laps of Gods: The Red Summer of 1919 and the Struggle for Justice That Remade a Nation.* New York: Three Rivers Press, 2009.

Wilkerson, Isabel. *The Warmth of Other Suns: The Epic Story of America's Great Migration*. New York: Random House, 2010.

Wood, Amy Louise. *Lynching and Spectacle: Witnessing Racial Violence in America: 1890–1940*. Chapel Hill: University of North Carolina Press, 2009.

The Civil Rights Movement and Massive Resistance

Arsenault, Raymond. *Freedom Riders: 1961 and the Struggle for Racial Justice*. New York: Oxford University Press, 2011.

Bartley, Numan V. *The Rise of Massive Resistance: Race and Politics in the South during the 1950s*. Baton Rouge: Louisiana State University Press, 1999.

Branch, Taylor. *At Canaan's Edge: America in The King Years, 1965–68*. New York: Simon & Schuster, 2007.

Branch, Taylor. *Parting the Waters: America in the King Years, 1954–63*. New York: Simon & Schuster, 2007.

Branch, Taylor. *Pillar of Fire: America in the King Years, 1963–65*. New York: Simon & Schuster, 2007.

Cruse, Kevin, and Stephen Tuck, eds. *Fog of War: The Second World War and the Civil Rights Movement*. New York: Oxford University Press, 2012.

Dudziak, Mary L. *Cold War Civil Rights: Race and the Image of American Democracy*. Princeton, NJ: Princeton University Press, 2000.

Frederickson, Kari. *The Dixiecrat Revolt and the End of the Solid South, 1932–1968*. Chapel Hill: University of North Carolina Press, 2003.

Jeffries, Hasan. *Bloody Lowndes: Civil Rights and Black Power in Alabama's Black Belt*. New York: New York University Press, 2009.

Klarman, Michael J. *From Jim Crow to Civil Rights: The Supreme Court and the Struggle for Racial Equality*. New York: Oxford University Press, 2004.

Lavelle, Kristen M. *Whitewashing the South: White Memories of Segregation and Civil Rights*. Lanham, MD: Rowman & Littlefield, 2015.

Lewis, George. *Massive Resistance: The White Response to the Civil Rights Movement*. New York: Bloomsbury, 2006.

Marable, Manning. *Race, Reform and Rebellion: The Second Reconstruction in Black America, 1945–1990*. Oxford: University Press of Mississippi, 1991.

Massey, Douglas S., and Nancy A. Denton. *American Apartheid: Segregation and the Making of the Underclass*. Cambridge, MA: Harvard University Press, 1993.

McAdam, Doug. *Freedom Summer*. New York: Oxford University Press, 1988.

McGuire, Danielle L. *At the Dark End of the Street: Black Women, Rape, and Resistance—A New History of the Civil Rights Movement from Rosa Parks to the Rise of Black Power*. New York: Knopf, 2010.

McWhorter, Diane. *Carry Me Home: Birmingham, Alabama: The Climactic Battle of the Civil Rights Revolution*. New York: Simon & Schuster, 2001.

Olson, Lynne. *Freedom's Daughters: The Unsung Heroines of the Civil Rights Movement from 1830 to 1970*. New York: Scribner, 2001.

Payne, Charles M. *I've Got the Light of Freedom: The Organizing Tradition and the Mississippi Freedom Struggle.* Berkeley: University of California Press, 2007.

Peltason, J.W. *58 Lonely Men: Southern Federal Judges & School Desegregation.* Chicago: University of Illinois Press, 1971.

Sokol, Jason. *There Goes My Everything: White Southerners in the Age of the Civil Rights, 1945–1975.* New York: Vintage Books, 2007.

Tyson, Timothy B. *The Blood of Emmett Till.* New York: Simon & Schuster, 2017.

Williams, Donnie, with Wayne Greenhaw. *The Thunder of Angels: The Montgomery Bus Boycott and the People Who Broke the Back of Jim Crow.* Chicago: Lawrence Hill Books, 2006.

X, Malcolm, with Alex Haley. *The Autobiography of Malcolm X.* New York: Grove Press, 1965.

Mass Incarceration

Abu-Jamal, Mumia. *Live from Death Row.* New York: HarperCollins, 1996.

Alexander, Michelle. *The New Jim Crow: Mass Incarceration in the Age of Colorblindness.* New York: The New Press, 2010.

Ayer, William, Bernardine Dohrn, and Rick Ayers, eds. *Zero Tolerance: Resisting the Drive for Punishment in Our Schools.* New York: The New Press, 2001.

Garland, David W. *Peculiar Institution: America's Death Penalty in an Age of Abolition.* Cambridge, MA: Belknap Press, 2010).

Hinton, Anthony Ray. *The Sun Does Shine: How I Found Life and Freedom on Death Row.* London: Ebury, 2018.

Houppert, Karen. *Chasing Gideon: The Elusive Quest for Poor People's Justice.* New York: The New Press, 2013.

Johnson, Paula C. *Inner Lives: Voices of African American Women in Prison.* New York: New York University Press, 2004.

Mauer, Marc, and Meda Chesney-Lind, eds. *Invisible Punishment: The Collateral Consequences of Mass Imprisonment.* New York: The New Press, 2002.

McCorkel, Jill A. *Gender, Race, and the New Politics of Imprisonment.* New York: New York University Press, 2013.

Patillo, Mary, Davide Weiman, and Bruce Western, eds. *Imprisoning America: The Social Effects of Mass Incarceration.* New York: Russell Sage Foundation, 2004.

Sarat, Austin. *When the State Kills: Capital Punishment and the American Condition.* Princeton, NJ: Princeton University Press, 2001.

Stevenson, Bryan. *Just Mercy: A Story of Justice and Redemption.* New York: Random House, 2014.

Stuntz, William. *The Collapse of American Criminal Justice.* Cambridge, MA: Belknap Press, 2011.

Von Drehle, David. *Among the Lowest of the Dead: The Culture of Capital Punishment.* Ann Arbor: University of Michigan Press, 2006.

Zimring, Franklin. *The Contradictions of American Capital Punishment.* New York: Oxford University Press, 2003.

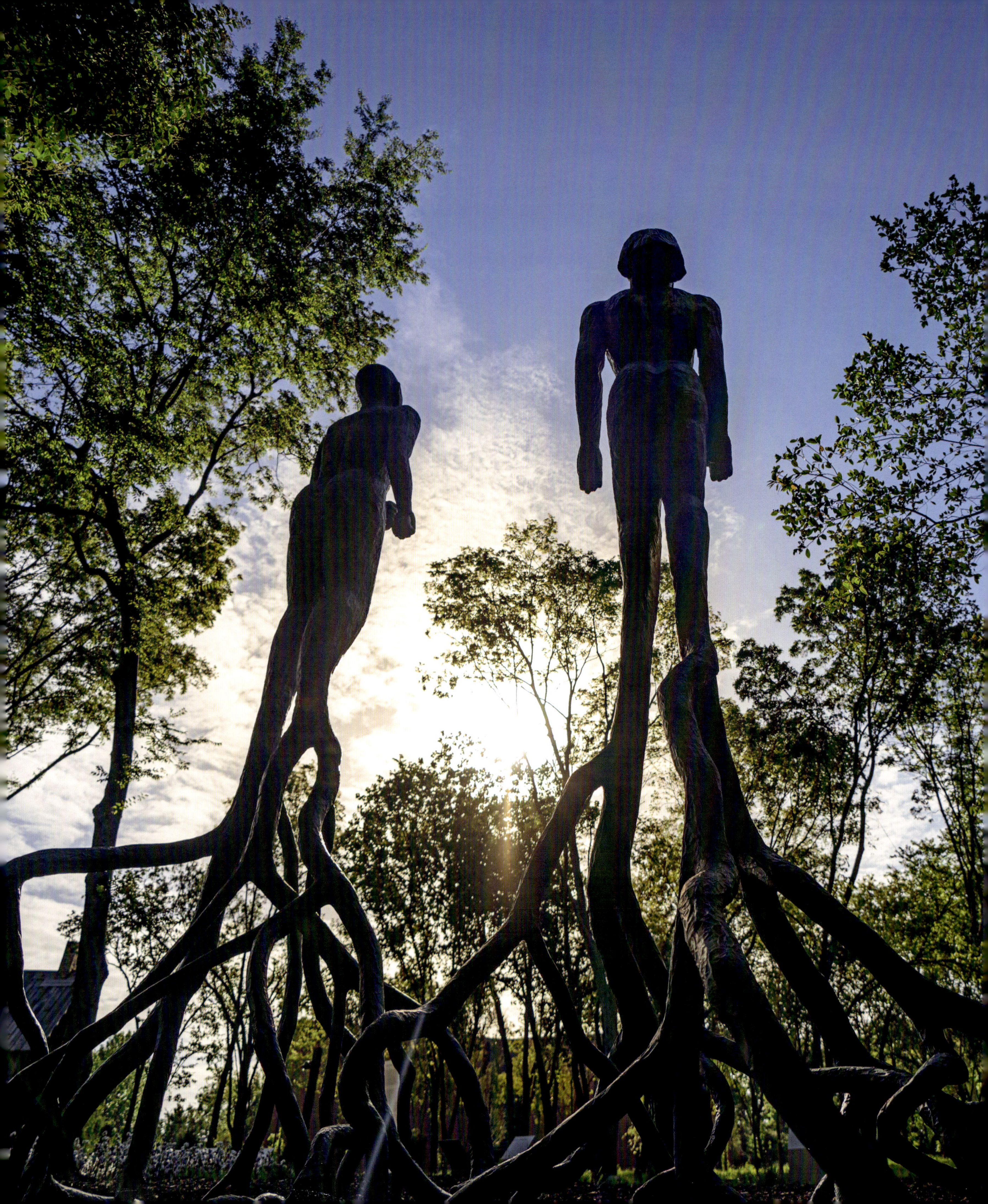

Photo Credits

Bryan G. Stevenson: 20–21, 46–47, 82–83, 91–95, 97, 98–99, 102–03, 124–25, 161, 174–75, 178–79, 191, 195–97, 201, 206–7, 218–19, 240–41, 244–45, 251–53, 256–57, 270

Human Pictures: Cover, 12, 14–16, 19, 22–25, 34–37, 40–41, 44–45, 48, 50–51, 56–58, 64–65, 70, 73–75, 88, 104, 109, 114–15, 126–27, 144–45, 150–51, 164–65, 172–73, 182, 184–85, 187–89, 192–93, 198, 204, 211–13, 216–17, 224–25, 226–31, 234, 236–37, 246–47, 260–63, 266–67, 268–69, 276, Back Cover

Jill Friedman: 54

Josh Cannon: 106–7, 120–21, 154–55, 180–81

Matt Odom: 27, 30, 32, 38, 43, 53, 60–61, 66–69, 76, 80–81, 84, 86–87, 100–101, 112–13, 116–17, 122–23, 128, 130–31, 134–35, 138–39, 141–43, 148–49, 156–58, 162–63, 166–71, 176–77, 202–3, 208–9, 220–21, 232–33, 236–37, 238, 254, 258–59

Stephen Gabris: 2–3, 6, 110–11, 136–37, 278–79

Acknowledgments

The Legacy Sites are narrative spaces that explore American history utilizing art, film, architecture, sculpture, scholarship, literature, and interactive technology. The Legacy Sites were conceived, created, curated, and designed by the Equal Justice Initiative staff. All historical research, content creation, text writing, and narrative construction were done by EJI except where noted. We are grateful to Keith Fox, Holly La Due, Jenny Mutch, Goto Design, and the entire Monacelli team. Special thanks to Sonia Kapadia, Danielle Carrasquero, and Tania Cordes at EJI for coordinating the production and editing of this book.

Alison Saar
Treesouls II, 1994–2024
Unique Bronze

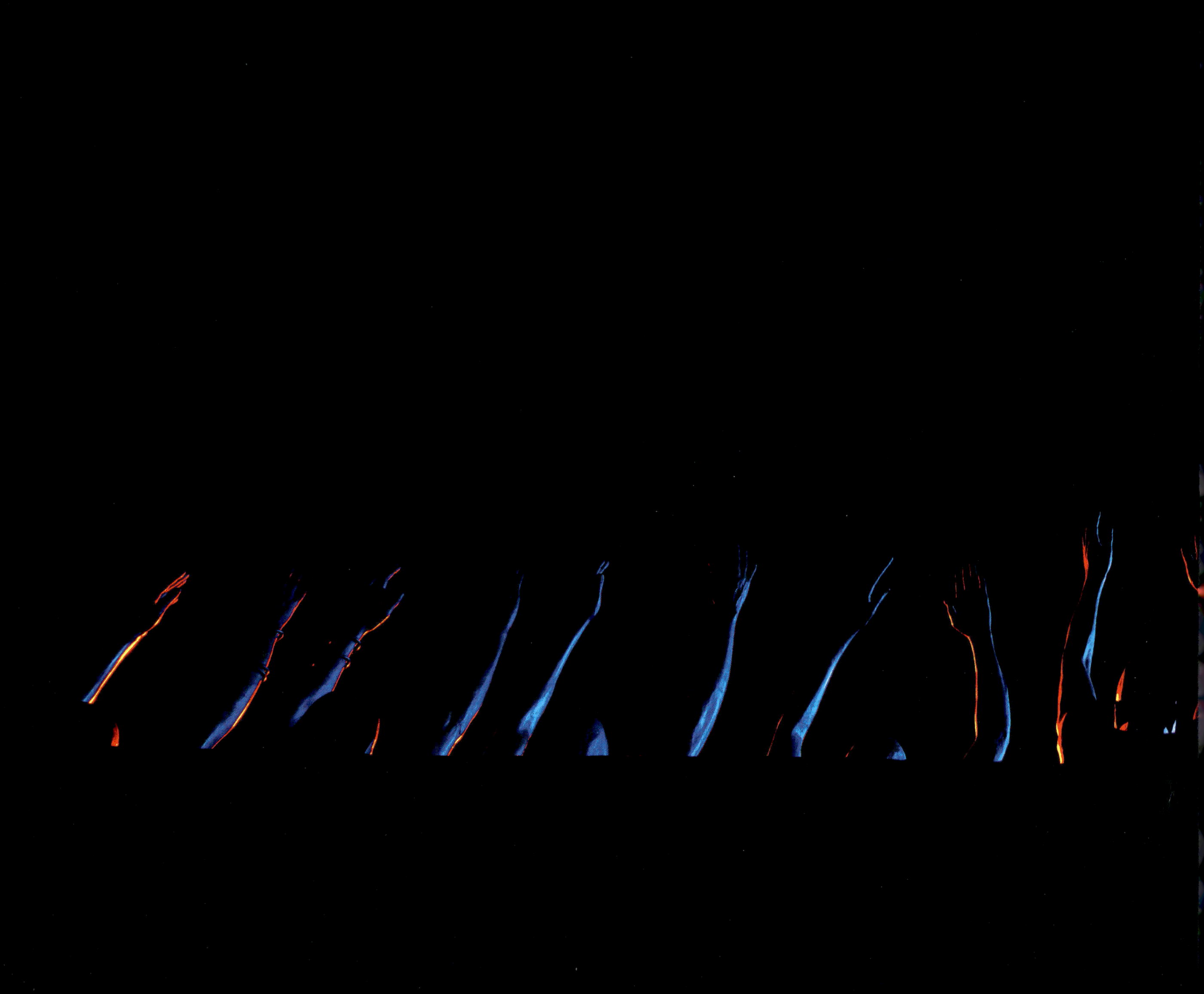

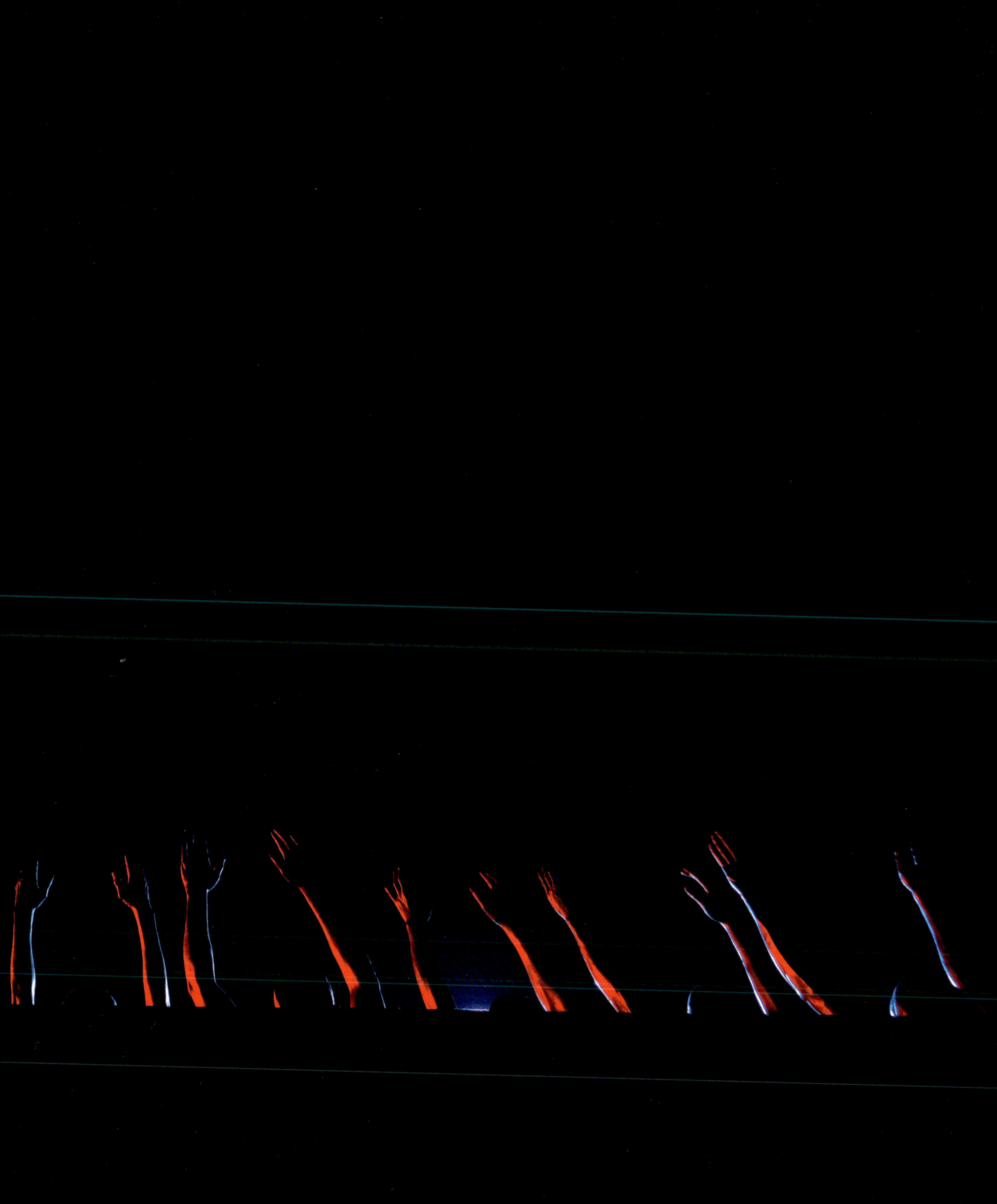

Front cover:
Hanging Monuments at the
National Memorial for Peace and Justice

Back cover:
Simone Leigh
Brick House, 2019
Bronze

Page 6:
Kwame Akoto-Bamfo
Nkyinkyim Installation (detail), 2018
Bronze

Page 12:
Kwame Akoto-Bamfo
The Legacy Museum Memorial
Bronze

Pages 278–79:
Hank Willis Thomas
Raise Up, 2014
Bronze

First published 2026

Library of Congress Control Number: 2025910037

ISBN 978-1-58093-732-0
Printed in China

Design by Goto Design, New York
Editor: Holly La Due, Jenny Mutch
Production: Michael Vagnetti

Phaidon Press Limited
2 Cooperage Yard
London E15 2QR

Monacelli
A Phaidon Company
111 Broadway
New York, NY 10006

Phaidon SARL
55, rue Traversière
75012 Paris

phaidon.com/monacelli

Equal Justice Initiative
122 Commerce Street
Montgomery, AL 36104